Forensics

FOR DUMMIES®

A Wiley Brand

2nd Edition

by D. P. Lyle, MD

Forensics For Dummies®, 2nd Edition

Published by: **John Wiley & Sons, Inc.,** 111 River Street, Hoboken, NJ 07030-5774, www.wiley.com

Copyright © 2016 by John Wiley & Sons, Inc., Hoboken, New Jersey

Published simultaneously in Canada

For general information on our other products and services, please contact our Customer Care Department within the U.S. at 877-762-2974, outside the U.S. at 317-572-3993, or fax 317-572-4002. For technical support, please visit www.wiley.com/techsupport.

Wiley publishes in a variety of print and electronic formats and by print-on-demand. Some material included with standard print versions of this book may not be included in e-books or in print-on-demand. If this book refers to media such as a CD or DVD that is not included in the version you purchased, you may download this material at http://booksupport.wiley.com. For more information about Wiley products, visit www.wiley.com.

Library of Congress Control Number: 2016930373

ISBN 978-1-119-18165-1 (pbk); ISBN 978-1-119-18168-2 (ebk); ISBN 978-1-119- 18166-8 (ebk)

Manufactured in the United States of America

V10004118_090418

Contents at a Glance

Table of Contents

Introduction

You probably purchased *Forensics For Dummies,* 2nd Edition, because you're fascinated by the marriage of criminal justice and science. I wrote this book because I have a similar fascination. And you and I are not alone. Shows such as *CSI: Crime Scene Investigation*, *CSI: Miami*, and *NCIS* have dominated network television ratings for many years, attesting to the fact that millions of people agree that forensics is an interesting subject. Every criminal investigation you see on the news or read about in the newspaper, it seems, hinges on some bit of forensic evidence.

This book is designed to give you an understanding of the techniques and procedures used by forensic scientists. The next time you read or view a mystery story or hear a news report about a crime, you can turn to this book for the science underlying the story.

About This Book

Forensics For Dummies, 2nd Edition, is an introduction to the field of forensic science, covering a broad range of forensic topics in a clear and concise fashion. I explain these often complex principles in plain English so that readers at all levels can gain a better understanding of forensic science. The book includes many examples of how these techniques are applied in real-life situations. In addition, I include case studies throughout the book to illustrate how forensic science has been used to solve famous cases.

If you know absolutely nothing about forensics, this book is an excellent starting point. If you're familiar with many forensic topics, this book serves to refresh and expand your knowledge.

Note: The conventional language used by scientists is foreign to most people, so I hold scientific jargon to a minimum in this book. Still, as with other areas of science, the study of forensics can be dry and boring at times. To avoid painting such an arid landscape, I added practical examples of how each technique works, and I included many famous cases that relied on forensic science for their solutions. I also threw in a little humor to liven things up a bit. If my humor falls flat, remember, I'm a physician, not a stand-up comedian.

Foolish Assumptions

As I wrote this book, I made some assumptions about you and what your needs may be, including that

- ✔ You have an interest in forensic science.
- ✔ You're a fan of the many forensic science shows that are aired on both network and cable television.
- ✔ You avidly follow criminal cases reported on TV and in newspapers.
- ✔ You're considering a career in forensic science.
- ✔ You love reading mysteries and want to better understand the science behind the stories.
- ✔ You're simply curious by nature.

Icons Used in This Book

Like other *For Dummies* books, this one has icons in the margins to guide you through the information and help you zero in on what you want to know. The following paragraphs describe the icons and what they mean.

This icon indicates that I'm giving you a look behind the scenes of a forensic practice or area of investigation. I use it to point out in-depth discussions of these concepts.

I use many real-life stories to illustrate the points in this book. This icon sets off these tales of crimes past.

Sometimes, to give you a clearer picture of how a forensic practice came about, I provide the historical background or a note about a related instance from long ago.

I flag certain pieces of information with this icon to let you know something is particularly worth keeping in mind.

Forensics deals with plenty of mind-blowing information about such things as the human body, evidence, and crime itself. For those of you who want just the juicy facts, look for this icon.

 This icon signals that I'm going to delve a little deeper than usual into a scientific or medical explanation. I don't mean to suggest the information is too difficult to understand — just a little more detailed.

Beyond the Book

This book is bursting with content, but you can go online and find even more. Check out the book's Cheat Sheet at www.dummies.com/cheatsheet/ forensics for tips on what to do if you witness a crime, tools of the trade in crime scene investigation, and more. And you can find some handy bonus articles related to forensics at www.dummies.com/extras/forensics.

Where to Go from Here

Forensics is a broad and diverse field that involves many areas of science and criminal investigation. In this book, you can find out about many but not all of its concerns. You may use this book as a reference and as a springboard for further investigation. The next time you see a news report, read a mystery novel, or watch a movie involving a crime, you can turn to this book to obtain a better understanding of the science behind the story.

Part I
Cracking Open the Case

In this part . . .

✔ Discover how forensic science works.

✔ Find out who makes up the forensics team and what they do.

✔ Figure out how to properly collect and protect evidence at a crime scene.

✔ Understand the inner workings of a criminal mind.

Chapter 1

Understanding the World of Forensic Science

Turn on the TV any night of the week, and you'll find crime scene investigators, or *criminalists*, tracking down criminals, crime lab technicians evaluating evidence, and even forensic pathologists conducting autopsies on shows detailing cases real or imagined. I don't think this newfound interest in all things forensic stems from some macabre fascination with death or a guilty enchantment with the criminal world. If you ask me, people simply are curious by nature and have a strong appetite for scientific knowledge. Remember everyone's fascination with the space program not too many years ago? The cool tools and magical feats of forensic science, such as making fingerprints appear from nowhere, identifying suspects by their shoeprints, sniffing out a forger by the unique signature of a laser printer, and finding even the most obscure poisons, are proving equally fascinating.

In this chapter, you get your feet wet with the basic definitions and organizational elements of the field of forensic science. Most of the topics that I touch on here are explored further in the chapters that follow.

Defining Forensics: The Science of Catching Criminals

If you lived in ancient Rome, you'd head to the forum when you wanted to discuss the news of the day. The town *forum* was a community meeting place for merchants, politicians, scholars, and citizens that doubled as a center for public justice. Steal your neighbor's toga, and the case would be tried at the forum.

The term *forensic* stems from the Latin word *forum* and applies to anything that relates to law. *Forensic science,* or criminalistics, is the application of scientific disciplines to the law.

The same tools and principles that drive scientific research in universities and identify cures in hospitals are used by forensic scientists to reveal how a victim died and, ideally, who was responsible. In the same way modern hospital laboratories employ professionals to deal with pathology (the study of diseases of the human body), toxicology (the study of drugs and poisons), and serology (the study of blood), modern forensic laboratories employ experts in forensic pathology, forensic toxicology, and forensic serology, all of whom use the principles and testing procedures of their medical specialties to help resolve legal issues and answer questions like

- ✔ When and how did the victim die?
- ✔ Does the suspect's blood match the blood found at the crime scene?
- ✔ Was a suspect's unusual behavior caused by drug use?

Integrating science into the practice of law

Not long ago identifying, capturing, and convicting criminals depended primarily upon eyewitnesses and confessions. The world was smaller, communities more closely knit, and the extent of travel basically only as far as you could walk. Whenever anyone witnessed a crime, he likely knew the perpetrator. Case closed.

Trains, planes, and automobiles changed all that. Criminals can now rapidly travel far and wide, and with this newfound mobility they are less and less likely to be recognized by an eyewitness. Besides, eyewitness evidence these days frequently is proven to be unreliable (see Chapter 3).

For law enforcement to keep pace with these changes, other techniques for identifying criminals had to be developed. Science came to the rescue with methods that depend less on eyewitnesses to identify perpetrators or at least link them to their victims or crime scenes. Fingerprinting (Chapter 5), firearms identification and gunshot residue analysis (Chapter 18), hair and fiber studies (Chapter 17), blood typing (Chapter 14), DNA analysis (Chapter 15), and many other scientific techniques now help solve crimes that would've remained unsolved in the past.

The marriage of science and law hasn't been without its setbacks. Many scientific breakthroughs are viewed with suspicion, if not downright hostility, until they become widely accepted. And before a science can ever enter the courtroom, it must be widely accepted. It should come as no surprise that before forensic science could develop, science in general had to reach a certain level of maturity.

Drawing from other sciences

The development of modern forensic science parallels general advancements in science, particularly the physical and biological sciences. Take a look at how a few milestones in science pushed forensic science several steps forward:

- ✔ The invention of the microscope enabled criminalists to analyze even the smallest bits of evidence and to see details in evidence that never before were imagined.

- ✔ The development of photography gave criminalists a crystal-clear representation of the crime scene without relying on memory or the slow process (and far less detailed results) of making drawings.

- ✔ The understanding of the physics of ballistic trajectories gave criminalists a much clearer idea of where a bullet may have come from, which, in turn, made crime-scene reconstruction more accurate.

- ✔ The discovery of blood typing and DNA analysis made matching suspect to crime scene far more exact.

- ✔ The expansion of our knowledge in basic chemistry allowed scientists to identify chemicals and poisons, particularly arsenic, and led to the development of forensic toxicology.

Getting the Big Picture: Forensic Science in Action

You witness a burglar sneaking away from a store late at night. You call the police, and when they arrive, you identify the thief as someone you know. That person is arrested. However, fingerprints from the store's broken window, cracked safe, and tools used to open the safe don't match those of the person you've identified. Instead, they match the fingerprints of a known safecracker. What do you think police, prosecutors, and more importantly, the jury are going to believe? After all, it was dark and raining, you were 100 feet away, you caught only a glimpse of the thief, and you'd just left a bar where you'd had a couple of drinks with friends. The fingerprints, on the other hand, match those of a known thief in each and every detail, meaning they came from him and only him. Which bit of evidence, the fingerprints or your eyewitness account, is more reliable?

This scenario represents what forensic science does, or at least attempts to do. Each and every forensic technique that you discover in this book is designed to either identify perpetrators or connect them to the crime.

Starting out small: Basic forensic services

Properly identifying, collecting, documenting, and storing evidence are at the heart of the forensic services offered by virtually all law enforcement agencies, from village cops to major metropolitan police departments. They need the basic services in the list that follows to be able to investigate and solve crimes and to convict the criminals who commit them:

- **Evidence collection unit:** This *crime-scene investigation unit* collects and preserves evidence from the crime scene and transports it to the lab. Regardless of whether they're individual police officers or highly trained professionals, members of this unit expose and lift latent fingerprints (Chapter 5), collect hair and fibers (Chapter 3), and gather any other articles of evidence at the scene.

- **Photography unit:** The *photography unit* takes pictures of the crime scene, all evidence, and the body (whenever one is present). These photos are crucial, serving as blueprints for crime-scene reconstruction and an excellent format for presenting evidence in the courtroom. Turn to Chapter 3 to find out more about photographing a crime scene.

- **Evidence storage:** A secure place for storing and preserving the evidence is essential. Evidence usually is stored in a locked room with restricted access that is housed at your local police station or sheriff's department. Evidentiary materials are kept in storage for years or even decades, and the chain of custody (see Chapter 3) must remain unbroken throughout that time, or the evidence can be compromised, losing its value.

Looking at physical forensic science

Tracking down trace evidence, checking the characteristics of bullets fired from a gun, examining the penmanship of a signature on an important document, and evaluating the swirling ridges of fingerprints under a microscope all are part of the physical side of forensic science.

- **Trace evidence:** Any small item of evidence, such as hair, fiber, paint, glass, or soil, for example, that places the suspect at the scene of the crime or in direct contact with the victim is considered *trace evidence*. Matching glass fragments found on the victim of a hit-and-run motor-vehicle accident to glass from the broken headlamp of the suspect's car is a prime example. Find out more in Chapter 17.

✔ **Firearms examination:** *Firearms examination* deals with the identification of weapons and the projectiles they fire, including ammunition, fired bullets, shell casings, and shotgun shells. Firearms experts use a microscope and various types of chemical analysis to identify the type of weapon used to commit a crime and match any bullets fired from that weapon or shell casings to a suspect weapon. I cover firearms examination in Chapter 18.

✔ **Document examination:** Whenever an important written document's age or authenticity is in doubt, a *document examiner* uses handwriting analysis to match handwriting samples to questioned documents or signatures. Document examination also may include analyzing the physical and chemical properties of papers and inks or exposing *indented writing* (the impressions made on the page beneath one that was written on). Typewritten or photocopied documents that may have been altered also fall under the document examiner's area of expertise. Check out Chapter 19 for the details.

✔ **Fingerprint examination:** *Fingerprint examiners* match prints to the fingers, palms, or soles of the people who left them at the crime scene. A print found at a crime scene can be compared with another taken from a database or from a suspect, victim, or bystander. Chapter 5 tells you all about fingerprint examination.

Delving into biological forensic science

Forensic science deals not only with physical evidence but also with biological evidence, which may take the form of a corpse, skeletal remains, drugs and poisons, teeth, bite marks, insects, and plant materials, to name a few. It also includes analysis of the criminal mind. Biological evidence is often what makes or breaks a case.

For example, an *autopsy* (postmortem examination of the body, which is discussed in Chapter 9) may reveal the nature and cause of any injuries, the presence of any poisons, and ultimately why and how the victim died. These findings alone may lead to the perpetrator. Blood and DNA analysis can positively identify suspects and link them to crimes. DNA and dental pattern records can be used to identify an unidentified corpse, and plant and insect evidence can reveal the time of death and link a suspect to the crime scene. Find out more about these sciences and the people who specialize in them in Chapter 2.

Investigating the Crime Lab

Although they use much of the same equipment and follow similar research procedures, forensics (crime) labs are quite different from medical (clinical) labs. The latter deal with the living by carrying out testing aimed at diagnosing and treating the sick. On the other hand, forensics labs are geared toward testing evidence with the hope of establishing links between a suspect and a crime.

Creating the first crime lab

The United States's first forensic laboratory was established in 1923 by August Volmer in the Los Angeles Police Department. Shortly thereafter, the first private forensic lab was created in Chicago in 1929 as a result of the investigation of Chicago's infamous St. Valentine's Day Massacre (see the nearby sidebar). This case involved the expertise of Calvin Goddard, then America's leading firearms identification expert, who was able to link the killings to Al "Scarface" Capone. Two businessmen who served on the coroner's inquest jury were so impressed with Goddard and his scientific use of firearms identification that they funded the development of a crime lab at Northwestern University. The lab brought together the disciplines of firearms examination, blood analysis, fingerprinting, and trace evidence analysis and served as a prototype for other labs.

In 1932, Goddard helped the Federal Bureau of Investigation (FBI) establish a national forensics laboratory that offered virtually every forensic service known to law enforcement across the United States. It, too, served as a model for future state and local labs. Now many states have networks of regional and local labs that support law enforcement at all levels.

The St. Valentine's Day Massacre

During the height of Prohibition, gang warfare raged over control of the illegal alcohol trade that sprang up in many U.S. cities. None was bloodier than the war between Chicago rivals Al "Scarface" Capone and George "Bugs" Moran.

On the night of February 14, 1929, seven of Moran's men were waiting for a shipment of hijacked liquor in a warehouse on Chicago's Clark Street. Unbeknownst to them, the shipment was a setup orchestrated by Capone in an attempt to kill his chief rival, Bugs Moran. Moran was supposed to be at the warehouse, but he arrived late. When he got there, he saw a police car pull up and five officers enter the warehouse. Moran retreated and heard machine gun fire, then saw the five cops come out and drive away.

The real police arrived and found that each of the seven men had been shot numerous times. They recovered 70 shell casings. Bullets later were recovered from the victims. Cardiologist Dr. Calvin Goddard, who became famous during the Sacco and Vanzetti case (see Chapter 20), was called in because of his expertise in firearms identification. He determined that the shell casings were from Thompson submachine guns. Using the newly developed comparison microscope, he tested casings from Thompsons belonging to police and determined that none of them were the murder weapons. Goddard's findings meant that the killers had impersonated police officers. Suspicion fell on Capone. Police raided the home of one of Capone's hit men, finding two Thompsons that later were identified as two of the murder weapons.

Identifying common procedures

Scientific services offered by modern crime labs and medical examiners' offices are varied and complex. The number of services supplied by a particular laboratory depends on its size and budget. State and regional labs may provide a wide array of services, whereas local labs may provide only basic testing. These smaller labs typically outsource more sophisticated testing to larger regional labs. In addition, the FBI's National Crime Lab offers services to law enforcement throughout the country. Not only does the FBI lab perform virtually every type of test, it also possesses or has access to databases on everything from fingerprints and tire-track impressions to postage stamps.

Larger labs often feature separate departments for each discipline, while smaller labs tend to combine services, perhaps even relying on a single technician to do all the work. Obviously, in this circumstance, a great deal of the work must be sent to larger regional labs.

HISTORICAL NOTE

From fiction to fact: Forensic scientists through the years

The first forensic scientist came not from the world of science but from the world of fiction. Sir Arthur Conan Doyle's character Sherlock Holmes frequently used the sciences of fingerprinting, document examination, and blood analysis to solve the crimes he investigated. In fact, in the first Sherlock Holmes' novel, *A Study in Scarlet,* Holmes developed a chemical that determined whether a stain was blood.

Similarly, Mark Twain employed fingerprint evaluation in two of his works *(Life on the Mississippi* and *Pudd'nhead Wilson)* nearly a decade before they became recognized investigational tools.

The first real-life forensic scientist was Hans Gross. In 1893, he published the first treatise on the use of scientific knowledge and procedures in criminal investigations. Others soon followed.

In 1901, Karl Landsteiner discovered that human blood could be grouped and devised the ABO blood groups that still are in use today. In 1915, Leone Lattes developed a simple method for determining the ABO group of a dried bloodstain and immediately began using it in criminal investigations. Today, ABO typing, though not able to absolutely identify a particular person, is used to exonerate some suspects, to refute paternity, and to reconstruct crime scenes.

Early in the 20th century, Calvin Goddard perfected a system for comparing bullets under a comparison microscope to determine whether they came from the same weapon. And, Albert Osborn laid down the principles of document examination in his book, *Questioned Documents,* which still is used today.

Common procedures conducted in a crime lab include

- Fingerprint analysis (Chapter 5)
- Tool-mark and impression analysis (Chapter 7)
- Blood analysis (Chapter 14)
- DNA analysis (Chapter 15)
- Toxicological testing (Chapter 16)
- Trace evidence evaluation (Chapter 17)
- Firearms examination (Chapter 18)

Peeking Inside the Criminalist's Toolbox

Crime-scene investigators are charged with finding, collecting, protecting, and transporting all types of evidence to the crime lab. Although each person or team may have different ways of doing things, typical equipment and supplies they take to the scene include the following:

- Crime-scene tape to demarcate and secure the scene
- Camera and/or video recorder to document the scene and the evidence
- Sketchpad and pens for scene sketches
- Disposable protective clothing, masks, and gloves
- Flashlight-alternative light sources such as laser, ultraviolet, and infrared lighting for exposing certain types of evidence
- Magnifying glass, tweezers, and cotton swabs for collecting hair, fiber, and fluid evidence
- Paper and plastic evidence bags and glass tubes to collect and transport evidence
- Fingerprint supplies, which include ink, print cards, lifting tape, and various dusting powders and exposing reagents such as luminol
- Casting kit for making casts of tires, footwear, and tool-mark impressions
- Serology kit for collecting blood and other bodily fluids
- Entomology kit for collecting and preserving insect evidence
- Hazmat kit for handling hazardous materials

The Cornerstone of Forensic Science: Locard's Exchange Principle

Every contact you make with another person, place, or object results in an exchange of physical materials. If you own a pet, this material exchange is well known to you. Look at your clothes and you're likely to see cat or dog hair clinging to the fabric — a pain in the behind if you want to keep your clothes looking sharp, but an incredible boon for forensic science. You may also find that you transfer these hairs to your car, your office, and any other place you frequent.

Known as the *Locard Exchange Principle,* after Dr. Edmond Locard, the French police officer who first noticed it, the exchange of materials is the basis of modern forensic investigation. Using this principle, forensic scientists can determine where a suspect has been by analyzing *trace evidence* (any small piece of evidence), such as fibers on clothing, hair in a car, or gunk on the soles of shoes.

Looking at Locard's principle in action

As an example, say that you have two children and a cat. You run out to take care of some errands that include stopping at a furniture store, the laundry, and the house of a friend who has one child and a dog. From a forensic science standpoint, this sequence of events can provide a gold mine of information.

You leave behind a little bit of yourself at each stop, including

- ✔ Hair from yourself, your children, and your cat
- ✔ Fibers from your clothing and the carpets and furniture in your home and car
- ✔ Fingerprints and shoeprints
- ✔ Dirt and plant matter from your shoes
- ✔ Biological materials, if you accidentally cut yourself and leave a drop of blood on the floor or sneeze into a tissue and then drop it in a trash can

But that's not all. You also pick up similar materials everywhere you go:

- ✔ Fibers from each sofa or chair you sat on at the furniture store ride away on your clothes, as do hair and fibers left behind by customers who sat there before you.

✔ Fibers of all types flow through the air and ventilation system and settle on each customer at the laundry.

✔ Hair from your friend, her child, and her dog latch on to you as do fibers from your friend's carpet and furniture.

✔ Fibers, hairs, dirt, dust, plant material, and gravel are collected by your shoes and pants everywhere you set foot.

In short, by merely running errands, you become a walking trace evidence factory.

Reading the trace evidence

An examination of your clothes and shoes after the preceding expedition essentially provides a travelogue of your errands. If someone robbed your friend's house that evening while your friend was away, criminalists would find your fingerprints, your hair (as well as that of your children and your cat), and fibers from the carpets in your house and car. They could place you at the scene of the crime.

Of course, you'd have an alibi (I hope) and a legitimate reason why your trace evidence was found at the scene. The thief would not be able to offer a legitimate reason for his trace evidence being at the scene, which means the presence of his prints, hair, and carpet fibers would need an explanation.

Determining who did what where

Placing a suspect at the scene of a crime is one of the basic functions of forensic science. The analysis of fingerprints, blood, DNA, fibers, dirt, plant materials, paint, glass, shoe and tire impressions, and indeed every test done by the crime lab, is performed to create an association between the perpetrator and the crime.

In many cases, the mere fact that a suspect can be placed at the scene is an indication of guilt. A fingerprint on the faceplate of a cracked bank vault, semen obtained from a rape victim, or paint from the fender of a car involved in a hit-and-run accident connects suspects to crime scenes where they have no innocent reason for being.

Chapter 2

Getting to Know the Forensics Team

TV forensics teams have it good: There's a specialist for every possible field of study and a fancy piece of equipment for analyzing whatever evidence comes in. Unfortunately, that's not the case even in larger, more sophisticated jurisdictions, much less in smaller ones where law enforcement officers or a single or very small number of criminalists perform all the required duties.

More often than not, this is due to funding shortfalls. The truth is that most crime labs are severely underfunded. This fact led author Jan Burke to create the Crime Lab Project (https://crimelabproject.wordpress.com), a site that helps raise public awareness of this national problem.

Police typically are the first officials to arrive at any crime scene. After they determine the nature and exact location of the criminal act and secure the scene, they call in various forensic specialists to document and gather evidence, and then transport it to the crime lab for further testing. Who shows up to handle these duties depends upon the resources and structure of the jurisdiction.

Larger crime labs may have a special crime-scene investigation unit (CSIU) that consists of individuals trained in evidence recognition, collection, and preservation. They are also skilled in performing many of the field tests and screening tests that must be done at a crime scene. Although their exact titles and duties vary from jurisdiction to jurisdiction, these specialists can be divided into two groups. I use the terms *criminalists* or *forensic investigators* for those who deal with the physical evidence and *coroner's technicians* to refer to those who deal with the body in cases of death.

Gathering the Evidence: The Criminalist at Work

Criminalist is a relatively new term and one that's not easy to define. It covers a wide range of abilities, responsibilities, and training. Some, such as serologists and chemists, are scientists, while others, such as fingerprint and firearms examiners, are likely to be ex-police officers who have no true scientific training. Still others are technicians with on-the-job training.

No matter what their specialty or education, the bottom line is that criminalists work with evidence. That can mean a lot of things, from looking for poisons in blood samples to authenticating written documents, but all of it falls under the banner of criminalist.

In spite of what you see on TV and in the movies, criminalists aren't cops (although, in some cases, they are *former* police officers). They don't carry guns, interrogate suspects or witnesses, or make arrests. They don't treat the injured or deal with a dead body. They collect and analyze evidence. That's it.

Common job titles for criminalists include the following:

- **Crime-scene investigator:** These are the CSI guys and gals who visit the crime scene to locate, collect, protect, and transport any and all evidence to the crime lab. They document the scene by sketching and photographing it, unless there is a sketch artist or photographer on the scene to take over this duty at their direction.

- **Latent print examiner:** These specialists examine fingerprints as well as palm and footprints and compare them with prints obtained from suspects, other crime scenes, or print databases. Chapter 5 gives you the skinny on fingerprints.

- **Firearms examiner:** The duties of this individual include examining and identifying firearms, comparing bullets and shell casings, and searching for and identifying gunshot residue. Chapter 18 gives you the details.

- **Tool-mark examiner:** Like fingers, tools leave behind distinct markings that may connect them to a crime scene. Tool-mark examiners compare these marks to suspect tools. I cover this practice in Chapter 7.

✔ **Document examiner:** These experts examine various documents to determine their authenticity and authorship and to look for any alterations in a document's original content. They may also be asked to identify whether a particular typewriter or copier produced a certain document. Check out Chapter 19 for more.

✔ **Trace evidence examiner:** These specialists analyze and compare hair, fibers, glass, soils, and paints to determine their type and origin. Chapter 17 tells you more about analyzing trace evidence.

Looking into the CSI Effect

I'm sure you're familiar with the TV series *CSI: Crime Scene Investigation* and its many spin-off shows. How could you not be? Though they more often than not get the science right, they create an unrealistic picture of what a crime lab looks like, how well equipped it is, and what CSI and lab techs actually do. But, like other more scientifically based shows like *Forensic Files*, for example, these shows have raised public awareness of forensic science and introduced viewers to the world of forensic investigation.

One unintended consequence of these shows and the raised public awareness of forensic science procedures is the *CSI Effect*. Though controversial as to whether it actually exists, many experts believe it does, while others feel it doesn't. Regardless, it makes sense that saturating the public with all this forensic science would naturally change its view on criminal investigation and prosecution. Those who support the existence of this effect point to three major areas: the public, and thus jurors; judges, prosecutors, and defense attorneys; and criminals.

Whenever a high-profile case pops up on the news, the public seems to immediately jump to whether there is DNA evidence or not.

If there is, the suspect must be guilty, and if not, he must be innocent. The facts are that DNA analysis is only relevant in a very small percentage of cases, perhaps as low as 5 percent. Most crimes are solved by good police work, not the crime lab. This attitude naturally enters the courtroom where jurors are asking the same question: Why is there no DNA? Did the police do something wrong by not collecting it? Is there no DNA because the defendant is innocent? You can see how this complicates the job of prosecutors and defense attorneys. If jurors expect forensic evidence to be presented to support their cases, these attorneys need to explain any absence of such evidence.

And what about criminals? They watch these shows. They learn what law enforcement and crime labs can do. They wear gloves when breaking into a home to avoid leaving fingerprints, they wear condoms in rapes to avoid leaving behind DNA evidence, and they take other steps to avoid detection. Fortunately, a little knowledge is a dangerous thing, and as you see in the remainder of this book, criminals may avoid leaving behind one type of evidence while ignoring other, equally damning, evidence. And that's a good thing.

From Analyzing Blood to Identifying Bugs: Forensic Science Specialists

If you need to find out how a victim died or identify a piece of a plant found at a crime scene, you call on a forensic scientist trained in pathology or botany, respectively. Professionals who work in the various forensic biological sciences are among the most highly trained and skilled members of the forensics team. They include the following:

- **Pathologist:** A *forensic pathologist* is a licensed physician with specialty training in *pathology,* which deals with the nature of disease and the structural and functional changes it causes in the human body. In addition, the forensic pathologist takes subspecialty training in forensic pathology, the application of pathological science to the law.

  The forensic pathologist is in charge of the body and all the evidence that is gleaned from its examination. He uses the autopsy, police report, medical records if indicated, suspect and witness interviews, the results of crime lab evidence evaluations, and much more in the pursuit of answers. The forensic pathologist also examines living victims to determine the causes and ages of injuries, particularly in cases of assault, rape, or abuse. Part III of this book focuses on forensic pathology.

- **Anthropologist:** The *forensic anthropologist* studies human skeletal remains to determine the age, sex, and race of the deceased, identify any illnesses or injuries that the victim may have suffered, and to estimate the time of death. The forensic anthropologist examines not only the recovered bones, but also the location and circumstances in which they were found. Toxicological, chemical, and DNA analyses also are used by the forensic anthropologist. Other responsibilities may include identifying victims of mass disasters and those interred in mass graves. You can find out more about forensic anthropology in Chapter 10.

- **Odontologist:** A *forensic odontologist* (or forensic dentist) helps identify unknown corpses by matching dental patterns with previous X-rays, dental casts, or photographs. Because dental enamel is the hardest substance in the human body, forensic dental services can help with identifying homicide victims, victims of mass disasters, and skeletal remains. Forensic odontologists are called upon to match a suspect's teeth with bite marks on the victim or on food products such as cheese or apples. Chapter 10 tells you more about forensic odontology.

- **Entomologist:** *Entomology* is the study of insects. The *forensic entomologist* uses knowledge of the life cycles of flies and various other insects that feed on corpses to determine the approximate time of death. Likewise, the forensic entomologist uses knowledge of insect habitats to determine whether a body has been moved from one location to another. Find out more in Chapter 11.

- ✔ **Psychiatrist:** The *forensic psychiatrist* may be asked to address someone's sanity or competence to stand trial, sign documents, or give informed medical consent. In suicide cases, forensic psychiatrists may be asked to conduct psychological autopsies to determine possible motivations of the deceased. A forensic psychiatrist may also be asked to provide a psychological profile of an unknown perpetrator. Check out Chapter 4 for the lowdown on forensic psychiatry.

- ✔ **Serologist:** The *serology* lab deals with blood and other bodily fluids such as saliva and semen, identifying the presence or absence of antigens and antibodies in those fluids. Blood typing, paternity testing, and in some labs even DNA profiling are conducted by the *serologist.* Turn to Chapter 14 for more.

- ✔ **Toxicologist:** *Toxicology* is the study of drugs and poisons. The *forensic toxicologist* determines whether drugs or poisons are present in the living and the deceased, often to assess how those substances contributed to aberrant behavior or death. The forensic toxicologist also determines whether drivers were intoxicated or workers violated company drug-use policies. Check out Chapter 16 for the full scoop on toxicology.

- ✔ **Botanist:** Examining plant residues, one of the tasks performed by a *forensic botanist,* is sometimes crucial to solving a crime. Plant fragments, seeds, pollen, and soil may be used to place a suspect at the crime scene. For example, pollen found on the clothing of a suspect can be matched to that of a rural crime scene, thus suggesting that the suspect was in the same area. Plant and pollen evidence also can reveal that a corpse has been moved. Find out more about forensic botany in Chapter 17.

Forensic Investigation's Head Honcho: The Medical Examiner

Coroners and medical examiners are charged with determining the cause and manner of death, overseeing the analysis of evidence, and presenting their findings in court. They often work with the police to help guide ongoing investigations by supplying them with the results of any forensic tests that have been performed. The responsibilities of these two offices cover every aspect of investigating a death.

The terms coroner and medical examiner (ME) are often used interchangeably, but they are, at least theoretically, quite different (see the following section for details). Regardless of which system is employed, in death investigations many of the duties of the coroner or the ME are similar. I use the term ME throughout the remainder of this book, even though some jurisdictions employ coroners for handling the legalities of death.

Looking at two forensic systems

In the United States, two types of forensic investigative systems exist: the coroner system and the medical examiner system. Fortunately, the trend is toward the latter system, though it is far from perfect.

The coroner is an appointed or elected position that, unfortunately, requires no special medical or forensic skills. The sole criterion seems to be the ability of the person seeking the office to be elected or appointed. The coroner could be the sheriff, a newspaper publisher, a neighborhood café owner, or the local funeral director. They too often possess little or no medical training or experience.

During the past several decades, the politics of the office have evolved so that today many jurisdictions require the coroner to be a licensed physician. He may be an internist, an obstetrician, or a dermatologist but doesn't necessarily have to be a pathologist and certainly not a forensic pathologist. Thus, the coroner may not actually be qualified to perform many of the duties of the office. This deficiency led to the creation of the medical examiner system.

In theory, a *medical examiner (ME)* is a physician licensed to practice medicine, and many are trained in pathology and forensic pathology, meaning that ideally they are medical doctors with special training in pathology and experience and training in forensic pathology. A *forensic pathologist* is a clinical pathologist who has taken extra forensic training. He usually heads up the crime lab and oversees all aspects of death and criminal injury. The heart of the forensic pathologist's job is performing *forensic autopsies,* which are designed to help determine the cause and manner of death.

In an ideal world, every jurisdiction would have a medical examiner who also is a board-certified forensic pathologist, qualified to fulfill all the duties of his office. The world, as you know, is not ideal, and even today in many jurisdictions nonmedically trained coroners and MEs continue serving as local public officials charged with investigating death. This solution is a practical, money-saving one because these areas simply don't have the population base to justify the presence of a forensic pathologist. Under these circumstances, the coroner/ME has several alternatives for acquiring the needed specialized pathological services.

If the coroner/ME is not a pathologist and not licensed to practice medicine, he must contract with larger regional or state medical examiner's offices for pathological examinations and laboratory testing or hire a forensic pathologist to serve as an assistant coroner or medical examiner. Under the legal umbrella of the coroner's or ME's office, the assistant coroner then performs autopsies, testifies in court, and oversees the crime lab.

Checking out the duties of a coroner or medical examiner

The duties of the coroner and ME are diverse, but many of them relate to the forensic investigation of death, including

- ✔ Determining the cause and manner of death
- ✔ Establishing the identity of any unnamed corpses
- ✔ Estimating the time of death
- ✔ Supervising the collection of evidence from the body
- ✔ Searching for any contributory factors such as disease
- ✔ Correlating wounds with the weapons that may have been used to inflict them
- ✔ Certifying or signing the death certificate

In fulfilling these duties, the coroner or ME uses any and all available information. Reviewing witness statements, visiting crime scenes, reviewing collected evidence and the results of crime lab testing, and, if a pathologist, performing autopsies are part of this endeavor.

In addition, the coroner or ME performs other duties not directly related to death investigations. These include

- ✔ Examining injuries of the living and determining their cause and timing
- ✔ Providing expert testimony in court
- ✔ Overseeing the crime lab (in some areas)

Following the medical examiner in action

When faced with an unexplained death, the ME takes a systematic approach to evaluating the case. This approach is similar to the one taken by physicians who treat the ill. Good physicians take a complete patient history, perform a thorough physical exam, order appropriate laboratory tests, and make an informed diagnosis. Only after this process can treatment begin.

The ME, on the other hand, obviously cannot obtain a direct history from the deceased but nevertheless can obtain information from police reports, medical records, witness statements, and interviews with family members, law enforcement, and other medical personnel. To help gather the needed information, the ME may possess (in some jurisdictions) or receive subpoena power from the court and can therefore legally require someone to provide information or evidence such as a blood sample, fingerprint, or shoe impression.

If no evidence of any potentially lethal trauma is seen, the ME then looks for natural causes of death by reviewing medical records, perhaps discussing the death with the person's physician or performing an autopsy when necessary. These investigations may lead the ME to conclude that the person died as a result of a natural cause, such as a heart attack, an infection, diabetes, or any number of other diseases.

When no natural cause is present or evident, however, the ME explores other manners of death, looking for less-obvious forms of trauma, poisons or drugs, or other signs of accidental, suicidal, or homicidal death.

After the analysis is complete, the ME files a report in which the essentials of the case are laid out and a conclusion is reached regarding the cause, mechanism, and manner of death.

The manner of death is an opinion expressed by the ME based upon all the circumstances leading to and surrounding the death. The ME's opinion may or may not be accepted by the courts, law enforcement, attorneys, or the victim's family. Even if the ME concludes that a death was a homicide, prosecutors may disagree and file no criminal charges. Likewise, surviving family members may sue the coroner's office for any number of reasons to change the manner of death, particularly in situations in which the manner of death has been ruled a suicide.

The ME's opinion is not written in stone and can change if new evidence comes to light that suggests a previously ruled natural death may not have been so natural after all.

Dealing with the Dead:
The Coroner's Technician

The *coroner's technician* is an extension of the coroner/ME and is indeed the ME's representative at the crime scene and works with the ME at the morgue. These technicians are often the ones who actually deal with the body at any crime scene where a death has occurred.

As an extension of the ME, the technician has legal authority over the body. The crime scene may be the domain of the police and the criminalists, but the body belongs to the medical examiner.

The coroner's technician may do the following:

- ✔ Make a cursory examination of the body
- ✔ Obtain a core (liver) body temperature, which is critical in determining the time of death (see Chapter 11)
- ✔ Direct the taking of photographs of the body
- ✔ Collect any trace or insect evidence from the body
- ✔ Wrap and transport the body to the ME's office

The technician may also assist the ME in all the examiner's duties at the morgue and may

- ✔ Perform or help with the performance of autopsies
- ✔ Prepare the autopsy report at the direction of the ME
- ✔ Communicate with the public, the media, and law enforcement on issues relating to the medical examiner's office
- ✔ Explain the autopsy procedure and its results to family members of the deceased
- ✔ Testify in court as the ME's representative

Testifying as an Expert

After they have analyzed the evidence, members of the forensics team may be called upon to explain it in court. Expert testimony can often make or break a case, and experts — be they medical examiners, crime-scene investigators, toxicologists, or other key players — can be called to testify by either the prosecution or the defense. In turn, their testimony may be refuted by the testimony of experts with different opinions.

The sworn duty of the ME is to present the facts in court and offer an unbiased opinion based on those facts. She is solely responsible for presenting evidence in court because she is in many ways an officer of the court. The ME may ask a member of her staff or of the crime lab to present evidence, but the ME is the one who is ultimately responsible to the court.

The ME may be asked to discuss and explain the forensic evidence and render an expert opinion regarding the evidence to the judge and jury. In this regard, the ME acts as an educator as well as a scientist. The ME often is the only person from whom a jury hears complex scientific information presented in an understandable way. At other times, the ME must pit knowledge and communication skills against other experts with different opinions.

Standardizing the science

Many of the procedures that are commonly employed in criminal cases, and that are discussed in this book, have never been adequately subjected to scientific scrutiny. Bite mark analysis, trace evidence such as hair and fiber analysis, and even fingerprints, to name a few, have been questioned in the courts and in scientific circles. The facts are that none of these techniques have ever been adequately tested for accuracy or reliability. Does this mean that they are no longer viable forensic scientific procedures? Not at all. It simply means that the techniques used in their analysis and the qualifications of the examiners must be better defined and standardized.

The 2009 study done by the National Academy of Sciences (NAS) titled *Strengthening Forensic Science in the United States: A Path Forward* started the ball rolling. Since then, organizations such as the National Institute of Standards and Technology (NIST), the Organization of Scientific Area Committees (OSAC), and others have made great strides in the standardization of forensic science. The goal is to make each scientific procedure reliable, reproducible, and uniform in every crime lab across the country as well as to establish standards and qualifications for experts in each area of forensic science. It's a tall order and will take time, but these organizations, and the working groups and committees they have established, are moving in the right direction.

Added to this is the problem of examiner bias, laziness, and corruption. Many cases of "experts" falsifying or "dry labbing" the evidence have cropped up in recent years. *Dry labbing* simply means coming up with results without actually doing the testing. We have seen this with DNA, fingerprints, bite marks, and other forensic techniques. Part of the work of the organizations previously mentioned is to identify and remove such individuals from the scientific community.

What does this mean for the current state of forensic science? Simply that the quality of the evidence uncovered and the expertise and honesty of the examiners is critical to the reliability of the results, and any move to improve that is a positive change. For example, if a good-quality fingerprint is found at a crime scene and it is examined and compared by a qualified expert, the results are very reliable. Even though no true scientific evaluation of fingerprint techniques has been done, the facts are that despite countless millions of fingerprints being obtained around the world, no two have ever been shown to be identical. Even identical twins have different fingerprints. So forensic science is sound; it simply needs to be standardized and uniformly applied.

Understanding the court system

The court system in the United States is adversarial by nature, meaning that each side attempts to outfox or outargue the other. The prosecutor and defense attorney attempt to present evidence that favors their respective side and spin any contrary evidence in a manner that supports their theory regarding the case. This locking of horns can put the forensic expert in a difficult position. Each side is likely to bring in outside experts to support or refute the testimony of the ME. These experts may even be other forensic pathologists, toxicologists, firearms experts, or someone from any of the other forensic areas.

Each expert can expect to be *qualified* before the jury, meaning that the opposing attorneys ask questions about the expert's credentials, training, experience, areas of expertise, teaching positions, publications in the field in question, and anything else they think will support or undermine the expert's true qualifications. In general, the side that calls on an expert as a witness asks easy, supportive questions, and the opposing side asks tougher questions aimed at impeaching, or refuting, the qualifications and any testimony the expert gives. Expert witnesses must be prepared for potentially unsettling questions.

Experts presenting testimony need to be honest and measured, trying not to oversell their points of view, but making their honest opinions clear, concise, and believable. That is, experts must appear neither too sure nor too unsure of their opinions. The former may alienate a jury, and the latter may undermine the expert's credibility.

Getting to the heart of the "truth"

The real goal of court proceedings is not so much to uncover the absolute truth as it is to provide enough evidence so a jury can reach an understandable version of the truth based on the applicable rules of law. Getting to that version is complicated by the fact that certain items of evidence may not be admissible (allowed into the courtroom at the time of trial) in court, because they were obtained improperly, contaminated, or overly inflammatory or prejudicial.

So, you may be wondering: "If some evidence is excluded, how can the absolute truth be found? Isn't that like trying to solve a math problem with only half the numbers?" You're mostly right, but the expert can't change but rather must work within the law. She can present only the information the court allows and must explain it as fully as possible in a true and unbiased opinion. Doing so helps the jury get as close to the truth as possible.

Understanding the role of expert testimony

Judges typically allow a great deal of leeway with regard to how expert witnesses present information to the jury. Most witnesses are permitted only to answer questions. If they attempt to move too far afield of the question, the judge will rein them in. Experts, on the other hand, are allowed to depart from the normal Q-and-A format because their often-technical testimony necessitates explanation. Indeed, the expert teaches the judge and jury. For example, understanding the impact of DNA evidence is difficult for the average juror when presented simply from a series of questions with *yes* or *no* answers. Enabling the expert to explain what DNA is, how it is tested, and what the results of the testing mean gives the jurors the knowledge they need to understand and evaluate the evidence.

Rarely will an expert witness express testimony as an absolute fact, especially when being challenged by the other side. Instead, the wise expert uses phrases such as "similar to," "consistent with," "not dissimilar from," "compatible with," or "shares many characteristics with." Why is this? The truth is that forensic evidence rarely, if ever, is absolute but rather states probabilities. For example, except for identical twins, no two people have the same DNA, but the testifying expert should never say the DNA "absolutely matches" that of the defendant. Instead, the expert should say that the probability that it matches someone other than the suspect is a billion to one. That is almost, but not quite, absolute.

Holding testimony to standards of acceptance

Regardless of who presents the information, by virtue of *Frye v. United States,* judges require that the science behind the evidence be real and not *junk science* coming from someone merely spouting personal beliefs without any scientific support.

In 1923, the District of Columbia Circuit Court addressed whether the results of a polygraph examination (lie detector test) were admissible as evidence in that case. The landmark decision in *Frye v. United States* set what later became known as the *Frye Standard* for presenting scientific evidence before the courts. The standard states that the court can accept expert testimony on "well-recognized scientific principle and discovery," if it is "sufficiently established" and has achieved "general acceptance" in the scientific community. This acceptance enables new scientific tests to be presented, but only after they've been thoroughly hashed out and accepted.

Although *Frye* was the standard for many years, and still is followed in many jurisdictions, it more recently was replaced by *Daubert v. Merrell Dow Pharmaceutical, Inc.,* or Rule 702 of the Federal Rules of evidence, which states that judges may use their discretion to admit expert testimony to "understand the evidence" and to "determine a fact in issue."

Rule 702 was upheld and amplified in 1993 by the United States Supreme Court, which held that the "general acceptance" clause in *Frye* was not absolute, thus handing judges wider discretion as to what expert testimony they can allow in any given case. To further help judges, the court offered several guidelines. For a new scientific technique or theory to be acceptable to the court, it must

✓ Be subject to testing and to peer review

✓ Be standardized with recognized maintenance of such standards

✓ Have a known and accepted error rate

✓ Attain widespread acceptance

The high court's ruling basically means that the technique or theory must be spelled out, tested, reviewed, accepted, and continually monitored for accuracy.

Whether scientific evidence and testimony are admissible often is hammered out by attorneys and the judge in pretrial hearings and motions that the jury never hears. If the evidence to be presented by the expert passes the *Frye* or *Daubert* standards, the judge allows the jury to hear the expert testimony. If not, the judge may exclude it from the trial.

Chapter 3

Collecting and Protecting the Evidence

Crime scenes are like puzzles and, when investigators are lucky, the pieces fit neatly together. In other cases, determining what happened is like trying to create a picture from two or three different puzzles where you have plenty of pieces, but they don't fit. And investigators often have to deal with pieces that just aren't there.

Because solving a crime and convicting a perpetrator depend upon evidence, investigators take a methodical approach to finding and handling evidence at crime scenes. They work hard to protect the evidence and to leave nothing important behind. Throughout the process, investigators formulate theories about what happened. If they do their jobs well, they end up with a complete picture of the crime. In this chapter, I fill you in on exactly how investigators deal with evidence and crime scenes.

Assessing the Scene of the Crime

From the moment the first police officer arrives at the scene, he follows a strict set of procedural guidelines designed to protect him and everyone else who's present; guard evidence against damage, contamination, or loss; and document everything that occurs at the scene. Following these procedures and maintaining control of the scene until the crime-scene investigators arrive offer the best chance of getting the evidence needed to identify and convict the perpetrator. Failure to follow these directives can result in the crime remaining unsolved or a known perpetrator walking free.

Distinguishing between primary and secondary crime scenes

There may be more to a crime scene than first meets the eye. In fact, more than one crime scene may exist, depending upon how the crime was committed, not to mention *where*. Crime scenes, therefore, are considered either primary or secondary. The *primary crime scene* is where a crime actually occurred. A *secondary crime scene* is in some way related to the crime but is not where the actual crime took place.

In a bank robbery, for example, the bank is the primary scene, but the getaway car and the thief's hideout are secondary scenes. In the case of a killer who commits a murder in someone's home but transports the victim's body to a river for disposal, the victim's home is the primary scene, and the killer's vehicle and the point along the river where the body was dumped are secondary scenes.

Primary scenes typically yield more usable evidence than do secondary scenes, but not always. Sometimes the only crime scene investigators have to work with is a secondary scene, such as the place where a serial killer dumps a victim's body, for example. Under these circumstances, investigators may not know where the actual murder took place and therefore use evidence they find at the secondary scenes to help them identify the killer or locate the primary scene. They may be able to use fibers from an expensive or unusual carpet they found on the victim to identify the manufacturer, the seller, and ultimately a list of buyers or locations where that particular product has been installed. Doing so can greatly narrow the focus of the investigation and lead police to the primary crime scene and the perpetrator.

Arriving at a crime scene

Regardless of whether the first officer to arrive at a crime scene found out about the crime via a phone call to the station, a radio call from a dispatcher, or directly from a concerned person, the officer must make every effort to detain the person who initially reported the crime and not allow that individual access to the crime scene. Anyone who reports a crime may have witnessed the incident or may have seen or heard something suspicious.

However, because the officer has no way of knowing whether the person reporting the crime is a witness or a suspect, allowing the informant access to the crime scene can mean losing or contaminating the evidence. After all, a perpetrator may

- ✔ Believe that reporting the crime makes him less likely to be a suspect
- ✔ Attempt to destroy or remove evidence

Neither of these situations is uncommon, so the officer who arrives first needs to approach the crime scene in a logical and organized manner, protecting the evidence and other people who may be there. Otherwise, harm may come to the officer, fellow officers, victims, witnesses, suspects, and even the perpetrator, or evidence may be damaged or destroyed.

The officer who responds first must make personal safety a primary concern and ensure that the perpetrator or perpetrators no longer are present or a threat. Whenever a perpetrator is present, the officer arrests and secures that person. Thereafter, the officer assists any victims who are present, offers first aid as needed, and mobilizes emergency medical services. After these important tasks are completed, the officer begins preserving the crime scene.

Additionally, the officer may need to detain suspects and witnesses and keep them separate to avoid *collusion,* meaning that the detainees work together to create a story to tell police. However, at this stage, the officer may not know who is who: A witness may become a suspect, and a suspect may actually be a useful witness. Furthermore, the officer may have no reason or legal right to detain some witnesses and thus must obtain accurate identification and contact information from each person who leaves the area.

At the heart of crime-scene protection is the principle of exchange. *Locard's Exchange Principle* (see Chapter 1) states that when any two people come in contact with each other, they exchange or transfer trace materials, such as hair, fibers, and prints. Every person who enters the crime scene can leave behind evidence of his presence; take away crucial trace evidence on his shoes, clothes, or hands; or otherwise damage or alter any evidence that remains. Thus, access to the scene must be restricted immediately and denied to all witnesses and suspects.

Preserving and processing the scene

The size of a crime scene can vary greatly and the police must be prepared to quickly determine its boundaries. This task is not as easy as it seems. A crime scene may be a single room, an entire house, everything on a property, or even a whole neighborhood. And that's just the primary scene.

At a minimum, the crime scene includes

- The exact spot where the offense took place

- Areas from which the site can be entered and exited

- Locations of key pieces of evidence, such as the body in a murder, a safe or cabinet in a burglary, or an entire structure in a suspicious fire

A crime scene can be cordoned off using crime-scene tape, barricades, automobiles, or even by police officers standing guard. Only personnel who are absolutely necessary for processing the scene are allowed in. This restriction often is more difficult to accomplish than you may think. A victim's family members or neighbors may be emotionally unstable and thus difficult to remove from the area. And, of course, members of the press often have clever ways of gaining access to a crime scene, to say nothing of a captain or other high-ranking official trying to push her way past a lowly patrol officer who's following orders to keep everyone without a reason for being there away from the scene. Furthermore, you can never underestimate the meanderings of the curious bystander.

After the scene is secured, the first officer to arrive establishes a *security log,* which basically is a sign-in sheet that must be signed by any and all visitors to the scene. This kind of crowd control helps the investigation in many ways, not the least of which is limiting the number of people who must be examined when stray fingerprints and shoeprints are found. If investigators can be ruled out, the print or prints remaining may point to the perpetrator.

A crime-scene investigator begins by doing a *walk-through examination,* getting a feel for the scene and organizing an approach to collecting evidence. During this overview, the crime-scene investigator typically doesn't examine any particular pieces of evidence, but rather looks at the big picture before beginning the tedious work of evidence examination and collection.

Documenting the procedure

While a crime scene is being processed, everything that transpires is documented in notes, sketches, and photographs, and perhaps even videoed. This documentation includes not only the scene and the evidence, but also the surrounding area, particularly the perpetrator's possible entry and exit points.

A designated note taker keeps an accurate account of all activities in and around the crime scene. Sometimes a tape recorder is used, and the verbal notes are transcribed later. Regardless of how they're taken, the notes must be detailed, including an overall description of the scene; an accurate list describing what each piece of evidence is; when, where, and by whom it was found; and who transported it to the crime lab. The note taker also identifies and comments on every photo that is taken at the scene.

Photographs of the scene need to be taken as soon as possible so that they show the scene preserved in an unaltered condition. Photos must be taken prior to moving or removing any evidence (or the body, if there is one). Taking several overview images of the area is a good idea, and if the scene happens to be outdoors, pictures of surrounding areas should be taken from multiple angles and points of view. Close-ups of each item of evidence, and, in murder cases, any and all visible injuries to the corpse (while it's still at the crime scene), are critical. Video possesses the advantage of including sound so that comments can be preserved. But whenever video is used, still photos nevertheless need to be taken because they offer much greater detail resolution.

Photos also are taken of any injured parties, including the suspect. Full-body and close-up shots of any injuries are obtained. Whether these pictures are taken at the scene or at the hospital (or even in the operating room) depends upon the nature of the injuries. Bumps, bruises, and scratches can be photographed at the scene, but photos of injuries such as gunshot and knife wounds probably have to wait until the victim is transported to the hospital.

In photographs where the size of the object or evidence being recorded is important, the photographer includes a point of reference. A ruler is ideal, but another common object, such as a cigarette pack, a ballpoint pen, or a car key, for example, works in a pinch.

Sketches also are extremely important, because they show the relationship of each item of evidence to other items or to the body (see Figure 3-1). Each piece of evidentiary material is mapped, or located by its distance from two fixed points, such as a wall, a lamppost, or a sidewalk. Doing so provides exact graphic coordinates of each item. Sketches made at the scene may be rough, but they need to be accurate. They can be redrawn later for clarity and aesthetics. Several computer programs are available that help generate clear drawings.

Reconstructing the crime scene

After doing an initial walk-through of the crime scene, the investigator begins mentally formulating a hypothesis of the crime, focusing on the likely sequence of events and the locations and positions of everyone present

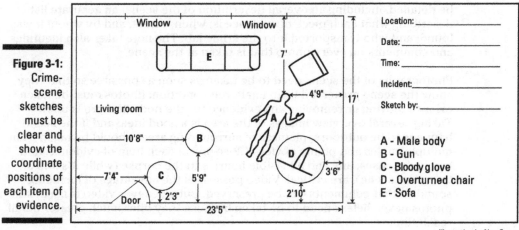

Illustration by Nan Owen.

Figure 3-1: Crime-scene sketches must be clear and show the coordinate positions of each item of evidence.

Window   Window

Living room

E - Sofa

A - Male body
B - Gun
C - Bloody glove
D - Overturned chair
E - Sofa

Location: _____
Date: _____
Time: _____
Incident: _____
Sketch by: _____

during the crime. Information like the following may be critical in determining the truthfulness of a suspect or the reliability of a witness:

- Shoeprints may reveal a perpetrator's every step.
- Fingerprints may indicate the things the perpetrator touched.
- Tool marks may signify points of entry or where safes or locked cabinets were pried open.
- Blood spatters, bullet trajectories, the angle and severity of blows and stabs, and the nature of the victim's injuries can reveal the actual and relative positions of the assailant, victim, and anyone else who was present during a crime.
- The physical changes that take place in a corpse (see Chapter 11) may indicate whether the body was moved several hours after death.

The investigator looks at each piece of physical evidence to assess whether it supports this theory, considering information obtained not only at the scene but also from the crime lab, medical reports of anyone who was injured, and the medical examiner's autopsy examination. Anything that doesn't fit in with or justify the investigator's theory of the crime must be reconciled; otherwise, the theory must change. As a result, the reconstruction of a crime scene is constantly evolving as more evidence is uncovered.

The investigator continually tests the developing crime theory against the evidence and avoids making any assumptions, no matter how logical they may seem. An investigator may logically believe that a piece of evidence ended up where it did because of a suspect's actions, but if the hard evidence doesn't support this belief, the theory must be held suspect.

If a gun is found just outside the rear door of a house where a homicide took place, logic suggests that the assailant dropped the gun while escaping. Although that's certainly a possibility, without solid evidence, ruling out other possibilities may be difficult. For all investigators know, the gun had been tossed there in an attempt to make a domestic homicide look like a murder committed by a burglar whom the victim supposedly caught in the act. Evidence like the spouse's fingerprints on the gun or the victim's blood on the spouse's shoes may, of course, change the theory, but until all evidence in a reconstruction is considered and explained, investigators can't reach any absolute conclusions.

Recognizing a staged crime scene

Staging is when someone who's committed a crime attempts to make the scene look like something that it isn't. The most common staging scenario occurs when someone tries to make a murder look like a suicide or an accident. The suspect may move the body or clean certain areas. Say, for example, a husband strikes his wife in the head with a blunt object, killing her. Then he cleans up the bedroom, moves her body into the bathroom, places her in the tub, and calls the paramedics, claiming that she fell while bathing.

Other common examples of staged crime scenes include the following:

- ✔ A murderer breaks a window or pries a lock and makes sure a prized piece of insured jewelry is missing in an effort to stage the crime so that it looks a burglar killed the victim.

- ✔ One spouse secretly feeds a deadly quantity of alcohol and sedatives to the other and then forges a suicide note in an attempt to make homicide look like suicide.

- ✔ A person committing insurance fraud stages a breaking and entering: Jewelry is missing, a window has been pried open, and of course, the jewelry was insured.

- ✔ A perpetrator sets a fire (thus committing arson) to cover up another crime, perhaps a murder, embezzlement, or even a burglary. The perpetrator hopes that the fire, which becomes a staged crime scene, destroys evidence of the underlying crime.

Classifying the Evidence

Evidence is anything that can be used to determine whether a crime has been committed. Evidence may link a suspect to a scene, corroborate or refute an alibi or statement, identify a perpetrator or victim, exonerate the innocent, induce a confession, or direct further investigation.

All evidence is not created equal. In fact, evidence is divided into numerous categories depending on its characteristics and reliability. For example, an eyewitness account falls into a different classification than left-behind hair or a piece of clothing.

Determining whether evidence is direct or circumstantial

Evidence can be either direct or circumstantial. *Direct evidence* establishes a fact. Examples of direct evidence are eyewitness statements and confessions. *Circumstantial evidence,* on the other hand, requires that a judge and/or jury make an indirect judgment, or inference, about what happened. For example, if a fingerprint or hair found at the crime scene matches that of a suspect, jurors may infer that the print or hair is indeed that of the defendant, and because it was found at the crime scene, links the defendant to the scene.

Circumstantial evidence is not absolute proof; instead, it provides a general idea of what happened. Most often, evidence identified through forensic science is circumstantial, though direct evidence such as witness and victim statements or suspect confessions may impact the ME's interpretation of test results or his reconstruction of the crime scene.

Circumstantial evidence often is much more reliable than direct evidence. Eyewitnesses are notoriously bad at identifying suspects or recalling events. After all, people tend to interpret what happened instead of simply playing it back like a film loop.

Furthermore, circumstantial evidence is more objective and is more likely to provide a reliable answer. An eyewitness may be wrong as much as half the time, but fingerprints and DNA evidence can, more often than not, accurately distinguish the individual in question from the other 7 billion people on Earth.

Discerning physical from biological evidence

Forensic evidence can be divided into two basic categories: physical and biological. *Physical evidence* may take the form of nonliving or inorganic items, such as fingerprints, shoe and tire impressions, tool marks, fibers, paint, glass, drugs, firearms, bullets and shell casings, documents, explosives, and petroleum byproducts or distilled fire accelerants. *Biological evidence,* on the other hand, includes organic things like blood, saliva, urine, semen, hair, and botanical materials, such as wood, plants, pollens and yes, Clarice, moth cocoons.

Understanding reconstructive evidence

Any evidence that helps law enforcement officers better grasp what happened at the crime scene is considered *reconstructive evidence*. Broken glass or pried-open doors and windows often reveal a perpetrator's points of entry and exit, and determining whether a window was broken from the inside or the outside tells which way the perpetrator went through it. Evidence derived from shoeprints, blood spatters, or the trajectory of bullets may pinpoint where in the room everyone was located and exactly how and in what sequence the events of the crime occurred. Whether the victim was attacked from the front or from behind, whether the life was taken quickly or after a struggle, and whether the prime suspect was at the scene at the time of the murder are important aspects in creating a clearer picture of the crime scene.

Another way of looking at reconstructive evidence is that it helps the crime-scene investigator determine who did what, where, when, and how. It may also help determine who is being truthful and who isn't.

Identifying associative evidence

Associative evidence, in a nutshell, ties a suspect to the crime scene, the victim, or some other bit of evidence. Fingerprints, footprints, hair, fibers, blood and other bodily fluids, knives, bullets, guns, paint, and many other objects and substances, even soil, can link a suspect to the scene.

Associative evidence also can have the opposite effect, proving a suspect's fingerprints, hair, or blood are not the same as those found at the crime scene, and thus someone else may have committed the crime.

Differentiating class and individual evidence

In general, all forms of evidence have class or individual characteristics. *Class characteristics* are not unique to a particular object but place the particular bit of evidence into a group of objects. *Individual characteristics* narrow down the evidence to a single, individual source.

The type of handgun with which a victim is shot is a class characteristic. For example, if the bullet came from a .38 caliber handgun, every .38 caliber handgun on the planet is the possible murder weapon. However, finding a suspect's fingerprint (an individual characteristic) on a .38 caliber handgun suggests that this .38, to the exclusion of all others, was the murder weapon. This is particularly true if the killing bullet can also be matched to this particular .38.

Alternatively, blood recovered from a crime scene that tests show is type B (a class characteristic) could have come from any of the tens of millions of people who share this blood type. If the suspect has type B blood, he remains a suspect. From there, DNA (an individual characteristic) from the suspect and DNA from the blood evidence are tested to determine conclusively whether they match. If, however, the suspect's blood is type A, he then is excluded as the source of the blood.

A single piece of class evidence rarely can be used to convict someone, but it can be and often is used to exonerate someone. However, when multiple types of class evidence associate one suspect with the crime and crime scene, the weight of that evidence can make for a stronger case, which is what happened to Wayne Williams.

In December 1981, Williams was tried for the Atlanta Child Murders based largely on class fiber evidence. Multiple fibers, 28 different types in all, were found on several of the victims. These fibers chemically and optically matched fibers taken from Williams's home and cars. Blue, yellow, white, and yellow-green fibers of various synthetic types were similar to fibers taken from Williams's kitchen and backroom carpets, bedspread, throw rug, and car liner. Hairs matching those of his dog also were found. Williams was convicted.

In the case against Wayne Williams, the sheer number of the pieces of class evidence made coincidence extremely unlikely. The odds that someone else left behind that particular combination of fibers and hair are astronomical. Although class evidence isn't absolute proof that a suspect is connected with a particular location and each bit of class evidence taken separately may not be strong, a large number of matching pieces of class evidence significantly boosts the probability that a suspect was present at the crime scene. A handful of class evidence is statistically equal to a single fingerprint.

The most individualizing types of evidence are fingerprints and DNA, because they're pretty much like snowflakes in that no two people have the same prints or, with the exception of identical twins, the same DNA. *Impression evidence* such as marks left on a fired bullet (see Chapter 18), shoeprints, tire tracks, and toolmarks may be unique and therefore have individual characteristics. Fracture or tear patterns can be individualizing; the way glass breaks, paper tears, and cloth rips is unique in each situation. When a piece of glass taken from a crime scene and a piece of glass removed from a suspect's broken headlight fit neatly together like the pieces of a jigsaw puzzle, the pieces share a common source.

The overriding principle in analyzing individual characteristics is that no two things are exactly alike. No two guns mark a bullet the same way. No two pieces of glass fracture in the same manner. No two pairs of shoes or sets of car tires wear in exactly the same way.

Analyzing the evidence

Forensic analysis of most physical and biological evidence is conducted for two purposes: identification and comparison. *Identification* determines what exactly a particular item or substance is. Is that white powder cocaine? Is that brown stain dried blood? After testing, a forensic examiner may state that the substance in question is present, not present, or that testing was inclusive and the presence of the substance can't be ruled in or ruled out.

Comparisons are made to find out whether a known and a suspect item or substance share a common origin. Did the fingerprint, hair, or blood come from the suspect? Does the paint smudge found on a hit-and-run victim's clothing match that of the suspect's car? After comparing a crime-scene fingerprint to one obtained from a suspect, the examiner may state that the two match, keeping the suspect in the hot seat, or that they don't match, thus exonerating the suspect as a source for the print. The examiner also may find the comparison inclusive, perhaps because the crime-scene print was of poor quality. When that happens, the suspect is neither cleared nor condemned.

Crime-scene investigators use evidence to create *linkage,* that is, a connection between a suspect and a person, place, or object. Finding a victim's hair on the clothing of the suspect, for example, suggests that they had some degree of contact and thus links the two together. A suspect's fingerprint, blood, or semen at the scene of a robbery, murder, or rape strongly links the suspect to the crime scene. A murder weapon on which a suspect's fingerprints are found requires a great deal of explaining. Each circumstance links elements (person, place, or object) of the crime to the suspect.

Investigators also attempt to link multiple crime scenes to a single perpetrator. For example, if a particular shoe impression or an identical fingerprint is found at two or more scenes, this evidence may link the scenes to a single suspect. Even if investigators don't have a suspect, such a linkage allows them to use other clues at the various scenes to create a better picture of the perpetrator they seek.

The skill of a crime-scene investigator in collecting evidence and the precision of the analytical procedures of the crime lab work in tandem to establish these links. When successful, evidence may find its way into court and result in a conviction.

Locating the Evidence

Locating evidence can be straightforward: Someone calls the police to report a burglary, and when the police arrive the victim invites them in and shows them the location of the pried-open window, the family safe, and the perpetrator's escape route. But, in other cases, the probable location of the evidence is not always associated with a crime scene, and police are not invited into the area where the evidence may be located.

For example, the murder weapon or other important evidence such as the victim's blood or hair may be in the suspect's home or car. Such items may provide important circumstantial evidence that the suspect is indeed the perpetrator of the crime. However, to enter and search the suspect's residence or vehicle, investigators need a reason for the search that is acceptable to a judge and, ultimately, a search warrant.

Obtaining a search warrant

The Fourth Amendment to the United States Constitution protects citizens "against unreasonable searches and seizures," which means that police personnel and crime-scene investigators need a warrant before they can search for evidence. This warrant must be specific about the time and place of the search, the items investigators are looking for, and it must be obtained on the basis of *probable cause,* a solid legal reason approved by a judge. Only a law enforcement officer can obtain a search warrant. Attorneys and private investigators can't, and neither can you.

The steps that are required to obtain a valid search warrant are

1. **Preparing an affidavit.**

   This affidavit must describe the location to be searched, the items to be searched for, and the reasons why the officer expects the items are at the location (probable cause).

2. **Preparing the warrant.**

   This step results in the official document that the judge must sign giving permission for the search to take place.

3. **Getting the warrant signed.**

   The officer must present the warrant and affidavit to the judge. If the judge thinks probable cause for the search exists, he signs the warrant, making it official.

Sounds simple enough, doesn't it? Often it is, but at other times, obtaining a search warrant can be difficult. Probable cause can be one of the first issues to raise a flag. The officer must have a strong, concrete reason for believing that the items to be searched for are at a specific location. A mere hunch or suspicion won't work. Say, for instance, that an arms dealer has a safe house from which he sells his wares, and police have observed known arms sellers coming and going with boxes and crates that potentially contain guns. Maybe police even know to whom one of the middlemen has sold illegal weapons. When combined, these factors are more than a hunch and provide solid evidence that packages arriving at and leaving from the house contain weapons.

Another problem is that the warrant must state exactly what police are looking for. Thus, police tend to add any and all items they think may be present. If police happen to find other evidence while they're conducting a legitimate search for the items listed in the warrant, then that evidence *can,* in most cases, be seized.

If the object of the search warrant is a gun crate, police can search only areas in which such a crate can be concealed. Rooms, attics, closets, and basements are searchable, but a kitchen drawer is not. So, if police open a drawer and find a gun, they can neither seize it nor use it in court. As a result, police try to include a number of small items in the warrant, because doing so enables them to conduct a much more extensive search. In the case of the arms dealer, police may include drugs, which can be hidden almost anywhere, in the warrant. If the judge believes police have probable cause to search for drugs, police then can look through the kitchen drawers and even the breadbox.

Creating yet another difficulty, the area to be searched must be explicitly defined. If a search warrant identifies a house, but doesn't specifically mention that the garage and storage shed can be searched, then those areas are off limits. If the warrant lists a garage but not the car inside, then the garage can be searched but not the car.

Searching without a warrant

Certain special circumstances allow police to search without a warrant. The Supreme Court has allowed *warrantless searches* to stand in the following situations:

- ✔ **Emergent situations:** When an emergency exists and someone's life or health is in danger, police may enter a building or other structure (including a vehicle) without a warrant. Any evidence that is found under such circumstance may be admissible in court. However, police officers cannot make an emergency entrance, leave, and return at a later date to search for evidence. This second entry requires a warrant.

✓ **Impending loss of evidence:** This exception applies in situations where a suspect or some other agent or outside influence, such as a structure fire, threatens to destroy evidence.

✓ **Lawful arrest:** Whenever someone has been arrested lawfully, the suspect and any property in the suspect's immediate control, such as a home or a vehicle, can be searched for evidence.

✓ **Consented search:** No warrant is needed when the parties who are subjected to a search of their person or property have given police their consent.

Collecting and Preserving the Evidence

Without evidence, even a heinous crime may go unpunished. Attorneys are called upon to prove beyond reasonable doubt that defendants committed the crimes with which they are charged, and that's no easy feat even in the best circumstances. Without evidence, it's virtually impossible. That's why protecting the scene and the evidence is of paramount importance.

In fact, the care (or lack of it) that is taken in handling evidence directly impacts law enforcement's ability to successfully investigate and prosecute a crime. Evidence can be damaged, contaminated, or even lost, and thus rendered useless to the crime lab and probably inadmissible in court. Even the most expensively equipped and sophisticated crime lab has little use for damaged or altered evidence, because courts rarely allow such evidence to be presented to the jury.

The size, budget, and organization of the crime lab or law enforcement agency often determine who is responsible for collecting evidence (see Chapter 2). Regardless of who actually gathers evidentiary materials, those people nevertheless need to be well schooled in proper techniques.

Searching the area

The first step in gathering evidence is finding it, and that means taking an orderly approach to searching the crime scene. Many items, such as corpses and weapons, may be readily visible, but others, particularly smaller materials or bits of trace evidence, require diligence on the part of investigators. In homicides, investigators target points of entry and exit and the area near the body; in robberies, open safes, cabinets, or drawers are good starting points.

The way investigators search for evidence depends upon the size and physical layout of the area in question. Scanning the floor of a broom closet for fiber evidence is much different than searching a half-acre lot for a shell casing. Yet in both situations the search must be thorough and orderly.

When searching a crime scene for trace evidence (see Chapter 17), investigators typically follow a geometric pattern (see Figure 3-2). They may use a crisscrossing grid, a shoulder-to-shoulder linear pattern, or expanding or contracting spiral patterns. The spiral may begin at the body or the cracked safe and move outward, or it may begin at the periphery of the crime scene and circle inward toward the spot where the actual criminal act took place. Larger areas are first divided into quadrants or zones so that each smaller area can be scanned using one of these methods. The goal is to carefully search every square inch of the target area.

Figure 3-2:
The pattern used to conduct a search depends on the size and location of the area being searched.

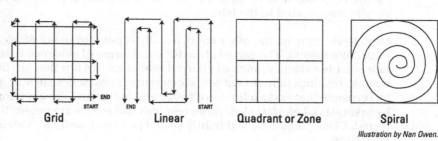

Grid   Linear   Quadrant or Zone   Spiral

Illustration by Nan Owen.

Gathering the evidence

When collecting evidence, investigators start with evidence that is particularly fragile or that is likely to be lost, damaged, or contaminated, such as blood, fibers, hair, fingerprints, shoeprints, and tire tracks. This method is particularly useful when gathering evidence from outdoor crime scenes, where wind and rain can complicate matters.

Investigators use the following techniques for gathering delicate evidence:

 ✔ Fingerprints are photographed and then lifted, or transferred to a material that investigators can take with them to the crime lab. Chapter 5 gives you the whole scoop on how investigators find and collect fingerprints.

- ✔ Toolmarks and shoeprints or tire impressions also are photographed before being lifted or cast (see Chapter 7).
- ✔ Fibers and hair are searched for with alternative light sources and gathered with tweezers.
- ✔ Carpets and furniture are vacuumed, using a fresh vacuum cleaner bag for each area. This often yields hair, fibers, and other trace material that escaped the investigator's eye at the scene.

Packaging the evidence

After evidence has been found and gathered, it must be protected. Each piece of evidence gathered is packaged separately to avoid damage and cross-contamination. Most dry trace evidence is placed in *druggist's folds,* which are small, folded papers. Envelopes, canisters, plastic pill bottles, and paper or plastic bags may also be used. Documents are sealed in plastic covers before they're transported to the lab.

Liquid evidence, on the other hand, usually is put into unbreakable, airtight, sealed containers. The same is true for solid forms of evidence that may contain volatile evidence, such as charred remnants of a fire that are believed to contain residues of hydrocarbon accelerants (substances such as gasoline or kerosene that make a fire burn faster and hotter and are commonly used by arsonists). Left unsealed, these residues can evaporate before they are tested. Clean paint cans and tightly sealed jars work well for evidence in solid form.

Moist or wet biological evidence must be placed in nonairtight containers so that it can air dry; otherwise, the moisture can cause mold, mildew, and bacterial growth, which, in turn, lead to decay and ultimately destroy the sample. Bloody clothing often is hung up and allowed to thoroughly air dry. After the biological evidence is dry, it is repackaged into sealed containers.

Sometimes removing evidence from the scene without damaging it is difficult or even impossible. A tool mark on the sill of a window that's been pried open can be processed at the scene, or the entire window or frame may be removed and taken to the lab. Similarly, bullet holes in a concrete wall may be processed on-site, or a portion of the wall may be carefully removed for later laboratory evaluation.

Collecting control samples

Another important aspect of collecting evidence is properly obtaining *control samples,* which are samples taken from a known source against which the examiner can compare samples taken from the crime scene.

Control samples may come from the victim, from the suspect, or from items found at the scene. A fiber found at the scene is most valuable when control fibers are available from the floor mats of the suspect's vehicle. That way, the *known* or control sample taken from the car can be compared with the *unknown* sample discovered at the crime scene. A match either puts the suspect at the scene or the victim in the suspect's car. Control samples of blood taken from the victim and the suspect can be compared with blood from an unknown bloodstain found at the scene to determine whether either of them shed the blood.

Control samples sometimes are materials that are identical to those on which evidence was found. For example, a sample of charred carpet that is suspected of containing residue from a fluid used to start a fire is best compared against the same kind of carpet that is known to be free of the suspect materials. A carpet sample taken from an area left undamaged by the fire can often provide the known sample. If a suspicious chemical is present in the charred carpet but not in the known sample, the laboratory examiner can be more certain that it is indeed a foreign chemical and not a component of the carpet or its adhesive.

Protecting the chain of custody

Without a continuous record showing that evidence has been kept safe and secure from the crime scene to the lab and ultimately the courtroom, evidence may be rendered inadmissible in court. Any competent defense attorney would rightly question the authenticity and integrity of any evidence for which outside contamination cannot be ruled out. That's why every person who handles the evidence must be accounted for and recorded as a link in this unbroken *chain of custody*, from crime scene to courtroom.

Whoever finds an item of evidence marks it for identification, which sometimes consists of writing or scratching his or her initials onto the item itself. Of course, this method is appropriate only when it won't damage the evidence or alter any of its specific identifying characteristics. For example, an investigator may scratch his or her initials on the side of a shell casing found at the scene. In court, the investigator can positively identify the shell casing as the exact one uncovered at the scene.

Not all evidence can be marked directly, however. An investigator probably wouldn't mark a bullet by scratching initials into it, because doing so can alter the striations on the side of the bullet that are used to identify the gun from which it was fired. Altering the bullet makes matching it with the gun more difficult. Therefore, evidence like a bullet is placed into an evidence bag, which is marked and initialed by the person who finds it. The identifying information on the evidence bag includes the case number, the name and description of the item, the name and initials of the person who found it, the names of any witnesses to the discovery and recovery, and the date, time, and location of the find.

Some items require special packaging before being placed in an evidence bag. For example, a blood sample may be taken using a moist, cotton-tipped swab. After drying, the swab is placed into a sealed glass tube, and the tube is marked with the collector's initials and date. The tube is placed into an evidence bag, which is similarly marked. The collector can then reasonably testify that that is the sample he obtained by identifying his initials on the sample tube and the evidence bag.

Each person who accepts an item of evidence initials or signs and dates the evidence bag and is then responsible for maintaining its integrity until it is passed along to the next person (or link in the chain). Here's how it works:

✔ A police officer finds a shell casing at the scene of a homicide; he collects it, marks it, places it into a marked evidence bag, and then signs it over to one of the crime-scene investigators.

✔ The investigator transports the evidence to the lab and signs it over to the crime lab technician.

✔ After the item is tested and evaluated, the lab technician signs the evidence over to the police department's custodian of evidence (the officer in charge of the secured evidence lock-up area at the police department).

✔ The custodian of evidence places the evidence in a secured area until it's needed again. From there, it may be signed over to the prosecuting attorney for presentation in court.

If the chain of custody remains intact, each witness, from the officer who found it to the custodian of evidence, can testify that the item presented in the courtroom is indeed the item that was collected at the scene and tested by the lab.

Locating a Missing Corpse

No body means no crime, right? Maybe so, but more often it means a body was well hidden. When a body (and the critical evidence it provides) can't be found, investigators rely on a few time-tested techniques for unearthing it. This branch of forensics is a particularly interesting one, and it's growing all the time.

When looking for a body, investigators use any and all evidence to narrow the search area, and statements by witnesses can be crucial. For example, a witness may have spotted a suspect's vehicle or found some of the victim's clothing in a remote area, pointing the investigation to a particular direction.

Investigators use a number of low- and high-tech methods when searching for a body that has gone missing, including

- ✔ **Looking downhill:** Say that a body is believed to have been buried near a remote roadway where the terrain rises above the road on one side and falls away on the other. When that's the case, investigators search downhill, because carrying a body downhill is much easier than carrying it uphill. It's just that simple.

- ✔ **Checking out variations in the terrain:** Freshly turned dirt, trenches, and elevations or depressions in the terrain may be helpful. Fresh graves tend to be elevated above the surrounding area, and older ones are often depressed because the soil covering the corpse settles naturally and as the body decays and the skeletal remains collapse, it settles further.

  Interestingly, the depth of the depression is greater whenever the body is buried deeply, which is likely because larger amounts of dirt have been turned and are then subject to a greater degree of settling. Another factor may be that with deeper graves, the increased weight of the dirt over the corpse causes earlier and more complete skeletal collapse.

- ✔ **Using tracking dogs:** Tracking dogs, when provided with an article of the victim's clothing, may be able to follow a scent trail to the burial site. Specially trained cadaver dogs search for the scent of decaying flesh. They often can locate bodies in shallow graves or even in water. Deeper graves, however, can be more problematic.

- ✔ **Looking for changes in vegetation:** Turning the soil during the digging process changes the soil conditions in the area covering the grave, as does the presence of a body. These changes in the compaction, moisture, aeration, and temperature of the soil may attract plant species that differ from those surrounding the gravesite. Similarly plants that are typical for a given area may be more abundant or grow thicker and richer because of changes in soil conditions. Not to mention that the decaying body can serve as a fertilizer, This kind of change may be visible, particularly from the air.

- ✔ **Checking out the scene from the air:** Aerial reconnaissance and photography, often coupled with thermal imaging, can be helpful. Freshly turned dirt loses heat faster than normally compacted soils and appears colder when scanned by such a device. Alternatively, a decaying body releases heat, which may reveal a measurable thermal difference when compared with the surrounding area.

✔ **Searching for byproducts of decay:** If an area is suspected of containing a body, it can be searched with special devices that locate sources of heat, nitrogen, and other byproducts of the decaying process or that measure changes in the physical properties of the soil. Ground-penetrating radar can essentially see into the ground and often locate a buried body.

✔ **Measuring the electricity:** Measurement of electrical conductivity can prove helpful. A buried body often adds moisture to the soil, and the moisture increases the soil's electrical conductivity. Two metal electrodes are placed in the soil, and an electrical current is passed between them and measured. Changes in this current may indicate where the body is buried.

✔ **Putting magnetic fields to work:** A simple metal detector can locate the victim's jewelry or belt buckle. A special device for measuring the magnetic properties of soil may also be helpful. Soil generally contains small amounts of iron and thus has a low level of magnetic reaction. Because the area where a body is buried has proportionally less soil, it exhibits an even lower level of magnetic reactivity. A magnetometer passed above the soil can help locate any areas that have low magnetic reactivity.

Chapter 4

Delving into the Criminal Mind

• •

• •

*U*nlike hair, shoeprints, or weapons, the motivations of criminals aren't visible, and they can't be studied under a microscope or analyzed in a chemistry lab. That makes psychiatry a different animal completely. Nonetheless, it's an ever-growing field that not only helps investigators sort fact from fiction but guides investigations by providing often astoundingly accurate descriptions of who the perpetrator is likely to be.

Investigators use physical and biological evidence to determine the *who, what,* and *how.* Forensic psychiatrists help flesh out the *why.* And the *why* is often the most valuable piece of information for solving the crime, because few, if any, crimes are committed without a motive, a *why.*

Defining the Role of the Forensic Psychiatric Professional

Where law meets the study of the mind, you'll find the forensic psychiatric professional. That juncture is a tricky place, however, because the medical and legal aspects of psychiatry often are at odds. Clinical, or medical, psychiatry and its forensic cousin have widely divergent goals and methods.

The forensic psychiatric professional (psychiatrist or psychologist) may be called upon to perform several functions, including

- ✔ Testing a suspect for mental illness
- ✔ Assessing a perpetrator's sanity
- ✔ Establishing a perpetrator's mental state at the time of the crime
- ✔ Determining an individual's competency to stand trial, offer testimony, sign contracts, and perform other actions
- ✔ Evaluating suspects for signs of deception and malingering (faking illness)
- ✔ Profiling perpetrators and victims

The psychiatric professional uses various medical records, examinations, and tests; psychiatric tests and interviews; police and witness reports; and crime-scene evidence to perform these duties.

Differentiating forensic from clinical psychiatry

In clinical psychiatry, the goal is to improve the patient's condition through a trusting relationship. If successful, the patient opens up and tells the psychiatrist what he needs to know to develop the proper treatment plan. The process is cooperative, and the psychiatrist doesn't make moral or value judgments about the patient.

Forensic psychiatry, in distinct areas, is just the opposite. It's adversarial, rather than cooperative. It's judgmental in that the legal system is designed to make moral judgments concerning responsibility. The goal isn't treating the individual but rather dissecting that person's personality to reveal hidden motives. In short, the subject and the forensic psychiatrist often are at odds.

In the clinical arena, the patient has every reason to be truthful. After all, the patient and physician want the patient to get better. In the forensic setting, however, subjects have many reasons to lie or deceive, wanting to hide the truth about their actions and thoughts, especially if they happen to be guilty. Subjects also want their possible motivations for committing a crime to remain buried within themselves. They may fabricate or exaggerate symptoms to create an insanity defense. They're likely to view the psychiatrist as an enemy rather than a friend and healthcare professional.

How the mind matters in forensics

Forensic psychiatrists can become involved in both criminal and civil matters. In the criminal arena, they may be brought to the case by the prosecution, the defense, or the judge. They're often involved in homicides, robberies, kidnappings, and cases of assault, battery, and sexual misconduct. They may be asked to

- Assess the role of alcohol and drugs in a defendant's conduct
- Determine sanity or competency to stand trial
- Assess a subject's understanding of reality and responsibility
- Offer a judgment regarding the suspect's state of mind at the time of the crime
- Offer investigators information for use in witness and suspect interrogations
- Create a psychological profile of the type of individual who likely committed the crime

In civil cases, the forensic psychiatrist may be asked to determine subjects' competency to sign wills and contracts, manage personal affairs, vote, care for themselves or others, offer testimony, or stand trial. Spousal and child abuse also are common areas of involvement, and so are disputes involving child custody, sexual harassment, disability, or emotional suffering.

In cases of apparent suicide, the forensic psychiatrist may be asked to perform a psychological autopsy (see the later section, "Profiling the victim: Victimology") to determine whether the victim likely took her own life and whether drugs and alcohol, financial problems, or social difficulties contributed to the death. Interviews with family, friends, and co-workers may reveal the victim's behavior during the period before the tragedy and point the forensic psychiatrist in the right direction.

Assessing the Brain

Understanding a suspect's state of mind often can have tremendous bearing on the legal proceedings that determine guilt or innocence. That state of mind may be affected by physical complications, like a stroke, or by significant psychiatric disorders, such as schizophrenia. Forensic psychiatrists use a wide variety of tests to determine what makes a subject tick.

The goal of psychiatric testing is to uncover any psychiatric disorders and to establish the subject's thought processes and cognitive abilities. Based on testing and interview results, the psychiatrist offers an opinion about the subject's psychiatric state, competence, and sanity.

Attorneys often argue that these tests are fraught with problems. They assess past and present mental states but don't necessarily determine the suspect's state of mind at the time of the crime, so any such determination is merely conjecture. This argument is in many ways true, but with properly conducted tests and interviews, the forensic psychiatrist most often can make an accurate assessment and formulate an opinion.

Getting started with a medical history and physical exam

When first examining a subject, the forensic psychiatrist determines whether the individual has any neurological or psychiatric problems that can alter his thinking and understanding. Medical problems, such as strokes, certain liver or kidney diseases, head trauma, and many medications can impact the assessment of the subject. For example, a stroke can alter your cognitive abilities so that you can't form complete and coherent thoughts. It may damage areas of the brain that control speech, hearing, emotions, and any other brain function. Because these medical conditions can greatly affect the subject's performance on the various psychiatric tests, they must be addressed before any psychological testing is undertaken.

Many prescription and illicit drugs alter brain function. Medications for seizure disorders, diabetes, heart disease, insomnia, and weight loss, in addition to essentially every known sedative and mood elevator, can affect psychiatric functional testing.

A review of the subject's medical, work, and military records is undertaken, and if the subject is a suspect in a crime, police and witness reports, crime-scene photos, and autopsy reports (in cases where a death was involved) also are reviewed and considered. Blood testing and perhaps specialized brain testing such as an electroencephalogram (EEG), magnetic resonance imaging (MRI), or computed tomography (CT) brain scan are next. If these examinations are normal, the psychiatrist proceeds with the evaluation and testing of the subject.

Digging into the psyche

Options abound for testing a subject's mental health, intellectual capacity, personality type, cognitive abilities, and mental competence. Each psychiatric professional chooses tests according to the particular situation and subject.

Tests fall into three categories:

✔ **Personality inventories** are designed to determine the subject's basic personality type, which includes his attitudes, behaviors, thought processes, beliefs, emotional responses, and social abilities. These tests, which may reveal antisocial tendencies, obsessive-compulsive disorders, and other disorders, are highly standardized and reliable.

Common personality inventories include the Minnesota Multiphasic Personality Inventory (MMPI), the Millon Clinical Multiaxial Inventory (MCMI), and the California Psychological Inventory (CPI). Chances are you've taken one or more of these tests at some point during your schooling.

✔ **Projective testing** is designed to evaluate the person's personality and thought processes. These tests are less standardized and more subjective than personality inventories. The examiner uses them to gain insight into how the subject thinks and how he views himself, others, and the world in general. They also often uncover any obsessions and fantasies that drive the subject's actions. The following tests are commonly used:

  • The *Rorschach test* is the famous inkblot exam. The subject views a series of abstract inkblots and is asked to describe what he sees. How the subject describes the images can reveal something about his personality, thought processes, and connections with reality. The test can also offer clues about the subject's inner fantasies.

  • *Projective drawing* is similar to the Rorschach test, except the subject produces the drawings, which then are analyzed. The person may be asked to draw a house, a car, a tree, a member of the opposite sex, or a frightening scene or situation. The drawings can reveal the subject's inner thought processes and fantasies. For example, if the subject draws images of a house that's on fire, a woman who's been stabbed, or a leafless tree with broken branches, such drawings may provide a look into the subject's inner world.

  • In the *Thematic Apperception Test (TAT)*, the subject is shown pictures of common situations and asked to make up stories to go with the images. Again, the subject's inner thoughts and fantasies may be revealed. For example, when shown a photo of a man and a woman talking, the subject may relate a tale of how the two are planning their wedding, arguing about money, or saying negative things about the subject. Each story indicates a different psychiatric state.

✔ **Intellectual and cognitive testing** is designed to assess the subject's intelligence, mental competency, thought processes, and ability to understand his own behavior. This information is critical in determining the subject's level of responsibility and competency to stand trial. The most common intelligence test is the Wechsler Adult Intelligence Scale (WAIS), which assesses the subject's intelligence quotient (IQ).

Asking the right questions

After these tests are completed and evaluated, the forensic psychiatrist interviews the subject, probing deeper into any areas of concern uncovered by the testing process.

In general, the psychiatrist first tries to get the subject to relax and to gain his confidence so the subject will speak freely. Simple, nonconfrontational questions about the subject's childhood, family, and social interactions usually do the trick. If the subject has suffered any illnesses or injuries that may impact his psychiatric state or mental health, these are explored.

The questions gradually become more probing as the psychiatrist works to determine the subject's attitudes toward past and current events in his life. Ultimately, the questions focus on the events that brought the subject to the psychiatrist in the first place.

The psychiatrist is more interested in the suspect's motivation than in the actual events. For example, if the subject has assaulted someone, the questions will be designed to determine why he did it and how he felt about it. If the subject is ashamed and apologetic and realizes that he was wrong, that will say something very different about him than if he feels anger, resentment, justification, and entitlement.

Employing dubious techniques

Two interview techniques, hypnosis and the use of drugs during the interview, are controversial but nonetheless show up in interrogations real and fictional.

Hypnosis, the induction of a trance-like, highly relaxed state, is used to help suspects and witnesses recall certain events and details. One problem: Faking hypnosis is not that difficult, so any information obtained by this technique requires corroboration. In addition, people who are under the influence of hypnosis often are highly susceptible to suggestion, such that merely asking them questions can alter their memories of certain events. It's possible for these *new memories* to become part of their *real memory,* thus jeopardizing any future interviews or court testimony they may provide. Not all courts allow testimony from previously hypnotized witnesses.

Although there's no such thing as a truth serum, certain drugs nevertheless can lower the subject's inhibitions and defenses. Sodium pentothal is the classic so-called truth serum. A short-acting barbiturate that causes drowsiness and euphoria, it can make the recipient quite chatty. As with hypnosis, however, any information gleaned in this fashion is suspect and is likely to face a challenge in court.

Though in real life it is very unlikely that any evidence gleaned by either of these techniques would be allowed in the courtroom, both are often found in fiction.

Dealing with Deception

Criminals lie. If they didn't, the job of a police investigator would be easy. Criminals would simply walk in and confess. But, of course, that isn't the case. Whether it's forgery, establishing a false alibi, staging a crime scene, or lying in court, criminals alter, distort, and manufacture the truth. In other situations, a witness's identification of a suspect is erroneous, or an innocent person offers a false confession. Although these people don't intend to lie, the result still is false information.

Recognizing lying perps

Distortion, exaggeration, and deception are the bane of the forensic psychiatrist's existence. Suspects are extremely likely to lie, regardless of whether they view forensic psychiatrists as enemies or possible allies in deception. After all, if suspects can convince forensic psychiatrists that they're telling the truth, that they remember nothing about the crime, or that they're insane, they ultimately end up with an ally in the courtroom.

Say, for example, that a suspect is indeed guilty of a horrid rape and murder but indicates that he likes and respects women, when the exact opposite is the case. The suspect may lie about past interpersonal and sexual experiences, alter or completely fabricate beliefs and feelings, or even exaggerate negative reactions and feelings, all in hopes of being declared incompetent or insane, and thus avoiding any responsibility. Often such exaggerations are imitations of symptoms the suspect believes will result in a well-known, though controversial, diagnosis, such as post-traumatic stress disorder, multiple personality disorder, or whatever else the suspect has recently seen in the news.

Malingering is a special form of deception in which the subject attempts to make any physical or mental defects appear worse than they actually are or to manufacture them completely. Alternatively, subjects may try to make a defect appear less severe than it actually is. Fortunately, the MMPI and several other tests include scales that indicate such deceptions.

Psychiatrists, police officers, attorneys, and many other individuals who deal with criminals and suspects on a regular basis become adept at detecting deception. There are no hard and fast rules for doing so, but several techniques, none of which are uniformly reliable, are used, including

- **Looking for signs of nervousness:** Many people become nervous when questioned by law enforcement officers, but sometimes signs of nervousness indicate that the person is lying. Sweating, dilated (wide open) pupils, tremors of hands and lips, failure to make eye contact, and hesitant or rapid speech can each indicate that the subject is lying.

- **Reading body language:** How the subject sits or moves can also betray her lies. Signs that may indicate lying include hand-wringing, slumping or slouching, finger-tapping, and fidgeting, among many others.

- **Using Neuro-Linguistic Programming (NLP):** NLP is a technique of reading a person's eye movements to determine her mental state. Looking up and to the side while answering questions, for example, may indicate that the subject is recalling something she has seen. However, this technique is extremely controversial and has little scientific backing.

- **Discerning micro expressions:** Micro expressions are very brief changes in the person's facial expression, usually lasting only a fraction of a second. They often result from the person attempting to repress emotions. The trick is distinguishing whether these movements are due to the natural fear many feel when talking with a psychiatrist or law enforcement officer or true deception.

Debunking the eyewitness

Eyewitnesses are notoriously unreliable. Unfortunately, memory isn't all that reliable. Your ability to recall the details of any particular event fades with time, and the natural tendency is to fill in any blanks with what you believe should've happened. This unconscious effort is further colored by your personal beliefs, prejudices, motives, and expectations. Add the stress of witnessing a frightening or threatening event to these factors, and conditions are ripe for false or altered memories. Nothing malicious, just the human brain at work.

Earwitness testimony waxes (how's that for a pun) even more unreliable. People occasionally are asked to identify a perpetrator by his voice. Unless the voice is unusual or exceptionally distinctive, this exercise is unreliable.

CASE STUDY

Hypnotizing Kenneth Bianchi

A series of brutal rapes and murders put Los Angeles on edge during the 1970s. Bodies were being dumped in plain sight on hillsides throughout L.A. County, so the killers became known as the Hillside Stranglers. After a long and complex investigation, police finally arrested Angelo Buono in Los Angeles and his cousin Kenneth Bianchi in Bellingham, Washington.

Using psychological knowledge that he'd gotten from college psychology classes and from the movies *Three Faces of Eve* and *Sybil*, Bianchi concocted an insanity defense in which he feigned having a multiple personality disorder (MPD). Bianchi said that his evil alter ego, Steve, made him kill the young women and that he was innocent, merely a pawn of the evil Steve.

Bianchi's act was so good that he fooled several psychiatric professionals. Finally, he was evaluated by Dr. Martin Orne, an expert in hypnosis. Dr. Orne managed to bring out Steve by

hypnotizing Kenneth. But, Bianchi made several mistakes. While he was Steve, he referred to Steve as "he" rather than "I" on several occasions. If he truly was Steve at that time, he wouldn't use the third-person pronoun "he." At one point Bianchi was introduced to an imaginary person whom Kenneth knew but Steve didn't. Bianchi acted out a handshake with the nonexistent person. Seeing an imaginary person, much less shaking hands with him, would mean that Bianchi was hallucinating, which isn't part of MPD. Finally, Dr. Orne told Bianchi how unusual it was for an MPD victim to have only one other personality and that most MPD victims had several. Almost on cue, Billy was born, giving Bianchi three separate personalities.

After his ruse was exposed, Bianchi confessed and agreed to testify against his cousin Angelo in exchange for favorable treatment by the court.

Dealing with false confessions

False confessions are more common than you may think. People who give false confessions don't necessarily intend to deceive police; they may simply be confused, tired, angry, or want to get the heck out of the room. They could have psychiatric problems and actually believe they did it, or maybe they've fantasized about the same type of crime so many times that they can't remember whether they did it or dreamed it.

STRANGE BUT TRUE

False confessions may not make sense to you, but they happen all the time. Whenever a sensational murder is reported in the newspaper, you can be sure that about two dozen people have called police to confess to it. Go figure.

Many false confessions arise because criminals think they can deflect police from another crime. For example, a suspect may confess to stealing a car or robbing a store but claim to know nothing about the murder that occurred at the same time but in another location. If guilty of the robbery, the suspect couldn't possibly be the killer. Likewise, a friend or family member may confess to a crime to protect the real culprit.

Some people, however, simply confess for no apparent reason. Many psychological factors come into play: low self-esteem, fear of the police, a need for fame, or a need to please the authorities or another person, for example. Many people have deep-seated feelings of guilt and may need to confess to something so they can be punished for their buried guilt, whether real or imagined.

In addition, the presence of alcohol or drugs can cloud judgment and lead to confusion, false memories, and fabrications, which in turn can make the individual unsure about whether he is guilty. With intoxicated suspects, the police may tell them that they were the only one in the house with the deceased and they may begin to believe that maybe they did commit the murder, even though they don't remember it. This can result in a false confession.

Certain police interrogation tactics also can lead to false confessions. Isolation and fatigue can break down a person's resolve so far that a confession seems easier than continuing with the interrogation. If interrogators employ a good cop–bad cop approach, the suspect may confess, erroneously thinking the good cop will provide protection from the bad cop and from the legal system.

Interrogators use tactics designed to trip up lying suspects. They may ask the same questions over and over in varying forms or go off on another topic and suddenly come back to a certain line of questioning. Sometimes, however, these techniques confuse innocent people to the point that a confession simply falls out of their mouth.

Assessing Competence and Sanity

The forensic psychiatrist may become involved in all three phases of the criminal justice process: pretrial, trial, and post-trial. During the pretrial phase, the psychiatrist often is asked to determine a suspect's competency to stand trial, to offer testimony, to understand his rights, and even to confess. The court won't accept a confession from someone who's incompetent or mentally ill.

Determining a defendant's competence

Competency to stand trial reflects the defendant's ability to understand the charges, the possible consequences of the charges, the workings of the courtroom, and the roles that the judge and attorneys play. Without an understanding of these matters, the defendant can't be fairly tried. For example, the defendant may harbor delusions that the judge is his grandfather or that the judge and attorneys are involved in a conspiracy to get him. Both delusions are counter to reality and can affect the defendant's ability to participate in his own defense. A competency examination also determines whether the subject is competent enough to confess, testify, waive Miranda rights (the rights to remain silent and be represented by counsel), accept or refuse an insanity defense, and even to be executed.

Commonly encountered mental disorders that lead to a determination of lack of competence include

- ✔ Mental retardation, which can be due to congenital or developmental abnormalities, brain injuries, or infections
- ✔ Severe drug or alcohol addiction
- ✔ Organic brain syndromes (structural or functional brain abnormalities) such as strokes, tumors, or infections
- ✔ Severe neuroses that lead to paranoid or severe anxiety states
- ✔ Psychoses and schizophrenias accompanied by an altered perception of reality

During the trial, the forensic psychiatrist may take the stand to offer an opinion regarding the suspect's mental state at the time of the crime and perhaps to address issues related to legal sanity, if the suspect's defense is in the form of an insanity plea. During the post-trial, or sentencing, phase, the psychiatrist may address the defendant's need for admission to a treatment facility as opposed to prison or may offer an opinion regarding how dangerous the defendant is or how likely the defendant is to commit crimes in the future. In death penalty cases, the psychiatrist may even be asked to comment on whether the convicted person is competent to be executed.

Defining insanity, loosely

Psychiatrists can't diagnose insanity, because it's a legal term rather than a medical condition. Insanity, therefore, is determined only by a judge or jury. Psychiatrists diagnose mental disorders and advise the court as to their findings, but the final say comes from the law, not medicine.

Insanity is a slippery, poorly defined term that means different things in different jurisdictions. However, most courts adhere to the *McNaughten rule,* which basically asks whether the suspect suffers from any mental disorder that prevents him from understanding the nature and the consequences of his actions. In other words, you can be found not guilty by reason of insanity if you didn't know at the time of the crime that your actions were illegal or if you were incapable of altering your illicit behavior.

In 1984, Congress adopted the Omnibus Crime Code for Insanity, which states that people can be found not guilty by reason of insanity if they didn't *appreciate* the illegality of their behavior. The term *appreciate* differs vastly from the word *know,* implying a higher degree of understanding than simple knowledge.

The McNaughten and the Omnibus definitions address the fact that a crime consists of two parts: the criminal activity, termed the *actus reus,* and criminal intent, known as the *mens rea.*

Diminished capacity is a special form of insanity. Its definition also varies among jurisdictions. The basic tenet of diminished capacity is that certain conditions during the commission of a crime reduced the criminal's ability to alter his actions or to distinguish between right and wrong. In other words, the perpetrator was incapable of forming a specific criminal intent or acting in a purposeful manner.

Claiming diminished capacity is an attempt to relieve the defendant of criminal guilt or at least reduce the degree to which he is held responsible for the crime. This may simply be a defense ploy or it may indeed be true. For example, someone who kills his wife over an adulterous affair may state that he did it in a fit of rage and was not responsible for his actions (temporary insanity) when, in fact, he had planned the murder for weeks. On the other hand, an individual suffering from paranoid delusions because of chronic cocaine or methamphetamine abuse may not have been capable of planning a murder, which changes that person's degree of liability from first-degree to second-degree murder.

Tracking Serial Offenders

Serial offenders create special problems for law enforcement. Regardless of whether you're talking about serial rapists, bombers, killers, or the perpetrators of other repetitive crimes, the episodic nature of their crimes and the fact that they often have no apparent connection to their victims, whom they appear to randomly select, forces law enforcement officials to continually develop new techniques for dealing with them.

Most murders have easily identifiable motives, such as financial gain, revenge, or covering up another crime. Thus, the earliest stages of any homicide investigation focus on people who know and may profit from the victim's death.

This approach makes perfect sense because the overwhelming majority of homicides occur between people who know one another. But most serial killers and rapists prey on strangers. Their motives are more private and personal, dwelling deep within the person's psyche, and may not be readily apparent. More often than not, even when a serial criminal's motive is discovered, it seems totally irrational . . . but not to the killer.

Classifying the multiple murderer

Multiple murderers are people who've killed more than one person. Multiple murders are classified according to the location and sequence of the killings:

- ✔ **Mass murderers:** These killers kill more than four people in one place at one time. They often have a clear agenda and want to send a message. Mass murderers are the kind of killers who walk into their workplace and shoot several people in a rapid-fire assault. The motive often is some perceived wrong committed by co-workers or an employer.

- ✔ **Spree killers:** These killers kill more than one person at two or more locations. The killings are linked by motive but without a cooling-off period between the acts. Rather, the killer is constantly killing, hiding, running, or planning his next attack. Spree killers go on rampages, moving from place to place, city to city, even state to state, leaving bodies in their wake. Such sprees often end in a suicidal confrontation with law enforcement.

- ✔ **Serial killers:** These killers kill more than one person at different times and locations with cooling-off periods between the killings. The cooling-off periods result from the killer having satisfied the driving need behind the killings. They can last weeks, months, and even years, and allow time for the killer to unwind, come down from the high, and relax — until the demons take over again. This cooling-off period distinguishes serial killers from spree killers.

Making the monsters

Society always has difficulty understanding and dealing with serial offenders. Serial rapists and serial killers seem so far removed from the rest of society that a rational method for dealing with them has been and still is out of reach. These individuals typically are *psychopaths* or *sociopaths,* two terms that are used interchangeably. Sociopaths tend to be self-centered (egocentric and narcissistic), manipulative, emotionally shallow, and devoid of empathy and remorse. They often lie with impunity, fooling even the cleverest interrogator.

CASE STUDY

Andrew Cunanan's killing spree

Andrew Cunanan often was described as a high-class male prostitute who catered to wealthy, older men. He lived and played among the wealthy and hedonistic until late 1996, when his world began to unravel. In mid-April 1997, he bought a one-way, first-class ticket to Minneapolis, and on the night of April 27, 1997, used a hammer to beat 28-year-old Jeffrey Trail to death in the apartment of Cunanan's lover, David Madson. Five days later at a lake some 50 miles away, Cunanan shot Madson in the head and fled in the red Jeep that the two had taken from Trail's home.

Cunanan then went to Chicago, where he took up with 72-year-old real-estate mogul Lee Miglin. After torturing and killing Miglin with pruning shears and a garden saw, Cunanan headed east in Miglin's Lexus. Then on May 9, he shot and killed William Reese in Pennsville, New Jersey, stole the dead man's red Chevrolet pickup, and headed south. By then, he was on the FBI's Ten Most-Wanted list.

Cunanan ended up in Miami, Florida, where on the morning of July 14, he shot world-renowned designer Gianni Versace twice in the head in front of Versace's residence, Casa Casuarina. Police were called to a boathouse by its caretaker, Fernando Carreira. There they found what's often true with many spree killers — Cunanan had taken his own life with the same gun he'd used to kill Madson and Reese.

Serial rapists and serial killers have a great deal in common. In fact, they may just be at different points on the slippery slope of sanity. Many serial killers begin their adventures with rape and then progress to murder in order to cover the crime or perhaps to increase their morbid enjoyment.

The psychosexual pathology that drives these offenders appears to become ingrained early in life, and it only grows in strength as the individual matures through puberty and into adult life. Many, but not all, serial offenders come from backgrounds of physical, psychological, and sexual abuse. They may insulate themselves from this abuse by creating a protective world that's rich in fantasy. As the fantasies develop, some serial offenders take on sexual and violent characteristics that can brew for years, or even decades, before the offender begins to act them out.

Fantasy plays a powerful role in the violent crimes of serial offenders. Early on, their fantasies may be amorphous and benign, but as they mentally play them out, again and again, year after year, the fantasies become more refined. Often the fantasies are simple, but in more imaginative offenders, they can become elaborately scripted plays. In many, sexual and violent themes tend to commingle until the two are inseparable.

When serial offenders go on the prowl for victims, they are, in fact, seeking characters in their respective fantasy plays. They may look for a certain type of person or one with a specific look. Ted Bundy, for example, sought women with dark hair that was parted in the middle; obviously they embodied the character he needed to fulfill his fantasy.

This example points out an important fact about these fantasies: They tend to be specific. Think about your own fantasies. When you daydream or fantasize about something, the details make the fantasy pleasurable, and these details typically remain the same no matter how many times you experience the fantasy. Why? Because this fantasy is comforting; it feeds some psychological need within you. So it is with the serial offender; however, serial offenders tend to have sexually violent fantasies that they may ultimately act out — and that's a mighty big difference.

The specific details of the fantasies enable forensic psychiatrists to develop profiles of the killers. Because a killer's fantasy is specific and repetitive, certain elements of the criminal act are also specific and repetitive. This concept shows up in the killer's signature (see the later section about "Distinguishing MO from signature").

Current thinking is that violent serial offenders cannot be reliably rehabilitated. This idea obviously is controversial, but one fact remains: Many laws have been placed on the books to protect the public from these criminals. They are given long sentences, and when they're released from prison or a mental facility, they're constantly monitored. Neighborhoods into which they move are notified of their presence.

As early as the 1930s, laws mandated that sexual offenders be evaluated and treated by medical professionals. By the 1960s, such programs were in place in virtually every state. It soon became clear to the people who were responsible for diagnosing and treating these sexual predators that they were different. These offenders neither fit into the usual diagnostic categories nor responded to the usual treatment regimens. By the 1990s, many states closed these specialized treatment centers, and longer sentences became the norm.

It is important to note that serial killers are motivated by varying drives. The nomenclature varies from expert to expert, but, in general, what I have described so far is termed a sexually sadistic serial killer. These killers are driven by sexually violent fantasies for the most part. Other types include those driven by anger (rage against a subgroup of people or society in general); profit (such as the little old lady who runs a boarding house and kills tenants while continuing to cash their support checks); power/control/thrill (those who kill for the love of the killing act); and psychosis (those driven by severe mental disorders), to name a few.

Profiling the Perpetrator

If you don't know what you're looking for, finding it is nearly impossible. Profiling, or looking at evidence and making a best guess as to the *type* of individual who would commit the crime in question, helps investigators get a firm grasp on who it is they're trying to track down. The *profiler,* usually a specially trained FBI agent, looks at the crime scene, autopsy data, victim, and likely precrime and postcrime behaviors of the killer to make this assessment. The profiler answers questions like

- How did the killer gain access to the victim?
- What did the killer do to the victim?
- Did the killer try to cover his tracks and, if so, how?
- What is it about this victim that attracted the killer?
- What motive or fantasy drove the killer to harm the victim in the particular manner at the particular time and location?

In serial murder cases, offenders often are termed *unknown subjects,* or *unsubs* for short. Analysis of the crime scene may offer clues to the type of unsub police should search for. That analysis has become known as *offender profiling.* Even though profiling may not lead to the exact individual, it often helps police narrow the focus of their investigation. In addition to predicting where other evidence is likely to be located, profiling may suggest the unsub's

- Physical and psychological makeup
- Areas of residence and work
- Behaviors that may have been exhibited before the crime
- Likely comings and goings after the crime

Lastly, the crime scene may reveal aspects of an unsub's modus operandi (MO, or method of operation) and signature. Check out the later section about "Distinguishing MO from signature."

Criminal profiling evolved from studies conducted by the FBI's old Behavioral Science Unit. The studies were designed to gain insight into violent criminals. As investigators' collective understanding of violent offenders increased, a useful investigative tool was born. Crime-scene analysis for clues to the offender's personality and motives and offender profiling continually gained popularity and now are considered critically important in tracking serial offenders. The premise that the perpetrator not only leaves behind physical evidence but also behavioral and psychiatric evidence is leading criminalists to understand that this evidence may be key to finding perpetrators.

Reading between the lines of the Mad Bomber's letters

The first major success of criminal profiling came long before the art of profiling was a tactic commonly used by police. On November 16, 1940, an unexploded bomb was found on a window ledge at the Manhattan office of Consolidated Edison, the power company known as Con Ed. Attached to the bomb was a hand-printed note that said, "Con Edison Crooks. This is for you." Although he took a break during World War II out of a sense of patriotism, the Mad Bomber struck several times and sent numerous letters to Con Ed between 1941 and 1956. After one of the Mad Bomber's explosions killed several people in a theater, police brought Dr. James Brussel in on the case. Brussel was a psychiatrist known for his uncanny ability to analyze crimes and speculate as to what type of individual the culprit could be.

After reviewing the Mad Bomber's letters and the police reports, Brussel concluded that the person responsible was a middle-aged male who was paranoid and introverted. Brussel hypothesized that the Mad Bomber's deep-seated grudge against Con Ed may have stemmed from his having worked there. Brussel also said the man was well-educated and probably of Slavic descent, lived with an older female relative, was extremely neat and meticulous in his work and good with tools. Brussel predicted that when captured, the suspect would be neatly dressed, likely in a buttoned, double-breasted suit.

Indeed, in one letter, the bomber had revealed that he was particularly enraged by an event that had taken place on September 5, 1931. Checking Con Ed's records, police found that a boiler explosion had occurred at Con Ed on that date and that George Metesky had been injured. Metesky had subsequently written a complaint letter to the company. Police compared that letter with those from the Mad Bomber and found many similar phrases. When police arrested Metesky at his home, they found that he was 54 years old, Polish, unmarried, and living with two older sisters. He was also wearing a buttoned, double-breasted suit.

More recently, the FBI's Behavioral Science Unit has evolved into the National Center for the Analysis of Violent Crime (NCAVC), which consists of five units: Behavioral Analysis Units 1, 2, 3, and 4 as well as the Behavioral Research and Instruction Unit. Each of these works to supply behavioral-based investigative support to the FBI and other law enforcement agencies.

One of the basic tenets of profiling is that behavior reflects personality. How people act depends upon their personality and psychological needs and fears. Profiling seeks clues to the perpetrator's personality from the behaviors exhibited at the crime scene. These clues can provide insight into the killer's motives, level of intelligence and sophistication, and reasons for selecting a particular victim.

Assessing the perpetrator's psyche

One basic method of characterizing offenders from crime-scene evidence divides them into the following three categories:

- **Organized offenders:** These criminals are more sophisticated in their approach, and their crimes show evidence of planning. These types tend to be of average or better intelligence, employed, and in active social relationships such as with spouses and families. Even though they're driven by their fantasies, they maintain enough control to avoid being impulsive. They prepare and even rehearse. They tend to target specific victims or types of victims and use control measures such as restraints to maintain victim compliance. They bring the tools they need to gain access to and control of the victim and avoid leaving behind evidence. As killers, they generally hide or dispose of the body and are likely to have a dumpsite already selected.

- **Disorganized offenders:** These criminals usually live alone or with a relative, possess lower-than-average intelligence, are unemployed or work at menial jobs, and often have mental illnesses. They act impulsively, or as if they have little control over their fantasy-driven needs. They rarely use ruses to gain the victim's confidence, but rather attack with sudden violence, overwhelming the victim. The crime scene often is messy and chaotic. This type of offender doesn't plan ahead or bring tools along, but rather uses whatever is handy. As killers, they typically leave the body at the scene and exert little effort to avoid leaving behind evidence. Some even have postmortem sexual contact with the victim.

- **Mixed offenders:** Some offenders leave behind mixed messages at crime scenes. They show evidence of planning and a sophisticated MO, but the assault itself is frenzied or messy, which may indicate some control over deep-seated and violent fantasies.

Profilers have developed categories of *descriptors,* or ways that they describe the types of individuals who commit the crimes. Some of the descriptors used in serial killer profiling are

- **Age:** Most serial killers are in their 20s or 30s.

- **Sex:** Most are male.

- **Race:** Most don't cross racial lines. That means, in general, white offenders kill whites, while black offenders kill blacks.

- **Residency:** Organized offenders are more likely to be married, have a family, and be well liked by their friends. Disorganized offenders, because of their mental instability and immaturity, tend to live alone or with a family member.

✔ **Proximity:** The location of the perpetrator's home in relationship to the crime scene is important. Most kill close to home, a factor that is particularly true with the first few victims. The area close to home is a comfort zone. With experience, however, the killer may move his predatory boundaries farther and farther from home.

✔ **Social skills:** Killers who use a ruse to ensnare their victims, like Ted Bundy did, typically possess good social skills, whereas those who use a blitz-style attack are less comfortable with conversation.

✔ **Work and military histories:** Organized offenders more often have a stable work history and are more likely to have left any military service with an honorable discharge. Disorganized offenders often are quite simply too unstable to hold a job in the long term or to complete military service.

✔ **Educational level:** Organized offenders tend to have more schooling than their disorganized counterparts.

Using these descriptors, profilers can create a pretty good picture, or profile, of the type of person who likely committed the crime. This profile can help police home in on a specific suspect and may play an important role during the interrogation of suspects. Knowing the type of individual who'd commit a criminal act helps investigators design the right questions and leverage any pressure points during interrogation that snare suspects in a web of lies or even produce a confession.

Profiling also plays an important role in determining whether a crime scene is staged. *Staging* means changing the appearance of the scene so that it looks like the murder took place in a different manner and for a different reason. A classic example: the husband who kills his wife in a fit of anger, then empties drawers and closets, knocks over furniture, and breaks a door lock or window to make it appear as though a burglar committed the crime. When investigators discover that the wife was severely bludgeoned and stabbed 20 times, the light of suspicion falls on the husband. A burglar wouldn't engage in such overkill, preferring instead to kill and run. Overkill usually is personal, with anger as the common, underlying drive.

Taking trophies and souvenirs

Many criminals take things from the crime scene. Money, jewels, electronic equipment, and other valuables that can be sold commonly are taken, as is incriminating evidence, such as the murder weapon or a used condom.

Serial offenders, on the other hand, tend to take objects that have no monetary or evidentiary value. But, regardless of what the object is, it holds some value to the perpetrator, and he will use it to relive the crime in later fantasies. Some killers take jewelry, clothing, or even driver's licenses. Some take body parts.

Distinguishing MO from signature

Modus operandi (MO, or method of operation) describes the tools and strategies a criminal uses to commit a crime. It isn't a new concept. It dates back to the 1880s and the efforts of Major L. W. Atcherley, a police constable in the West Riding Yorkshire Constabulary in England, who developed a 10-point system for identifying a perpetrator's MO. Scotland Yard later adopted many of his techniques.

Atcherley considered the following factors:

- Location of the crime
- Point of entry
- Method of entry
- Tools that were used during the crime
- Types of objects taken from the crime scene
- Time of day the crime was committed
- The perpetrator's alibi
- The perpetrator's accomplices
- Method of transportation to and from the scene
- Unusual features of the crime, such as killing the family dog or leaving behind a note or object to taunt the police

All these factors address the perpetrator's method of doing things. They are the things the killer sees as necessary to committing and getting away with the crime.

An MO often evolves over time as the unsub finds better ways to commit the murders or other crimes and to avoid detection. Perpetrators change their mode of entry, ruse, disguise, when and where the attacks take place, and whatever else makes their efforts more effective.

In contrast to an MO, a *signature* is an act that has nothing to do with completing the crime or getting away with it. Signatures are important to the offender in some personal way. Torturing the victim, overkill, postmortem mutilation or posing, and the taking of souvenirs or trophies are signatures. These actions are driven by the killer's psychological needs and fantasies.

Reading clues in the Carmine Calabro case

In 1979, the body of a 26-year-old school-teacher, Francine Elveson, was found on the roof of her apartment building. She was nude and had been object raped with a pen and an umbrella and mutilated. Her body was placed in a position that reflected the shape of the *Chai* (the Jewish symbol of good luck). She was known to wear a Chai pendant, but the killer apparently took it as a souvenir.

An FBI profile suggested that the killer was disorganized, because little planning seemed to be evident and the crime scene suggested a fantasy-driven murder. The killer was likely an unemployed white male, 25 to 35 years of age, who knew the layout of the building and the victim's habits. These factors meant that he probably knew the victim, or had at least seen her. He also knew that the roof of the apartment house

was private enough to complete the assault and murder and escape without detection. The ritualistic and sadistic nature of the murder and the fact that the perpetrator used objects to commit the rape suggested that he was sexually inadequate and had no stable relationships with women. The perpetrator probably suffered some form of mental illness and probably had been in a psychiatric hospital at some time.

This profile caused police to focus on Carmine Calabro, an unmarried, unemployed 30-year-old male who often visited his father, who lived in the same apartment building as the victim. Calabro was undergoing treatment at a psychiatric hospital from which he was absent without permission at the time of the murder. He was convicted when his dental anatomy matched bite marks on the victim's body.

Unlike an MO, a signature never changes. It may be refined over time, but the basic signature remains the same. For example, if a serial killer poses victims in a religious manner, praying or as a crucifix, details such as candles, crucifixes, or other ceremonial objects may be added later. The signature has changed, but its basic form and theme remain the same.

A CLOSER LOOK

The reason for the stability of the signature lies in its driving force. The signature is derived directly from the unsub's fantasies. These fantasies develop early in life and are refined into an obsession from years of mental reenactment. During the crime, an unsub forces the victim to respond according to the script from his fantasy. The signature is solely for the killer to live out his personal fantasy. Because the fantasy never changes, the signature remains intact.

Profiling the victim: Victimology

Evaluating the victim often adds to the offender profile. Studying victim characteristics is called *victimology*, which basically is establishing a measure of their risk of becoming a victim as a result of their personal, professional, and social life. A detailed understanding of the victim's lifestyle and habits provides clues as to why this particular victim was selected at a given time and location. This information divides victims into the following risk categories:

- ✓ **High-risk** victims frequently live in high-risk situations. Prostitutes, particularly the ones who walk the streets, obviously fall into this category. They typically work at night, interact with strangers on a regular basis, willingly get into cars with strangers, and thus are easy targets. Other high-risk behaviors include drug use, promiscuous lifestyles, nighttime employment, and associations with people who possess criminal personalities.

- ✓ **Low-risk** victims stay close to work and home, don't visit areas unfamiliar to them, and lock their doors at night. They have steady jobs and many friends.

- ✓ **Medium-risk** victims fall between these two extremes. A medium-risk victim may work close to home and lock her doors but be promiscuous and occasionally venture out at night alone.

Offenders select their particular victims based on their fantasies and the victims' vulnerability. Some victims merely are grabbed as victims of opportunity. High-risk victims place themselves in vulnerable positions much more often than low-risk victims, but either can simply be in the wrong place at the wrong time. Other victims are taken because they fit the starring role in the perpetrator's fantasy. Offenders may spend days or weeks cruising for just the right victim, the one who most closely matches the perpetrator's fantasy. Other potentially easy victims are ignored because they're just not right.

A special form of victim profiling is the *psychological autopsy,* which is performed when the manner of a victim's death isn't clear, that is, investigators don't know whether the victim's death was an accident, suicide, or homicide. To help make this determination, the forensic psychiatrist looks into the victim's medical, school, work, and military histories; interviews family, friends, and associates; and evaluates autopsy, police, and witness reports. The goal is to assess whether the victim was the type of person who was living in a stressful enough situation to commit suicide or living a lifestyle that made the victim an easy target for a killer.

Drawing boundaries: The killer's domain

You've no doubt watched nature shows on TV where the narrator discusses a certain predator's domain or hunting range. Game wardens use these boundaries to narrow their searches for elusive lions or tigers. Profilers do the same with serial killers.

Analysis of the pattern of the perpetrator's assaults can yield valuable information that ultimately leads to the apprehension of the assailant. Known as *geographic profiling,* this technique is based on the premise that serial offenders, like lions and tigers, have certain comfort zones within which they feel free to carry out their crimes. The geographic profiler likes to know where the victim was abducted, where the actual assault or murder took place, and where the body was dumped. Whenever several assaults have occurred, profilers have several such locations with which to work and can then locate the points on a map and thus define the killer's domain.

The killer's domain may show murders clustered in a small area, which may indicate the killer isn't very mobile and thus may not possess a car or have a job. Conversely, if the range is broad, the perpetrator likely is highly mobile and possesses a vehicle with high mileage from its use to troll for victims. Regardless of whether the range is narrow or broad, the perpetrator likely resides or works within or near this comfort zone.

In general, disorganized killers, because of their inability to hold a job, maintain social connections, or make sophisticated plans — as well as their mental illness — tend to have narrower comfort zones and thus more confined boundaries. Organized killers are able to plan and travel and as a result tend to have much larger domains.

Determining which victim was killed first is important for investigators because the comfort zones for most serial killers usually begin small and grow with each killing. The first victim probably was abducted closer to the killer's home or workplace.

Determining the order of the crimes is straightforward if the victims are found shortly after the crime. However, if the victims are street dwellers or prostitutes, whose disappearance may go unnoticed, the dates of their abductions may not be known. Likewise, if the bodies are dumped in remote places, the order in which the victims were killed may not be the order in which the bodies are found. In such cases, a forensic anthropologist may be brought in to assess approximate times of death. Having this knowledge can be crucial in identifying the killer.

Linking Criminals and Crime Scenes

Serial offenders are the most difficult criminals to apprehend. They attack strangers, have no obvious motives, and frequently are highly mobile. In the same way the Automated Fingerprint Identification System (AFIS; discussed in Chapter 5) enables authorities to match fingerprints from various crime scenes and suspects, the FBI databases also match serial offenders with crimes and profiles.

The first such database was the National Center for the Analysis of Violent Crime (NCAVC). It serves as a repository for violent-crime data throughout the country. It led to the development of the Violent Criminal Apprehension Program (VICAP), a web-based tool, which maintains profiles that help link homicides, sexual assaults, missing persons, and unidentified remains.

Data from crime scenes are entered into the VICAP database. Investigators confronted with a murder or series of murders can create profiles of the crime scenes and compare them with others from across the country, hoping to link the crimes they're investigating with another. An investigator analyzing a murder scene where the victim was strangled with a knotted rope, had her hands cut off, and was dumped in a lake can plug this information into a profile and compare it with other profiles stored in the VICAP database. Any crimes with similar characteristics are identified, and the investigator can look at them to determine whether the same perpetrator may have committed both crimes. If other evidence shows that to be the case, linking the two murders may ultimately lead the investigator to the killer.

Part II
Analyzing the Evidence

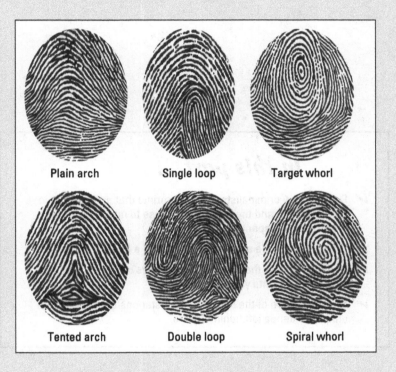

Plain arch   Single loop   Target whorl

Tented arch   Double loop   Spiral whorl

web extras

Can people actually lose their fingerprints? Head to www.dummies.com/extras/forensics to find out!

In this part . . .

- ✔ Find out how criminalists find fingerprints that are invisible to the naked eye and the methods they use to match up those prints with a suspect.

- ✔ Discover what the shape and location of a bloodstain reveals.

- ✔ Understand how the way you walk shows up in your shoes — and the shoeprints you leave behind.

- ✔ Become aware of the special circumstances created and the unique evidence left behind by fire.

Chapter 5

Fingerprints: Your Personal Signature

In This Chapter

▶ Defining fingerprints

▶ Classifying and matching prints

▶ Exposing and collecting prints

*I*f you read, watch TV, or go to the movies, you know that fingerprints play a vital role in many mysteries, whether real-life or fictional. Fingerprints often are how police identify criminals and solve crimes, even crimes that are decades old.

Although fingerprint identification is now standard practice, acceptance of the individuality of fingerprints by police, scientists, and the courts didn't happen overnight.

In this chapter, I explain the science behind fingerprinting, a little bit of its history, and some of the methods used for finding and lifting prints at the crime scene.

Getting a Grip on Fingerprints

Using a bright light and magnifying glass, take a close look at your *finger pads* (the fleshy surface of your fingers that you use for touching and gripping). You'll see very fine lines that curve, circle, and arch. These lines are composed of narrow valleys called *grooves* and hills known as *friction ridges*. When you see an inked fingerprint, you're looking at the pattern made by the friction ridges.

Friction ridges give your fingers traction, and this traction enables you to pick up a glass, pin, piece of paper, or speck of lint. Imagine trying to turn the pages of this book without being able to grip the paper. Without friction ridges, a glass would easily slip from your hands, and you'd have trouble gripping the broom you need to sweep up the mess. Without friction ridges, we'd all be butterfingers.

HISTORICAL NOTE

Developing the science: A trip through fingerprint history

Fingerprints moved from being marks of authenticity in artwork to criminal signatures over a 3,000-year period that includes the following highlights:

✔ **Prehistory:** Early potters identify (or sign) their works with an impressed fingerprint.

✔ **1000 BC:** The Chinese sign legal documents (even criminal confessions) with hand and fingerprints. Whether the practice was ceremonial or a true method of identification is unclear.

✔ **1685:** Marcello Malpighi, a professor of anatomy at the University of Bologne, first recognizes fingerprint patterns and describes them in terms of *loops* and *whorls* when writing about the "varying ridges and patterns" he saw on human fingertips.

✔ **1823:** Johannes Purkinje of Breslau University establishes nine basic fingerprint patterns and rules for classifying them, thus forming the basis for modern classification systems.

✔ **1858:** English civil servant Sir William Herschel requires natives in Bengal, India, to sign contracts with a hand imprint to prevent fraud in contracts and pension distributions. Perhaps the first European to note the individuality of handprints, he finds that his prints are unchanged after 50 years, an important fact in developing fingerprints as a forensic tool.

✔ **1880:** Henry Faulds, physician and surgeon at Taukiji Hospital in Tokyo, Japan, writes that fingerprints can be used for personal identification and suggests they can be useful in identifying criminals. Faulds discovers that dusting latent (invisible) prints with powder exposes them. He uses that method to exonerate an accused thief whose prints don't match one left on a window by the real thief, who later confessed based on the evidence.

✔ **1892:** Sir Francis Galton publishes his classic textbook, *Finger Prints,* the first book on the topic, in which he describes patterns within the prints that he calls loops, arches, and whorls. More importantly, Galton offers convincing evidence that no two prints are identical.

Juan Vucetich, a police official in La Plata, Argentina, devises the fingerprint classification system that's still in use in most of South America and ultimately publishes a book on the subject in 1894.

Argentina is the first country to report using fingerprints to solve a crime, the June 18, 1892, murders of the children of a woman named Rojas. She tries to pin the murders on a man named Velasquez, but an investigator discovers Rojas's lover said he'd marry her if she had no children and finds a bloody fingerprint at the scene matching Rojas's right thumb. She confesses.

✔ **1897:** Herman Welcker finds that his own prints taken in 1897 are unchanged from the ones he'd taken 41 years earlier (1856), thus supporting the findings of Sir William Herschel.

✔ **1899:** Sir Edward Henry devises a classification system based on five types of prints. His system is the basis for the ones used today in Britain and America.

✔ **1910:** Thomas Jennings becomes the first person convicted in the United States on fingerprint evidence. Tried for murder in Chicago, Jennings is convicted, and the verdict is upheld on appeal, making his case a landmark in the use of fingerprint evidence in court.

These ridges evolved so that human beings would be less clumsy and more efficient when working with their hands. In fact, the ability to grip sticks and throw stones was a matter of survival to your remote ancestors. After all, how can you hunt and kill an elk if your weapon continually slips from your fingertips or that stone you hurl lacks any predictable direction? The evolutionary development of friction ridges makes a tough and perilous existence just a little easier. Modern-day people use these ridges to twist doorknobs, hold pens, grasp a steering wheel, and throw baseballs.

Fingerprints have a utility beyond gripping a doorknob or throwing a baseball, however, and that utility became evident as the need for a reliable method of identification arose.

When the world was sparsely populated and people lived in small nomadic communities of 30 to 50, everyone knew everyone else. If you were an outsider and wanted to know who Joe was, anyone in the group you were visiting could easily point him out. But as populations grew, settled into ever-expanding cities, and developed systems of government, identifying others became much more difficult. No longer did everybody know Joe. A reliable method for identifying people became necessary, not only for fingering criminals, but for detecting fraud in contracts and pension payments and other situations where identity is important.

Measuring bodies: A precursor to fingerprinting

One of the first attempts to identify and record differences among people was through *anthropometry,* the science of measuring humans.

Using anthropometry, French police officer Alphonse Bertillon developed the first truly organized system for identifying individuals in 1883. Believing that the human skeleton didn't change in size from about age 20 until death and that each person's measurements were unique, he created a system of body measurements that became known as *bertillonage.* According to Bertillon's calculations, the odds of two people having the same *bertillonage* measurements were 286 million to one.

Bertillon thought everyone could be distinguished from one another by key measurements, such as the diameter of the head and the span of the outstretched arms. For many years, this system was accepted by many jurisdictions, but by the dawn of the 20th century, bertillonage was losing its luster. The inexact measurements varied according to who made them. And because the measurements of any two people of the same size, weight, and body type varied by fractions of a centimeter, the system's flaws quickly appeared, and it soon was discontinued.

Anthropometry's death knell sounded as a comical coincidence in the Will West Case. On May 1, 1903, Will West arrived as a new inmate in Leavenworth Penitentiary in Kansas. The records clerk apparently thought he looked familiar, but the new inmate denied having been in the prison before. Imagine the surprise among prison officials when Will's anthropometry measurements exactly matched those of William West, another inmate at Leavenworth. The two men did indeed look eerily similar . . . as if they were twins. They were brought together in the same room, but they said they weren't brothers. Fingerprints helped authorities distinguish between the two Wills. So much for measuring the diameter of a person's head. Leavenworth immediately dumped anthropometry and switched to a fingerprint-based system for identifying prisoners. New York's Sing Sing Prison followed a month later.

The similarity between Will and William West was not merely a bizarre coincidence. A report in *The Journal of Police Science and Administration* in 1980 revealed that the two actually were identical twins who had many fingerprint similarities and nearly identical ear configurations (unusual in any circumstance except with identical twins). Furthermore, each wrote letters to the same brother, same five sisters, and same Uncle George.

Toward the end of the nineteenth century, Bertillon reluctantly agreed to add fingerprints to his *bertillonage* profile. However, he added only those of the right hand. Big mistake.

On August 21, 1911, Leonardo da Vinci's famous painting *Mona Lisa* was stolen from the Louvre Museum in Paris. The thief left a clear thumbprint on the glass that had protected da Vinci's masterpiece. Alphonse Bertillon added his profiles to the investigation, but unfortunately, he had no classification system to aid investigators searching through his thousands of data cards. He and his assistants spent several months digging through his files to no avail. Two years later, police apprehended the thief, Vicenzo Perugia. His prints matched the one found at the crime scene. It turns out that Perugia's prints were among those in Bertillon's possession all the time. No match had turned up because the print found at the scene was from Perugia's left thumb, and Bertillon's files contained only that of Perugia's right thumb.

Taking a suspect's prints

You may have had your fingerprints taken at some time. Hopefully as a job requirement and not as part of a criminal investigation. If so, the pads of your fingers are inked by pressing the fingertips to an ink pad and then pressing them on a fingerprint card. Messy. Now there are many types of digital scanners that can collect the same information without the mess. And handheld digital devices can now be used by law enforcement to collect prints in the field.

CASE STUDY

Dillinger's indelible fingerprints

John Dillinger, one of America's most notorious criminals, attained the moniker of Public Enemy Number One. In an effort to evade the cops, he underwent facial plastic surgery and tried to remove his fingerprints with acid. After he was betrayed by the infamous Lady in Red, Dillinger was shot to death outside Chicago's Biograph Theater. Despite Dillinger's efforts, prints taken at the morgue still matched the ones on file, thus proving that the dead man was indeed Dillinger.

REMEMBER

Using ridge patterns

The usefulness of fingerprints for identification depends upon three principles:

✓ **A fingerprint is individual and is not shared by any two people.** Every person has a unique set of fingerprints. Even though identical twins have the same DNA, they have different fingerprints.

✓ **A fingerprint remains unchanged throughout life.** The fingerprints you're born with are the same ones you die with. If someone burns or shaves off the pads of his fingers, the prints disappear for a while, but as the skin repairs itself and wounds heal, the print reappears.

However, more severe damage that involves deeper layers of the skin may leave permanent scars and prevent prints from reemerging. Nonetheless, completely obliterating a print is difficult, and any scars left behind by attempts to do so create new individual characteristics that an examiner can use for making a match.

✓ **Fingerprints exhibit general patterns that provide a basis for classification.** General patterns exist within every person's prints, and all people share these patterns to varying degrees. Prints therefore can be systematically classified, reducing the number of records that must be searched when looking for a match.

Making Matching Easier: Classifying Prints

The purpose of any classification system is to add order to chaos by finding common traits among items. For instance, libraries organize books by subject matter, which keeps readers from having to wander aimlessly through the shelves for hours or (more likely) days. Lumberyards categorize wood by type, width, and length, and grocery stores stock pasta sauce with the linguine and spaghetti. You get the idea.

The same is true of fingerprint files. They're useful only if they can be stored in great numbers and quickly searched for a match. The Federal Bureau of Investigation (FBI) has more than 200 million fingerprint files. Imagine slogging through those! Organizing the prints into groups makes searching for a match to an unknown print much easier.

Grouping by arches, loops, and whorls

In 1685, Marcello Malphigi recognized patterns in fingerprints and named them loops and whorls. The arch pattern followed more than 200 years later, when Sir Francis Galton identified it in 1892.

Whorls, loops, and arches (see Figure 5-1) are still the basis for fingerprint matching and identification, because although everyone has them, *how* they have them is unique. Each person has a different number of these types of patterns, and the patterns vary from fingertip to fingertip on each person.

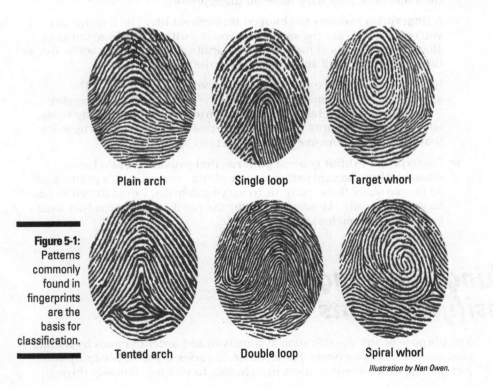

Plain arch   Single loop   Target whorl

Figure 5-1: Patterns commonly found in fingerprints are the basis for classification.

Tented arch   Double loop   Spiral whorl

Illustration by Nan Owen.

Arches

Arches are ridgelines that rise in the center to create a wavelike pattern. Arches are subgrouped into plain and tented varieties. Tented arches have a sharper central rise than do plain arches. Only 5 percent of all pattern types are arches.

Loops

Loops are comprised of one or more ridges that double back on themselves. About 60 percent of patterns in human fingerprints are loops. They're subdivided into two types depending upon the direction the ridges flow in relation to the two bones of the forearm, the radius and the ulna:

- ✔ Radial loops flow toward the radius or the thumb side.
- ✔ Ulnar loops flow toward the ulna or little finger side.

Whorls

Whorls look like little whirlpools of ridgelines. They make up 35 percent of patterns seen in human fingerprints and are subgrouped into four categories:

- ✔ Plain whorls are either concentric circles like a bull's-eye or spirals like a wound spring.
- ✔ Central pocket loop whorls resemble a loop with a whorl at its end.
- ✔ Double loop whorls include two loops that collide to produce an S-shaped pattern.
- ✔ Accidental loop whorls are slightly different from other whorls and are irregular.

Developing the Henry System

Sir Edward Henry, an inspector general of the British police in India's Bengal province, worked on a fingerprint classification system for many years. The Henry System, which he completed in 1899, still is used (with a few modifications) in the United States and Great Britain.

Using the Henry System, individual prints are assigned scores based on where whorls show up within a ten-finger set of prints. Whorls on certain fingers get higher scores than whorls on other fingers. The total score is used to narrow down matches into all the sets with the same score.

This system separates fingerprint files into 1,024 groups, thus narrowing the focus of fingerprint searches. The actual matching still is done by hand, meaning the system doesn't make the match but simply reduces the number of files the fingerprint examiner must wade through.

Now, in the computer age, prints are digitized and stored as computer data. This allows for much faster sorting and matching. Still, if a match is found, the final determination is made by a human visually comparing the prints in question.

Speeding up identification: AFIS

Because criminals almost never leave behind a full set of prints, systems that rely on prints from all ten fingers are less than perfect. Enter the Automated Fingerprint Identification System (AFIS).

AFIS came about during the 1960s as a result of collaboration between the FBI and the then National Bureau of Standards (now the National Institute of Standards and Technologies, or NIST). With growing numbers of print sets being housed in the FBI's database, a better method for storing, retrieving, and matching fingerprints became a necessity. Imagine hundreds of agents sitting at hundreds of desks looking through thousands of print cards, searching for a match to only a partial print left behind by an accused serial killer. The wheels of justice would indeed move slowly.

Putting AFIS to work: The Night Stalker case

Between June 1984 and August 1985, a series of brutal rapes and murders occurred throughout Southern California, putting the entire region in a state of fear and shock. The killer became known as the Night Stalker.

The Night Stalker entered victims' homes at night through unlocked doors, often after cutting the phone line. After shooting and killing any adult males present, he then raped the female victims. The assaults often took place in the bed where the woman's spouse lay dead. The Night Stalker sometimes, but not always, killed the female victims. His final victims were a couple from Mission Viejo, California. The Night Stalker raped the woman while she lay in bed next to her husband, who had been shot in the head. Both she and her injured husband survived the attack. As fate would have it, a teenage neighbor saw a man in black drive away from the murder scene and wrote down the license plate number. The vehicle, which had been stolen earlier, was found abandoned two days later, and a partial fingerprint was lifted from the vehicle's interior.

At that time, the Los Angeles Police Department had just installed a new AFIS that was capable of comparing more than 60,000 prints per second. The partial print from the car registered a match within minutes. Performing a similar search by hand (without AFIS) and finding a match against the 1.7 million print cards in Los Angeles would have taken a fingerprint expert 67 years.

The Night Stalker was Richard Ramirez, a 25-year-old drifter from El Paso, Texas. After his picture went out over the media, residents of East Los Angeles recognized and overpowered him as he attempted to steal another car. Police arrived in time to save him from an angry mob. On November 7, 1989, a jury sentenced him to death.

The AFIS computer scans and digitally encodes fingerprints, storing that information in massive databases. It can search thousands of these files every second while attempting to match them to an unknown ten-print set or even a single or partial print. Current AFIS computers search through a batch of 500,000 prints in less than a second.

After the computer establishes a match, an agent trained in fingerprint evaluation then hand-checks the file or files. Even in the computer age, the final match is made by the trained eye of a fingerprint expert.

Not only can the computer match prints with dizzying speed, it can improve the quality of the print through minor digital manipulations. Brightness and contrast can be enhanced, and fuzzy images can be made sharper, all of which results in a clearer print that is more easily used in matching.

Despite this system's incredible power, all is not rosy in AFIS Land. Early in the system's development, several different AFIS manufacturers designed and supplied the computers, and not all of these computers are compatible. Added to this, not all jurisdictions subscribe to the AFIS system. This means that a set of prints in New York may belong to a criminal whose prints are stored in a Chicago database, but because the two systems can't search each other's databases, no match can be found. The FBI, which has a national database within the United States, is working with NIST to standardize the different systems so that searches can be conducted of fingerprint databases in all jurisdictions. Still not perfect, the system continues to improve year by year.

Locating Those Sneaky Prints

Fingerprints come in three general types that depend on how and where they were left. For example, a print left in grease on a wall is easier to find than one left on a garbage bag without any visible substance present to enhance its visibility.

Here's the breakdown of what types of prints investigators are likely to find and where:

- ✔ **Patent prints** occur when a substance such as blood, ink, paint, dirt, or grease on the fingers of the perpetrator leaves behind a readily visible print.
- ✔ **Plastic prints** have a three-dimensional quality and occur when the perpetrator impresses a print into a soft substance such as wax, putty, caulk, soap, cold butter, or even dust.
- ✔ **Latent prints** are invisible and can't be seen without special lighting or processing.

Patent and plastic prints can be photographed, and the photo can be used for matching. Often the print is lighted at an angle to increase contrast, but little else is needed to make these prints recordable. If a criminal doesn't leave behind a visible print, however, identification still is possible, but it's certainly a lot trickier. Tools for tracking down prints can be as simple as a flashlight or black powder, as sophisticated as chemical reactions and lasers, or as goofy as Super Glue.

Which method investigators use depends upon the surface beneath the print. For harder surfaces, powders typically are used, and chemicals often are needed on more porous surfaces. Some prints show up under ultraviolet light or even a plain old flashlight.

Seeking latent prints

Just because you don't see it right away doesn't mean it isn't there. Fingers constantly are coated with sweat and oils that are left behind on everything you touch.

The inner surfaces of your fingers, palms, and even the soles of your feet contain friction ridges lined with pores that serve as outlet openings of your sweat glands. Although these particular glands secrete sweat that has fewer oils, your fingers nevertheless pick up oils, salts, and grime when you touch your hair, face, or any area of your body served by more oil-rich sweat glands. You deposit these residues whenever you touch another surface.

The best surfaces on which to find latent prints are hard, smooth surfaces, such as a murder weapon, tools, or objects left behind or potentially touched by a criminal, opened drawers, out-of-place furniture, and entry and exit points. In short, any place the perpetrator may have touched and therefore left a print.

The simple approach is best when trying to reveal a latent print. An angled light from a flashlight, with or without the aid of a magnifying glass, may bring it into focus. Because the ridge pattern of a latent print actually fluoresces (glows) when exposed to laser and ultraviolet lights, these light sources may pop it into view. Think back to the '70s, if you're old enough: This effect is just like looking at black-light posters. A print exposed in this manner can be photographed and then matched with a known print on a database.

Powdering the print

Fingerprint powders adhere to moisture and oils of the residue in a latent print and thereby expose the pattern of the friction ridges. The powders come in a variety of colors and types. Criminalists use the color that gives the greatest degree of contrast with the background surface. Black powder, which is made from carbon black or charcoal, and gray powder, made from aluminum or titanium powder, are used most often.

Magnetically sensitive powders also are used, and they too come in varying colors. These powders are used with a special magnetic brush that is not actually a brush at all. It has no bristles, and thus doesn't come into contact with the print, making it less likely to damage or smear the print. It is more like a magic wand that loosely holds the powder by a weak magnetic force. This so-called brush deposits the powder when it's passed over the print, and the print snaps into view.

Other specialized powders are fluorescent. After they are applied, the print fluoresces (glows) under a laser light.

After the powdering process is complete, the print is either photographed or lifted. *Lifting* is done by gently laying the sticky surface of a strip of transparent tape over the print. As the tape is peeled off, the print pattern sticks to the tape, which is then placed on a card for later examination and matching. Because smears can render a print unusable, lifting a print takes a very steady hand. If the print is on an irregular surface, where tape lifting can be a problem, technicians may employ a gel-lifter or the silicon-based Mikrosil Casting Kit. This is also used for collecting tool-mark impressions.

Using chemistry to expose prints

Latent prints found on more porous surfaces are treated with chemicals that reveal print patterns by reacting with some component of the print residue. The reaction creates another compound that is more clearly visible. Common chemicals used for exposing prints include: cyanoacrylate vapor, iodine fuming, ninhydrin, and silver nitrate.

Cyanoacrylate vapor

What is cyanoacrylate? You probably know it by its trade name, Super Glue. Yes, *that* Super Glue . . . the kind you can buy in virtually any hardware or hobby store. It turns out Super Glue is 98 percent cyanoacrylate, which has become an extremely useful forensic tool. When heated or mixed with sodium hydroxide, cyanoacrylate releases vapors that bind to amino acids that are present in print residues, thus forming a white latent print.

After a print has been exposed with cyanoacrylate, it can be photographed as is or treated with a fluorescent dye that binds to the print. The print then glows under a laser or ultraviolet light.

The item that's to be checked for prints in this manner often is exposed to the vapor in something called a fuming chamber. The resulting fumed print is quite hard and stable, as you'd probably expect from Super Glue. Instead of setting up a fuming box at the crime scene, police now frequently use a hand-held, wand-shaped gadget that heats a small cartridge of cyanoacrylate mixed with a fluorescent dye. The wand releases fumes that are directed at the latent print, enabling the criminalist to fix and dye the print at the same time.

Iodine fuming

When heated, solid crystal iodine releases iodine vapors into a fuming chamber, where the iodine fumes combine with oils in the latent print to produce a brownish print. This kind of print fades quickly, so it must be photographed right away or fixed by spraying it with a solution of starch in water, which preserves the print for several weeks or months.

Ninhydrin

Ninhydrin (triketohydrindene hydrate) is a staple of law enforcement investigators and has been used for years to reveal latent prints. The object with the supposed latent print is dipped in or sprayed with a ninhydrin solution. Because the reaction between the ninhydrin and the oils of the print is extremely slow, the latent print may take several hours to appear as a purple-blue print. Heating the object to a temperature of 80 to 100 degrees Fahrenheit speeds up this process. Ninhydrin is very useful in exposing prints left on paper.

Silver nitrate

Silver nitrate is a component of black-and-white photographic film. When investigators expose a latent print to silver nitrate, the chloride in salt (sodium chloride) molecules present in the print residue reacts with the silver nitrate and forms silver chloride. This colorless compound develops, or becomes visible, when it's exposed to ultraviolet light, revealing a black or reddish-brown print.

Cleaning up the print: Digital techniques

More often than not, a print or partial print is unclear. Its minute details may be fuzzy or difficult to see. Digital technology has stepped up and helped remedy this problem. Prints are scanned into a computer and then subjected to one of many programs that can enhance, improve, and clean up the computer-generated image of the print. Changing the light, contrast, clarity, and background patterns can make a previously obscured print jump into clear view, speeding up the matching process and making it more accurate, to boot.

Digging deeper into fingerprints

With modern forensic techniques, fingerprints can reveal more than simply the friction ridge patterns. Prints are made up of body oils, amino acids, salts, grime, and cellular debris. This cellular debris contains DNA, and with modern DNA analysis (see Chapter 15 for DNA details), this DNA can be profiled, thus giving law enforcement very useful identifying information. This is often called *Touch DNA,* as it is left behind by simply touching an object.

Additionally, the print residue can be subjected to toxicological analysis (see Chapter 16 for the full scoop). From this material it can be determined whether the person has handled or used various drugs, such as cocaine, marijuana, or nicotine.

Chapter 6

Painting A Gruesome Picture:
Bloodstain Analysis

- -

In This Chapter

▶ Diving into the characteristics of blood

▶ Recognizing bloodstain patterns

▶ Checking out a hypothetical case

- -

*N*o doubt you'd prefer to keep your blood *inside* your body, but it's somewhat reassuring to know that blood can be extremely useful on the outside, as well. Forensic investigators can figure out a great deal about a crime from blood found at the crime scene. Bloodstains left at an accident, suicide, or crime scene may be the key to determining what happened, helping investigators solve a crime, or, for that matter, determining whether a crime was even committed.

The shape and location of bloodstains provide clues about where the victim and suspect were when the crime took place and where they went afterward. Blood also reveals the presence of disease, drugs, or alcohol, and it can be used to determine the identity of the victim and the suspect through DNA analysis.

Understanding Blood's Character

In addition to the revealing blood type and DNA evidence it leaves, blood is important to crime scenes because of the way it moves and clots. These characteristics stem from blood's composition. Knowing how blood operates, inside and outside the body, enables investigators to get to the bottom of how a bloodstain got there.

Thicker than water

Blood is a complex substance, consisting of liquid and solid components. As a liquid, blood shares many of the same physical properties as other liquids, including water. It moves and flows as gravity dictates and tends to pool in low-lying areas. Blood spreads to cover a surface or to conform to the shape of a container. It possesses *viscosity* (a measure of its thickness) and *surface tension* (an elastic-like property that results from the attraction of a liquid's molecules to each other). Surface tension holds a liquid together and pulls a falling drop of that liquid into a spherical shape.

Unlike water, blood is a living, breathing liquid. It really is thicker than water, and, of course, it clots. You can find cellular elements, such as red blood cells, white blood cells, and platelets, as well as various proteins, in blood's liquid plasma. The clotting process involves many of these elements. When blood clots, it separates into a solid dark-red clot and a clear yellow liquid known as serum.

Plasma and serum look similar to the naked eye, but they differ in important ways:

✔ *Plasma* is the liquid portion of whole, unclotted blood that contains proteins involved in the clotting process. You can separate plasma from whole blood in a *centrifuge,* a device that rapidly spins a test tube of blood, causing cells to settle in the bottom, leaving the plasma on top.

✔ *Serum* is the liquid that remains after the blood's proteins have done their job and the blood has clotted and retracted into a clump.

Blood remains a liquid as long as it's moving inside the body. At death, the heart stops pumping blood through the body, and the blood stagnates and clots. When blood leaves the body, it clots within a few minutes.

Looking into blood clotting

As you've no doubt seen after a mishap with a bread knife or a fall from your bike, whenever blood leaves your body, it begins to pool and clot. Normal clotting time for blood is from 3 to 15 minutes, but clotting time is extremely individual and can be affected by certain diseases, such as hemophilia and some types of leukemia, and various medications, including blood thinners.

When blood first begins to clot, it forms a dark, shiny, jelly-like mass. With time, the clot begins to contract and separate from the yellowish serum. Investigators use the state of blood clotting as a rough guide to estimate how much time has passed since the blood was shed. If the blood is still liquid, the bleeding occurred only a few minutes before. If it's a shiny, gelatinous pool, bleeding occurred from less than half an hour to an hour earlier.

And if the blood is separated into clot and serum, an hour or more has probably passed. These are very broad and general timelines, as each situation is different.

Bloodstains that resulted from blood spurting or gushing must have happened before death, when blood was still moving through the body. Impact spatters and splashes can occur after death, but only the assailant (or a clumsy investigator) can cause these kinds of stains, for example by continuing to strike the victim after that victim is dead or stepping into a pool of blood.

Oozing, gushing, and dripping

Blood can leave your body in many ways. Depending on the situation, blood can drip, ooze, flow, gush, or spurt. Each kind of blood movement leaves a recognizable bloodstain pattern or spatter. I tell you more about each of these in the later section "Analyzing Bloodstain Patterns." Left unchecked, any continuous blood loss can lead to death from *exsanguination* (bleeding to death).

The mechanisms by which blood leaves the body can be divided into two categories: passive and projected. *Passive* bleeding depends upon the action of gravity alone. This kind of bleeding includes oozes and drips. Blood is *projected* when a person or object applies some force other than gravity. Arterial spurts, cast-off blood, and impact spatter are examples of projected blood. The next section tells you more about each of these patterns.

Analyzing Bloodstain Patterns

Investigators can learn a lot from the pattern of bloodstains at a crime scene. Who shed the blood? How did it get where it was? What was the sequence of events that must have occurred for this particular pattern to be present? A careful analysis of the pattern can answer these questions and help solve the crime.

The information bloodstain patterns provide includes

- ✔ The origin of the bloodstains
- ✔ The type of instrument that caused the bloodstains
- ✔ The direction from which an object struck the victim
- ✔ The relative positions of the victim, assailant or assailants, and bystanders

> ✔ The locations and movements of the victim and assailant during the attack
>
> ✔ The number of blows or gunshots the victim received
>
> ✔ The truthfulness of any suspects and witnesses

Finding clues in passive bloodstains

Passive bloodstains form not because of force but because of the laws of gravity. Blood that oozes, drips, or gushes from the body moves downhill and collects in the lowest areas on or near the injured or deceased person. Stairs, ramps, or even slight inclines can carry blood considerable distances before it clots. Gushing or fast-flowing blood obviously gathers in larger amounts and can travel farther from the body than dripping or oozing blood. A slow ooze clots before blood moves too far from the body.

Blood can drip from an injured person's wounds, a blood-covered weapon, the assailant's hands, a tabletop, or any elevated object. Getting shot or stabbed in the shoulder can cause blood to run down your arm and drip from your fingers. Similarly, an escaping assailant can drip blood from a knife, bludgeon, or other weapon.

Typically, a drop forms when a small amount of blood breaks away from a larger blood source. Because of surface tension, drops remain spherical until they strike a surface or until they're struck by another object. Drops don't break into smaller drops simply by falling through the air. If a drop hits the edge of a table, or if a swinging arm or weapon strikes it, the drop breaks apart. Otherwise, it falls as a sphere until it reaches the floor or some other surface.

When a falling drop of blood strikes a surface, it splashes in all directions, spattering in a circular pattern around the point of impact. The shape and size of the blood spatter pattern depend upon the size of the drop, how fast it falls, at what angle it hits the surface, and the kind of surface it strikes.

A blood drop picks up speed as it falls until it reaches *terminal velocity*, its maximum free-fall speed. The terminal velocity of blood is approximately 25 feet per second, and a drop can reach that speed only after a fall of 20 to 25 feet. But the circular spatter pattern produced by a drop of blood increases in size when it falls from an inch up to about 7 feet. The diameters of spatter patterns from drops falling from higher than 7 feet don't significantly increase. The size of the diameters of spatter patterns for single drops typically varies from 13 millimeters to 22 millimeters, depending on the distances the drops travel and the sizes of the drops.

When a drop strikes a surface at a right angle (90 degrees), the spatter pattern forms an even circle around the point of impact. If the blood strikes from a smaller angle, the spatter creates an elongated oval pattern with the narrow or pointed end aiming in the drop's direction of travel (see Figure 6-1).

90°   45°   10°

Figure 6-1:
The size and
shape of
stain
patterns
reveal the
angle at
which they
struck the
surface.

Illustration by Nan Owen

The surface that the blood hits can change the size and shape of the spatter (see Figure 6-2). Hard, smooth surfaces like glass, tile, or polished marble create much smaller spatters than rough, irregular surfaces like unfinished wood or concrete.

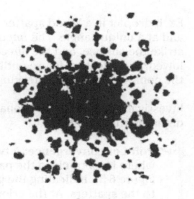

Figure 6-2:
Blood
behaves
differently
according to
the type of
surface it
strikes.

Glass   Concrete

Illustration by Nan Owen

Secondary or satellite spatters often create confusion when criminalists analyze bloodstains (see the next section). If a large drop of blood falls onto a hard surface, small secondary droplets may surround the original circular stain. Because these droplets hit the surface at angles that are less than 90 degrees, the secondary stains are elongated, but the elongated tails of these satellite droplets tend to point toward the direction from which they came, not the direction in which they were traveling.

Analyzing projected blood spatters

Projected blood spatters happen when something other than gravity applies force to a blood source. This force may be a naturally occurring internal activity like the heartbeat or the victim's breathing, or it may be an external force like a gunshot or a blunt-force trauma.

Spatters can be produced by several different mechanisms, including stabbings, beatings, gunshots, arterial bleeding, cast-off blood, splashing, and expired blood. *Expired blood* describes blood the victim expels from his lungs or airways. Each time the victim exhales, blood sprays from his mouth and nose.

Determining where the deed went down

Spatter patterns aid the medical examiner (ME) in determining the source of the blood, the source's location at the crime scene, and the mechanism that produced the bloodstains. This critical information can show investigators the positions of the assailant and the victim when the attack occurred.

Each droplet in a blood spatter strikes the surface from a unique direction and at a unique angle. The *impact angle* is the slant at which the blood drops strike the surface, and the *directionality* is the course the blood drop followed. Investigators figure out the impact angle using a protractor or one of the computer programs developed for that purpose.

Investigators use the directionality of each stain to make the following determinations:

✔ **Point of convergence:** A two-dimensional representation of the point where lines tracking the pathways of two or more spatters meet (see Figure 6-3), indicating the general location of the blood source in relation to the spatters. At the crime scene, investigators stretch strings from each stain according to the angle of impact; where those strings meet is the point of convergence.

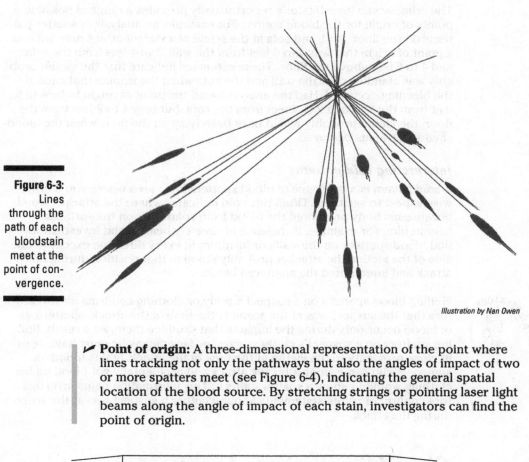

Figure 6-3:
Lines through the path of each bloodstain meet at the point of convergence.

Illustration by Nan Owen

✔ **Point of origin:** A three-dimensional representation of the point where lines tracking not only the pathways but also the angles of impact of two or more spatters meet (see Figure 6-4), indicating the general spatial location of the blood source. By stretching strings or pointing laser light beams along the angle of impact of each stain, investigators can find the point of origin.

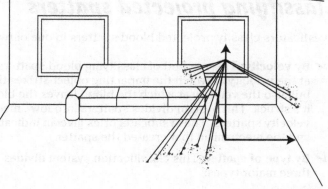

Figure 6-4:
Directionality and angle of impact reveal the point of origin of bloodstains.

Illustration by Nan Owen

The crime scene investigator's report usually provides a range of possible points of origin for the blood source. For example, an analysis of spatter patterns on the floor, wall, and sofa at the scene of a violent attack may indicate a point of origin that was 4 to 6 feet from the wall, 2 to 4 feet from the sofa, and 4 to 6 feet above the floor. These estimates indicate that the victim probably was standing near the wall and the sofa when the trauma that caused the bleeding occurred. Had the analyst found the point of origin to be 4 to 6 feet from the wall and 2 to 4 feet from the sofa, but only 1 to 2 feet from the floor, the victim probably would have been lying on the floor when the blood-shedding trauma occurred.

Interpreting void patterns

A *void pattern* is an absence of blood spatters in an area where you'd otherwise expect to see them. Often this void indicates where the attacker stood because his body prevented the blood from spattering on the surfaces behind him. For example, if someone is severely beaten, and investigators find blood spatters on the walls or furniture in every direction except to one side of the victim, the attacker probably stood in that position during the attack and intercepted the spattered blood.

Finding blood spatters on a suspect's body or clothing confirms for investigators that the suspect was at the scene at the time of the attack. Spatterings of blood occur only during the impacts that produce them. As a result, finding spatters on a suspect's clothes, arms, or face means he must have been in close proximity to the victim at the time of the attack. Stains found on someone who came along after the attack and accidentally got blood on her clothing wouldn't show a spatter pattern. This information helps investigators confirm or refute statements about whether a suspect was at the scene during the attack.

Classifying projected spatters

Investigators classify projected blood spatters in one of two ways:

- **By velocity:** This method of classifying blood spatters looks not only at the velocity at which the impacting object strikes the blood source but also the velocity at which the blood leaves the blood source when it's struck. This system divides spatters into low-, medium-, and high-velocity spatters. These subcategories give an indication of the object and the mechanism that created the spatter.

- **By type of spatter:** This classification system divides spatters into these three major types:

- *Impact spatters* typically occur with beatings, stabbings, gunshots, or any other circumstance where a foreign object impacts the victim.

- *Projection spatters* result from arterial bleeding, cast-off blood, and expired, or exhaled, blood. The next section provides details about these patterns.

- *Combination spatters,* which include impact and projection spatters, often are found at crime scenes. A victim who gets stabbed in the chest or neck may leave a combination of impact spatters from the force of the attack and projection spatters from arterial bleeding, expired blood, and cast-off blood.

Investigators find both methods of spatter classification useful because these methods overlap in many areas.

Low-velocity spatters

Low-velocity spatters occur when an object moving less than 5 feet per second strikes a surface. This impact results in fairly large spatters, typically 4 millimeters or greater in diameter.

Several mechanisms produce low-velocity spatters. Common examples include drops dripping under the influence of only gravity from a wound or a blood-soaked weapon. If the dripping blood source is standing still, the drops fall vertically and create circular stains. But if the source is moving, such as an injured victim taking flight or an escaping assailant carrying a blood-covered weapon, the drops strike the floor at an angle, producing elongated stains with spines or projections of blood extending in the direction of movement.

Suppose that an assailant with blood on his hands stands near the body of his victim. He drips blood onto the floor, leaving a round bloodstain pattern for each drop. If he begins to move around in the house, the drops that fall no longer strike the floor from a 90-degree angle. The direction in which the assailant moves influences the direction in which the drops leave his hands. These drops hit the floor at an angle, resulting in oval stains with elongated tails that point in the direction of travel, like those shown in Figure 6-1. Criminalists follow the tails to determine the assailant's movements within the crime scene and perhaps his escape route. Along this path investigators are likely to find other useful evidence, such as a discarded murder weapon or bloodied clothes.

Arterial bleeding is also considered low velocity. If an artery is damaged during an assault, suicide attempt, or accident, the blood loss may take the form of gushes or spurts, depending upon the size of the artery, the extent of the damage, and whether clothing or some other object covers the injury. A freely spurting artery results in a linear and cascading spatter pattern (see Figure 6-5). The pattern's distance from the wound, length, and volume may decline steadily as the victim continues to lose blood, causing his blood volume and blood pressure to decline.

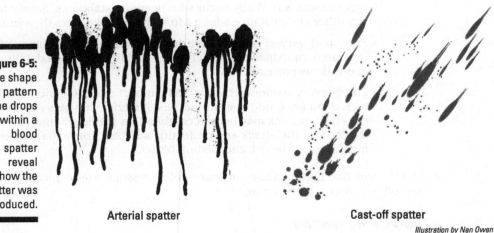

Illustration by Nan Owen

Figure 6-5: The shape and pattern of the drops within a blood spatter reveal how the spatter was produced.

Arterial spatter   Cast-off spatter

Another low-velocity blood source is *cast-off blood*, or blood that is flung from an object because of centrifugal force. Cast-off patterns usually occur when an attacker uses a weapon to deliver a series of arcing blows. Investigators typically find these patterns on walls and ceilings.

The spatter pattern associated with cast-off blood tends to be a fairly uniform trail of droplets, which reflects the arc that the object traveled in (see Figure 6-5). Determining the point of convergence and the angle of impact of these cast-off stains reveals the assailant's position at the time he swung the weapon. In some cases, estimating the perpetrator's height and even whether the assailant is right- or left-handed — or at least which hand struck the blows — is possible.

Also, the number of these cast-off patterns investigators find indicates the minimum number of blows to the victim. Because not every swing of the weapon necessarily produces cast-off stains, the assailant may have delivered more blows, but fewer can't have been delivered.

Medium-velocity spatters

Medium-velocity spatters come from objects moving between 5 and 100 feet per second. These spatters are typically smaller than spatters from low-velocity droplets and vary from 1 to 4 millimeters in diameter. Medium-velocity spatters come from impacts with blunt or sharp objects and from expirated blood.

Spatters from impacts with a blunt object distribute blood in all directions from the area of impact. As with low-velocity spatters, an analysis of directionality and impact angle of the stains can help locate the point of origin. See the section "Determining where the deed went down" earlier in this chapter for a discussion of directionality and impact angle.

If the wounds are to the face, throat, or lungs, blood mixes with the exhaled air, creating a fine spray and producing a mist spatter pattern. This mist pattern may be found on and around the victim and on the attacker.

High-velocity spatters

High-velocity spatters result when an object strikes the victim at a speed faster than 100 feet per second. The resulting spatters tend to be very small, usually less than 1 millimeter in diameter, and appear as mist-like stains.

A bullet travels at high velocity and thus produces a high-velocity spatter pattern. These patterns show up near entrance and exit wounds, but blood behaves differently according to whether the bullet is coming into the body or heading back out.

A bloodstain associated with an entrance wound is called *blowback* or *back spatter,* meaning the droplets travel in a direction opposite to the path of the bullet. Blowback often is found on the shooter or the weapon, even inside the barrel of the gun in very close-range shots. A bloodstain found near the exit wound is called *forward spatter.* In the case of forward spatter, the blood droplets follow the direction of the bullet.

If you tossed a glass of water through a window screen, the water would keep right on going through the screen. That's forward spatter. Toss that same glass of water against a wall, and the water splashes back toward you, just like back spatter.

Latching on to transfer patterns

Transfer patterns result when an object soaked with blood comes into contact with an unstained object. Bloody fingerprints and shoeprints fall into this category. The perpetrator may brush against or kneel in a bloodstain, or wipe the weapon or his hands or his shirt, transferring the victim's blood to his clothing. Matching the blood from such a transfer stain to the victim's blood may help solve the crime.

Like fingers and shoes, a blood-soaked fabric can leave behind a recognizable pattern. Say a perpetrator knelt on the floor next to his victim and unknowingly transferred blood to the knee of his pants. After his escape, he leaned against his car door and transferred the stain. The weave pattern of his pants may be transferred, also. If investigators find this pattern, they may be able to use the fabric pattern to determine what type of clothing the attacker wore. Regardless, analysis of the transferred blood on a suspect's clothing can link the suspect to the crime scene and the victim if they can match the DNA of the bloodstain to the suspect. Chapter 15 tells you more about DNA.

CASE STUDY

Reconsidering evidence in the Sam Sheppard case

Marilyn Sheppard was bludgeoned to death in her home on July 4, 1954. Her husband, Dr. Sam Sheppard, survived what he called an attack by an intruder. He reported that he had been knocked unconscious as he tried to protect his wife and himself. The home appeared to have been ransacked, as if the murders were part of a home-invasion robbery.

Investigators noticed that Sheppard had no blood on his hands, body, or clothing, and he denied having cleaned up before summoning the police. Normally that would seem to exonerate Sheppard, but this complete absence of blood disturbed the police. Because of the brutal nature of the attack, the killer would have been covered with blood, and some of that blood should have been transferred to Sheppard during their struggle. In addition, Sheppard had no blood on his hands — impossible if he had checked for a pulse in his wife's blood-covered neck, as he said he had. Further, Sheppard said that his watch, wallet, ring, and keys were missing, and he believed that the killer must have taken them. Indeed, police found a bag with the missing items not far from the house. But the bag and wallet had no blood on them. Would they not have stains from the killer's bloody hands? And wouldn't Sheppard's pants, wrists, and hands have blood transfers from the killer removing Sheppard's wallet, keys, watch, and rings? No such stains were found.

Sheppard's watch, however, had blood spatters from flying blood droplets, indicating that the watch had been near the victim at the time the fatal blows were struck. If they had come from contact with the victim's neck as Sheppard felt for a pulse, the stains would have been transfer smears and not spatter droplets.

Police determined that most likely Sheppard had bludgeoned his wife to death; cleaned the blood from his hands and body; trashed the house to make it look as though a burglary had occurred, thus staging the crime scene; placed his watch (without noticing the blood spatters) and the other items in the bag; and tossed the bag where police would find it. Based in large part on the blood evidence — or lack thereof — Sheppard was convicted of murder.

But the story doesn't end here. After spending ten years in prison, Sheppard was released when the U.S. Supreme Court overturned his conviction, primarily on the grounds that the massive pretrial publicity had made a fair trial impossible. A second trial commenced on November 1, 1966, and again the blood evidence played a crucial role, but this time it became a case of dueling experts. A representative from the coroner's office again stated that the blood on Sheppard's watch represented a spatter pattern and meant that Sheppard must have been present at the time the fatal blows were struck. The defense, headed by a young F. Lee Bailey, avoided the error of the first trial, in which the defense had no expert to refute the prosecution's blood expert, and countered with Dr. Paul Kirk, a renowned criminalist. Kirk testified that the blood on the watch was a transfer pattern that resulted when Sheppard checked his wife's neck for a pulse.

On November 16 the jury returned a "not guilty" verdict, and Dr. Sheppard became a free man. The controversy surrounding this case continues to this day, and the contrast between the two trials shows that experts' opinions differ, and so do juries'. Dr. Sheppard's story inspired the popular television series and major motion picture *The Fugitive*.

Reconstructing the crime scene from bloodstains

Contaminated evidence is no evidence at all, so investigators have to document bloodstain and spatter patterns in a timely and logical fashion. Police, fire, and rescue personnel can alter or contaminate the blood evidence, as can any unnecessary foot traffic at the crime scene. For that reason, investigators need to take control of the scene immediately and consistently. Unless they're high-traffic public places, indoor scenes usually can be preserved long enough for investigators to obtain needed information. Outdoor scenes, however, are subject to environmental influences, and public places require investigators to gather information more urgently.

Investigators carefully photograph bloodstains. Initial photographs capture an overall view of the scene. Subsequent pictures gradually move in on individual stains. The photographer takes pictures of individual stains close enough to reveal all needed detail, and should include a ruler or other measuring device to provide a scale reference. In homicide cases, investigators check out the body and any associated bloodstains or spatters first. After the body is removed, investigators turn their attention to other spatters.

Some bloodstains are *latent* (invisible to the naked eye). Investigators often use luminol to expose these hidden stains. *Luminol* is a chemical that reacts with the hemoglobin in blood to produce a complex substance that *luminesces* (glows). Luminol is extremely sensitive, detecting blood in concentrations as low as one part per million. Investigators darken the room and spray luminol over areas where they suspect blood to be. When blood is present, stains glow a bluish-white, and the photographer takes pictures of the glowing pattern.

Luminol also can reveal bloody tracks that indicate the perpetrator's movements or escape route and drag marks that show whether anyone moved the body. Luminol is so sensitive that it can uncover blood in cracks, crevices, and even areas where someone has tried to clean it.

It's important to note that many substances can interfere with or confuse luminol pattern analysis. Bleach and other cleaning agents, certain paints and varnishes, and even some fruit juices are examples.

After photographers take an adequate number and variety of photographs, crime-scene analysts complete their analyses and create a report that may include implications of the victim's and assailant's locations at each stage of the crime, the number and types of injuries inflicted, and the exact sequence of events (see the next section to understand how analysts gather this information).

Putting It All Together: A Hypothetical Case

Joe and Bill have a serious disagreement, and the two men reach a point of true hatred for one another. Bill, carrying a 2-foot piece of metal pipe, kicks in Joe's door and steps into the entryway of Joe's home. But Joe is expecting him and shoots Bill in the left arm with a .32 caliber pistol.

Angered more than injured, Bill strikes Joe in the face with the pipe. Joe staggers, drops the gun, and turns to run away. Bill hits him several more times in the head with the pipe as Joe retreats across his living room and down a hallway, both of which have hardwood flooring.

The blows finally bring Joe to his knees at the far end of the hall, where he crawls into his bedroom, which is carpeted. He collapses facedown near his bed and a nightstand. Bill continues his attack until Joe is dead. He then runs back up the hallway, through the kitchen and out the back door. Gruesome, but all too common.

After photographers take pictures of the scene and forensic pathology technicians (see Chapter 22) remove the body, the crime scene investigator examines each and every piece of evidence available to him. Here's what he finds and where he finds it:

- ✔ **The entryway:** High-velocity blood spattering from the gunshot to Bill's arm is on the entry wall and the front doorjamb. Later DNA analysis reveals that this blood matches a sample obtained from Bill. The blow to Joe's face causes bleeding from his nose and mouth, and blood falls to the floor, producing circular stains. Joe also expirates blood in a fine mist over the wall, the floor, and Bill.

- ✔ **The living room and hallway:** Joe continues to expirate a mist of blood as he runs. The spray is found on the carpet, walls, and furniture he passes on his retreat toward his bedroom. He also continues to bleed from his facial wounds. However, the drops that reach the floor no longer leave circular stains because he's now on the move. The stains become oblong and have spikes or projections pointed along his line of retreat. As Bill continues to strike Joe in the head, medium-velocity impact spatters radiate in all directions. Some reach the floor, and others pepper the wall, the furniture, and Bill. The directionality and impact angle of the drops show that the blood source (Joe's head) was 5 to 6 feet above the floor and moving toward the bedroom. At the end of the hallway where Joe collapses, the point-of-origin analysis shows that the blood source is less than 3 feet off the floor.

✔ **The bedroom:** The carpet shows dripped and expirated mist patterns, but they are less clear because of the texture of the carpet. The same is true for the continued impact spatter from Joe's blows. The bed, wall, and nightstand show medium-velocity impact and expirated spatter as Bill continues his assault and Joe breathes his last breaths. Investigators find the expirated pattern only in the direction Joe's head is turned, although the impact spatters occur in all directions. Investigators find a void area where Bill stands over the fallen Joe and delivers his final blows.

✔ **The escape route:** Investigators find bloody shoe prints leading back down the hallway, through the kitchen, and out the back door. Low-velocity spatters with projections indicating movement toward the back door show where blood dripped from Bill's hands and the pipe during his escape.

✔ **Bill:** If the police apprehend Bill before he can clean up and change his clothing, he will have blood on his hands and probably his face. Even if he has time to clean himself, his clothing may be recovered, and it will show impact spatter stains over the sleeves and front of his shirt, the front of his pants, and the tops of his shoes. His shoe soles retain blood in the crevices and treads, and the tread pattern matches those shoe prints left at the scene in blood. Then, of course, Bill has his gunshot wound to explain away.

Based on the bloodstain evidence, the criminalist can reconstruct the scene and determine the exact sequence of events. If Bill tells a story that varies from the truth, the spatters will trip him up.

Chapter 7

Leaving Impressive Impressions: Shoes, Tires, and Tools

In This Chapter

▶ Using shoeprints to identify the perpetrator

▶ Identifying tire tracks as evidence

▶ Analyzing and using tool-mark evidence

▶ Recognizing fabric patterns

"*W*atch where you step" is good advice for a criminal. For a farmhand, too. Many suspects have been connected to crime scenes by the tracks of their shoes. Even though shoes are manufactured in vast numbers, and the same shoe brand and size may be worn by any number of people, your particular walking pattern still may give you away.

Tires and tools also leave impressions that usually are classified as class evidence (see Chapter 3), meaning that they can exclude certain types of shoes, tires, or tools but can't absolutely identify a particular one. The tread pattern of a shoe or a tire may identify the size and the manufacturer of the product, and that information narrows the search for the perpetrator by focusing the investigation on sellers and buyers of the particular product.

Stepping Out: Shoeprints as Evidence

When the shoe fits, criminals often find themselves walking right off to prison. Shoeprints and impressions are useful to criminalists for many reasons. Not only can they suggest that a particular person was at the crime scene, they may also confirm or refute a suspect's alibi. For example, a neighbor claims that when he walked next door to borrow a cup of sugar, he found the woman who lived there lying on the kitchen floor bludgeoned to death. He says that the door was unlocked, so he checked for the woman's pulse, called 911, and waited for police to arrive. The neighbor says that he went nowhere else in the house. If police discover the neighbor's shoeprint elsewhere in the home, say on the hardwood floor of the woman's bedroom, near where her empty jewelry box is found, his story doesn't ring true.

Prints also can indicate the points of entry and exit at a crime scene. Shoeprints in the soft soil of a flower garden beneath a pried-open window that match dirt and grime prints on the floor inside the home indicate the point of entry. Bloody prints leading through a rear door suggest an exit portal. Prints left on tile or wooden floors, stairs, countertops, windowsills, ladders, and even chair seats can reveal the perpetrator's movements within the crime scene.

Following shoeprints through a crime scene helps investigators focus their search for evidence. When prints are found in several rooms of a house that has been burglarized, investigators concentrate their search in those areas. Following an exit trail can lead investigators to where the perpetrator tossed a weapon or articles of clothing, such as a mask or gloves. The best evidence tends to be left in the perpetrator's wake.

A shoeprint also can link several crimes. Finding identical prints at several different crime scenes indicates that the same perpetrator may be involved in each crime. This linkage (see Chapter 3) often is crucial to solving the crimes. Each separate scene may provide evidence that when taken alone is of little help, but when combined with evidence from the other scenes may become significant.

For example, suppose that investigators find a dark brown hair at one crime scene, blue carpet fibers from a Chevrolet at another, and, at a third crime scene, blood spatter patterns that suggest the killer was left-handed and approximately 6 feet tall. Viewed separately, each item of evidence tells investigators little about the crimes, but when the same shoeprints link the crimes and suggest that the same person committed all the crimes, a much clearer picture emerges. That picture is of a 6-foot-tall, left-handed male with dark brown hair who drives a Chevrolet with blue carpet. Although this profile still doesn't provide conclusive identification, it nevertheless constructs a better description of the perpetrator.

Multiple shoeprints can indicate whether more than one person is involved and may even help determine exactly how many. When investigators find three distinct types of prints, they can state that at least three people are involved. More people may have participated but failed to leave behind any shoe impressions.

Characterizing and using shoeprints

Cinderella may have been the only belle at the ball wearing tiny glass slippers, but few suspects wear shoes that are so easily identifiable. Most shoes are mass-produced in a wide assortment of sizes and shapes for different genders and age groups, and that makes matching a suspect to a shoeprint quite a challenge, to say the least. Investigators start by identifying the size and manufacturer of a shoe before moving on to the characteristics that make the track unique. Individualization comes from the varying wear patterns, damage, or debris either lodged in the shoe tread or left behind by the perpetrator. Shoeprints are so important to crime fighters that the FBI works with shoe manufacturers to maintain a database of sole patterns.

Your shoes travel across a wide array of surfaces every day — hardwood, tile, carpet, soft soil, and rain-soaked or snow-covered sidewalks, for example. As you walk, the soles of your shoes are worn, nicked, and scuffed, and they pick up dirt, oil, grease, moisture, and debris. Much of this material then is tracked across other surfaces, leaving behind your distinctive shoeprints.

The three basic kinds of shoeprints include the following:

✔ **Patent:** The term *patent* means visible. These prints are the result of tracking through a substance, such as dirt, paint, or blood, and leaving some of it behind as you walk.

✔ **Plastic:** Walking through mud, snow, or other soft, malleable substances leaves *plastic*, or three-dimensional tracks.

✔ **Latent:** Latent shoeprints are invisible to the naked eye and result when you transfer a thin layer of accumulated yet invisible oils and grime from the soles of your shoes to a hard surface, such as glass, pieces of paper, cardboard, or polished wooden, tile, or even concrete floors.

Matching sole to soul — so to speak

Shoeprint impressions often are considered class evidence because they identify only the manufacturer and size of the shoe, which narrows the search to a suspect list rather than identifying a specific suspect.

A few specific characteristics may, however, point to a particular person. Everyone wears out the soles of their shoes in a distinct manner, as shown in Figure 7-1. Some people walk more on the outsides of their feet, others favor the heel, and still others shuffle along on the balls of their feet. How your foot strikes the ground determines how the sole of your shoe will wear.

Furthermore, from one day to the next, people routinely walk over the same kinds of surfaces during the normal course of their activities; however, the types of surfaces they walk on vary from person to person. As a result, the shoe sole–wear patterns of an office worker, who walks across carpets most of the day, will vary greatly from those of a construction worker who frequently stomps through gravel or across rough concrete.

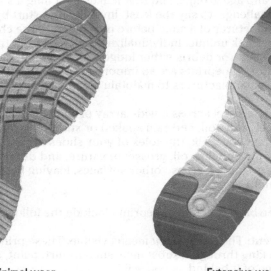

Minimal wear   Extensive wear

Illustration by Nan Owen

Noticing wear patterns

Check out the bottoms of a pair of your old tread-soled shoes. The original
tread pattern will be worn more in some areas than in others. Maybe it's
your heel or the outside area near the ball of your foot that wears down more
severely than the rest of your shoe.

Now check out the soles of someone else's shoes. Although comparing the
same brand, style, and size of shoe offers a better example, you still can distinguish a wear pattern that is much different from yours.

Differences in tread wear patterns essentially mean that everyone leaves a
unique shoeprint. And often the print made by one shoe can be matched to
that shoe to the exclusion of any others. The wear pattern makes a shoeprint
individual evidence (evidence that points to one suspect — see Chapter 3)
and not just class specific. Such an individualized pattern may enable the
criminalist to positively identify a suspect's shoe as the exact same shoe that
left the crime-scene impression.

Cuts, nicks, scratches, and gouges in the sole or a stone trapped in the tread
also can make a particular shoeprint very distinctive. Whenever a print found at
a crime scene reveals a size; style; worn, nicked, or gouged sole; and perhaps a
small, imbedded rock pattern that exactly matches an impression of a suspect's
shoes, it strongly suggests that that shoe was the one that left the print.

Of course, after months have passed, the wear pattern may have changed,
the gouge mark may have lost some of its characteristics, and the rock may

have come loose. When those things happen, individualizing characteristics can be lost or altered to the point where a positive match can't be made.

Figuring out gait patterns

Shoeprints also offer insight into the gait, walking style, length of stride, and stance of the person wearing the shoes. They can even tell investigators whether that person is pigeon-toed or slew-footed. Although generally unreliable as evidence, stride length and step width can help investigators estimate the shoe-wearer's height or expose whether that person has a limp or walks with any other unusual characteristics. A tall, thin suspect is not likely to leave a widely spaced, short stride-length impression, for example.

Collecting shoe impressions

Protecting the crime scene means protecting all evidence, including shoeprints and impressions. Investigators must be mindful of where perpetrators have or even may have walked so they can avoid those areas of the crime scene until the prints can be recovered. Likewise, *exclusionary shoeprints* are obtained from all law enforcement personnel who visit the crime scene before prints are secured. Doing so prevents confusion later on when prints are examined back at the crime lab, because an examiner therefore can exclude prints belonging to investigators. To avoid such confusion, investigators should slip surgical booties over their shoes while they're checking out the crime scene.

Patent prints often are simply photographed. Those left by tracked mud or blood typically are easily captured on film. Others, however, may need to be enhanced by using an angled or high-intensity light source to produce a clear-enough ridge pattern for a photograph. Regardless of how they're lighted, photographs of prints must be taken head-on, at a 90-degree angle relative to the surface of the print, and centered in the camera's viewing screen. Doing so lessens the amount of distortion in the image, which, in turn, means that more accurate comparisons can be made. Including a small ruler or other measuring device in pictures helps investigators more accurately determine the size of the print.

Looking for latent prints

Latent prints are not readily visible to the naked eye and tend to be deposited by shoes that are relatively clean. The soles of your shoes constantly pick up and deposit substances and debris, such as oils, dust, and fine particles of dirt. When your shoe comes into contact with a clean surface, it leaves a faint print. Even clean, dry shoes can leave prints on glass, floors, tables, countertops, or other surfaces that have been polished, waxed, or otherwise left with a faint film of grease or grime.

Searching for latent shoeprints is a task that is as meticulous as searching for latent fingerprints. Hard-surface flooring, sheets of paper, magazines, and larger pieces of broken glass make excellent surfaces for finding shoeprints. The areas near the victim and close to points of entry and exit are typically the most fruitful places to search for shoeprints.

Latent shoeprints are handled in a manner similar to latent fingerprints. They can often be dusted with fingerprint powder and either photographed or lifted with special adhesive tape. For latent dust or fine dirt prints, investigators may use an electrostatic lifting device, which creates an electrostatic charge that actually transfers the print to a lifting film specifically designed for this purpose. Latent shoeprints in blood often are exposed by using luminol (see Chapter 6).

Recording plastic prints

Plastic shoeprints are made in soft, malleable material such as mud or snow. These prints can be photographed, using an angled light source to bring out depth and detail. Impressions in snow and sand create special problems because they're light in color, and this makes achieving any contrast in the photographic image more difficult. You can resolve this issue by lightly coating the shoe impression with a dark spray paint.

After the impression is photographed, a criminalist usually makes a three-dimensional casting of the print, which then can be used for making a better match between the impression and the suspect's shoes. First, a metal or wooden frame is placed around the impression. Dental stone, a hard durable plaster, is then carefully poured into the shoe impression and allowed to set. Before the dental stone hardens completely, the initials of the person making the casting are scratched into its base so that later in court it can be identified easily and accurately.

When making a casting of a print in soft mud or sand, the weight of the plaster can deform or change the impression. Spraying the print with shellac or an acrylic lacquer before making the casting helps harden and support the impression to prevent any damage or distortion caused by the plaster.

Impressions left in snow create special problems because they're easily deformed and, of course, snow melts. Dental stone is of little use for prints in the snow. However, all is not lost. *Snowprint Wax,* a product that works a lot like shellac and stabilizes snow impressions, can be applied before a casting is made.

A special form of three-dimensional shoe impression occurs when someone steps on a carpet, leaving behind faint indentions in the pile. The indention fades with time, but sometimes an angled light reveals these footprint indentations.

Interference holography also may be used to reveal footprints in carpet. This technique uses a split laser beam to create a holographic image of the print that is then recorded on photographic film. Although interference holography doesn't reveal great detail, it helps determine the size and overall structure of the shoe.

Making the match

After photographing, lifting, or making a casting of the crime-scene shoeprint, investigators compare it with a print obtained from a suspect's shoe. The sole of the suspect's shoe is coated with ink, and its pattern then is transferred to a sheet of paper or acetate. An investigator compares the prints, first by eyeballing them to determine whether the shoes have the same tread and general wear patterns, and then by using a magnifying glas — or sometimes even a low-power microscope — to look for small cuts and scars, which are key to matching any individual characteristics.

The expert examining the shoeprints determines whether the impressions match or don't match, or whether the results are *inconclusive,* which means the examiner can't say with certainty one way or the other.

Tracking Down Tires

A hundred years ago, criminals didn't stray too far, prowling only their local neighborhoods or towns on foot or horseback. They had fewer means of traveling far from home to commit their crimes. Think about it: How far can *you* walk or ride a horse in an hour or two? The advent of the automobile, however, dramatically changed the distances that criminals are able to roam. Cars make criminals extremely mobile and enable them to travel from city to city, state to state, and even country to country, committing crimes across more widespread areas.

Hot on the heels of the automobile came a new world of forensic investigation. Vehicles often leave behind or carry away trace evidence. Glass and paint from an automobile can be left at the scene of an accident or hit-and-run and can help investigators identify the manufacturer, model, color, and year of the vehicle and narrow their search for the owner. Careful processing of a car's interior can reveal blood and many other types of trace evidence connected to a perpetrator or victim. And just like fingerprints and shoeprints, a vehicle's tires can leave behind impressions that connect them with vehicles, crime scenes, and hopefully their owners and drivers.

Although automobile tires can't leave impressions in firm asphalt or concrete, tracks nevertheless may be present. When a car rolls through mud, paint, or blood, these substances can be picked up by the tires and transferred to the pavement. Tires also pick up grease and grime from the roadway, and if they then pass over a piece of paper or a cardboard box along the roadside, a clear tire track may be left behind.

Many of these impressions, such as those made by tar or paint, are durable, whereas others made by fragile materials, such as mud or blood, will deteriorate over time. Impressions therefore should be photographed at the scene before the paper or cardboard is moved.

Latent (invisible) tire tracks can be left on concrete or paved roads. Likewise, tires can leave behind *extender oils* — substances tire manufacturers use to make their products more pliable — on the surface of the roadway.

The amount of extender oils present in a given tire varies from manufacturer to manufacturer and according to the age of the tire. Because they fluoresce under ultraviolet light, these oils can expose a tire tread pattern, which then can be photographed and compared with other tire tracks. However, because tar also fluoresces under ultraviolet lights, this technique is not useful where tar-covered roads are prevalent.

Tires leave *plastic* or three-dimensional tracks when they are driven across soft dirt roads, soft shoulders, mud, snow, and many off-road surfaces, including lawns or fields.

Analyzing tire-track evidence

Like shoeprints, tire tracks tend to be class evidence. Although the tread design may point to a particular manufacturer and tire size, it doesn't usually indicate the exact tire that made the impression. Matching a tire impression from a crime scene to that of a known design stored in a database narrows the field of suspects by focusing the attention of investigators on vehicles with similar tires. Several databases of tread designs, including an extensive one maintained by the FBI, are available to aid in this process.

Determining the manufacturer

A good tire track or impression yields information about tire size, tread design, manufacturer, and even the turning radius of the vehicle on which it was mounted. Tracks may also reveal the relative positions of all four tires, which is particularly important when tires on a particular vehicle vary in design, manufacturer, and tread wear. This variation is not uncommon because tires frequently are replaced one or two at a time, and replacement tires often differ from the original-equipment tires.

Tires have several design features that help with classification and identification (see Figure 7-2):

 ✔ **Texture:** Tire tread is wrapped around a tire's circumference in alternating *ribs* (high points or ridges) and *grooves* (depressions), which are crisscrossed at approximately 90-degree angles by *transverse grooves* (called *slots*). This cross-hatching effect breaks up the ribs into more-or-less square islands called *lugs*. On the contact surface of the lugs are small grooves called *sipes*. Though the exact pattern varies greatly, these basic features are fairly standard and appear on most tires.

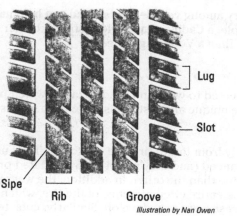

Figure 7-2:
Investigators take a close look at these common features when trying to match tracks to the tires that made them.

Lug

Slot

Sipe

Rib

Groove

Illustration by Nan Owen

- **Wear bars:** Bars of rubber called *wear bars* or *wear indicators* are placed in the grooves at scattered points around the tire. They rise above the floors of the grooves approximately 1/16 inch, which is much lower in height than the tread ribs and lugs. Their purpose is to show the degree of tread wear, and, when fully exposed, they indicate that the tire should be replaced. A tire has to be significantly worn before these bars can contribute to a two-dimensional impression. However, wear bars should be visible in the casting of a three-dimensional impression.

- **Noise treatment:** If you look carefully at a car tire, you can see that the tread design is not simply a monotonous repetition of ribs, lugs, and grooves. Minor variations exist in the sizes of each of these design elements. Typical lugs tend to be of three different sizes, but on better tires you may find as many as nine. The purpose of these variations in lug size is to improve traction and to reduce noise. At high speeds, tires tend to vibrate. Whenever the tread design is completely uniform, vibration increases because of the development of harmonic waves, which, in turn, create more tire noise. A slight variation in design pattern prevents the buildup of vibration and harmonic waves, and thus decreases tire noise.

Besides helping to determine the exact type and style of the tire, track evidence also can reveal other information about the car:

- Track width, or *stance,* can be measured from the center of one tire to the center of the tire opposite it.

- *Wheelbase,* or distance between the center of the front wheel hubs and the center of the rear wheel hubs, can be measured if the car was turning when it left the tracks.

- *Turning radius*, a measure of the tightest circle in which the vehicle can turn, also may be measurable if the tracks were left as the car turned.

These characteristics vary among vehicle models and can help narrow the field of search. For example, a Cadillac has a wider stance, longer wheelbase, and wider turning radius than a Volkswagen Beetle.

Matching track to car

Tires constantly are subjected to wear and road hazards, which produce defects that make the tire unique and distinguishable from others of the same model and size.

Wear patterns vary greatly from tire to tire and car to car. Tires usually aren't perfectly aligned and balanced (and they're not always inflated properly), so they wear more on one side than the other. In addition, the wear pattern may not be uniform around the entire circumference of the tire, which means that *flat spots* or islands of excess wear may develop. Similarly, cuts, tears, and gouges can occur, and accumulated debris, such as rocks, nails, and sharp glass, add a unique quality to the tread impression.

At times, impressions from two, three, or even all four tires are recovered from a crime scene. Collecting each of them and determining the respective locations of the tires on the vehicle that made them is important. A new car with new tires usually has the same brand of tires at all four positions, but older cars may have one or more replacement tires. The owner of a suspect vehicle with tires matching crime-scene impressions of a vehicle that has a different brand of tire at each position is in very hot water, indeed. If the wear and defect patterns on the tires also match up, he's just about cooked.

Obtaining tire impressions

Drive your car over a firm surface or a material like cardboard, and you'll leave a two-dimensional tire track. Careen across your neighbor's lawn after a light rain, and you'll likely create three-dimensional tracks. The same kind of tracks would show up in any malleable surface, such as mud or snow. Investigators have different techniques for handling these different types of tracks.

Two-dimensional

Investigators typically photograph two-dimensional impressions from a 90-degree angle, which is important for preventing any distortions. They also place a ruler near the track to capture the size of the tire and its tread patterns in the photograph.

Some two-dimensional tracks are latent, in which case investigators often use laser light and other alternative light sources to snap the tracks into view so they can be photographed.

Tread patterns from the tires of suspect vehicles are obtained by inking the tires and then rolling them down long pieces of white paper, which then are compared with tire impressions from the crime scene. Capturing the entire tread pattern is important because recording noise reduction patterns and patterns caused by defects are the keys to making a match. Obtaining only a foot or so of the pattern may exclude this critical information.

Three-dimensional

Investigators photograph three-dimensional impressions under an angled light source, which can add detail and depth to the photo. After taking the photos, they make a casting of the impression, using techniques similar to the ones used for plastic shoe impressions. Castings are better for comparisons than photographs because they show more detail, accurately reflect tread depth and design element contours, and expose any unevenness in wear pattern of the tire tracks. Photographs are less likely to reveal these types of details.

Castings can also be inked and used to make two-dimensional impressions on paper, which then can be matched against any other two-dimensional impressions found at the scene or against those obtained from a suspect vehicle.

Prying Clues from Tool Marks

Although they may look identical, two tools of the same kind made by the same manufacturer bear tiny variations that make them as unique and distinguishable as fingerprints. Even mass-produced products, cut from the same mold, have minor flaws that distinguish them from one another. And after they've been used, tools develop nicks, scrapes, striations, and other minor defects that further set them apart. These minor, even microscopic, defects are individual characteristics that may be recognized whenever the tools are put to use.

Characterizing and using tool marks

Marks that are found on and often transferred from tools are classified into the following three categories:

- **Indentation marks** occur when a tool is pressed into a soft material such as putty, caulking, or thick paint. A screwdriver tip wedged into a caulked window seal during a break-in may leave behind an indentation in the soft caulking or even the wood, vinyl, or metal parts of the window itself. Class characteristics, such as the width and depth of the tool, are often revealed by these impressions. For example, investigators may even be able to determine that a screwdriver of a particular size made the pry marks on the window. Matching the indentation marks with a particular screwdriver, however, is difficult, if not impossible.

- ✔ **Sliding marks** occur when a tool slides or scratches across a surface. Chisels, screwdrivers, and crowbars often produce sliding marks when wedged into a doorjamb or window seal. These tools can leave behind a pattern of lines or striations in wood, metal, paint, or other materials. These striations vary from tool to tool and often reveal manufacturing and use defects. These defects may be distinct enough to yield a conclusive match with a tool belonging to a suspect.

- ✔ **Cutting marks** are left by tools that slice through materials. Wire and bolt cutters often leave behind lines and striations along the cut edges of wires, bolts, and lock shackles. And because many of these cutting tools are ground or sharpened by hand, the resulting striation pattern may be unique to a particular tool. An examiner may therefore conclude that the tool in question produced the pattern. The best cut surfaces to use for comparison are soft metals, such as copper and lead, because they more readily retain the microscopic detail of the cut marks left by the tool's blade.

The best places to look for prying tool marks at a crime scene are at points of entry into a building or any enclosure. Windows, doors, cabinets, and safes are common locations. Cutting marks typically are found on chains and lock hackles or hasps.

Capturing tool impressions

After carefully examining and photographing tool marks, investigators remove them (if they can) and take them to the lab for further analysis. A door, window, lock, or chain can be taken in its entirety to the lab. Investigators make castings of any indentation marks that cannot be moved. Several casting materials are available, but the most versatile appear to be rubberized or silicon-based materials such a Mikrosil, as these tend to retain minute details of the impression.

Under no circumstances whatsoever should the suspect tool be placed into contact with the impression. In other words, investigators can forget about making any effort to fit the suspect tool into the indented tool mark. Doing so can alter the impression or mark and thereby render it useless in court.

In the lab, a *comparison microscope* (see the nearby sidebar, "Using two, two, two microscopes in one") enables an examiner to place two images side by side so that the finer details are more easily compared. Close examination of indentation, scrape, and cut marks from a crime scene reveals microscopic lines, grooves, and striations that can be matched by an examiner with a suspect tool. The examiner makes a cut using the suspect implement, preferably into a soft material that will retain the unique striations caused by defects in the working surfaces of the tool but won't damage the tool. The cut surface from the crime scene then is compared under the comparison microscope with the cut surface produced in the lab, as shown in Figure 7-3.

Using two, two, two microscopes in one

Comparison microscopes are a crime lab staple that enable examiners to make side-by-side comparisons of two objects. They come in handy when tool-mark and other detailed comparisons of physical evidence are necessary.

The comparison microscope basically is made up of two regular microscopes joined by a bridge. The bridge contains a series of lenses and mirrors that project images of each object into a single binocular-like viewing device. The viewer sees a circular field divided in half, with the object under the microscope on the left side shown on the left half and the one under the microscope on the right shown on the right half, as shown in Figure 7-3. Microscopic details of the two specimens then are compared. The comparison microscope is used most often in tool-mark and bullet comparisons but is also employed when comparing hair and fibers.

Figure 7-3:
Tool-mark striations from a crime scene and suspect tool as seen through the comparison microscope.

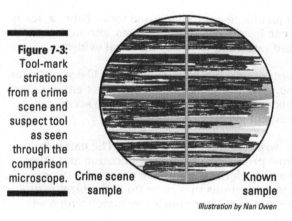

Crime scene sample

Known sample

Illustration by Nan Owen

Sometimes a comparison cut in soft lead isn't adequate for making an accurate comparison. To re-create the crime scene cut as accurately as possible, the examiner must cut the same material in the same manner. For example, if a bolt cutter was used to cut a lock hackle and the lab has the cut lock and a suspect bolt cutter, the examiner can cut a similar lock hackle with the bolt cutter, trying to do so at the same angle and with the same pressure used by the perpetrator. The separate crime-scene and lab-produced cuts then are compared under the comparison microscope.

Bolt cutters and similar devices can cause special problems for crime labs because their cutting edges are bigger than the items they cut. For an accurate comparison to be made, the lab-produced cuts must be made by the same portion of the cutting blade that was used in the crime. The examiner can make several cuts using different areas of the tool's working surface, but doing so is time consuming and may damage the blade, thus making further comparisons impossible.

Fortunately, chemical tests can reveal traces of the cut object or material on the cutting edge of the tool. For example, many locks have zinc coatings. Testing the blade for zinc may reveal exactly where on the blade the cut was made and enable the examiner to make a cut at the same spot, thus making a more accurate comparison. To avoid contamination of the cutting edge, such chemical testing should take place before any comparison cuts are made.

Investigators or lab technicians also may be asked to evaluate pressed imprints. Many illegal drug labs compress their products into tablets. Presses used for this purpose often leave behind distinguishing marks on the surfaces of the pills. Microscopic examination of the press and the suspect pills may lead to a match.

Finding Facts in Fabrics

Prints and impressions aren't just for fingers, shoes, and tools. Fabrics, leathers, and other materials also can leave behind impressions, although these are not as commonly found and rarely are used as individual evidence.

The most common fabric impressions come from gloves. Just like your fingertips, gloves can pick up grease, dirt, and grime and then deposit either patent or latent prints on surfaces. Sometimes patterns left at a crime scene can be used for comparison with a suspect glove.

Leather gloves tend to crease, wrinkle, and crack with use. The pattern of these defects can make a unique print. Gloves made from cotton and other fabrics also can leave behind an imprint of their weave patterns, and any pulls, snags, tears, and other imperfections that show up in the print may make it possible for an investigator to make a conclusive match with a suspect glove.

Glove prints are handled in a manner similar to the way fingerprint evidence is gathered. Patent prints are photographed, and latent prints are dusted with fingerprint powder and then photographed and lifted. An electrostatic device (see the earlier section, "Looking for latent prints") can be used to lift glove prints left in dust.

Other fabrics may also leave impressions. For example, when blood, oil, grease, or dirt get on clothing, they can be transferred by contact to a wall or other object. Fabric impressions from the clothing of hit-and-run victims have been found in the dirt and grease on car fenders.

Chapter 8

Burning Down the House: Is It Arson?

....

In This Chapter

▶ Understanding the basics of fire

▶ Identifying why arson happens

▶ Using accelerants

▶ Investigating the fire scene

▶ Wiring explosives

....

Fire is great for roasting marshmallows or cooking a steak, but it wreaks havoc on evidence. Evaluating scenes where fire or explosions have occurred is difficult, at best. This task usually falls to specialized arson investigators, who are trained in suspicious fire analysis. They often face crime scenes where the evidence is severely damaged, if not completely destroyed, by the fire. In addition, the efforts of the firefighters themselves can destroy evidence.

A successful arson investigation overcomes these obstacles to answer two basic questions: Where was the fire's point of origin, and what was the cause of the fire? The investigator uses physical and chemical evidence to uncover the answers. Based on those findings, the investigator may determine, in general, whether the fire was accidental or *incendiary* (intentionally set).

Simply bringing together oxygen and a potentially flammable fuel source, such as paper or gasoline, doesn't produce fire. You need something else — heat. Remove any of the three components — fuel, oxygen, or heat — and no fire occurs.

Striking the Match: Looking into Fire-Starters

Fire is just plain fascinating, and humans have a nearly universal attraction to it. Whether it's admiration for the beauty of a fireplace or for the practicality and tastiness of food grilled over an open flame, most of us find fire captivating. Maybe it derives from our ancestors' close relationship with fire, which served as their only source of heat and light. Maybe it's fire's ethereal nature that draws us to it. In cases of arson, it may simply be fire's raw destructive power that fuels the attraction.

The reasons people intentionally set fires are many and varied, but arson invariably has a payoff. The most common reasons criminals set fires include the following:

- ✔ **Covering their tracks:** Arsonists often use fires to cover another crime, such as theft or even murder. An embezzler may use fire to destroy company financial records; an employee who stole goods from a company warehouse may hope that a fire will hide this indiscretion. After all, if you destroy the records or the inventory, how can anyone determine whether anything is missing? Because of this possible motive, arson investigators always search a fire scene for signs of a break-in and theft.

- ✔ **Insurance fraud:** Maybe the arsonist needs quick money, or perhaps the insurance on the home or warehouse is greater than the property's market value. Arsonists sometimes file insurance claims on valuables they actually removed from the building before setting the fire, hoping to get an insurance settlement for the valuables without actually having to lose them. Greed is a great motivator.

- ✔ **Psychological reasons:** An individual who has a pathological love of fire may start a forest or structure fire simply because he finds it exciting. The resulting destruction and the beauty and power of the fire itself feed some deep-seated psychological need. This kind of fire-starting often becomes a serial offense.

- ✔ **Revenge:** A grudge or deep-seated hatred for another person may drive a hot-headed arsonist to torch that person's house or business.

- ✔ **Suicide or murder:** Fire rarely is used as a means of committing suicide or murder, because it's simply too painful for suicide and too unpredictable for murder. Bodies found in fires usually were killed before the fire was started.

- ✔ **Terrorism:** Someone, or some group, may burn structures to create fear or make a political statement.

Trying to sweep the ashes under the rug

A murderer who sets a fire in an attempt to disguise or cover up the murder doesn't know his chemistry. Structure fires typically don't burn hot enough or long enough to completely destroy a body. When cremated, bodies are exposed to temperatures around 1,500 degrees Fahrenheit (815 degrees Celsius) for two hours or more. These sustained temperatures reduce the body to ashes and bone fragments. A structure fire may reach temperatures of 500 to 2,000 degrees Fahrenheit (260 to 1,100 degrees Celsius), but because fire rapidly consumes its fuel (the structure), the high temperatures don't last long. Therefore, a structure fire is unlikely to completely destroy a human body. In fact, bodies that are significantly charred in a fire often remain remarkably well preserved internally. The medical examiner (ME) can still search for signs of trauma, poisons, and often DNA.

Determining Where and How the Fire Started

A fire scene is a dangerous place and one fire investigators must approach with great caution. Collapsing floors and falling beams aren't uncommon. Broken glass, sharp nails, smoldering materials, noxious gases, and asbestos (in older buildings) are other common hazards. Before an investigation can proceed, a structural engineer must give the okay.

The investigation and collection of evidence must begin as soon as possible after the fire has been extinguished and the engineer has declared the structure safe to enter. Time is the enemy: Many of the volatile substances that cause or accelerate a fire rapidly dissipate.

Locating where a fire began is the cornerstone of fire and arson investigation. Evaluating materials found where the fire started can help investigators determine whether it was accidental or incendiary.

A point of origin near an overloaded wall outlet points toward an accidental fire, but finding a point of origin in a corner of a warehouse, far removed from any electrical source and near a charred gasoline can, suggests the work of an arsonist. Of course, an arsonist may purposely overload a wall outlet in the hopes that a fire would start. But this method is unpredictable, so most arsonists resort to more direct methods for starting fires.

Using other people's eyes and ears

While members of the arson investigation team inspect and collect samples from the scene, the chief fire investigator or fire marshal interviews witnesses, who can provide many important clues. Someone may have seen the fire in its earliest stages, and that person's description can lead investigators to the point or points of origin. Many accelerants and combustible materials produce characteristic flame and smoke colors, so witness descriptions of what the fire looked like may help determine its cause. For example, gasoline produces a yellow flame and white smoke.

Investigators may use witnesses' reports to help

- ✔ Locate the point of origin
- ✔ Determine whether the fire was accidental or intentional
- ✔ Figure out whether the arsonist used an accelerant

Locating the point of origin

Determining a fire's point of origin requires an understanding of how fire moves through a structure. Fires typically spread out and up from the point of origin, but that pattern can be influenced by structural and decorative elements of the building — stairwells may pull the fire in one direction, and the chemicals in synthetic carpet can cause unusual burn patterns. Usually, however, the largest amount of damage occurs near the point of origin. Investigators often find any igniters or accelerants that were used in this area.

Notice I said that the area of worst damage is *usually* near the point of origin. That's not always the case. The worst damage tends to occur where the best combination of fuel, oxygen, and heat is concentrated. It may be that the ventilation is actually poor at the point of origin, but as the fire spreads, it reaches an area with better ventilation and the fire burns more briskly, thus causing more damage. Things are never simple with fires.

Not only drafts from open windows or stairwells but also materials used to construct or decorate the building are among the many factors that can result in greater damage in an area remote from the true point of origin, thus further confusing fire investigators.

After locating the point of origin, an investigator sometimes can retrace the fire's path even when the structure is heavily damaged. Conversely, backtracking along the fire's route may lead to the point of origin.

Investigators also can find the point of origin by looking for a *V pattern* of burned material. Fire tends to rise and spread so that it burns a wall or other vertical surface in a V-shape, with the foot or bottom of the V pointing to the origin of the fire.

Stored fuels and other flammable liquids likewise can interfere not only with locating the true point of origin but also with the search for arson-related accelerants, simply because they too are accelerants. Similarly, an arsonist may have started multiple fires within a building or sloshed a path of gasoline or other accelerant throughout or around the structure, thus creating a fire with multiple or widespread points of origin.

A CLOSER LOOK

Investigators estimate the intensity of the fire at any particular location by assessing the fire's effect on structural materials. Steel beams buckle whenever the fire is extremely intense, and glass melts at around 1,500 degrees Fahrenheit. Cracking and flaking *(spalling)* on walls and floors indicate areas of high heat. Similarly, wooden beams, floors, and walls may char, leaving a pattern that looks like alligator skin. When that happens, smaller scales tend to be near the hottest point of the fire. For years, investigators believed that spalling and alligatoring meant that an accelerant had been used, but these myths have been debunked. These findings, for reasons I state earlier, simply mean that the fire was hot enough in that area to produce these changes; they can occur without the presence of an accelerant and can be far removed from the actual point of origin.

If the building is equipped with a system of smoke detectors, the time at which each alarm was set off can help investigators determine the path that the fire took through the structure and help locate the point of origin.

Liquid and gaseous fuels present special problems for investigators, because they spread more readily and conform to the shapes of their containers. If an arsonist pours gasoline on a floor, the gasoline spreads across the room, runs down the stairs, and seeps into the baseboards. When ignition occurs, the fire follows the liquid and spreads rapidly, making the point of origin widespread. Gaseous fuels, such as natural gas, diffuse in all directions until they fill their containers. When the arsonist adds an ignition source, these fuels can explode. In this example, finding an exact point of origin may be impossible.

Figuring out how it happened

After investigators find the point of origin, they search for potential causes. They examine the circumstances and factors that enabled the fire to start and spread. Human factors, accidental or intentional, top the investigator's list of potential causes.

Investigators conduct a thorough search of the area near the point of origin for igniters and accelerants. Potential ignition sources include electrical wiring, oil lamps, candles, cigarettes, fireplaces, sophisticated electrical timers, and spontaneous combustion.

Spontaneous combustion (an internal chemical reaction that starts a fire) is rare but can occur when combustible materials are contained in a tight space — when oil-soaked rags are kept in a small, closed pantry, for instance. Slow oxidation of the oils releases heat. If the rags are in an enclosed space, the heat has nowhere to go and may reach the ignition temperature of the oil or the rags.

Analysis of these possible sources aids fire investigators in categorizing fires as natural, accidental, or intentional. A natural fire results from events like lightning. Accidental sources include frayed wiring or a smoldering cigarette. The presence of an electrical or combustible timing device suggests arson, of course.

Igniting the blaze

Ignition devices range from simple to complex. A match is perhaps the most common ignition device. Arsonists often light fires and toss their matches aside, believing that the resulting fire will completely destroy them. But getting rid of matches isn't quite so easy.

The heads of matches contain *diatoms,* which are single-celled organisms found in the kind of earth used in match production. The shells of these tiny creatures contain *silica,* a tough compound that survives fires. Interestingly, match manufacturers use different materials, so different diatom species show up in their matches. Because each species of diatom has a unique shell structure, identifying these shell remnants often identifies the brand of matches used by the arsonist.

Another low-tech but effective igniting device can be made by placing a candle on a pile of paper. When the candle burns down, the flame ignites the paper, and the fire takes off. An arsonist may even create a crude timing device by laying a lit cigarette across an open book of matches beneath flammable curtains.

The ignition device also may be a complex electrical timing device. Either commercial timers or a modified clock can be used to time when a circuit closes and switches on an initiator. The construction of these devices is limited only by the creativity of the arsonist.

If a thorough search of the scene reveals candle residue, a cigarette butt, or the remains of an electrical device, investigators have unearthed a possible igniting device.

Heating Things Up: Accelerants

Whenever investigators can't find a natural or accidental source for a fire, arson must be considered. Like an ignition device, the presence of an *accelerant,* or something that makes the fire burn faster, suggests an intentional act.

Arsonists almost always use accelerants, because simply dropping a match onto a pile of paper or tossing a cigarette on a bed is too unpredictable. Arsonists want to be sure that the fires they start actually burn.

Accelerants can be solids, liquids, or gases. Solid accelerants include paper, black powder, and kindling wood. Liquids include gasoline, kerosene, alcohols, and paint thinners. Typical gaseous accelerants include natural gas and propane.

Arsonists most commonly use liquid accelerants, particularly gasoline and kerosene, as fire accelerators; however, even when a structure has been severely damaged, traces of these accelerants often remain. They soak into carpets and brickwork, seep into baseboards and crevices, and settle into areas beneath the fire. Remnants survive most fires, and investigators diligently search for these remnants at the scenes of any suspicious fires.

Collecting samples at the scene

Investigators take samples from the area around the point of origin for chemical analysis. Sometimes, specially trained dogs aid investigators in obtaining the best samples by sniffing out traces of accelerants. Investigators also use chemical detectors, such as a Vapor Trace Analyzer (VTA), which screen materials for accelerant residues (see the nearby sidebar "Sniffing out accelerants with a VTA" to find out more about how it works).

The sooner investigators gather materials for testing, the better. The accelerants of choice for arsonists generally are petroleum-based hydrocarbons, such as gasoline and kerosene, whose vapors dissipate with time. To prevent the loss of this crucial evidence, investigators place any materials they gather in nonporous, sealed containers, such as clean paint cans and glass jars. Plastic bags don't work because the plastic can react with the hydrocarbons, giving the volatile gases a chance to escape through the damaged material.

Sniffing out accelerants with a VTA

A *Vapor Trace Analyzer (VTA)* is an extremely sensitive specialized gas chromatograph (discussed in the section, "Digging deeper into iffy samples") that tests for flammable hydrocarbon residues in the air around the site of a potential accelerant residue. The VTA has a nozzle, a heating element, and a temperature gauge.

An investigator draws a sample of the air near the site of the suspected accelerant through the VTA's nozzle. The sample passes over the heating element. If the sample burns, it raises the temperature in the device, a fluctuation that registers on the temperature gauge.

A bump in the temperature provides investigators with presumptive evidence that a flammable residue is present in that area. Investigators take further samples of structural materials from the site to the crime lab for more thorough analysis.

In addition to taking samples from the area of the fire, investigators take samples of the same materials from unburned areas. If, for example, the sample suspected of holding an accelerant residue happens to be a section of charred carpet, investigators take a piece of the same carpet from an unburned area, whenever possible, for comparison purposes.

Many carpets, linoleum flooring, and tile adhesives already contain volatile hydrocarbons that may show up when investigators test for accelerant residues. An unburned section of carpet usually provides an uncontaminated sample against which to compare the suspect sample. Comparing the burned and unburned segments enables lab personnel to separate a foreign hydrocarbon from the ones that already were present in the carpet or other material.

Taking it to the lab

Investigators take the materials they collect to the crime lab for analysis. These materials may include charred wood, pieces of carpet, or even empty bottles. The first step in the analysis is extracting any possible chemical accelerants from the debris.

Lab technicians use several methods to single out any questionable compounds, including the following:

- **Headspace vapor extraction:** The material is placed in a closed container. The natural volatility of the hydrocarbons creates a vapor-rich gas in the *headspace,* or the air-filled area above the material in a closed container. Heating the sample accelerates this process. The vapor is then removed from the container with a syringe and tested.

- **Solvent extraction:** The sample is placed in a container with a solvent, such as chloroform, carbon tetrachloride, methylene chloride, or carbon disulfide. The solvent dissolves the sample material, separating out the hydrocarbons, which are then analyzed.

- **Steam distillation:** The charred material is heated, and the steam is collected and condensed. The resulting liquid then is checked for volatile hydrocarbons.

- **Vapor concentration:** The sample is heated in a closed container that also contains charcoal, which absorbs the volatile hydrocarbons as they leave the sample. Just as an open box of baking soda in your refrigerator absorbs "odor molecules" and freshens your fridge, charcoal readily absorbs hydrocarbon molecules from the air. The charcoal is then removed, and the hydrocarbons are extracted using a solvent, after which the hydrocarbons are analyzed to determine their nature and type.

Digging deeper into iffy samples

After technicians have isolated the suspicious compounds using one of the techniques in the preceding section, they look more closely at them using one or more of the procedures discussed in the following sections.

Gas chromatography

One way to identify a compound is to identify how far each part of it moves through an inert gas, or carrier gas. *Gas chromatography* (GC) rapidly separates mixtures of compounds into individual components in this manner.

A technician injects a liquid sample into one end of the column, where it is heated and vaporized. The vapor enters the column and flows with the moving carrier gas until it reaches a detector. Various compounds move at different speeds and thus separate from one another. During this transition, the separate compounds arrive at the detector at different times. The detector signals a recorder that prints a graph that represents each of the compounds detected. The graph is called a *chromatograph* (see Figure 8-1).

Often, technicians need only the results from the GC to determine the composition of the unknown sample. But if they need further information, they can combine the GC results with either mass spectroscopy or infrared spectrophotometry results (see the sections that follow).

Figure 8-1:
A gas chromatograph.
Each peak represents a different component of the unknown substance being tested.

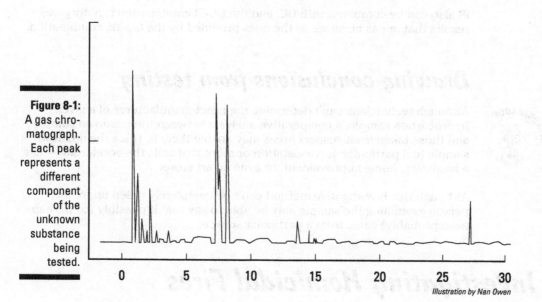

Illustration by Nan Owen

Mass spectroscopy

No two substances have the same chemical fingerprint, and each compound's fingerprint can be determined with *mass spectroscopy* (MS).

The mass spectroscope bombards a compound with a beam of high-energy electrons that break up, or fragment, the compound. These fragments pass through an electric or magnetic field that separates them according to their respective masses. The fragmentation pattern of the unknown compound is then compared by computer to known fragmentation patterns and reviewed by a technician in hopes of finding a match that reveals the composition of the unknown substance.

The GC and MS can be directly connected. This combination is called a *gas chromatograph-mass spectrometer* (GC-MS). The GC feeds each gaseous compound it separates directly into the MS, and the MS determines the compound's mass spectrum. Virtually any substance can be identified using this combination.

Infrared spectrophotometry

Each compound has a different infrared absorption spectrum and can be identified by its spectrum using *infrared spectrophotometry* (IR). This test determines the amount of infrared light absorbed by the compound in question and results in a chemical fingerprint of the compound in question.

IR also can be combined with GC, and the GC-IR combination rapidly gives results that are as accurate as the ones provided by the GC-MS combination.

Drawing conclusions from testing

Although technicians can't determine the exact manufacturer of a given hydrocarbon sample, a comparative analysis between the unknown sample and those taken from suspect areas may enable them to trace the unknown sample to a particular service station or store that sells the accelerant — like a hardware, home improvement, or even an art store.

Although this investigative method can't be completely relied upon, the person examining the sample may be able to say that it possibly (or perhaps even probably) came from a particular source.

Investigating Homicidal Fires

Arson may not be the only crime at fire scenes, which unfortunately often contain a body or two. Just because a body is found at a fire scene, however, does not mean the victim died because of the fire. The cause and manner of death is a matter for the medical examiner (ME) and homicide investigators, who are called in whenever a body turns up at a scene. They work to identify the victim and figure out how he died, using clues like the location of the body and evidence of smoke inhalation.

The ME must answer one all-important question: Was the victim alive at the time the fire started and burned? If the victim was alive, the fire may have been an accident, though murder is still possible if the killer/arsonist thought the victim was dead when in fact he wasn't. If the fire was indeed arson and the ME determines the victim was dead prior to the fire beginning, then murder is obviously more likely.

Determining the cause and manner of death depends upon careful evaluation of the fire scene and the corpse during autopsy. The ME looks at several aspects of the body to help make this determination, including the position it was in, the carbon monoxide (CO) levels of its blood and tissue, and the presence or absence of soot in the lungs and airways.

Location, location, location

The position of the body is extremely important. Where the victim died, the state of the body, and the items around the body provide investigators vital information about that person's death (and about the fire itself).

Say, for example, that the corpse is found on a bed, and the ME determines that the cause of death is smoke inhalation. Investigators conclude that the fire's origin was a cigarette in contact with bedding. Under these circumstances, the death may be accidental. But did the victim smoke? If no one is able to clear up this question for investigators, the ME can measure the nicotine level in the victim's urine. A high level indicates that the victim was indeed a smoker. If not, the cigarette may have been an instrument for arson.

Curl up and die: The boxer's posture

Many people believe that a body found curled into a fetal position shows that the victim was alive at the time the fire reached him and suffered great pain before death. This assumption simply is not true.

A burning corpse often assumes a *pugilistic position,* or boxer's posture. Legs and arms flex, and fists tuck beneath the chin. You can interpret this position as that of someone who curled into a ball from severe pain; however, during a fire, the body actually reaches this posture when the fire dehydrates the body's muscles, causing them to contract.

Poisoned by air

Asphyxia (or suffocation) from inhaling smoke and carbon monoxide (CO) causes most fire-related deaths. The ME tests the victim's blood and tissues for CO. A normal level is less than 5 percent, but it can be slightly higher in smokers. In victims of CO asphyxiation, the level ranges from about 45 to 90 percent. Finding a high CO level suggests that the victim died from smoke and CO inhalation, but a low level implies that the victim died before or at the time the fire started.

Interpretation of the CO level also depends upon evaluation of natural disease in the deceased. An older person with severe coronary artery disease will die from a lower level of CO than a young person with a healthy body.

Carbon monoxide intoxication (excessive CO in the bloodstream) not only causes death, but also often prevents victims from escaping before the fire kills them. As the CO level in the blood increases, the person loses the ability to think and move properly. At a CO level of 20 percent, dizziness and confusion occur; at 35 percent, weakness, loss of coordination, and disorientation appear; and at levels above 50 percent, the victim experiences loss of consciousness and death. So even if the victim is alive and has time to escape when the fire starts, the toxicity of the CO may prevent her from doing so.

During an autopsy, victims of CO intoxication exhibit several characteristics, one of which is unique coloring. As you inhale CO, it combines with the hemoglobin in your red blood cells to produce *carboxyhemoglobin,* which is a bright red compound. If the victim's blood, muscles, and organs are a bright, cherry-red color, the victim likely died from CO inhalation, but the CO levels in the blood and tissues provide the real proof.

Besides a high blood CO level, finding soot in the mouth, throat, lungs, and airways suggests that the victim was alive as the fire burned and inhaled these materials in a struggle for oxygen. Conversely, if the CO level is low and no soot is present in the airways, the ME considers other causes and manners of death, and homicide becomes a strong possibility.

What if a burned body is found bound, gagged, and shot? The ME performs blood CO levels to determine the cause of death. Did the gunshot or the fire do in the victim? Finding high blood CO levels and soot within the airway and lungs leads the ME to conclude that the victim lived through the gunshot and died as a result of CO inhalation caused by the fire. If the victim has a low blood CO level, the gunshot is the more likely cause of death. This finding can be critical to prosecutors if there were two perpetrators in the crime. If one pulled the trigger and the other started the fire, one is the murderer and the other an accomplice.

Evaluating Explosive Situations

Fires and explosions are similar reactions in that both result from a combination of fuel and oxygen. The difference is simply the rate of that reaction. Fires consume their fuel (wood, paper, trees) more slowly than explosions, which consume their fuel (gasoline, dynamite) almost instantaneously, in part because the material is confined. If ignited in an unconfined space, the material simply burns, but if you tightly pack the material into a container, it explodes when you ignite it.

Explosions create numerous problems for investigators. The explosive device and any surrounding structures are heavily damaged, if not completely destroyed. Unless a secondary fire occurs, investigators usually can determine the point of origin with ease; however, finding fragments of the device or any igniters or timers may be difficult.

Defining explosives

Explosives are categorized as either high or low by the speed of their resulting pressure wave. *Low explosives* typically move at rates of 1,000 meters per second or less, and *high explosives* may reach speeds as high as 8,500 meters per second.

The most readily available and commonly used low explosives are black powder and smokeless gunpowder. A combination of sugar and potassium chlorate makes another easy explosive. Bombers need not be very sophisticated.

High explosives can be subdivided into two categories, depending upon their sensitivity to heat, friction, or mechanical shock:

- ✔ **Initiating explosives** are very sensitive to these effects. Because of the potential for unexpected detonation, home-manufactured bombs rarely use initiating explosives. These explosives more often appear in primers and blasting caps, where they initiate other, less-sensitive noninitiating explosive materials. Mercury fulminate and lead azide are commonly used in this way.

- ✔ **Noninitiating explosives** are less sensitive and more commonly used in commercial and military applications. These explosives include dynamite, TNT (trinitrotoluene), RDX (pentaerythritrol tetranitrate), and PETN (cyclotrimethylenetrinitramine). Although you can still find dynamite, it and other nitroglycerine-based explosives have largely been replaced by ammonium nitrate–based explosives. ANFO, an easily made explosive material, is a mixture of ammonium nitrate and fuel oil.

Ammonium nitrate is an oxygen-rich oxidant that can be found in fertilizers. Bombs produced from this substance were involved in the Oklahoma City and 1993 World Trade Center bombings.

Investigating a bombing scene

Searching the scene of an explosion requires the same attention to detail as does the search of a fire scene. Finding fragments from the explosive device, igniter, and timer can be crucial to determining the type of explosive used and, ultimately, the person responsible for the bombing. In addition to locating these fragments, investigators direct their searches toward collecting debris to test for unexploded residue, which almost always is present.

Microscopic examination of the debris may reveal black powder or gunpowder, both of which are easily recognizable by the color and shape of their particles. After the microscopic inspection, the lab technician rinses the debris with a solvent in which most explosives are soluble (acetone is a common one) and then analyzes the resulting solution, using thin-layer or gas chromatography and mass and infrared spectroscopy. Identification of the explosive is made through a combination of these tests.

After finding out what particular explosive was used, investigators focus on finding the seller and buyer of that explosive.

Part III
Examining the Body

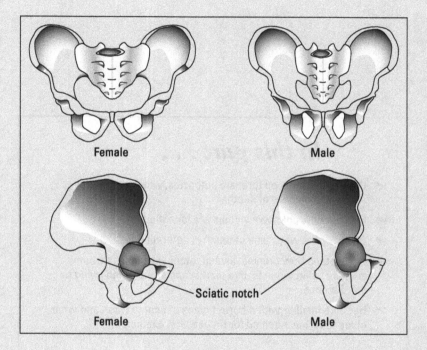

Female   Male

Sciatic notch

Female   Male

web extras

Find out more about cause and manner of death, and how they sometimes don't seem to go together in a free article at www.dummies.com/extras/forensics.

In this part . . .

✔ Get the lowdown on forensic autopsies, which determine cause and manner of death.

✔ Find out how unknown victims are identified.

✔ Discover the ways time of death is determined.

✔ Understand how criminal investigators use signs of trauma, such as bullet wounds, bite marks, and more, when trying to solve a case.

✔ Become familiar with different types of asphyxiation and what clues they leave behind for the medical examiner.

Chapter 9

Determining the Cause and Manner of Death: Forensic Autopsies

. . . .

In This Chapter

▶ Introducing death: Its causes, manners, and mechanisms

▶ Understanding the role of a forensic pathologist

▶ Digging in to a forensic autopsy, step by step

▶ Summing up the findings in an autopsy report

. . . .

The dead do "talk," but only figuratively. Changes that take place in the body before and after death reveal which diseases victims suffered, what trauma they endured, which toxins were present at the time of death, and much more. *Autopsy,* or examining a corpse to determine how death occurred, is the method used to interpret exactly what a body says.

Defining Death and Declaring It as Such

Picture yourself being buried alive. People living prior to the nineteenth century had good reason to worry about such matters, because stethoscopes hadn't been invented, and determinations of death were more a guessing game than a scientific pursuit. A weak heartbeat meant you'd probably be pronounced dead — only to wake up while your body was being prepared for burial. Fortunately, those days are gone, but plenty of trial and error took place before they could be laid to rest.

Searching for a definitive method

Determining death never has been straightforward. Alcohol, drugs, heart attacks, serious infections, bleeding, shock, dehydration, and other situations can render supposed victims comatose, cold to the touch, and with weak respiration and pulse, and they might appear dead when in fact they aren't.

Because signs of life can be difficult to accurately interpret, several methods for determining whether a person died were devised and used long ago, when science was in its infancy. Among them were

- ✔ Tongue and nipple pulling
- ✔ Tobacco smoke enemas
- ✔ Insertion of hot pokers into various bodily orifices

Finally, in the 17th century, a system of *waiting mortuaries* — known as *vitae dubiae asylums* before Latin kicked the bucket — was established. In waiting mortuaries, the suspected dead were placed on cots and watched until decay set in. Although this process was unpleasant for the family of the deceased, it at least enabled a confident proclamation of death and avoided premature burials, which weren't unheard of at the time.

The invention of the stethoscope enabled physicians to determine the presence or absence of breathing and a heartbeat, thus making death a little easier to pronounce. The development of the electrocardiogram (EKG), a device that records the electrical activity of the heart, followed, and the combination of these two devices gave physicians a much more objective measure of death. The 20th century saw the development of cardiopulmonary resuscitation (CPR) followed by the use of ventilators and pacemakers that are capable of keeping the heart and lungs working even after death. And the water suddenly became muddier. These advancements brought about the concept of *brain death,* which means that although the heart and lungs may be working, the brain is dead.

Currently, a death pronouncement in someone who has a heartbeat or a pacemaker and is on a ventilator requires the absence of electrical activity in the brain, which is measured on a device known as an *electroencephalogram* (EEG), or determination of loss of blood flow by radionuclear scanning. And even then, a pronouncement of death under those circumstances is controversial and has resulted in varying definitions for brain death.

If a person on a ventilator was shot in the head, hit by a drunk driver, or otherwise ended up in that condition as a result of suspicious means, determining death becomes an issue for the coroner or medical examiner. Charges that can be filed against the shooter, driver, or other perpetrator become measurably more serious if the victim dies. Before physicians caring for the victim actually pull the plug on the ventilator, they must be absolutely sure the victim has no hope for survival. Otherwise, doctors can be implicated in the death.

Determining the causes and mechanisms of death

Simply put, the *cause of death* is the reason the individual died. A heart attack, a gunshot wound, and blunt force head trauma with intracranial bleeding are causes of death. They are the diseases or injuries that altered the victim's physiology and led to death. The *mechanism of death* is the actual physiological change, or variation in the body's inner workings, that causes the cessation of life.

A gunshot to the heart, for example, is a cause of death that can lead to one of several mechanisms of death, including cessation of the heartbeat (cardiac arrest), *exsanguination* (bleeding to death), or *sepsis* (infection that enters the bloodstream). Similarly, the victim of blunt force head trauma can die from direct trauma to the brain *(cerebral contusion),* bleeding into the brain itself *(an intracerebral bleed),* or bleeding around the brain (a subdural or epidural hematoma), all of which can lead to compression of the brain and result in a stoppage of breathing *(asphyxia).* Again, one cause can lead to death by several mechanisms.

Conversely, one mechanism can result from several different causes. A gunshot wound, stabbing, bleeding ulcer, or a bleeding lung tumor can cause you to bleed to death. In each case, blood loss and shock are the abnormal physiological changes.

For example, say that a man is struck by an intoxicated driver's car and is severely injured. The paramedics arrive and transport him to the hospital, where he dies as a result of his injuries. The blunt trauma from the car may have caused lethal brain injuries, and the driver could be charged in the man's death. On the other hand, if the injuries weren't that severe, and the victim died from a heart attack that paramedical and hospital personnel failed to recognize and treat appropriately, who then is responsible for the man's death? Was the cause of death blunt trauma from the automobile impact or a mismanaged heart attack?

In cases in which the mechanism of death is unclear, the medical examiner or coroner (see Chapter 2) assesses the evidence to determine the true cause and mechanism of death, which can impact what criminal or civil actions follow, if any.

Uncovering the four manners of death

The manner of death is the root cause of the sequence of events that leads to death. In other words, it answers these questions:

- How and why did these events take place?
- Who or what initiated the events and with what intention?
- Was the death caused by the victim, another person, an unfortunate occurrence, or Mother Nature?

The four manners of death are

- **Natural:** Natural deaths are the workings of Mother Nature in that death results from a natural disease process. Heart attacks, cancers, pneumonias, and strokes are common natural causes of death. Natural death is by far the largest category of death that the ME sees, making up over half of the cases investigated.

- **Accidental:** Accidental deaths result from an unplanned and unforeseeable sequence of events. Falls, automobile accidents, and in-home electrocutions are examples of accidental deaths.

- **Suicidal:** Suicides are deaths caused by the dead person's own hand. Intentional, self-inflicted gunshot wounds, drug overdoses, and self-hangings are suicidal deaths.

- **Homicidal:** Homicides are deaths that occur by the hand of someone other than the dead person.

- **Undetermined or unclassified:** These are deaths in which the ME can't accurately determine the appropriate category.

Just as causes of death can lead to many different mechanisms of death, any cause of death can have several different manners of death. A gunshot wound to the head can't be a natural death, but it can be deemed homicidal, suicidal, or accidental.

Though the ME can usually determine the manner of death, it's not always easy, or even possible. For example, the manner of death of a drug abuser who overdoses is most likely to be either accidental or suicidal (it also could be homicidal, but it's never natural). When the cause of death is a drug overdose, autopsy and laboratory findings are the same regardless of the victim's or another's intent. That is, the ME's findings are the same whether the victim miscalculated the dose (accidental), intentionally took too much (suicidal), or was given a lethal dose (homicidal). For example, perhaps the victim's dealer, thinking the user had snitched to the police, gave the victim a purer form of heroin than he was accustomed to receiving, so that his "usual" injection contained four or five times more drug than the unfortunate soul expected. Simply put, no certain way exists for determining whether the person overdosed accidentally, purposefully, or as the result of another's actions. For these reasons, such deaths are often listed as Undetermined.

Only natural deaths are caused by disease. The other categories involve trauma or drugs and may lead to civil or criminal court proceedings. Of course, even a natural cause of death may be deemed accidental, homicidal, or even suicidal. For example, people with certain serious medical disorders might become confused about their medications, miss doses, and succumb to their disease (accidental). Or the person might simply give up, stop taking her meds, and die as a result (suicidal). Additionally, if a critically ill person is prevented from visiting a doctor or hospital, and an inheritance is at stake, the individual who prevented the victim from receiving healthcare could be charged with homicide.

Death from a heart attack because of an error during surgery is another example of a "natural" death that isn't natural. Although heart attack is a natural cause of death, the manner by which the heart attack occurred could be deemed accidental (often euphemistically termed a "medical misadventure") and malpractice litigation could follow. Likewise, a person with severe heart disease might be assaulted on the street, and, while struggling with the assailant, could suffer a heart attack and die. The cause of death again is a heart attack, but the manner could be deemed homicidal.

Shadowing the Forensic Pathologist

As you may suspect, determining the cause, mechanism, and manner of death takes a thorough knowledge of the ins and outs of human biology. Autopsies therefore should be performed by *pathologists,* medical doctors who specialize in determining how disease affects the body.

The medical specialty of *pathology,* or the study of disease, dates back to the 1800s, and by the mid-twentieth century pathologists began branching out into separate subspecialties. *Forensic pathology* became a board-certified specialty in 1959.

The forensic pathologist is concerned with the study of medicine as it relates to the application of the law and, in particular, criminal law. Furthermore, the forensic pathologist is more likely to deal with injuries. Nevertheless, more than 50 percent of the cases he deals with involve death caused by disease. He performs the kind of autopsies (forensic) that produce evidence that often must be presented as testimony in court as the findings and opinions of an expert. Find out more about expert testimony in Chapter 1.

A pathologist who wants to become a forensic pathologist typically serves a one- or two-year fellowship in forensic pathology — in addition to the 13 years of college, medical school, and specialized training it takes to become a clinical pathologist. Turn to Chapter 22 for the details.

Discovering what makes an autopsy forensic

Forensic pathologists typically perform medical-legal autopsies, although in some areas, hospital pathologists may be designated medical examiners and charged with this duty. And in some jurisdictions, the local undertaker performs the autopsies, even though he isn't trained in forensic pathology.

A medical autopsy is conducted to determine the medical factors relating to death and to search for any illnesses the deceased may have suffered. The forensic autopsy, on the other hand, is performed initially to determine not only the cause of death and any illnesses the deceased had, but also the time, mechanism, and manner of death.

Deciding who gets autopsied

The ME typically investigates any death that is

- **Traumatic:** Occurring from an injury that could be accidental, homicidal, or self-inflicted
- **Unusual:** Occurring in circumstances that appear to be unnatural or suspicious
- **Sudden:** Taking place within a few hours of the onset of symptoms
- **Unexpected:** Occurring in someone who wasn't thought to be ill

The laws governing situations in which an ME performs an autopsy vary from one jurisdiction to another but usually are similar. In most areas, approximately 1 percent of the population dies every year. About 25 percent of those deaths are brought to the attention of the ME. In most deaths, the physician who has cared for the deceased person signs the death certificate, and the ME accepts that doctor's determination that the death was by natural causes. When an attending physician is uncomfortable with a particular situation or considers the death suspicious in any way, the ME becomes involved.

The terms *reportable death* and *coroner's case* refer to any death that must be referred to the coroner or ME for investigation. Circumstances that constitute a reportable death vary among jurisdictions, but the following are common situations in which the coroner or ME typically becomes involved and a postmortem examination, or forensic autopsy, is performed:

- Violent deaths (accidents, homicides, suicides)
- Deaths that occur in the workplace, usually as a result of traumatic circumstances, poisoning, or exposure to toxins
- Deaths that are suspicious, sudden, or unexpected
- Deaths that occur during incarceration or while the deceased was in police custody
- Deaths that are unattended by a physician, that occur within 24 hours of admission to a hospital, or that occur in any situation where the deceased is admitted while unconscious and never regains consciousness prior to death
- Deaths that occur during medical or surgical procedures
- Deaths that occur during an abortion, regardless of whether the procedure was performed by a medical professional, by the pregnant woman herself, or by some unqualified person
- When a known or unidentified body is discovered unexpectedly (a *found body*)
- Prior to disposal of a body by means of cremation or burial at sea
- Upon the request of the court

Not all cases that fall into one of these categories require an autopsy. The ME has the final say. Whenever reviewing a case, the ME has several options for handling it.

If the cause of death is obvious and the circumstances aren't suspicious (a patient with severe heart disease dies at home, for example), the ME may accept a cause of death reported by any of the victim's physicians before issuing and signing a death certificate.

If the death is unusual or suspicious, the ME may employ the autopsy to help determine the true cause and manner of death. In this situation, the ME may perform a complete or partial autopsy. For example, if a young, healthy person dies from blunt head trauma, the ME may decide a complete autopsy isn't necessary, and the exam may be confined to only the head. A partial autopsy can save time and money, so the ME often does the minimal work necessary to make the needed determination. It's completely up to the ME.

Performing an Autopsy

Autopsies are designed to determine how, when, and why someone died. During an autopsy, the ME uses a wide variety of tools and a fair amount of intuition to determine what happened. Everything from the debris found under a victim's fingernails to the contents of his stomach can lend clues. The investigation proceeds from the big picture to the fine details and from the outside of the body in.

Getting to work on a given case as soon as the ME's workload permits is vitally important because a corpse deteriorates rapidly; however, a four- or five-day stay in a refrigerated vault usually won't cause any damage to the body that inhibits an investigation.

Every pathologist has a unique way of doing things, but for the most part, the forensic autopsy follows a common protocol. Many of the steps overlap, and some are performed in a different order, depending upon the circumstances surrounding the death.

Identifying the body

Whenever a death becomes the subject of a criminal proceeding, the identity of the deceased cannot be left in doubt. If the identification is unconfirmed, any evidence gleaned from the body is of little use in court.

Generally, however, the identity of the person is not open to question. Family members or friends usually come forward to confirm this information. If not, photos, fingerprints, and dental records may be used to make a positive identification. See Chapter 10 for more about how investigators unearth the identity of a Jane or John Doe.

Conducting an external examination

Whenever possible, a thorough external examination of the body, which includes a search for evidence of obvious trauma or illness, begins at the crime scene. Practical considerations, such as adequate light and space, limit this practice in many instances. The ME or one of the coroner's technicians nevertheless should visit the scene before the body has been moved or removed to observe the body's position and its relationship to other crime-scene evidence, such as the perpetrator's points of entry and escape, weapons, shoe impressions, fingerprints, blood spatters, or any other crime-scene discoveries.

The ME is careful not to touch the body or move it any more than is absolutely necessary during a crime-scene examination primarily to avoid losing or contaminating any evidence related to the body.

For the same reasons, the ME or the technicians must be especially careful whenever they remove a body from a crime scene. In traumatic deaths, particularly if an altercation with another is suspected, the hands of the victim are covered with paper bags to protect any trace evidence, such as tissues or blood beneath the victim's fingernails, before the body is moved. The body usually is wrapped in clean sheets or plastic and then placed in a clean body bag. This procedure traps or collects any trace evidence that falls from the body and keeps out foreign materials that can confuse or contaminate evidence later retrieved.

After arriving at the morgue, the body is removed from the transport wrappings and placed on an autopsy table. Crime lab technicians transport the sheets and the body bag to the crime lab, where they search for trace evidence such as hair, fibers, dirt, paint chips, and other materials.

Measuring and weighing

The first step in the actual postmortem examination of any body is to determine the corpse's height and weight. The ME records this information along with age, sex, race, and hair and eye colors.

Photographing the body

The body also is photographed, both clothed and unclothed, and at various stages during the autopsy. Frontal and profile pictures of the face and body are important, particularly if the victim's identity hasn't been thoroughly established. Every scar, birthmark, tattoo, and unusual physical feature is documented. Every injury must be adequately recorded.

Checking out the victim's clothing

The ME next examines the clothed corpse, searching for

- ✔ Trace evidence, such as hair, fibers, gunshot residues, semen, saliva, or blood stains. Any findings are photographed and then collected.
- ✔ Damaged clothing that may correspond with injuries on the body. For example, do the defects in the victim's shirt match the gunshot or stab wounds found on the body?

After this initial exam, the clothing is removed carefully, to avoid losing any trace evidence, and sent to the crime lab for processing.

Establishing the time of death

Next, the ME determines the state of rigor mortis (stiffening of the muscles) and whether and where lividity (settling of the blood) is present (see Chapter 11 for more on determining time of death). Knowing the position the body was in at the time it was discovered and the location of lividity may indicate whether the body was moved after death.

Taking X-rays

Although they're not obtained in every autopsy, X-rays can supply critical evidence. X-rays of wounds can reveal the extent of injuries and the general shape and size of whatever object created them, which can help identify the murder weapon. For example, X-rays sometimes reveal that the tip of a knife has broken off and remains behind in the wound.

X-rays are particularly useful in gunshot wounds (GSWs), because bullets are unpredictable and can move in unusual paths through the body, especially if they strike bones. For example, a bullet may enter the victim's chest, strike a rib or the spinal column, deflect downward through the diaphragm, and settle in the pelvic area. An extensive search of the chest will not find the bullet, but an X-ray reveals its location.

Bullets tend to deform and break up inside the body, leaving behind chips and fragments that further show the bullet's path through the body. X-rays often help follow the bullet's travels and help locate the bullet's final resting place so that it can be retrieved for examination.

Looking for trace evidence

Hair, fibers, and other foreign materials, as well as blood and semen stains, are examined, photographed, and collected. In traumatic deaths, the victim's fingernails are clipped or scraped because hair, blood, or tissue from the assailant may be found if the victim struggled with the attacker. In sexual assault cases, the victim's pubic hair is combed to search for hair from the rapist, and vaginal and anal swabs are obtained to check for the presence of semen. The ME also takes hair samples from the victim's head, eyebrows, eyelashes, and pubic area for comparison with any foreign hair that's found on or around the body. All the trace evidence collected from the body is sent to the crime lab for further evaluation.

Fingerprints are taken after all trace evidence, particularly fingernail clippings or scrapings, has been obtained, because small bits of evidentiary material can be lost merely by prying open the hand to take the fingerprints.

Examining injuries

Injuries, whether old or recent, are the next items on the ME's autopsy agenda. Each injury is examined, photographed, and marked on a diagram, indicating its location on the body and its position relative to anatomical landmarks like the top of the head, the heel of one foot, the midline of the body, or the nipple on the same side as the wound.

These details may be important factors in reconstructing the crime scene. The exact location of a wound can often suggest that the assailant was a certain height or was either right- or left-handed, which, in turn can help pin down or exonerate a suspect. For example, the suspect may simply be too short to have stabbed the 6-foot-tall victim in the neck with a downward motion.

Three of the common injuries MEs encounter are

- ✔ **Lacerations and contusions:** *Lacerations* (cuts and slices) are photographed and measured. The depth of each is determined, and a search for retained weapon fragments, such as the tip of a knife, is conducted. Bruises, or *contusions,* from blunt trauma are measured and photographed.

  When they are widely scattered over the arms, legs, and torso of the victim, bruises and cuts suggest that a struggle took place or that the victim was tortured before death. Bruises and cuts on the arms and hands may indicate that the victim tried to fend off the attacker. Such injuries are called *defensive wounds.* Contusions may be seen around the throat in cases of manual or ligature strangulation.

- ✔ **Stab wounds:** In stabbings, the ME carefully determines how many wounds are present and then measures the width, thickness, and depth of each. The ME also tries to determine which wound was the killing thrust and whether the wounds were caused by a single- or double-edged blade or blades. This information can be critical in cases where more than one assailant took part in the crime, because it can have a direct impact on how charges are leveled against the perpetrators. The one who actually did in the victim faces the more serious charges.

  In some passionate or overkill homicides, so many wounds may have been inflicted that an accurate count isn't possible. When that's the case, the ME determines the minimum number of wounds.

  Hesitation wounds often accompany suicide attempts involving a knife. These are small nicks and cuts inflicted by someone who's gathering the courage to make a fatal cut.

- ✔ **Gunshot wounds:** Entry wounds from gunfire are measured and photographed. The bullet's angle of entry and the gun's distance from the body when it was fired are estimated (see Chapter 18). X-rays are helpful for following the bullet's path through the body and for locating its final resting place. This information is used during the dissection not only to find the bullet but also to assess the extent of any internal organ and tissue damage it may have inflicted.

If the murder weapon is available, the ME compares it with the injuries to determine whether it is the device that actually caused the injuries. X-rays provide considerable help in making this determination. A depressed skull fracture or a series of fractured ribs whose dimensions mirror that of the suspected murder weapon can be important evidence.

Dissecting the body

Dissection is the part of an autopsy that usually makes its way into horror movies and cop shows, because that's when the body actually is opened up for internal examination. The steps taken by the ME during the autopsy dissection include the following:

1. Making the incision.

The ME makes a Y-shaped or similar incision (see Figure 9-1) to the front of the body. This incision has three arms, two extending from each shoulder down to the lower end of the sternum (breastbone) and the third continuing down the midline of the abdomen to the pubis. The ribs and clavicles (collarbones) are then cut with a saw or shears and the breastplate is removed, exposing the heart, lungs, and blood vessels of the chest.

Figure 9-1:
The Y-shaped incision used during most autopsies enables the ME to remove the breastplate to examine and remove the heart and lungs.

Y incision

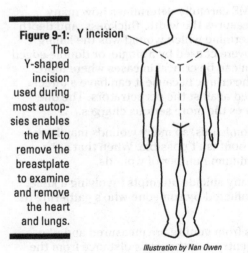

Illustration by Nan Owen

2. Removing the heart and lungs.

The heart and lungs can be removed sequentially but more frequently are removed *en bloc,* or as one unit. Blood for typing, DNA analysis (when necessary), and toxicological testing is often taken from the heart, the aorta, or a peripheral vein.

3. **Examining the abdomen.**

   After the heart and lungs are removed, the ME focuses on the abdomen. Each organ is weighed and examined, and tissue samples are taken for microscopic examination.

4. **Collecting samples.**

   The contents of the stomach are examined, and samples are taken for toxicological examinations. Stomach contents can help the ME determine the time of death if the content and timing of the victim's last meal can be determined (see Chapter 11). In addition to stomach contents, ocular (eye) fluid, bile from the gall bladder, urine, and liver tissue samples are taken and submitted for toxicological testing (see the next section "Sniffing out clues in chemicals: Toxicology").

5. **Opening the head and peeking at the brain.**

   The ME looks for evidence of head trauma and/or skull fractures and then opens the skull to view the brain. First, an incision is made from just behind one ear, over the top of the head, to just behind the other ear (see Figure 9-2), so that the scalp can be peeled forward, exposing the skull. A saw is used to remove a portion of the skull to expose the brain. The ME examines the brain first *in situ* (in place) and then removes it for a thorough inspection and for taking tissue samples.

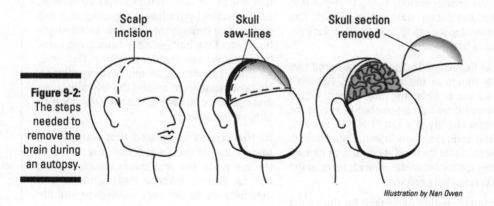

Figure 9-2:
The steps needed to remove the brain during an autopsy.

Scalp incision

Skull saw-lines

Skull section removed

Illustration by Nan Owen

6. **Returning the organs and suturing the body.**

   After each organ has been examined and samples have been taken for later microscopic examination, the organs are returned to the body, and the incisions are sutured closed. The body is then released to the family for burial.

Sniffing out clues in chemicals: Toxicology

Body fluids and tissues collected during the dissection are sent to the toxicology lab for drug and poison testing. Here's what they may show:

- Stomach contents and ocular fluid may reveal any drugs the victim ingested during the hours before death.

- Urine and bile may indicate what drugs the victim used during the past several days.

- Hair may show signs of chronic heavy metal (arsenic, mercury, and lead) ingestion as well as other drug use such as GHB.

- Blood is particularly useful for determining levels of alcohol and other drugs.

CASE STUDY

Getting creative: The Kenneth Barlow case

On the evening of May 3, 1957, nurse Kenneth Barlow of Bradford, England, called a doctor to his residence. The doctor found Barlow's wife lying dead in the bathtub. Barlow reported that he had woken up at 11 p.m. and found her like that. After unsuccessfully trying to revive her, he called the doctor. Barlow said his wife had been vomiting, sweating, and feverish for several hours that evening.

Medical Examiner Dr. David Price noted two unusual things at the scene. First, Barlow's pajamas were neat and dry, which would be unusual if he had attempted to revive his wife while she lay in a tub of water. Second, two used syringes were found in the kitchen. Barlow said that he used them to give himself penicillin for a carbuncle. Indeed, tests of the syringes revealed penicillin.

The autopsy yielded no reason for the young woman to have died. Dr. Price remained convinced that Barlow, a nurse who had access to syringes and drugs, had injected his wife with something that killed her. Using a magnifying glass, he went over every inch of the woman's body and located two tiny injection marks on her buttocks. Her symptoms, as described by Barlow, suggested that she had died of hypoglycemia (a low blood-sugar level) and thus had possibly been given insulin. There was no test for insulin at that time, so Price carried out an unusual experiment: He took tissue from around the injection sites and injected it into mice. The mice quickly died of hypoglycemia.

At trial it was suggested that Barlow had given his wife insulin and had placed her in the tub while she was unconscious, leaving her to drown. Price's thoroughness and ingenuity led to Barlow's conviction and life sentence.

Filing the Official Autopsy Report

After the ME uncovers everything he can from the autopsy, he summarizes his findings in an autopsy report, which is a legal document that may become part of any court proceeding and can be requested by the prosecution, the defense, or the judge. It also may be released to the public (or not) at the discretion of the ME and the court.

The ME's final official report consists of all the details uncovered during the examination as well as any conclusions the ME drew about the cause and manner of death.

The ME typically is cautious whenever filing any kind of report regardless of whether it's preliminary or final. The ME may wait for lab results (toxicology reports, for example) to be returned or file a preliminary statement that will be updated when the rest of the results arrive.

Because the ME's findings and opinions often make or break a case, every pathologist has a particular method and style of preparing the final report, but certain information must be included.

A typical report includes the following:

- ✔ Complete description of the body and its external examination

- ✔ Description of any visible injuries

- ✔ Description of any illnesses or injuries to the central nervous system (brain and spinal cord)

- ✔ Detailed descriptions of the internal examination of the neck, chest, abdomen, and pelvis, which include any abnormalities or injuries found in any of the internal organs

- ✔ Description of any abnormalities found during microscopic examination of organ tissues removed at autopsy

- ✔ Results of all toxicological examinations

- ✔ Results of other laboratory tests

- ✔ Pathologist's opinion, which includes assessment of the cause, mechanism, and manner of death

It's important to note that the official autopsy report and the ME's final conclusions are not written in stone. If new evidence is uncovered or if a delayed test result arrives that changes the ME's opinion, the report can be altered or amended to reflect this.

Chapter 10

Identifying Unknown Victims

In This Chapter

▶ Outlining how bodies are identified

▶ Finding answers in skeletal remains

▶ Determining the time and cause of death

▶ Using facial reconstruction and photographic techniques

Not every corpse that comes into the coroner's office is conveniently carrying a driver's license and Social Security card. All too often police are confronted with identifying an unknown corpse. In movies, this process usually takes only a few minutes of screen time, but in reality, it may take weeks, months, or even years. Some bodies never are identified.

The corpse in question may have been dead for hours, days, months, years, or many decades. An extended time since death and many other factors can complicate the identification process, which usually involves several different forensic disciplines and techniques, all of which are coordinated by the medical examiner (ME).

Getting rid of the body

Criminals don't like to leave behind evidence, although they usually do. In a murder, the primary bit of evidence is obviously the body. Sometimes a murderer attempts to completely destroy the body of a victim, reasoning that no body means no conviction. Not true, as convictions have been obtained even when no body is found. Regardless, destroying a body is no easy task. Fire seems to be the favorite tool of murderers looking to cover their tracks, but it's almost never successful. Short of a crematorium, creating a fire that burns hot enough and long enough to destroy a human corpse is nearly impossible. Check out Chapter 8 to find out why.

Another favorite is quicklime, which murderers often have seen used in the movies. Knowing the chemistry behind it may make them think twice about this one. Quicklime is calcium oxide. When it contacts water, as it often does

in burial sites, it reacts with the water to make calcium hydroxide, also known as slaked lime. This corrosive material may damage the surface of the corpse, but the heat produced from its activity kills many of the putrefying bacteria and dehydrates the body, thereby preventing decay and promoting mummification. Thus, the use of quicklime actually may help preserve the body.

Acids also are commonly used by ill-informed criminals hoping to dissolve the body, which is not only difficult but extremely hazardous. Acids that are powerful enough to dissolve a body exist, but they require a great deal of time to complete the task. They also eat the tub the body is in and destroy the plumbing. They release fumes that peel the wallpaper from the wall and chew up the perpetrator's skin, eyes, and lungs, thus wreaking havoc and leaving behind evidence of a different kind.

Identifying the Body

Neither Mother Nature nor time is kind to the dead. Not only is a dead body subjected to internal digestion (autolysis) and bacterial action (putrefaction), but extreme weather, insects, predators, and environmental bacteria conspire to destroy it.

The condition of a body when it's found depends on how long ago the death occurred and whether it is left exposed to the elements or buried. The general rule: One week in the open equals two weeks in water or eight weeks in the ground. The more decomposed the body, the greater the medical examiner's challenge in making an ID.

If the body is more or less intact, its size, sex, race, scars and tattoos, facial features, dental examinations, fingerprints, DNA, and clothing may help authorities identify who it is. So an intact or partially decayed body gives the ME a great deal to work with and in many cases, a facial photograph of the corpse can be taken and compared with photos or descriptions of missing persons. Problem solved. However, when the body is skeletal, help from a forensic anthropologist, forensic odontologist (dentist), forensic artist, or all three may be needed.

Once a presumptive (possible or likely) match is made, family or friends may be asked to make the final identification. If no missing person matches the general characteristics of the corpse, descriptions and photos are circulated to law enforcement agencies and the media. To help in this regard, a forensic artist or anthropologist may be asked to sketch or computer-generate a best-guess likeness of the individual (more on this in the later section "Reconstructing Faces").

Sifting through the artifacts

Sometimes items buried with or found near the body are helpful. Clothing, jewelry, materials used in the burial, and other artifacts can point to who the deceased is. Finding a wallet or ID card is ideal, but even if that sort of information is found, the forensic team may be involved in the ID process if the person cannot be positively identified visually. Many other items, however, offer clues:

- ✔ Rings or jewelry often are inscribed with names, initials, or dates.
- ✔ Clothing may be distinctive in either style or manufacturer. For example, designer clothes and shoes can point the police in one direction, while ragged and worn clothes like those worn by a homeless person point them in another.
- ✔ A coffin, blanket, or some other material may have been used to bury the victim by a criminal hoping to keep animals away and make the body harder to find.
  - A makeshift, wooden coffin may provide information from its construction materials and methods as well as from any distinct markings it bears.
  - Blankets or sheets likewise may bear tags identifying the manufacturer or seller.
  - A plastic bag may offer up the perpetrator's fingerprints, which, in turn, can lead to the identity of the corpse.

Examining scars, birthmarks, and tattoos

Distinguishing marks on the body, such as tattoos, birthmarks, and surgical or other scarring, often are helpful in suspect and corpse identification. Many are so distinctive that they alone supply positive identifying evidence. Could you mistake former Soviet President Mikhail Gorbachev for anyone else? Probably not, because the port wine stain on his noggin makes his face one of a kind.

Birthmarks are irregular and distinctive, making them perfect identifying characteristics. The tattoos and other body marks of arrested criminal suspects often are sketched or photographed as part of the booking process; however, this procedure is far from universal. If photos from a previous arrest exist, they can be compared with the body marks on a suspect or corpse.

Tattoos, even when they're not readily identifiable, may be traced to the artist by style, chemical composition, or both. Many tattoo artists use black pigments that contain carbon, reds that contain mercuric chloride, and greens that contain potassium dichromate. Others use aniline-based dyes. Extracting and analyzing some of the pigment from the tattooed skin of a corpse makes confirming or excluding the work of a specific tattoo artist possible and takes investigators one step closer to identifying the victim.

Certain gangs boast their own tattoos, and many jurisdictions keep files of these tattoos. In California, for example, the CALGANG database stores such data, and often a query results in a hit, which leads to identifying the victim. If the deceased had a previous brush with the law, a former cellmate, corrections officer, or arresting officer may be able to supply a presumptive ID.

Chumming around: The Shark Arm Murder

In April 1935, two fishermen caught a large tiger shark off the coast of Sydney, Australia. They donated the creature to a local aquarium. The shark refused to eat for several days, and then regurgitated the well-preserved, muscular arm of a Caucasian human. The shark was sacrificed so that autopsy could be performed, but no other human remains were found.

The arm, which bore a tattoo of two boxers squaring off, appeared to have been severed from its owner by a knife rather than by the shark's teeth. Furthermore, the knife wounds appeared to have occurred postmortem. Through meticulous work, forensic investigators obtained fingerprints. The investigation indicated that the victim might be James Smith, an ex-boxer with a criminal past. His wife identified the tattoo, and the fingerprints confirmed the identity of Smith's arm.

Smith's wife said that when she last saw her husband, he and Patrick Brady, a known forger

and drug trafficker, were off to a seaside cottage for two weeks of fishing. Investigators searched the cottage, and its owner reported that a trunk, mattress, three mats, and some rope were missing. Police theorized that Smith was killed, hacked to pieces on the mats, and stuffed into the trunk, which then was dumped into the ocean. His arm apparently had slipped loose in the water and was swallowed by the unfortunate shark.

Under questioning, Brady implicated Reginald Holmes, who unfortunately was shot and killed on the day before an inquest into Smith's death was set to begin. Brady's attorneys obtained an injunction from the Supreme Court, halting the inquest on the grounds that an arm was not sufficient evidence to bring murder charges. Police charged Brady with murder anyway, but the jury likely was influenced by the high court's ruling and ended up acquitting him. This case became known as The Shark Arm Murder.

Finding evidence of wounds or disease

During an autopsy, the ME may discover that the deceased suffered from a disease or sports a scar from a surgical procedure. This information narrows the search for identification. If the victim has a scar from an appendectomy or gall bladder removal, for example, a search through missing-person reports for people who are the same age and sex and have the same medical history may lead to identification, particularly if the surgery was a fairly recent event. The ME often can determine the age of surgical wounds.

Any wound, regardless of whether it's from surgery, a knife fight, or other means, follows the same healing pattern. During the first week, surgical and repaired knife wounds usually require sutures (or stitches). For several months following the removal of the sutures, a telltale pattern caused by the suturing can be seen. The pattern, however, may fade after several months.

For several weeks, any scar remains slightly pink to brownish-red because of microscopic blood vessels supplying blood to the area to aid in the healing process. During the next few months, the body continues to repair the damage by laying down *collagen* (thick strands of connective tissue), the color gradually fades, and the scar shrinks considerably. As scars mature, they finally become faint white lines after four to six months. The collagen layering continues to shrink over the next year or so. Thereafter, the scar remains pretty much the same. Thus, the age of a scar can be approximated within the first four to six months, but thereafter, all bets are off.

Certain surgical appliances provide another means of identification, because they are uniquely marked. The ME may discover through an X-ray exam or during the autopsy that the deceased had a hip replacement surgery, for example. The artificial hip is removed and examined for an engraved serial number, which then can be traced to the hospital where the surgery took place and ultimately to the name of the person who received it. Pacemakers, implantable defibrillators, heart valves, and other cardiac devices have traceable serial numbers.

Fingerprinting the dead

Unless a corpse is severely deteriorated, fingerprints can be obtained and matched against known missing persons and national fingerprint databases. Fingerprints often lead to quick and absolute identifications.

Saline sometimes is injected into the tips of the fingers, causing the pads to swell and potentially reveal the friction ridges (see Chapter 5). Alternatively, skin over the pads of the fingers can be carefully sliced away, viewed under a microscope, and even photographed for matching purposes.

Fingerprints can even be obtained from mummified bodies in some circumstances. The finger pads of such corpses are shriveled and have the texture of old leather, but soaking them in water or glycerin may cause them to swell enough for fingerprints to be obtained.

Checking out the choppers

Everyone's teeth are different. Although you and I may have the same number and types of teeth, their lengths, widths, and shapes show great variability. Missing, misaligned, and reconstructed teeth can be matched with dental records to establish an identity. Chips, furrows, and fillings add even more individuality to the patterns of your teeth. Today, dental records often are used to identify human remains. DNA also plays a role here as the pulp of the teeth often supplies DNA-containing tissues.

Using teeth as a method of identity isn't new. In the first century A.D., the Roman Emperor Claudius demanded to see the teeth of his beheaded mistress to assure her identity. He knew she had a discolored front tooth. William the Conqueror used his crooked teeth to bite the wax seals on his letters to prove they came from him. The first time teeth were used to identify victims of a mass disaster was after the 1849 fire at the Vienna Opera House.

When faced with an unidentified corpse, the ME often makes a set of dental X-rays that can be compared with the most recent dental X-rays of a missing person. With a match, the identity of the body is confirmed.

The ME uses any and all evidence she can glean from a corpse in order to ID the deceased. Even stomach contents can be of use in rare instances.

Recognizing the teeth of Paul Revere's patient

Paul Revere is a well-known figure in American history primarily for his dramatic horseback ride that alerted the colonists of the approach of British forces. Less known, however, is that he had been schooled in the art of dentistry and in 1775 made a set of dentures for his friend Dr. Joseph Warren.

Dr. Warren fell in the Battle of Bunker Hill in June of that year and was buried in a mass grave for those killed in action. When Warren's family wanted his body disinterred for a private burial, the first task was, of course, to distinguish Dr. Warren's corpse from the others. A positive identification came from Paul Revere, who recognized the dentures he had made for his friend.

CASE STUDY

The truth is in the canapés

Abraham Becker and his wife Jennie had a rocky marriage at best. On April 6, 1922, they attended a party at a friend's home in New York City. Jennie ate canapés, almonds, grapes, and figs. The couple left the party, and Jennie never again was seen alive. Becker claimed that she'd run off with another man. The police investigation led to Reuben Norkin, a business associate of Becker's. Under pressure, Norkin admitted that he had helped Becker bury his wife's body. He told police that Becker had killed Jennie with a wrench and buried her body in a shallow grave, sprinkling it with lime in hopes of hastening its destruction. Norkin led police to the shallow grave.

When confronted, Becker said the corpse was not that of his wife, claiming that his wife was larger than the corpse found in the grave and that the clothes were not the ones she had been wearing when she last was seen. During an autopsy, medical examiner Dr. Karl Kennard found that the victim's stomach was well preserved, and within it he found almonds, grapes, figs, and meat-spread canapés. Becker countered that any woman could've eaten those foods, but when the meat spread was tested, the ME discovered that it was identical to the kind served at the party, which had been made from an old family recipe. Both men were convicted of first-degree murder.

Using DNA To Make the ID

DNA is also used in identifying unknown remains in many cases. But, like fingerprints, it is only useful if there is a DNA profile available against which it can be compared. DNA taken from the corpse's tissues, or from bones and teeth in the case of skeletal remains, can often be analyzed and compared to DNA from a missing person — if it's available. It can also be entered into DNA databases such a CODIS in the hopes of getting a "hit" — a match with someone who is already in the system.

Besides nuclear DNA, other DNA analyses, such as mitochondrial DNA, Y-chromosomal DNA, and familial DNA, can be very useful in these situations as each can narrow the possibilities. Each of these techniques is discussed in Chapter 15.

Dem Bones, Dem Bones: Working with Skeletons

Sometimes a forensic team doesn't have a complete body to work with. They may have only a skeleton (at best) or simply a single bone. In these situations, the expertise of a forensic anthropologist and a forensic odontologist usually come into play. They're asked to answer several questions:

- ✔ Are the bones human?
- ✔ What are the biological characteristics (size, age, sex, and race) of the individual?
- ✔ How long has the person been dead?
- ✔ What is the cause and manner of death?

With an intact adult skeleton, determinations of sex can be made essentially 100 percent of the time, age to within 5 to 10 years, height to within 1.5 inches, and race much of the time. The problem: Often only a portion of the skeleton or only a few bones are available to the anthropologist.

Any hope of identifying an unknown corpse rests with determining the deceased individual's biological characteristics; age, stature, sex, and race narrow the field greatly. After these characteristics are determined, the search turns toward individualizing characteristics. The presence of bony evidence of disease, congenital defects, or trauma is important.

Determining whether bones are human

The first question that must be answered is whether the bones are human. Time and the effects of nature and predators can scatter and destroy portions of a skeleton, leaving investigators with little to go on and no room for assumptions.

Determining the species (let alone the specific identity) of a bone is challenging, to say the least. The front paw bones of a bear are eerily similar to those of a human hand, for example, and shell fragments from some turtles can be mistaken for skull fragments. Ribs from sheep and deer resemble human ribs. If the victim is an infant or young child, determining that the bones are human can be even more difficult. Infant bones are much smaller and easier to confuse with the bones of small animals. An infant's skull is not fully fused (joined together into a single structure) and some of these fragments can be scattered and lost, so a complete view of the skull is not apparent. Infant teeth also resemble those of small animals.

Bones are more complex structures than you may realize. They have bumps, grooves, indentations, and other characteristics according to their function in the body and what species that body belongs to. The forensic anthropologist uses these features, as well as overall size and thickness, to assess the species of origin. Yet, even with years of experience, species identification can prove difficult.

Determining age

When only bones are available, the forensic anthropologist can only make a best guess (which is, after all, a scientific opinion) about age, but that estimate is more accurate for younger victims than it is for mature victims. Teeth and bones in children and adolescents follow a predictable growth and maturation pattern. By assessing the stage of this development, a fairly narrow age range can be determined. Later in life, after the maturation process is complete, changes in the teeth and skeleton occur at much slower rates, thus leading to age assessments across much wider ranges.

Details that are particularly useful include

- ✔ **Teeth:** Tooth development begins before birth and progresses through the formation, appearance, and loss of baby teeth (20 altogether) and ultimately the appearance of 32 permanent teeth. The appearance of permanent teeth is complete usually by about age 12. The last teeth to appear, the wisdom teeth, typically erupt by age 18. This general timeline helps with assessing the age of anyone who's 18 or younger at the time of death.

- ✔ **Skull:** In adults, the skull is of little use for age estimation, and in infants it can be of some help, but not as much as once believed. The skulls of infants actually are in several pieces. With time the pieces fuse or meld together along jagged lines of separation known as *suture lines*. Although it seems logical to conclude that the pattern of the closure of the suture lines is useful, unfortunately suture line fusion occurs in such a widely variable pattern that age estimation is not as accurate as investigators would wish.

- ✔ **Long bones of the legs and arms:** These bones change as the body ages. The growth plates within them remain open as they grow, but then close when growth comes to an end. These changes can help determine the ages of people younger than 25, when the bones have completed their growth.

- ✔ **Pelvis:** The *symphysis,* a thin band of cartilage, fuses together the front of your pelvis. It has a zigzag shape in the beginning, but it straightens as you age, stopping when you reach about 50.

- ✔ **Ribs:** Areas where ribs join the breastbone, or sternum, are smooth and rounded when you're young, but they become pitted and sharp as you age. Examination of these junctions can narrow age prediction to within 1 and 1/2 years up to age 30 and within 5 years up to age 70. After that, these changes are of little use.

- ✔ **Bone density:** As you age, your bones lose calcium and become less dense. X-ray examination of the bones reveals the density of the calcium and may help with determining age. Malnutrition and diseases such as osteoporosis lessen the bone density at any given age, so those factors must be considered when determining age from skeletal remains.

Estimating stature

You may think that simply measuring the skeleton from top to bottom provides its height and general build. When a complete skeleton is present, that's entirely possible; however, more often only partial remains are found, making such measurements out of the question. Remember that height is but one part of your stature, which also includes body shape, bone thickness, and degree of muscular development.

The long bones (legs and arms) can help provide an estimate of height. Tables matching length of long bones to the expected height of the person from which they came are available to help in this regard. For example, height usually is equal to five times the length of the *humerus* (upper arm bone). Even fragments of long bones can be useful in determining stature. Other formulas have been developed to enable investigators to estimate bone length from fragments. Such estimates make possible a rough calculation of the person's overall height.

The thickness of the bones gives investigators a rough idea of whether the person was of slight or muscular build, as thicker bones often indicate thicker muscles. The thickness may also reveal handedness, because right-handed people usually have thicker, stronger bones on their right side, and vice versa for southpaws.

Determining sex

Determining sex from skeletal remains of infants and children is more difficult than it is with adults because gender-specific changes in the skeleton don't appear until puberty, after which male and female bones grow differently and begin to take on sex-identifying characteristics.

The overall size and bone thickness of the adult male skeleton usually is greater than that of the adult female. However, bone size and thickness is related to many things other than sex: Better nutrition and heavy physical activity lead to stronger bones regardless of sex. So the skeleton of a female who ate well and performed manual labor may look more like that of a male than the skeleton of a poorly nourished male who rarely worked physically.

Nevertheless, the thickness of certain areas of certain bones can be used to distinguish between males and females. In general, the diameters of the heads of the humerus (upper arm bone), the *radius* (lower arm bone on the thumb side), and the *femur* (upper leg bone) are larger in males.

The most reliable bones for determining sex are those of the pelvis (see Figure 10-1). The male pelvis is designed only for support and movement, while the female pelvis is adapted for childbirth. The female pelvis is wider and has a wider pelvic outlet, which allows passage of the infant during childbirth. The *sciatic notch* (which the sciatic and other nerves pass through on their way to the leg) is wider in females than it is in males. In addition, the backside of the pubic bone of a woman who's delivered a child may have pregnancy pitting, or scarring and irregularities caused by the tearing and regrowth of ligaments that occur during and after childbirth.

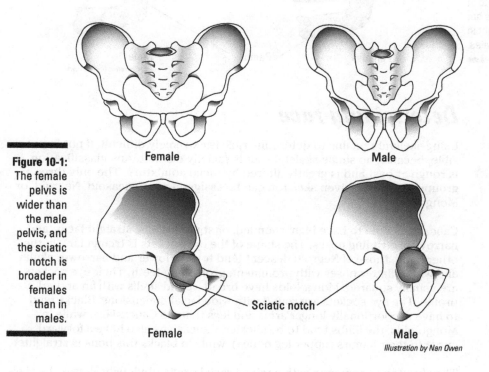

Female   Male

Sciatic notch

Female   Male

Illustration by Nan Owen

Figure 10-1:
The female pelvis is wider than the male pelvis, and the sciatic notch is broader in females than in males.

The skull also offers useful clues to the sex of an individual. Male skulls tend to have more distinct ridges and crests and to be larger and thicker, particularly in areas where facial and jaw muscles attach. In addition, the *posterior ramus* (back branch) of the *mandible* (jaw bone) in males is slightly curved, but in females it tends to be straight (see Figure 10-2).

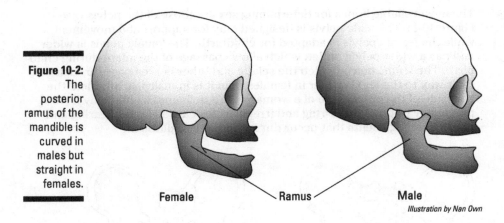

Figure 10-2:
The posterior ramus of the mandible is curved in males but straight in females.

Female   Ramus   Male

Illustration by Nan Own

Determining race

Using skeletal remains to determine race is extremely difficult, if not impossible, because no single skeletal trait is racially distinct. Any classification is rough at best and is greatly altered by racial admixture. The only three groups to which a given skeleton can be assigned are Caucasoid, Negroid, or Mongoloid.

Caucasians tend to have high, rounded, or square skulls, straight faces, and narrow, protruding noses. The shape of the eye sockets is triangular. On the other hand, those of Negroid descent tend toward lower and narrower skulls and wider, flatter noses with prominent, protruding teeth. Their eye sockets are usually squared. Mongoloids have broad, round skulls with an arched profile. The eye sockets are round with wide facial dimensions. Blacks tend to have proportionally longer arms and legs than do Caucasians, while in Mongoloids, the limbs tend to be shorter. Caucasians also have a forward curve to their femurs (upper leg bones), while in blacks this bone is straighter.

The skeleton of someone with a mixed racial origin obviously shares the skeletal characteristics of its ancestors. This racial admixture frequently makes racial determinations impossible.

Seeking individual characteristics

Estimates of the age, stature, sex, and race of the remains greatly narrow the search for the identity of the unknown person, but establishing the true identity requires much more information. Just knowing that the remains are those of a 12- to 18-year-old, 5-foot-tall, left-handed Caucasian female doesn't absolutely identify the individual. Far from it. But these factors narrow the focus to a manageable number of individuals.

Other details that can be compared with medical records or X-rays of potential matches to make identification more certain include

- Evidence of previous injuries, such as healed fractures
- Evidence of knife or gunshot wounds, which can fracture and nick bones
- Surgical appliances, such as artificial hips and pacemakers
- Skeletal evidence of disease, such as the characteristics of bone cancers, tuberculosis, or rickets
- Dental patterns
- DNA extracted from bones or teeth

One newer technique that is being used for identifying remains is matching mitochondrial DNA (mtDNA — see Chapter 15) from a corpse with that of a survivor. Mitochondrial DNA is inherited and unchanged along maternal lines for many centuries. It is very hardy, survives for long periods of time in decayed and skeletal remains, and is found in all the cells of the body, the pulp of the teeth, and even in shafts of hair, which don't contain normal, or nuclear, DNA. If the victim is believed to be a particular individual, then the mtDNA obtained from close relatives can be compared with that of the deceased person. If they share a common maternal ancestry, the mtDNA from each will match. Other useful DNA techniques include Y-chromosomal DNA and familial DNA analyses.

Estimating time since death

Taphonomy is the study of what happens to the human body after death. How the body decays, if it does, and how it becomes *skeletonized* (deteriorated to the point that only bones remain) are areas of interest to the student of taphonomy. As you've seen so far in this chapter and can discover in Chapter 11, estimating the time of death may involve not only the forensic anthropologist and odontologist, but also an ME, archeologist, climatologist, botanist, entomologist, and others (Chapter 2 gives details about each of these positions).

When confronted with skeletal remains, the forensic anthropologist first works to determine how old the bones are. The answer is critical to any forensic involvement. Bones that are hundreds of years old have little forensic use, but bones that are between 2 and 40 or so years old may have significant import.

Estimating the time since death is never easy, and it becomes increasingly more difficult with each passing hour. Chapter 11 looks at determining time of death of more-or-less intact corpses, a task that falls within the expertise of the ME. With skeletal remains, the forensic anthropologist determines the approximate time lapse since the death occurred, using any or all of the following methods:

- **Examining artifacts from the burial site:** Clothing, jewelry, casket materials, and burial artifacts may indicate the period of the burial. For example, arrowheads or musket balls suggest a different time frame than do synthetic materials and plastic objects.

- **Chemical analyses:** Measuring the nitrogen level in bones, which decreases as they deteriorate, is one such method. This kind of analysis is inexact, however, because the rate of protein and nitrogen loss is affected by temperature and moisture, the same two factors that most affect the decay rate of the body. Nonetheless, because a high level of nitrogen suggests that the bones are a few years and not several decades old, this determination can be of some help.

  Another chemical measurement is based on different amino acids disappearing from bones at different rates. Analysis of fresh bones may yield as many as 15 different amino acids, but bones that are a hundred or more years old often yield only seven.

- **Ultraviolet (UV) light:** Fresh bones fluoresce (glow) a pale blue color under UV light. A cross section of the bone reveals this glow across the full thickness of the bone. Time causes this fluorescence to diminish from the outside in, so a bone that is less than 100 years old may glow across its full thickness, whereas one that is several hundreds of years old shows no fluorescence at all. In between, the fluorescence may be confined to a narrow band within the bone's cross section. This band narrows decade by decade until it disappears.

- **Radioactive isotopes:** Carbon-14 (C-14) dating is of little use in forensics because its ranges are too broad; however, other radioactive materials may be helpful. Continuous testing and use of nuclear weapons from World War II through the '50s and '60s caused global increases in the amounts of C14, strontium 90, cesium 137, and tritium (a radioisotope of hydrogen). Finding increased amounts of one or more of these substances in bones means that the person died after about 1950.

Handling burned bones

Bones that have been burned present special problems for the anthropologist. Direct exposure to the fire chars and blackens bones and may cause them to crack or splinter. Prolonged direct contact with fire can calcinate bones, reducing them to white ashes. Under those circumstances, an anthropologist may have only a few remnants to work with.

On the other hand, the texture and color of the bones provide clues about the intensity and the duration of the fire. Indirect or brief exposure to the fire may cause only yellow-brown discoloration of the bones with or without streaks of soot.

Desiccation, or drying out of the bones, causes them to shrink, thus making an accurate estimate of stature very difficult.

Determining cause and manner of death

Occasionally, skeletal remains offer clues to the cause and manner of death. Fractures, fragmentation, and impact marks (dents and depressions) on the bone may reveal blunt-force injuries, indicating the victim likely fell or was hit with a blunt object. Sharp-force injuries, such as from an axe or knife, may show up as cut surfaces where the blade sliced into the bone. Metallic remnants from the weapon occasionally remain along cut surfaces. Similarly, gunshots may leave entry and exit holes in the skull, and gouges and other defects in the ribs, spine, and other bones. Finding a bullet or two among the bones helps. Measuring an entrance hole in a bone sometimes enables investigators to estimate the caliber of the bullet that caused the injury.

Tracking injuries to more than one bone or finding an imbedded bullet may also enable investigators to estimate the path of the bullet and thus determine which organs may have been damaged. Of course, blunt objects, knives, and bullets can lead to death without impacting the skeleton, and, unfortunately, many strangulations and most natural deaths leave behind no skeletal evidence, meaning that a skeleton may not offer any clues to the cause and manner of death.

One problem facing the ME is whether the bone injuries occurred around the time of death or at some earlier point in time. For example, a skull fracture that occurred years before death and one that occurred at the time of death mean two entirely different things. Fortunately the forensics team often can make such a distinction.

Fractured bones heal, evidence of which can be seen by way of *callus* (scar) formation in the area of injury. Callus formation takes months to complete, and, of course, no healing occurs after death. So a fracture that sports a robust callus probably occurred months before death. *Perimortem* fractures (ones that occur close to the time of death), on the other hand, show no signs of healing and no callus formation. Thus, a skull fracture that shows no sign of healing may have occurred around the time of death and may, indeed, be related to the cause of death. Conversely, well-healed fractures can't be directly related to the cause of death.

Bones left in nature undergo trauma from natural forces and from predators and can suffer fractures years after the victim's death. Forensic anthropologists recognize postmortem fractures as such in large part because living bones possess moisture, living protein, and fat, and that makes them less brittle than bones from a long-dead victim.

Fractures to living bones tend to be *spiral* (twisting down the bone's shaft) or *greenstick* (splintered, like when you snap a green twig in half). Desiccated (dried out) bones are brittle and tend to crumble more readily and break cleanly, usually parallel or at a cross section to the long axis of the bone. By examining the nature of any fractures, a forensic anthropologist may be able to distinguish premortem fractures from those that occurred postmortem.

Based on the timing and nature of skeletal injuries, forensic anthropologists and MEs sometimes can determine cause of death and perhaps even whether it was self-inflicted, accidental, or homicidal in nature. Determining the manner of death, however, is not always easy or accurate. When findings suggest that someone died from a skull fracture, determining whether the fracture was caused by a blow to the head (homicidal), a fall (accidental), or as the result of a fall brought on by a heart attack or stroke (natural) can be difficult.

Reconstructing Faces

Forget Michelangelo. For the poor victims who end up dead and unidentified, great artists are those who re-create faces based on skeletal remains. Whether through drawings, sculptures, or computer-generated images, these artists help identify a body by creating a likeness of the victim that is circulated in hopes of finding someone who can identify him. *Facial reconstruction,* or re-creating a likely image of the unidentified victim's face, comes into play when other methods have failed to identify the remains.

The skull, or a casting of the skull, serves as the framework for this fascinating art and often must be constructed from just portions of a skull. Once this is accomplished, a drawing, clay model, or computer image is created one layer at a time. These sketches, computer graphics, and three-dimensional clay models require the hand and eye of an artist and a great deal of experience. Not to mention guesswork.

Artists who work in clay rely on studies that have determined average skin thicknesses over certain bony landmarks on the human skull. They place small spacers of these thicknesses in the corresponding areas and then connect them with strips of clay. This latticework then is filled in and contoured.

However, many problems plague this process. The structure of the eyelids, hair and eye colors, hairstyle, and the presence or absence of facial hair are not known. The victim's race also is likely unknown, though DNA analysis can often suggest racial origin (see Chapter 15). Features such as the nose and ears, which are made of cartilage, are often absent. Drawing or sculpting these features requires the artist's best guess. Similarly, the thickness of the skin and the amount of body fat also must be estimated, and any errors in these estimations can greatly affect the final picture.

Digging into mass graves

Mass disasters, war, genocides, and events such as the 9/11 destruction of the World Trade Centers in New York can lead to mass graves, either intentionally constructed or as a result of rubble. Locating and identifying the victims of such events is challenging, and forensic anthropologists, forensic dentists, and DNA experts may be brought in to help identify the remains. These remains can be decayed corpses, body parts, skeletal remains, or even body parts and bones and teeth scattered far and wide in pieces of varying sizes. It is a painstaking process, and often not all the remains can be identified.

Whenever the characteristics of a missing person fit the general characteristics of the remains, a photograph of the missing person can be superimposed with images of the skull to confirm an ID using a technique known as *skull-to-photo superimposition*. Basically, the photo of the missing person is superimposed over a similarly sized photo of the skull, and the bony landmarks are compared.

This technique rarely provides a conclusive match, but it can eliminate certain candidates. For example, the missing person's photo can reveal eyes that are too widely spaced, a nose that's too long, or a chin with a contour that's different from the one on the skull. On the other hand, when all the features match, the missing person cannot be excluded.

Comparing Photographs

When they're not digging into bones, forensic anthropologists may be asked to use their knowledge of what lies beneath the skin to determine whether two photos are of the same person. Although everyone's face undergoes age-related changes, certain features do not change, and the forensic anthropologist can compare the bone structure of people in photographs, even if the photos were taken years or even decades apart and vary widely in quality and technique. One photo may be from a surveillance camera and the other from a professional portrait studio, for instance.

The examiner superimposes one photo over the other and compares fixed structures, such as orbital ridges (eyebrow area), nasal openings, and chin contours. A match suggests that the photos possibly are of the same individual. Matching superimposed photos is not conclusive but rather is suggestive evidence.

A forensic anthropologist or artist may also be asked to *age* a photograph when a suspect or a missing person has not been seen for years or decades. Using an old photograph of the individual, an attempt is made to determine what the individual looks like years later. This technique has been successful in finding missing persons and tracking down suspects on many occasions. This aging process mostly is guesswork, but in recent years a number of individuals have gained experience and abilities, becoming quite skilled in this area. Computer programs also have been developed to aid the process.

A psychiatric profile (see Chapter 4) often is developed for the missing person before the aging process is applied to the old photograph. A profile provides a look into the type of personality, habits, beliefs, and many other factors the person may have possessed. For example, if a missing person has a social or religious bias against plastic surgery, the artist can reasonably assume that the person didn't alter her appearance. Likewise, if the victim led a sedentary lifestyle, facial changes from aging would be more pronounced than they would be if the victim had been athletic when last known. In short, the artist uses the information from the psychiatric profile to theorize what facial changes the individual is likely to have experienced through the years.

CASE STUDY

Identifying the "Angel of Death"

Josef Mengele, the "Angel of Death," conducted an array of unspeakable human experiments and atrocities on prisoners of Hitler's Third Reich. He alone oversaw the deaths of perhaps as many as 400,000 people.

Throughout the '60s, '70s, and '80s, Mengele was the world's most hunted war criminal. In 1985, rumors of his impending capture reached a fevered pitch, and many wondered whether the "Angel of Death" finally would be brought to trial and forced to answer for his crimes. Unfortunately, he wasn't. A German couple living in Brazil showed authorities a grave near the village of Embu and told them that the body beneath the soil was Josef Mengele.

Scientists from the United States, Germany, and Austria took part in the examination of the skeletal remains. They determined that the bones were those of a Caucasian male whose size and age matched that of Mengele. Unfortunately, Mengele's Nazi SS file was sketchy at best and, in particular, his hand-drawn 1938 dental chart was inexact. The chart revealed that Mengele had 12 fillings but didn't pinpoint their locations and made no mention of his gap-toothed smile.

German forensic anthropologist Richard Helmer, who had been working with photographic superimposition, took a photograph of the skull from the grave and marked more than 30 identifying points before superimposing a known photo of Mengele over the skull photo. Helmer determined that the match was perfect and was convinced that the bones were those of Mengele. He was right. In 1992, DNA materials obtained from the bones and compared with samples taken from Mengele's relatives proved to be a match. The "Angel of Death" had been found.

Chapter 11

Estimating the Time of Death

▶ Understanding the intricacies of timing death

▶ Looking at physical changes after death

▶ Using bugs and other telling evidence

A husband says that he left home for a business meeting at 2 p.m. and returned at 8 p.m. to find his wife dead. He says that he was at home all morning and that she was alive and well when he left. Maybe, maybe not, but establishing the wife's time of death will refute or support his story. If the medical examiner (ME) determines the time of death was between 10 a.m. and noon, the husband has a great deal of explaining to do. On the other hand, if the estimation reveals that the death occurred between 4 and 6 p.m., and he has a reliable alibi for that time period, the investigation will move in a different direction.

In criminal cases, an accurate determination of the time of death eliminates some suspects and focuses attention on others. Determining the time of death, however, is an inexact art, and to make a best-guess estimate, the ME uses each and every means available, from witness statements to body temperature to (egad!) bugs on the body.

Defining Time of Death

Time of death seems like a simple and straightforward concept. It's the exact time that the victim drew a last breath, right? Wrong. Time of death actually comes in three different forms:

✓ **Estimated:** The best guess as determined by the ME.

✓ **Legal:** The time when the body was discovered or pronounced dead. The legal time of death also is the time that's recorded on the death certificate.

✓ **Physiological:** The time at which the victim's vital functions actually ceased.

These three times of death can differ by days, weeks, even months, if the body isn't found until well after physiological death has occurred. For example, if a serial killer kills a victim in July, but the body isn't discovered until October, the physiological death took place in July, but the legal death is marked in October. The ME's estimated time of death could be July, or even June or August. The ME's estimate is always a best guess.

The only absolutely accurate determination of the time of death is under the uncommon circumstance in which a person dies with a physician or other skilled medical professional present. Many deaths, however, are not witnessed by anyone. Natural deaths may occur during sleep, and accidental and suicidal deaths often occur when the victim is alone. In homicides, the perpetrator typically is the only witness, and even if he checks his watch, he's not likely to pass on that information.

Examining the Body to Estimate Time of Death

After death, bodies begin to decompose, and they do so in a somewhat predictable pattern. The ME uses this pattern to estimate the physiological time of death. Unfortunately, these changes don't take place within a rigid time frame, and they occur in widely variable ways. No single factor accurately indicates the time of physiological death. It's always a best guess.

Measuring body temperature

Normal living body temperature in most people is 98.6 degrees Fahrenheit (37 degrees Celsius). After death, the body loses heat at a rate of about 1.5 degrees per hour until it reaches *ambient temperature* (the temperature of its environment). This rate varies, however, depending upon the environment surrounding the body: A body in a warm room loses heat much slower than one in an icy, flowing stream.

The criminalist who processes the scene takes a body temperature and measures the temperature of the surrounding air, water, snow, or soil (if the body is buried). Ideally, body temperature is taken rectally. Another method is taking a liver temperature, which may be a more accurate reflection of the true core body temperature.

The sooner after death that the body is found, the more accurately time of death can be assessed by this method. Once the body reaches ambient temperature, all bets are off.

Obesity; clothing; warm, still air; exposure to direct sunlight; and an enclosed environment slow heat loss. Fat and clothing make good insulators. A thin, unclothed corpse exposed to cold or moving air or water, or one deposited in an area shaded from direct sunlight, loses heat faster. Children and the elderly tend to lose heat more rapidly, as do people who are chronically ill or emaciated. Whenever the body is in contact with cold surfaces such as marble or cool concrete, heat loss is greater.

As with all methods for determining the time of death, heat loss is fraught with inaccuracies. Nevertheless, with early and careful measurement of the core body temperature and with consideration for the conditions surrounding the body, the ME can make a reasonably accurate estimate.

Stiffening up: Rigor mortis

You've probably heard the term *stiff* used in reference to a corpse. I can almost hear Bogart mumbling it right now: "Who's the stiff?" Although the term may not be kind, it is accurate. It refers to *rigor mortis,* or the stiffening and contraction of muscles caused by chemical reactions that take place in the muscle cells after death.

The reason the body becomes rigid after death is the loss of adenosine triphosphate (ATP) from the muscles. ATP is the compound that serves as energy for muscular activity. Through a chemical reaction that converts ATP to adenosine diphosphate (ADP), energy is produced and this energy causes the muscle to contract. The presence and stability of ATP depends on a steady supply of oxygen and nutrients, which are lost when the heart stops. In turn, the ATP then converts to ADP and the muscles stiffen, producing the rigidity of rigor mortis. The later loss of rigidity and appearance of flaccidity of the muscles occur when the muscle tissue itself begins to decompose as part of the putrefaction process.

Rigor mortis begins throughout the body at the same time, but the muscles become rigid at different rates in a predictable pattern. When conditions are normal (ambient temperature is about 70 degrees Fahrenheit), rigor mortis sets in as follows:

✔ Beginning about two hours after death, rigor mortis is first detectable in the small muscles of the face and neck and progresses downward in a head-to-toe fashion to the larger muscles.

✔ The entire contracting process takes about 8 to 12 hours, after which the body is completely stiff and is fixed in the position of death.

✔ The body remains fixed for another 12 to 18 hours, a state that is called the *rigid stage* of rigor mortis.

- The process reverses itself, and rigidity is lost in the order in which it appeared, beginning with the small muscles and progressing to the larger ones.

- After another 12 hours or so, the muscles become relaxed in the *flaccid stage* of rigor mortis.

The general rule is 12-12-12. Rigor comes on over 12 hours, remains for 12 hours, and then resolves over 12 hours. More or less, anyway.

Because of this process, rigor mortis is useful only for estimating time of death during the first 36 to 48 hours after death — under normal conditions, that is.

Sometimes rigor mortis comes on very quickly after death, especially when ATP levels have been reduced before death, usually by intense physical activity or body heat, both of which can rapidly deplete ATP levels. Examples include the following:

- A victim who ran from an assailant prior to death may show the first signs of rigor in the legs, which is where the ATP would be most depleted.

- Victims of strychnine poisoning may develop rigor almost immediately because strychnine causes convulsions and muscular spasms that mimic intense physical activity.

- Because an elevated body temperature also causes increased ATP consumption, victims of *sepsis* (infection throughout the bloodstream), pneumonia, or any other *febrile* (fever-causing) process, or those who succumb to heat stroke may rapidly develop rigor mortis.

Cold conditions, on the other hand, slow the process of ATP loss considerably and delay the onset and development of rigor. A victim who dies from exposure in a cold climate or one who is frozen immediately after death may not develop rigor for days, perhaps not even until the body is warmed or thawed.

Rigor is one of the least reliable methods for determining the time of death because it is extremely variable. Heat quickens the process, and cold slows it. Obese people may not develop rigor at all, and in thin victims it tends to occur rapidly. If the victim struggled before death and consumed much of his muscular ATP, the process also is hastened.

The stiffness associated with rigor can be "broken" by bending and stretching the corpse. This stretches and breaks up the muscle fibers. Once broken, rigor won't return.

STRANGE BUT TRUE

Get a grip: Cadaveric spasm

Cadaveric spasm, which often is confused with rigor mortis, is the instantaneous onset of stiffness throughout the body. A corpse that's affected by cadaveric spasm is locked in the exact posture it was in at the moment of death. The corpse can be frozen sitting, kneeling, reaching, or virtually in any position. Cadaveric spasm occurs under extremely violent physical and emotional circumstances. A victim may be fighting to get hold of a knife at the moment of death, for example, and cadaveric spasm causes her hand to get a death grip on the weapon.

Getting the blues: Lividity

In movies, the dead are beautiful, with perfect makeup and not a hair out of place. Real corpses are considerably less attractive, in large part because of the dark, purplish discoloration of portions of the body that comes from *lividity.* Also called *livor mortis* or *postmortem hypostasis,* lividity can help determine the time of death and indicate whether a body was moved after death.

Lividity is caused by stagnation of blood in the vessels. At death, the heart stops beating and blood ceases to move. Stagnant blood goes where gravity leads it. A corpse lying on its back develops lividity along the back and buttocks. A corpse lying on its left side shows lividity along the downside of the left shoulder, arm, hip, and leg.

However, any part of the body that presses against a firm surface appears pale and is surrounded by the lividity. For example, a corpse lying on its back shows lividity along its entire lower surface except where the body actually made contact with the hard floor. The shoulder blades, buttocks, and calves show pale points of contact, because the weight of the body compresses the blood vessels in these support areas and keeps stagnant blood from pooling. Tight-fitting clothing can do the same thing. A belt or brassiere can leave a pale track through an area of lividity.

The color of the lividity also can provide clues to the ME. Normal lividity is bluish or grayish in color, but red or pinkish lividity often is seen in deaths caused by carbon monoxide or cyanide poisoning or by exposure to cold temperatures after death. Alternatively, people dying from severe heart failure, shock, or asphyxia may develop deep purple lividity. The blood in these situations is usually poorly oxygenated and is thus deeply purple in color, which means any lividity also is deeply purple.

Lividity typically appears within 30 minutes to a couple of hours and reaches its maximum by 8 to 12 hours after death. During the first four to six hours after death, the discoloration can be shifted by rolling the body to a different position. When a body is supine (on its back) for a couple of hours and then rolled onto its left side, the lividity that began accumulating along the back shifts and begins accumulating along the left side. But after six to eight hours, the lividity becomes fixed because the blood vessels begin breaking down, and the blood escapes the confines of the blood vessels and settles in the surrounding tissues, permanently staining them. Moving the body after this does not shift the lividity.

The ME uses shifting and fixed lividity to estimate time of death and determine whether the body has been moved — something the dead don't do without assistance.

The fixing process is not an all-or-nothing phenomenon. It occurs gradually, meaning that four to six hours after death, some of the lividity may be fixed and some still may be shifting. Whenever the ME finds that the corpse has some faint areas of fixed lividity along the back and true fixed lividity along the front, he may conclude that the body was lying on its back for four to six hours before it was moved and placed face down.

Of course, all these mental gymnastics presume normal circumstances. Because body decay and the breakdown of blood vessels depend primarily on the ambient temperature and because the fixing of lividity is caused by leakage of blood from decayed blood vessels, anything that hastens or slows the decay process has a similar effect on the fixing of lividity. In hot and humid environments, lividity may become fixed in as little as 3 or 4 hours, and in colder climates it can take as long as 36 hours.

Determining the rate of decay

The decomposition of the human body involves two distinct processes:

- **Autolysis** basically is a process of self-digestion. After death, enzymes within the body's cells begin a chemical breakdown of the cells and tissues. As is true of most chemical reactions, the process is hastened by heat and slowed by cold.

- **Putrefaction,** which is a more destructive process, is caused by bacteria, which destroy the body's tissues. The responsible bacteria come mostly from the intestinal tract of the deceased, but environmental bacteria and yeasts also may contribute.

Bacteria thrive in warm, moist environments but become sluggish in colder climates. Freezing stops their activities completely. A frozen body will not undergo putrefaction until it thaws. Occasionally the destruction of bacteria by freezing is so effective that putrefaction does not occur, and the body continues to desiccate, or dry out, a process that may lead to the eventual mummification of the body (see the section "Dealing with other possibilities" later in this chapter).

Breaking down the bacteriological breakdown

Putrefaction is an ugly and unpleasant process. (The faint of heart may want to skip ahead to the next section.) Under normal temperate conditions, putrefaction follows a fairly predictable sequence:

✔ After the first 36 hours, the abdomen takes on a greenish discoloration that spreads to the neck, shoulders, and head.

✔ Bloating, caused by the accumulation of gas produced by bacteria within the body's cavities and skin, follows. Bloating begins in the face, where the features swell, and the eyes and tongue protrude.

✔ The skin begins to develop blisters or large areas of accumulation of liquid or serum.

✔ The skin next begins to marble, meaning that it reveals the weblike pattern of blood vessels in the face, chest, abdomen, and extremities caused by the breakdown of red blood cells that release hemoglobin, which stains the vessel walls.

✔ As gasses accumulate, the abdomen swells, and the skin continues to blister. Skin and hair begin to slip from the body, and fingernails start to slough off.

If you were to pull on the body at this point, to move an arm, for example, you'd likely come away with a handful of skin instead.

✔ The body takes on a greenish-black color, and the fluids of decomposition (purge fluid) begin draining from the nose and mouth. As the body swells, the skin and tissues break open, releasing gas and decomposition fluids — much like an overripe tomato splitting open.

Internal organs also decay in a known order, and the ME uses this pattern to estimate time of death. The intestines, which hold many bacterial species, decay first, followed by the liver, lungs, brain, and then the kidneys. Stomach decomposition is often delayed because the stomach may contain food mixed with a significant amount of acid that slows the growth of the bacteria and may even kill many of them. Lastly, the uterus or prostate succumbs to invading bacteria.

I told you it wasn't pretty.

Speeding up or slowing down decay

Environmental and internal body conditions can alter the process of decay. Obesity, excess clothing, a hot and humid environment, and the presence of sepsis can speed up the process so much that 24 hours can do the damage of five or six days. Sepsis is particularly destructive to the body, because not only is the body temperature higher at the time of death, but the septic process also spreads bacteria throughout the body.

Conversely, a thin, unclothed body lying on a cold surface with a cool breeze follows a much slower decomposition process. Very cold climes can slow the process so much that even after several months, the body appears as though it's been dead only a day or two. Freezing protects the body from putrefaction only if the body is frozen before the process begins. Once putrefaction sets in, however, even freezing the body may not prevent its eventual decay. If frozen quickly enough, the body can be preserved for years.

Left unchecked, the decomposition process ultimately leaves behind only a skeleton. Obviously, the time required for a body to skeletonize is determined by the same conditions that dictate how fast putrefaction occurs. In a Louisiana swamp in August, the process may take only a week or two, but in February in Minnesota, putrefaction may be delayed until spring.

An important factor in the rate of decay is the location of the body. A body that's exposed to the environment decays faster than one that is buried or in water. The general rule is that one week exposed above ground equals two weeks in water and eight weeks in the ground. Bodies left exposed or in shallow graves also are subject to the actions of predators and parasites, which can consume the tissues and scatter the bones.

Estimating the time of death for a corpse that is more than a few weeks old is particularly challenging for the ME because body temperature, rigor mortis, and lividity no longer are of any use. What's left? The expected stages of postmortem decay, but even that timeline must be modified according to the conditions at the site where the body is found.

Temperature and humidity are only two of the factors the ME must consider. But these factors are inexact and may be significantly altered if the body's location and degree of exposure change at any point after death. For example, a buried corpse decomposes or is reduced to a skeleton at a slower rate than one that is exposed to the open air. Bacterial growth is less vigorous in a buried corpse, and predators and climatic changes are less likely to damage a buried body. The passage of several days between the death and burial of the victim complicates things greatly for the ME, because the changing conditions to which the corpse was exposed need to be considered. A body that is retrieved and buried two days after being dumped into a lake or a body that is buried for a week and then dug up and moved to another burial site with entirely different soil and water conditions are a couple of situations that can give the ME fits.

CASE STUDY

Operation Iceman and the cyanide sandwich

In September 1983, the corpse of a man was found in a wooded area of Rockland County, New York. Although the body was wrapped in plastic and appeared to have suffered a single gunshot wound to the head, things were not quite as simple as they seemed for medical examiner Dr. Frederick Zugibe. Dr. Zugibe performed an autopsy and was shocked to find that the body seemed to be decaying from the outside in, rather than the inside out, which is the normal pattern. Moreover, the internal organs were remarkably well preserved, and the heart contained ice crystals. The body obviously had been frozen in an attempt to disguise the true time of death.

By soaking the victim's hands in water and glycerin, Dr. Zugibe was able to rehydrate them enough to obtain fingerprints and subsequently identify the body as that of 58-year-old Louis Masgay, a Pennsylvania storeowner who had been missing since July 1, 1981. Because Masgay was found wearing the clothes in which he was last seen, Dr. Zugibe concluded he probably had been killed on that day.

Police determined that on the day he disappeared, Masgay had an appointment with Richard Kuklinski. As the police began investigating Kuklinski, a disturbing pattern emerged. Many people who had dealings with Kuklinski had ended up dead or missing. Police set up a sting they called Operation Iceman to trap Kuklinski in an attempted murder. Dominick Polifrone, an agent with the Bureau of Alcohol, Tobacco, and Firearms, went undercover and convinced Kuklinski that he could supply him with 10 kilos of cocaine and asked him whether he had any ideas about how to get rid of a bothersome competitor.

Kuklinski took the bait, telling Agent Polifrone that cyanide was his weapon of choice, but that he didn't have ready access to any. Polifrone said he could supply it, so they arranged to meet the target at a motel, where Kuklinski planned to add cyanide to sandwiches and get the target to eat one. Fearful that an accident might occur, Polifrone supplied a jar of quinine, telling Kuklinski it was cyanide. Kuklinski was arrested for attempted murder and ultimately convicted of killing two of the other missing men. He later confessed to several others, including the murder of the unfortunate Louis Masgay.

Dealing with other possibilities

Though the ME is most often confronted with bodies in various stages of putrefaction, decomposition is not the only way that a body can change after death. Under certain circumstances the following situations may occur:

- **Mummification** occurs when the body desiccates (dries out) in a hot, dry environment. Low humidity inhibits bacterial growth, and thus putrefaction, while at the same time sucking the moisture from tissues. In ancient Egypt, spices and salts were rubbed on corpses to hasten the drying process and ensure the bodies would mummify rather than decay. A leathery, dark-colored corpse results. The flesh looks like it was shrink-wrapped over the bones. Internal organs may dry and shrivel or become a dark, brownish-black, puttylike material. Mummified corpses tend to remain intact for long periods of time, which makes the determination of time since death difficult, if not impossible.

The process of mummification actually is similar to the process of making beef jerky. In both situations, moisture is removed, causing drying (mummification) of the body's tissues or the meat. Bon appétit!

✔ **Adipocere formation** occurs in very wet environments within the body's adipose (fatty) tissues. The fat literally turns to soap. The result is a white, greasy, waxy substance. It gives the body an unreal, mannequin-like appearance. Adipocere formation most often occurs in bodies found in swamps, bogs, and other damp and acidic or alkaline areas. It takes at least three to six months to form, so a body with significant adipocere formation must have died several months earlier.

Bodies may not decompose uniformly, so a corpse may be found partially skeletonized and partially mummified or changed to adipocere. Incomplete embalming likewise can lead to partial preservation and partial skeletonization.

Breaking the surface: When sinkers become floaters

Bodies that die in water or are dumped into water shortly after death initially sink, but they eventually rise to the surface because of putrefaction gases that accumulate in the body's tissues and cavities. The temperature of the water has a significant effect on how long this process takes. In the warmer waters of the Gulf of Mexico a body may float after only a few days or a week, while in colder waters it may take weeks or months.

In general, bodies found in temperate water display

✔ Swollen hands and face after two to three days

✔ Separation of skin from the body after five to six days

✔ Loss of fingernails after eight to ten days

✔ Floating after eight to ten days in warm water and after two to three weeks or more in cold water

Gazing into the eyes

After death, *corneas* — the clear coverings over your pupils — become cloudy and opaque. This process may take only a few hours if the eyes were open at death or up to 24 hours if the eyes were closed.

The concentration of potassium within the *vitreous humor,* the thick, jellylike substance that fills your eyeballs, increases slowly during the first few days. As opposed to many other postmortem changes, this process is independent of ambient temperature; however, any determination from vitreous potassium isn't very accurate and is useful only within the first three or four days.

Gathering Other Clues

Determining the time since death is not an easy task, and every bit of information helps. The ME uses not only the above techniques but any other information he can glean from the body and from the site where it was found. Three very useful types of information include the victim's stomach contents, the actions of various insects on the corpse, and materials found near the body.

Discovering what was on the menu

The ME often uses the contents of the victim's stomach to help determine the time of death. After a meal, the stomach usually empties itself in approximately two to four hours, depending on the type and amount of food ingested. If a victim's stomach contains largely undigested food material, then death likely occurred within an hour or two of the meal, but this is extremely variable from person to person. If, on the other hand, the stomach is empty, the death likely occurred several hours after eating. Additionally, if the ME finds that the small intestine also is empty, death probably occurred at least 24 hours after the victim's last meal. If the colon is empty, no food had been ingested for 48 to 72 hours before death.

These calculations depend upon a number of factors. Heavy meals and those that are rich in protein and fat digest more slowly than smaller meals and those that are high in carbohydrates and sugars. The consumption of alcohol and drugs, and even certain medical conditions, may affect digestion and gastric emptying. The rate of digestion also greatly varies from one individual to the next, which means that gastric contents are of only marginal help in determining the time of death.

Getting buggy

In addition to animal predators, numerous insects show up on a corpse to feast not only on the body itself but on other insects that are attracted to it. The ME uses these insects to aid in determining the time of death. Although bugs usually show up on a predictable schedule, these patterns vary greatly depending upon geographic region, locale, time of day, and season. Because of the complex nature of the bug world, the ME often asks for assistance from a forensic entomologist, who studies insects to uncover clues.

One example is the blowfly, which shows up early, often within the first hour after death. Blowflies seek the moist areas of the corpse to lay their eggs. The nose, mouth, armpit, groin, and open wounds are favored locations. Eggs hatch to larvae (maggots) within 24 hours. These larvae usually reach a length of a half-inch (one centimeter) after the first three days. During the next six to ten days the larvae feed, grow, and repeatedly molt, finally becoming pupae, when their outer covering hardens. Approximately 12 days later adult flies emerge, and the cycle continues.

In general and under normal circumstances, if the ME or entomologist finds only eggs, death likely occurred less than 24 hours earlier. If fully grown maggots but no pupae are found, death occurred less than 10 days earlier. Finding pupae indicates that six to ten or more days have passed, and the presence of mature hatchlings indicates that death occurred two to three weeks earlier.

Naturally, certain circumstances can throw off this schedule. Blowflies, for example, don't deposit eggs at night and are less plentiful during winter. So, if the victim was murdered at midnight, blowflies may not appear until dawn, and if it's cold outside, they may not appear at all. If conditions are unfavorable — extremely cold, for example — maggots may go dormant for extended periods of time. For example, if the body is in an area that's warm during the day and very cold at night, maggots may be dormant during half of each 24-hour period. If it turns cold for several days, the developmental process may be put on hold during that time period. This can greatly complicate the determination of time since death.

Because the weather plays such an important role on the behavior of insects, the entomologist may also consult a climatologist. Information regarding the weather conditions during the past days and weeks can help the entomologist better understand his findings, which in turn helps the ME estimate the time of death.

Insect studies most often provide only a minimum time that's elapsed since death occurred. Pupae cannot appear in fewer than six days, for example. To add to the confusion, insects appear in waves and new generations all the time. Adults produced after two weeks lay their own eggs, which then follow a similar cycle. So a three-week-old corpse may show fly eggs, maggots, pupae, and adults. I told you it wasn't easy.

The ME collects live maggots, pupae, and empty pupal cases. Samples of the recovered maggots need to be placed in alcohol or a mixture of alcohol, kerosene, and other chemicals to preserve them in the state they were in when they first were observed at the scene. The criminalist may be asked to collect samples of the soil around the body to recover insects that pupate (develop) in the ground. The entomologist reviews all of the samples to determine

- ✔ The types of insects present
- ✔ Where each insect is within its developmental cycle
- ✔ How many development cycles have occurred

Checking other scene markers

The ME uses all the information at his disposal to estimate the time of death, including many nonscientific findings. *Scene markers* are any information found at the scene or taken from witnesses or family and friends. The last time the person was seen alive, for example, serves as a starting point for the ME. Family and friends can report the deceased's habits and any changes they may have observed.

Missed work or forgotten appointments, not going on a regular daily walk or visit to the coffee shop, mail or newspapers left uncollected, and dated sales receipts all can be useful clues. Here are some examples:

- ✔ A broken watch or clock may indicate the time an assault took place.
- ✔ A victim who missed work for two days and is found at home, dressed in work attire and holding car keys, probably was heading to work at the time of death.
- ✔ A victim who never showed for a scheduled racquetball game and was found in the garage wearing exercise gear is likely to have died while leaving for the game.

Of course, the ME uses all the information from other parts of the investigation to confirm or refute this evidence.

Planting the dead: The Body Farm

At a farm in Tennessee, bodies are planted in shallow graves, left lying on the ground with only a light blanket of brush, and tied upright to tree trunks. The site is not the playground of a serial killer but a university facility that conducts macabre experiments designed to determine exactly what happens to bodies after death.

In the 1970s, William Bass III, a forensic anthropologist, established the University of Tennessee Forensic Anthropology Facility (also known as The Body Farm) in Knoxville to study the rate and pattern of decomposition under various environmental conditions. It's basically an outdoor laboratory for studying *taphonomy* (what happens to human bodies after death).

Bass began with a single body but since has studied hundreds. At any one time, the farm may have bodies decomposing in the open in either sun or shade, buried at various depths and in varying soil conditions, in water, in the trunks of cars, or hanging from scaffoldings. With each one comes a better understanding of the decay process.

The Federal Bureau of Investigation (FBI) regularly uses the expertise of Bass and information obtained from research performed at The Body Farm, and directors at the farm teach taphonomy classes for the FBI.

Researchers at the farm plan to produce an atlas of body decomposition for law enforcement, help perfect ground-penetrating radar and other body-locating techniques, and understand the chemistry of decomposition better so that more accurate estimations of the time of death become the norm. And that's just for starters. Several other such sites now exist in various parts of the country to enable researchers to study decomposition under varying climatic conditions. Sites include Texas State University, Western Carolina University, Southern Illinois University, and other locations.

Chapter 12

Ouch! That Hurts: Traumatic Injuries and Deaths

How is a bite like a gunshot wound? For that matter, what do walking into a door, cutting your finger, and being struck by lightning have in common? Each of these injuries is classified as *trauma,* which is a catchall term for just about anything that hurts or leaves a mark. Bumps and bruises resulting from your own klutziness and slipping on a banana peel rarely result in a criminal investigation. Crimes that result in trauma — physical and sexual abuse, murder, assaults, or even car crashes, for example — often do, and they can leave a wealth of information for investigators.

Unleashing the Power of Guns and Gun Evidence

Most people have seen guns only on TV or in movies. This artificial reference point gives no indication of the true power of the weapon. When properly maintained and used, guns are a great source of sport and fun, but when handled carelessly or in an unlawful manner, they can cause injury and death. And they can do it in a heartbeat. The fired gun cannot be unfired. The sudden explosive force is shocking. Even more shocking is the damage a bullet can do to a human being.

Gunshots wounds (GSWs) are a common cause of death in accidental, suicidal, and homicidal shootings. The mechanism of death depends upon the location and severity of the injury the bullet produces. For a gunshot to be immediately fatal, extensive trauma to the brain, heart, or upper spinal cord must occur. Otherwise death is slower and typically is caused by *exsanguination* (bleeding to death) or a secondary wound infection. The manner of death depends upon the intent of the person discharging the weapon. Death from a GSW obviously can't be a natural death, but shootings never intended to harm anyone are likely to be deemed accidental, while intentionally inflicted lethal GSWs are either suicidal or homicidal.

Tracking those tricky bullets

Bullets are tricky and behave in all sorts of odd ways. They may strike the skull, sternum (breastbone), or rib and be deflected away from vital organs beneath. A bullet that ricochets off the skull may leave the body completely or burrow beneath the scalp and be found at some distance from the entrance wound. A bullet that enters the chest may strike the spinal column and be defected downward into the abdomen. This can make a bullet's final resting place difficult to locate.

Bullets that cannot readily be located are visible under X-rays, which the surgeon or medical examiner (ME) uses to locate them. Long story short: Bullets are unpredictable, and the ME may have a hard time tracking their path through the victim.

Studying entry and exit wounds

Even when a bullet enters a body, leaving an *entry wound*, it does not necessarily come back out, or create an *exit wound*. More often than not, the bullet remains within the victim. When evaluating GSWs, an ME searches for and examines entry and exit wounds and tracks down any bullets retained within the victim. Although the distinction isn't always apparent, the ME also attempts to distinguish between entry wounds and exit wounds because doing so can be critical in reconstructing a crime scene. Knowing the paths the bullets followed can implicate or exonerate suspects or help determine which bullet caused lethal injury.

The character of a wound produced by a gunshot depends upon several factors, including

- ✔ The distance between the victim and the muzzle of the gun
- ✔ The caliber and velocity of the bullet
- ✔ The angle at which the bullet enters the body (if it does)

✔ Whether the bullet remains within the victim or passes completely through, exiting the body (a *through-and-through gunshot wound*)

The ME can estimate the distance from which a single bullet was fired by looking closely at the entry wound (see Figure 12-1):

✔ If the muzzle was 2 or more feet away from the victim, the entrance wound usually is a small hole, with an *abrasion collar* (a blue-black bruising effect in a halo around the point of entry). Some black smudging can also occur where the skin literally wipes the bullet clean of the burned gunpowder, grime, and oil residue it picks up as it passes through the barrel of the gun (see Figure 12-1a).

✔ If the muzzle was between 6 inches and 2 feet from the point of entry, the skin may appear *tattooed* or stippled. This effect is the result of tiny particles of gunpowder discharged from the muzzle embedded in the skin, in a speckled pattern around the wound (see Figure 12-1b).

✔ If the muzzle was less than 6 inches from the victim, the gunshot produces a hole, a more compact area of stippling, a surrounding area of charring (from the hot gases expelled through the muzzle), and a bright red hue to the wounded tissues (see Figure 12-1c).

✔ If the muzzle is pressed against the victim when the gun is fired, hot gases and particulate matter are driven directly into the skin, producing greater charring and ripping the skin in a star-shaped or *stellate* pattern (see Figure 12-1d).

Figure 12-1:
The anatomy of a gunshot entry wound depends upon the distance between the gun muzzle and the point of entry. Wounds may have an abrasion collar (a), tattooing (b), charring (c), or a stellate pattern (d).

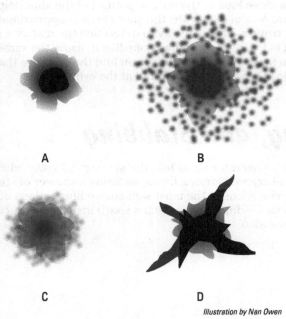

A

B

C

D

Illustration by Nan Owen

Exit wounds, on the other hand, typically are larger than entry wounds because the bullet lacerates (cuts or tears) the tissues as it forces its way out through the skin. The shape and size of an exit wound depend upon the size, speed, and shape of the bullet. For example, soft lead bullets are easily deformed as they enter and pass through the body, particularly if they strike any bony structures along the way. When that happens, the bullet may become severely misshapen, which, in turn, produces more extensive tissue damage that often results in a gaping, irregular exit wound.

Distinguishing entry wounds from exit wounds is not always easy for the ME, particularly when the exit wound is *shored,* which means clothing or some other material supports the wound. The ragged nature of most exit wounds is caused by the bullet ripping its way through the skin. However, if the victim's skin is supported by tight clothing or the victim is against a wall or other structure, the skin is less likely to tear. The exit wound therefore will be smaller and less ragged, and it will look more like an entry wound.

Analyzing shotgun patterns

Generally speaking, a shotgun expels a group of projectiles, or *shot,* and not merely a single bullet, so it creates multiple entry wounds. Because a shotgun is not *rifled* — that is, the inside of the barrel doesn't have grooves (see Chapter 18) — no identifying markings are found on the shot.

In a murder where the victim is shot with a shotgun, determining the distance between the muzzle and the victim can be critical to the outcome of the case. Taking a close look at the spread pattern of the shot helps make this determination. As a general rule, the shot spreads approximately an inch for every 3 feet it travels. The best way to determine the distance from which the gun was fired is to fire it, or perhaps one like it, using the same type of ammunition, from several distances until you find the distance that comes closest to matching the shot pattern found at the crime scene.

Slicing, Dicing, and Stabbing

When Janet Leigh's character steps into the shower in *Psycho,* she steps right into the clutches of crazed Norman Bates, suffering a shower of stab wounds. That gruesome scene is one of the most well-known illustrations of *penetrating* or *sharp-force injuries* — injuries in which a sharp instrument, such as a knife, actually pierces the skin.

Sharp-force wounds can be divided into three general types:

✔ **Stab wounds** most often are homicidal and result from a pointed instrument like a knife or sword. Stab wounds usually are deeper than they are wide and are more likely to be distorted by the victim's twisting and turning to fend off the attacker. By looking at the characteristics of the wound, an ME usually can determine the type of instrument that was used. Distinguishing a knife wound from one made with an ice pick or a screwdriver is usually easy, but identifying the exact weapon that caused the injury is virtually impossible. Two notable exceptions make things a lot easier:

- If the tip of the weapon's blade breaks off and remains in the wound, the crime lab may be able to match the broken edge from the tip with that of a suspect weapon in a jigsaw puzzle fashion.

- If the victim's blood can be DNA-matched (see Chapter 15) to blood found on the weapon, the evidence tells a powerful story.

✔ **Incised or cut wounds** are caused when a sharp instrument is drawn across the skin. Unlike stab wounds, they have no characteristic width or depth and thus reveal little of the nature of the weapon. These wounds are rarely fatal, but when they are, they usually are suicidal or homicidal.

- Suicidal wounds typically are found on the victim's wrists and, rarely, on the neck. Suicidal incised wounds frequently are accompanied by hesitation marks — smaller, shallower cuts created by the person gathering the courage to make the fatal cut.

- Homicidal incised wounds typically are seen on the neck. If the assailant is behind the victim, the cut usually extends from high up on one side near the ear, sweeps downward across the front of the throat, and then back up on the opposite side. The path of this sweep is left to right in a right-handed assailant and the opposite for a left-handed one. If an attacker is facing a victim, the cut usually is shorter and more horizontal.

- Defensive wounds can be incised in nature. As a victim attempts to fend off an attacker, the knife blade may slice the victim's hands, wrists, forearms, and even feet.

- Accidental cuts typically involve the hands and rarely are fatal. Accidental cuts that involve the neck are extremely rare. Falling or flying glass fragments make up the majority of such neck wounds.

Accidental, suicidal, and homicidal incised wounds usually are in different areas of the body and show different cut patterns. Knowing these locations and patterns helps the ME reconstruct the death scene and determine the manner of death.

✔ **Chop wounds** are produced by heavy, sharp-edged implements, such as axes and meat cleavers. These wounds tend to be deep and wedge-shaped. Fractures and grooves often are seen in underlying bones. Lethal chop wounds usually are accidental or homicidal and rarely are suicidal. If an accidental blow (when chopping wood, for instance) severs a major artery in the leg, death can follow quickly from extensive blood loss unless immediate medical help is available.

When evaluating fatal penetrating injuries, the ME must make several determinations. First off, the ME must examine the corpse and locate each and every wound and then determine what types of weapons were likely used and which wounds were potentially lethal. One goal is to find out the sequence of the injuries and to estimate which one was the likely killing wound. In homicides, this determination becomes critical when more than one assailant is being investigated, because the person delivering the fatal wound faces more serious charges. Sometimes these determinations are obvious, and other times they're not.

Next, the ME works to determine the manner of death. Stabs, cuts, and chopping wounds can be accidental, suicidal, or homicidal in nature, and the ME must make this distinction whenever possible by evaluating the nature, location, and number of wounds.

Determining the type of blade that made the wound is next to impossible, but often the ME can measure the depth and width of the wound and occasionally can determine whether the blade was straight, curved, or serrated on one edge. The depth of the wound can be used to estimate the minimum length of the blade. The blade could be longer if incompletely thrust into the victim, but it can't be shorter. However, if the knife was thrust deeply enough to leave a patterned abrasion that mirrors the knife's hand guard around the wound, the ME may then be able to determine the blade's actual length. The *hand guard* is the piece of metal between (usually perpendicular to) the handle and the blade that prevents the user's hand from sliding down on to the blade. Whenever the hand guard impacts the skin with enough force, it can leave a bruise or abrasion that matches the guard in shape and size.

Taking the Hit: Blunt-Force Trauma

If you've ever bumped into a table, hit your head on a cabinet, or caught a baseball with your face, you've experienced blunt-force trauma. *Blunt-force trauma* occurs whenever you make contact with a hard, dull object in a way that hurts you. It can come from an assault, a fall, an automobile accident, or a number of other situations, and the impact may scrape or bruise your skin, break your bones, or even damage your internal organs.

Scraping and abrading

Abrasions are injuries that result in the removal of the superficial layer of skin. Although most people call all abrasions *scrapes,* physicians and MEs refer to them in several different ways:

- **Sliding abrasions** occur when an object scrapes or brushes away the skin. *Road rash* is a common example that results when a pedestrian slides across pavement after being struck by an automobile. Rope nooses and other materials used for strangulation can cause scrape abrasions on the neck.

- **Stamp abrasions** occur when a blunt object strikes the skin, crushing it and leaving behind a raw area. These types of abrasions tend to be small and discreet and may reflect the general shape of the object that made them — a baseball bat, wooden board, or car bumper, for example.

- **Patterned abrasions** are a special type of stamp abrasion where the blunt object that strikes you leaves behind its pattern or the pattern of clothing or any other material between the object and your skin. A chain may leave abrasions that reveal the pattern of its links; the pattern of a car's grillwork may be seen on the body of a hit-and-run victim. If the victim is wearing clothing with a coarse weave, the impact may likewise imprint the pattern of the weave on the victim's skin.

Establishing when an abrasion occurred is difficult and rests on the *usual* healing patterns for such injuries. Unfortunately, the process doesn't always move at a *usual* pace. Pathologists visually inspect these wounds in living and deceased victims and may take samples for microscopic examination from the latter.

The healing process can be divided into these five stages:

- **Scab formation** begins almost immediately but is not noticeable until after about six hours. The wound may ooze serum for the first 24 hours. Red blood cells are usually caught up in the dried red-brown serum that becomes the scab. The abraded area appears dark red, and when viewed under the microscope, reveals the presence of large numbers of specialized white blood cells called *polymorphonuclear cells* (PMNs).

- **Cell regeneration,** which is the reappearance of lost epithelial (skin) cells, begins about 36 hours after the injury but isn't clearly visible until after about three days. Regeneration begins at the edges of the injured area.

- **Cell growth** and thickening progresses during the next five to nine days. The cells divide, grow in number, and continue the healing process.

✔ **Remodeling** occurs by about day 12, when the skin has thinned and taken on a slightly pale appearance.

✔ **The skin completes its repair,** and all remnants of the wound disappear, leaving a bleached-out color. Over the next few months the pigment regenerates. The skin regains its normal appearance by about day 20. Abrasions rarely leave permanent scars.

Abrasions inflicted after death have a characteristic color and character that identify them as postmortem injuries. Because circulation has stopped, blood cells and serum don't accumulate at the injury, so these scrapes take on a light brown, parchment-like appearance. If the abrasion occurs in an area of lividity (see Chapter 11), it may show some red discoloration, but cutting into the tissue will reveal the absence of hemorrhage (blood in the tissues).

The ME analyzes abrasions and scrapes with these general stages in mind; however, the stages can vary greatly from one person to the next and from one injury to another. The ME can only estimate the general age of an abrasion, but this information still may be helpful in supporting or refuting suspect and witness statements.

Bruising and battering

Contusions, or bruises, result from damage to small blood vessels in tissues at the site of a blunt-force trauma. These injured vessels leak blood, which imparts a blue-black color to the tissues. Blood collecting in a pocket beneath the skin is called a *hematoma,* or goose egg.

Not every trauma leaves a mark, and the absence of a visible contusion doesn't necessarily mean that injury didn't occur. Bruises can be so deep that they are not apparent on the skin's surface. Some people, particularly children and the elderly, bruise more easily than others.

Like abrasions, contusions may reflect the object that caused them: A chain, for example, can leave behind a contusion in the shape of its link pattern, a board can leave a broad clear or uninjured area with a marginal bruise that has straight and parallel edges, and a handprint often becomes visible after a slap on the face or body.

In blunt-force injuries, internal organs also can be contused. In falls, automobile accidents, and serious attacks, the liver, spleen, muscles, and other organs and tissues can be bruised. The liver and spleen are particularly prone to such injuries, which are easily identified during an autopsy.

Bruising a corpse, strangely enough, also is possible; however, because a contusion depends upon blood leaking from injured vessels, creating a bruise in a body through which the blood has stopped flowing isn't easy. A sufficiently forceful blow to a corpse can damage blood vessels and cause the stagnant blood to leak into the area of impact.

When determining when, how, and why a contusion occurs, the ME considers the following factors:

- ✔ **Color:** A contusion goes through a predictable color-change process as the body reabsorbs it. The color typically goes through a sequence from dark blue to a lighter blue to a greenish-yellow to a brownish-yellow, and it fades by about day 14.

  Bruises change color as enzymes in the body break down the hemoglobin in the blood. Scavenger cells from the tissue, called *macrophages,* in conjunction with the circulatory system, then remove these remnants, and the contusion fades.

- ✔ **Size:** If a victim suffers a contusing blow many minutes or hours before death, the resulting bruise is fairly diffuse and widespread (larger) around the area of impact. However, if the blow is struck *perimortem* (the period within a few minutes before or immediately after the time of death), the bruise is smaller and more clearly defined, primarily because the blood didn't have time to seep into and spread through the tissues before death occurred.

- ✔ **Organ trauma:** Sometimes no evidence of bruising shows up on the surfaces of a body that's suspected of suffering from blunt-force trauma. Such is the case if bruising occurs deep within the tissues and muscles and if the victim doesn't live long enough for bruising to seep to the surface. When the ME suspects this kind of bruising, a series of deep cuts into the muscles and down to the bones along the back, arms, and legs can sometimes reveal deeper contusions as well as contusions of the internal organs.

  Bruises to internal organs vary according to which organ was injured, but most appear as dark, blue-black areas at the point of impact. The ME may also notice bleeding or a *hematoma* (a collection of clotted blood).

- ✔ **Defensive wounds:** When attacked with a blunt object, the victim almost always attempts to block the blows. For example, if being pummeled with a baseball bat, victims raise their arms to prevent the blows from striking their heads. The blows impact against the *ulnar* (little-finger) side of the victim's forearm, wrists, and hands. Abrasions and contusions in these areas are termed *defensive wounds.*

✔ **Lacerations:** *Lacerations* from blunt-force trauma occur when skin is torn or ripped by the force of the impact and are more common in areas like the scalp, where the skin lies close to the bone. Blunt-force lacerations occur not only to the skin but also to internal organs. An *avulsion* is a severe laceration where a section of the skin or other tissue actually is torn away from underlying tissues or bone. Avulsions most often occur when the blow strikes the skin at a shallow angle.

Breaking bones

Fractures are breaks in bones that result from direct or indirect trauma. A *simple fracture* is a single break, a *comminuted fracture* is where the bone breaks in two or more places, and a *compound fracture* is one in which the bone protrudes through the skin.

When an object makes direct contact with a bone, it causes either a *single-transverse fracture* (one that occurs across the long axis of the bone) or a *crush fracture* (one that is composed of several fracture lines).

A crush fracture often produces a *compression wedge* (see Figure 12-2), which can indicate the direction of the blow. The wedge points in the direction of the force. Knowing the direction of the force helps the ME reconstruct the blow and perhaps even the sequence in which multiple injuries occurred. In automobile-pedestrian accidents, this type of fracture often is termed a *bumper fracture,* because it results from the impact of a vehicle's bumper against the victim's legs or arms.

Figure 12-2:
Crush frac-
tures often
produce a
compres-
sion wedge
that may
indicate the
direction of
the force
causing the
injury.

Direction of force

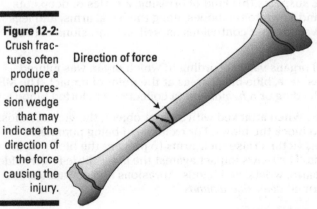

Illustration by Nan Owen

Indirect fractures are not caused by a direct blow to the bone, but rather occur when an indirect force is applied to the bone with sufficient force to cause it to break. Traumatic indirect fractures are divided into four basic types (see Figure 12-3):

- **Angulation fractures** are simply transverse fractures that occur when a bone is bent to the point of breaking, which may occur when someone falls while his arm is trapped or held stationary. This type of injury commonly happens to children playing on playground monkey bars.

- **Rotational fractures** arise when a bone is twisted, causing a *spiral fracture* that twists down the long axis of the bone. The direction of the spiral indicates the direction of the twisting force. A child yanked or thrown by the arm can suffer such fractures.

- **Compression fractures** result when force is applied along the long axis of the bone, driving the bone into its end and resulting in a *T*- or *Y*-shaped break. Such fractures are sometimes seen in automobile accidents in which the victim's knee is driven into the dashboard.

- **Combination fractures** are any combination of angulation, rotational, and compression fractures.

Figure 12-3:
Indirect
trauma may
result in
broken
bones that
are referred
to as
angulation
(A), rota-
tional (B),
compres-
sion (C), or
combination
fractures.

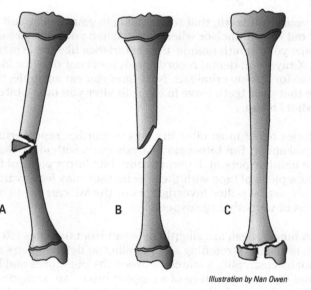

A   B   C

Illustration by Nan Owen

Determining the age of a fracture is slightly easier than determining the age of an abrasion or contusion. Fractures heal according to the following pattern:

- Initial bleeding into the fracture site is followed by the accumulation of various types of blood cells.

- By the end of the first week, *osteoblasts*, which are bone-forming cells, appear.

✔ By the second or third week, a *callus* forms. This fibrous capsule-like structure surrounds the area of the fracture.

✔ Bone formation and the closing of the fracture within the callus take four to six weeks.

✔ Complete healing may take five months.

This sequence of events varies with age and from person to person. Healing is faster in the young and slower in elderly people. Determining the age of fractures is extremely important when evaluating individuals who have suffered multiple injuries over a period of time. In cases of child or elder abuse, this evidence may be critical. X-rays of severely abused individuals may show fractures that are years old as well as those that are only weeks or days old. As with bruises, whenever a physician sees a child or elderly person with fractures of varying ages, the likelihood of repeated abuse must be considered.

Getting toothy: Bite marks

The angle of your front teeth, that rough filling in your molar, and the chip you knocked out of your incisor when you crashed your bike are characteristics that make your mouth unique. Characteristics like these make dental impressions, X-rays, and dental records great tools not only for identifying bodies but also for finding criminals. Next time you eat an apple, take a look at the outline that your teeth leave in the fruit after you take a bite, and you'll see exactly what I mean.

Bite-mark injuries occur most often in cases of murder, rape, torture, and child or spousal abuse. But bite-mark analysis deals with more than injuries inflicted upon another person. If perpetrators bite into a piece of fruit or cheese or tear a piece of tape with their teeth, they may leave valuable clues at the crime scene that police investigators or the ME can use to match the dental patterns of virtually any suspect.

Bite marks on human flesh are slightly different from the ones left in food because flesh is elastic, stretching and recoiling so details of any marks that are left are not as clear. Still, a match between the punctures and bruises left on the skin and the dental pattern of a suspect often can be made. If an individual's teeth are damaged, chipped or are shaped in an unusual pattern, an individualizing match sometimes can result.

Because there is a lack of sufficient scientific research into bite mark analysis as well as questions about the qualifications of many examiners, this technique has recently been brought into question. Still, if the biter's dentition shows unique features, such analysis can offer useful identifying information.

Matching bite marks to teeth

On August 7, 1867, after an all-night search, the body of missing 15-year-old Linda Peacock of Biggar, Scotland, was found in a cemetery. She had been beaten and then strangled with a rope. No evidence of rape was found, but a bruise near her right breast turned out to be a bite mark that appeared to indicate one of the killer's teeth was unusually jagged.

Police interviewed virtually all of the 2,000 residents of Biggar and extended their interrogations to members of nearby communities. The investigation ultimately led police to a local low-security detention center for juvenile offenders. Twenty-nine residents at the center were asked to give dental impressions, which then were compared with the bite mark found on the girl. Visual inspections of the impressions eliminated all but five of the suspects. These young men were called in for further examination, which enabled police to narrow the suspect list to one person — Gordon Hay.

Hay suffered from *hypocalcination,* a rare disorder that causes pits and craters in the teeth. These pits and craters were matched with the pattern of the dental abrasions on the girl's corpse, and Gordon Hay was convicted of murder.

The ME often can determine whether bite marks were inflicted before death, around the time of death, or after death, by evaluating the degree of bruising. Check out the earlier "Bruising and battering" section for more about determining when bruising occurred.

After suspects are identified, molds are made of their teeth so that a model can be created. This casting then is compared with bite marks found on the victim. The lack of a match excludes the suspect, but when a match is made, it suggests, but doesn't confirm, that the suspect is the perpetrator. More definitive follow-up testing, such as DNA matching, is required.

Bite marks on a victim should be swabbed for saliva, which can provide investigators with the perpetrator's blood type and often a DNA profile. Chapter 15 has the details about DNA.

Moaning and groaning: My aching head

Even though most blows to the head produce injury rather than death, the head nevertheless is the most dangerous location for blunt-force trauma to occur. The brain is easily injured, and many of these injuries cause permanent damage and can lead to paralysis, blindness, loss of mental abilities, and even long-term psychiatric problems. Head and brain injuries and skull fractures most often are accidental — from falls or motor vehicle accidents, for example — but they also can be attributed to assault, homicide, or suicide.

Blunt-force head trauma can result in anything from a simple bump on the head (contusion) to concussion, which is often accompanied by a loss of consciousness, to death. To cause death, blunt-force head trauma would most likely have to cause *intracranial bleeding,* which occurs when an artery, vein, or many small capillaries rupture.

Bleeding into the head

REMEMBER

The brain is covered by several membranes: The most important one is the *dura mater.* The space between the dura and the skull is called the *epidural* space, and the space between the dura and the brain is the *subdural* space.

Intracranial bleeds (see Figure 12-4) are of three basic types, all of which are potentially lethal:

- **Epidural bleeds** take place between the dura and the skull and originate in the epidural arteries, which are often torn by fractures of the skull. Automobile accidents, falls, and assaults with blunt objects can lead to such injuries.

- **Subdural bleeds** usually originate in the veins and occur in the space between the dura and the brain. Any blunt-force trauma to the head, even minor injuries, can lead to subdural bleeding.

- **Intracerebral bleeds** occur within the brain tissue itself and are most often spontaneous and caused by the rupture of abnormal or diseased arteries rather than inflicted injury.

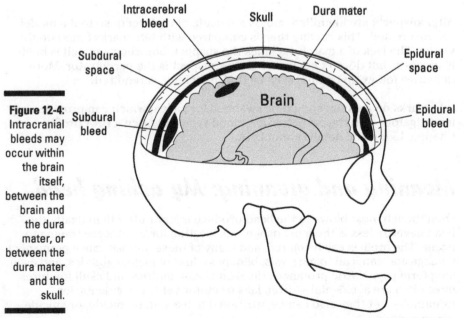

Figure 12-4: Intracranial bleeds may occur within the brain itself, between the brain and the dura mater, or between the dura mater and the skull.

Illustration by Nan Owen

The skull is a rigid capsule that protects the brain. Because the skull cannot expand, intracranial bleeding causes the pressure inside the skull to rise rapidly, effectively squeezing the brain. Mounting pressure alters brain function and ultimately pushes brain material into the *foramen magnum,* the opening at the base of the skull where the spinal cord exits, causing the victim to lose consciousness. The part of the brainstem that controls breathing also shuts down, respiration stops, and death follows. This process can occur within minutes, hours, or days.

During an autopsy, the ME can easily determine that a blow to the head occurred by finding a contusion or abrasion of the scalp and then locating bleeding into and around the brain. The ME may then conclude that the cause of death was blunt-force injury to the brain with bleeding. The manner of death depends upon whether the blow was accidental or intentional.

Cracking the skull

Significant brain injury can occur with or without a fracture of the skull. Similarly, a fractured skull may or may not be associated with injury to the brain. Skull fractures fall into one of the following four categories (see Figure 12-5):

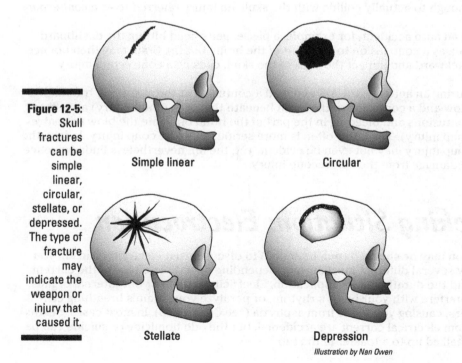

Figure 12-5: Skull fractures can be simple linear, circular, stellate, or depressed. The type of fracture may indicate the weapon or injury that caused it.

Simple linear

Circular

Stellate

Depression

Illustration by Nan Owen

- ✔ **Simple linear fractures** occur with low-impact injuries such as falls.

- ✔ **Circular fractures** require more force and may result from a blow with a pipe, hammer, or similar object. The circle can be complete or incomplete.

- ✔ **Stellate fractures** have a star-like shape and result from localized blows that bend the skull inward and cause it to fracture along lines of stress.

- ✔ **Depressed skull fractures** are the result of a section of the skull being pushed inward against the brain. This fracture requires a blow of enough force to fracture the skull throughout its depth.

Bouncing the brain: Coup and contrecoup

During blunt-force trauma to the head, the brain may be injured at the site of impact, an injury known as a *coup,* or it may be injured in a slightly more complicated way.

The brain sits within the skull and is surrounded by several layers of membranes and fluid, so that it is suspended within the skull like an egg yolk inside an eggshell. It can move inside the skull, but not much, so if the skull is moving and suddenly stops, the brain may continue to move. It may move enough to actually collide with the skull, an injury referred to as a *contrecoup.*

In an auto accident, for example, a passenger's head hitting the dashboard causes a coup lesion to the front of the brain, but the brain may then bounce backward and impact the back of the skull, causing a contrecoup injury.

During an autopsy, the ME may find a contusion at the site of the traumatic blow and a contusion of the brain beneath that area (coup injury) as well as contusions and bleeding in the part of the brain opposite the blow (a contrecoup injury). The latter often is more serious than the coup injury. In fact, the coup injury may not even be evident; yet, the ME nevertheless finds evidence of damage from the contrecoup injury.

A Shocking Situation: Electrocution

You may be shocked (pun intended) to discover that electricity can kill you by several different mechanisms, depending upon the voltage of the current and the duration of its application. Electricity can burn your internal organs, interfere with your heart's rhythm, or paralyze your brain's breathing centers, causing you to die from asphyxia (see Chapter 13). In most cases, deaths from electrical current are accidental, but the odd homicide or suicide can be chalked up to a toaster in the tub.

Wreaking havoc: Electricity's path through your body

When electricity enters your body, it flows along the shortest path from the point of entry to the point where it's grounded. Whether the current turns out to be deadly depends on its amperage (a measure of the amount of electric current) and the duration of contact. A low-voltage current can take several minutes to do any harm, but a high-voltage current can kill instantly.

The greatest danger from low-voltage shocks is their effect on the heart. A normal heartbeat is caused by a rhythmic pulse of electrical current that originates in the heart's internal pacemaker and flows through the heart muscle. A low-voltage shock from an alternating-current (AC) electrical source — any device you plug into an outlet — can interfere with this natural rhythmic pulse and lead to deadly *cardiac arrhythmias* (changes in heart rhythm). Death is typically instantaneous when this occurs.

Death can result from even brief shocks if a current flows directly through the body to the ground. Fatal shocks from low-voltage AC cause only minor superficial burns. In half of the cases of low-voltage electrocution, no external damage from the current is evident.

High-voltage (1,000 to 8,000 volts) electrocutions occur in industrial settings and from the high-tension lines that carry current across the country and into neighborhoods. Direct contact with such lines is not necessary because the current can *arc,* or jump, several inches from the line to someone standing nearby. Any tall metallic object, such as a ladder or a crane arm, also can carry the current to the victim. Accidents like these frequently occur where *cherry-pickers* (mechanized lifts) are inappropriately used for tree trimming or TV cameras.

Shocks from high-voltage AC sources usually result in severe internal and external burning, even with only brief exposures. However, they are less likely to cause dangerous changes in the heart's rhythm.

High-voltage currents are defibrillatory rather than fibrillatory, meaning that they convert an abnormal rhythm back to a normal one, rather than the other way around. During a cardiac arrest, the external shock that physicians give to the victim with those paddles you see on every hospital show is higher voltage and is intended to restore a normal rhythm where a deadly abnormal rhythm exists. Note, however, that high-voltage shocks can paralyze the respiratory center of the brain, causing death from asphyxia.

Assessing the damage

During an autopsy, the ME may uncover several signs of electrical injury. In some low- and all high-voltage deaths, the skin can be charred at the point of contact, the point of grounding, or both. In low-voltage electrocutions, charring may not occur, but the skin at the contact point is likely to be red and blistered.

An interesting phenomenon of electrocution deaths is the appearance of localized rigor mortis. The spasm of rigor mortis results when the adenosine triphosphate (ATP) in the muscles falls low after death. Electrocution causes muscular spasms that can consume the ATP and cause a more sudden onset of rigor in the affected area. For example, if someone grabs an electrical line with her right hand, the current passes down the right side of the body and out through the right foot; therefore, the right arm and leg may show signs of rigor long before the rest of the body.

The rare cases in which electrocution is used as a tool for homicide usually involve an electrical device being tossed into a tub of water in which someone is sitting. When that happens, no burns are found on the body, and if the device is removed before the body is found, the ME may not be able to determine the cause of death. These circumstances are less common than in the past, because electrical devices now are required to have ground-fault interrupters (GFIs), which turn them off whenever a spike in the current or resistance is detected.

Lightning's electrifying potential

Lightning, which thus far has not been harnessed for homicidal purposes, causes accidental deaths with a direct current (DC) in voltages that range from 3 million to 200 million volts. Fortunately, when lightning strikes, the current is very brief, averaging between 1 and 100 milliseconds (thousandths of a second).

Injuries caused by lightning primarily are caused by the body's conversion of electrical energy into heat. The current can burn and char the skin, scorch the clothing, and fuse or melt metal objects in the victim's pockets, shirt buttons, belt buckles, and even dental fillings.

All the tissues of the body are susceptible to injury from lightning. The heart, liver, kidneys, bone marrow, brain, spinal cord, and muscles can suffer permanent damage in people who survive.

One sure way to tell when someone's been struck by lightning are occurrences of something called *Lichtenberg figures,* which first were described by German physicist Georg Christoph Lichtenberg in 1777. He discovered a painless, red, fernlike or arborescent pattern across the back, shoulders, buttocks, or legs of victims, which tended to fade within 12 to 48 hours, leaving behind no scars or discolorations. Lichtenberg figures rarely occur, and their cause is unclear, but when they're seen, they're *pathognomonic* (absolutely indicative) of lightning strikes.

The R Word: Dealing with Rape

The trauma caused by rape goes far beyond physical trauma inflicted during a violent act and may cause long-lasting psychological trauma. Rape is a heinous crime that, although it involves sex, is about aggression, control, and possibly humiliation.

For rape to be charged, the three things that must occur are

- ✔ Actual penetration
- ✔ The use of force
- ✔ The lack of consent

Penetration doesn't need to be complete because only slight penetration is needed to meet the definition of rape. Force often is applied through violence, the threat of violence, or coercion.

All too often, rape is accompanied by homicide, either as part of the violent act or following it to prevent the victim from identifying the assailant. Rape often is part of the act of homicide committed by a serial killer, particularly where sexually sadistic types are the perpetrators. In such cases, rape almost always is part of the killer's fantasy or part of the killer's need to humiliate the victim.

Conducting a rape exam

Completing a rape examination of a surviving rape victim as soon after the act as possible is critical. Unfortunately, because the act often is so devastating, the victim may wait days, if not months or even years, before reporting it. On the surface, this may seem to be odd behavior for an assault victim, but rape is nothing at all like a punch in the face. It carries with it an array of emotions and social baggage that no other crime comes close to rivaling. Victims often feel ashamed, even guilty, and want to avoid the inappropriate but real feelings of social stigmatization. Remnants of Puritanical thinking and a court system that all too often puts the victim "on trial" also play roles in propagating these feelings.

The victim should be examined by a medical doctor with experience in conducting rape examinations or a specially trained nurse practitioner. Whenever possible, a female law enforcement officer should be present so that the evidence chain of custody can be maintained. The examination consists of the following:

✔ The physician or nurse practitioner examines the victim's entire body, including the genitalia for evidence of trauma such as bruises, abrasions, or lacerations, carefully noting and photographing each.

Note: The absence of signs of trauma or violence in no way negates or diminishes any claims that a rape has occurred.

✔ The victim's hands are examined, and nail clippings and scrapings are collected. The assailant's hair, blood, or skin tissues often are found clutched in the victim's hand or beneath the fingernails.

✔ Any bite marks are photographed and swabbed for saliva, which may yield DNA evidence.

✔ Any stains found on the victim are likewise swabbed, because they may contain saliva or semen.

✔ As guided by the victim's account of the assault, the examining physician obtains vaginal, anal, and oral swabs to check for DNA-containing materials.

✔ The victim's pubic hair is combed for foreign hairs and fibers.

✔ Samples of any stains found on the victim's clothing are taken, and the clothing is packaged and taken to the crime lab for further evaluation.

All evidence collected during the examination is turned over to law enforcement officials for transport to the crime lab for further study.

Even if no overt trauma is found, the examining physician looks for signs that sexual intercourse took place. Vaginal fluids are examined for evidence of semen. Tests for *acid phosphatase,* an enzyme found in abundant quantities in semen, and a *P30 immunodiffusion test* for a semen-specific glycoprotein, are conducted. Acid phosphatase can be present for up to 72 hours after intercourse. A problem arises, however, whenever the victim has had consensual sex during the two or three days prior to the assault. No method exists for differentiating whether elevated levels of acid phosphatase are remnants of the consensual act or the rape itself.

A search for spermatozoa also is undertaken. Motile sperm can be found in rape survivors for up to about 24 hours after intercourse, but they rarely survive longer than 12 hours. Nonmotile sperm can persist for two or three days. As sperm die off, they initially lose their tails, leaving behind only sperm heads, which can be found for up to seven days after intercourse. So, if the victim states that she last had consensual intercourse three days earlier, finding nonmotile sperm or sperm heads is of little help; however, the presence of motile sperm has nothing to do with that episode and therefore must be related to the rape.

Sperm survive longer in a dead body than they do in a living victim. The reason: Vaginas produce certain chemicals that destroy sperm, but this action stops when the heart stops, so sperm inside a dead body are destroyed only through decomposition. Sperm can be found for up to two weeks in a corpse.

Even if no sperm are found, intercourse cannot be ruled out. The assailant may have used a condom, had a previous vasectomy, failed to ejaculate, or he may be azoospermic. *Azoospermia* is a condition in which no sperm is present in the seminal fluid.

After the examination is complete, the victim's injures are treated, and she is given medications to prevent pregnancy and treat any potential venereal diseases — a wait-and-see attitude has no place in cases involving rape. The victim is tested for HIV immediately, and the test is repeated during the next several months. A rape counselor usually becomes involved immediately to help the victim with the psychological fallout from the assault.

Dealing with fatal assaults

In rape-homicides, many of the same examinations are conducted, except that an ME, rather than a treating physician, performs the examination.

At the lab, the ME initially examines the victim while clothed, looking for trace evidence and stains and attempting to match any defects in the clothing with injuries to the victim. Afterward, the victim's clothing is removed, packaged, and sent to the crime lab for further processing. The ME's attention then turns to the body, following the process outlined in the earlier "Conducting a rape exam" section, and conducting other necessary tests.

Chapter 13

Gasping for Air: Asphyxia

. . . .

In This Chapter

▶ Understanding deaths by asphyxiation

▶ Checking out causes and mechanisms of suffocation

▶ Taking a look at strangulations and hangings

▶ Sniffing out deadly gases

▶ Dealing with drowning deaths

. . . .

*E*ver attempt to hold your breath for two minutes? Try it. It's not as easy as it sounds. Two minutes can seem like an eternity. Now, imagine that you can't breathe. What if something prevented you from taking a breath or the air that you *could* breathe in had no oxygen or was laced with a toxic gas? What if the next breath never came? That's *asphyxia* — when the body's cells can't get oxygen. It can happen in several different ways, each leaving a clue or two for the medical examiner (ME).

Understanding Asphyxia

The air we take into our lungs contains oxygen (O_2). After it's in the lungs' air sacs, the O_2 crosses into the blood, combines with the hemoglobin of the red blood cells, and travels with those red blood cells throughout the body.

Normal air contains approximately 21 percent oxygen. When this percentage drops to 10 to 15 percent, judgment and coordination suffer. You lose consciousness when the O_2 concentrations in the air fall below 10 percent, and death occurs at around 8 percent.

An interruption of the supply of O_2 at any step in its path from the environment to the cells of the body can lead to asphyxia. For example:

✔ **Suffocation:** The air may contain little or no O_2, or something (like a suffocating gas) may prevent that O_2 from reaching the bloodstream.

✔ **Strangulation:** A blockage or obstruction prevents air from entering the airways and the lungs.

> ✔ **Drowning:** The lungs fill with water, thus preventing oxygenation of the blood.
>
> ✔ **Inhalation of toxic chemicals:** Certain toxins can interfere with the uptake of O_2 by the blood or the cells' use of oxygen in the body.

Gasping for Oxygen: Suffocation

You can't see it, and you probably rarely think about it, but oxygen in the air keeps your body operating and your mind at its peak. Whenever you can't get enough oxygen into your bloodstream, suffocation occurs. It may happen because the air has very little O_2 (at the top of Mt. Everest or in a tiny, air-tight, enclosed space) or because some object (a suffocating gas, for example, or a peanut that got stuck in your throat) keeps the O_2 from reaching the lungs and ultimately the bloodstream.

Suffocating environments

Deaths from *environmental suffocation,* which occur when someone cannot get sufficient oxygen from his surroundings (usually in a small space or one in which the air quality is poor), are most often accidental, but homicidal incidences are not unheard of. The classic example of an accidental death from environmental suffocation is a child trapped inside an old refrigerator. With no fresh air available, once the oxygen inside has been consumed, the child dies from asphyxia.

A determination of the cause and manner of death in an environmental suffocation relies on an analysis of the circumstances surrounding the death and on the fact that no other cause of death turned up at autopsy. In other words, if someone finds the victim in an oxygen-poor environment or an airtight enclosure with no evidence of trauma or toxin exposure (and if the medical examiner rules out natural causes), the ME may deem the death an accidental suffocation.

Smothering

Smothering occurs when some external device prevents air from entering the nose or mouth. You can distinguish smothering from choking (see the following section, "Choking sensations," for more about that form of death) because, in smothering, the obstructing material is *outside* the mouth or throat.

Common examples of smothering include the following:

- ✔ Suicidal smothering usually employs a plastic bag, which the individual places over his head and secures with tape or a rope.

- ✔ Plastic bags may also account for accidental smothering, particularly in children. On rare occasions, an intoxicated individual can lose consciousness face down on a pillow and die from smothering.

- ✔ Homicidal smothering usually employs a pillow, bedding, plastic bag, or the killer's own hands. When the killer uses a pillow or a plastic bag, the victim typically has no visible marks unless he struggles, in which case the victim's face or arms may show abrasions or bruises left by the killer's attempts to control the victim.

Choking sensations

Choking results when an obstruction occurs *within* the airways. The cause of death may be natural, homicidal, or accidental.

A natural choking death may result from an acute infection and inflammation of the *epiglottis,* which is the flap at the upper end of the trachea (main airway) that closes to prevent the aspiration of food and water when we swallow. With severe inflammation, the epiglottis can rapidly swell and block the airway. This is a true medical emergency and must be treated immediately, usually with a tracheostomy. This is an incision into the trachea below the larynx (Adam's apple) that creates an alternate pathway for air to reach the lungs.

Diphtheria, which can cause a natural choking death, is now, thanks to widespread immunization programs, rare in the United States. Diphtheria is a bacterial infection of the throat that is associated with the formation of a thick, tenacious pseudomembrane that can peel away from the throat and obstruct the airway.

Homicidal choking deaths also are rare. However, if an assailant gags the victim by placing a sock, cloth, ball, or other object in the victim's mouth before applying the gag, the victim may choke and die. As with deaths from smothering, if the choking device is not found in the victim's mouth or near where the body is found, the ME may not be able to determine the exact cause of death.

Most choking deaths occur accidentally. Children get small objects, such as pieces of balloons, parts of toys, and food materials, into their airway and choke. With adults, the culprit is almost always food. In fact, choking to death on food occurs so commonly that physicians have given it the moniker "Café Coronary." Typically, the victim is eating, suddenly stops talking, perhaps grabs her throat, and collapses. On the surface, it looks like a heart attack, or *coronary*. In reality, the airway is obstructed, the victim can't breathe, the blood oxygen level drops dramatically, and the victim collapses and dies.

With natural and accidental choking deaths, the ME usually has little difficulty in determining the cause of death. However, finding food material within the victim's airway does not absolutely indicate that the victim choked to death. Many individuals who are eating at the time of death suck food into their airways and lungs as they die. Investigators can take a detailed history of what actually happened from witnesses, giving the ME what may be the most useful information in determining the cause of death. If a piece of meat or other firm food product completely obstructs the airway, the ME may be able to state, on that evidence alone, that the victim indeed died from choking.

Applying pressure: Mechanical asphyxia

Mechanical asphyxia results when some external force applied to the body prevents the expansion of the chest and leaves the victim unable to breathe. A person trapped beneath a heavy object, such as a car or a collapsed wall or ceiling, can die because the force of the external pressure prevents the victim from taking in a breath.

CASE STUDY

Suffocation by "Burking"

Experts have come to know a particular form of mechanical suffocation as *Burking*. William Burke was a merchant of sorts around Edinburgh, Scotland, in the early 1800s. In 1827, he hooked up with William Hare, who ran a beggars hotel in the village of Tanners Close. In December of that year, a resident of the hotel died, and Burke arranged to sell the body to a Dr. Knox, who needed corpses for his dissection demonstrations. Burke and Hare loaded a coffin with bark and buried it in front of many witnesses. They then delivered the body to Dr. Knox and received seven pounds and ten shillings. The men struck an arrangement whereby Burke and Hare would deliver the doctor more bodies for eight pounds in summer and ten in winter. (Apparently grave robbing was more difficult when the ground was cold.)

Burke and Hare began digging up fresh corpses for their new enterprise, but the local populace refused to die fast enough for the greedy men. They began kidnapping and killing people who were not likely to be missed. Burke sat on his victims, holding their mouths and noses closed until they suffocated, after which Burke and Hare delivered the corpse and collected their fee.

A lodger at the hotel notified authorities when she discovered the sixteenth and last victim beneath a bed. Police arrested the two men. Hare then cut a deal and testified against Burke. Burke was convicted and experienced asphyxia for himself when he was hanged on January 28, 1829, an event attended by as many as 40,000 people.

A boa constrictor kills in exactly this way. This muscular species of snake wraps itself around its prey. Each time the prey exhales, the snake coils a little tighter. So, each successive breath becomes increasingly shallower until the prey can't take another breath. Death follows quickly.

Suffocating gases

Suffocating gases aren't toxic or poisonous in and of themselves, but their presence diminishes the percentage of the oxygen in the air. Any gas added to air lowers the percentage of oxygen in the air. Room air contains approximately 21 percent oxygen. Whenever you add another gas to the air, it mixes with the gases already there, and the percentage of oxygen available drops in proportion to the amount of gas added. Oxygen levels below 15 percent can lead to lethargy, confusion, disorientation, and ultimately coma and death.

Carbon dioxide and methane are common examples of suffocating gases. Each is nontoxic and odorless. Methane is the principal component of natural gas. By law, an odor is added to household natural gas so that residents can detect leaks.

At autopsy, the ME rarely uncovers specific findings that prove the death was from suffocating gases. However, in methane-related deaths, the crime lab may find high levels of methane in the victim's blood. Carbon dioxide is another story. Because carbon dioxide is normally found in our blood and the blood's carbon dioxide levels often rise around the time of death, the ME may find determining the cause of death impossible when carbon dioxide is the culprit.

Grasping Strangulation

The next time you stand in front of a mirror, take a look at your neck. It's not very big, is it? Yet, it's basically the conduit of life: All communication between the brain and the body passes through the neck by way of the spinal cord, and all the brain's blood supply from the heart must pass through the arteries of the neck. Thus, the neck provides a vital link between brain and body. But it's exposed and vulnerable to injury, both accidental and intentional.

Strangulations are forms of asphyxia in which an outside force compresses the airways and blood vessels of the neck. This compression prevents blood from reaching the brain and air from entering the lungs.

Finding common threads in strangulations

The mechanism of death in most strangulations is *cerebral hypoxia,* which means a low level of oxygen in the brain. Strangulation blocks the airway, preventing the victim from breathing. It also prevents the flow of blood to the brain by blocking the *carotid arteries,* which pass from the aorta to the brain by way of the neck and are the major source of blood supply to the brain. In reality, most strangulation deaths are due to this interruption of blood supply rather than obstruction of air passage. And it can happen very quickly, a fact that is operative in many accidental strangulation deaths.

If you are inspired to feel around for your carotid arteries, be careful: Putting pressure on both carotid arteries at once can cause sudden death by activating a sensitive baroreceptor (pressure receptor) in the arteries that can induce a sudden drop in blood pressure and heart rate and lead to cardiac arrest.

Examiners often find *petechial hemorrhages* in all types of strangulation. Those hemorrhages are caused by blood leaking from ruptured capillaries and appear as small red dots or streaks in the whites of the eyes *(sclera)* and the pink parts around them *(conjunctivae).* These markings appear when the pressure within the veins of the neck rises suddenly and dramatically. This pressure transmits to the capillaries of the eyes, causing them to leak blood.

In many strangulation deaths, the victim's face becomes *congested.* Fluid collects in the tissues, and the face appears swollen and often takes on a dusky hue.

Hands on: Manual strangulation

Manual strangulation occurs when someone applies pressure to the victim's neck with a hand, forearm, or other limb, compressing the airway and the carotid arteries. The ME may be able to uncover any of several indications of manual strangulation:

✔ **Contusions:** The pressure from the assailant's fingers and thumbs may leave bruises in the shape of fingers or, more often, round bruises that match the tips of the fingers and the pads of the thumb. The ME typically finds these bruises on the sides of the victim's neck, but not always. If the assailant is facing the victim, he may use both hands and press his thumbs into the recesses where the carotid arteries lie. In this case, the major bruising appears on either side of the *trachea* (wind pipe), with smaller finger bruises on either side or the back of the victim's neck.

- **Abrasions:** The assailant's fingernails can cause abrasions on the victim's skin. Because assailants tend to use the tips of their fingers to grip the victim's neck, their nails may dig into or scratch the victim's flesh. If the assailants' nails aren't closely clipped, abrasions may appear as linear scratches or as thin, semicircular or linear marks where the nails "dug into" the victim's flesh.

- **Injuries to the neck:** Because most assailants use a great deal more force than they need to, they may cause injury to the neck muscles. The ME often finds bleeding in these muscles at autopsy. Also, the assailant often injures the small bones of the neck. Fractures of the *cornu* (horn) of the *thyroid cartilage* (Adam's apple) and the tiny *hyoid bone* (a delicate C-shaped bone above the thyroid cartilage) often occur in manual assaults.

When the police locate a suspect, they need to examine the suspect carefully for signs of injury. Victims often put up a fight and scratch or bruise their attacker. The ME typically sees such injuries on the assailant's fingers, hands, forearms, and face. If the attacker committed a rape-strangulation, the ME may find scratches along the attacker's flanks or back.

Another form of manual strangulation is the *chokehold,* often employed by law enforcement officers to subdue a combative subject. The purpose of the chokehold is to collapse the carotid arteries and render the subject unconscious. Two forms exist:

- **Bar arm hold:** The officer places one forearm across the front of the subject's throat and, using the other hand, grasps the wrist and pulls back, applying forearm pressure to the subject's neck. The officer may use a baton rather than a forearm to apply the pressure.

- **Carotid hold:** The officer places the crook of one elbow against the center of the subject's neck, and again grasps the wrist and pulls back. This produces a pincher or scissors effect, which occludes (blocks) the two carotid arteries.

Both of these maneuvers are dangerous and should never be performed by anyone who has not been trained to use them. The unconsciousness is caused by a restriction of blood flow to the brain, which, if applied too aggressively for too long, can lead to death or permanent brain injury. Police officers use these holds as a last resort to restrain extremely violent or uncontrollable people.

The ME often becomes involved in situations where these holds have been used and a police brutality complaint is filed. If too much force is used, the thyroid cartilage and the hyoid can fracture, and bleeding can occur in the strap muscles of the neck. In either a living or deceased subject, the ME must evaluate the injuries and develop an opinion.

Applying a ligature

Ligature strangulation occurs when someone tightens a constricting band around the neck. The tightening comes from some force other than the victim's own body weight, as occurs in hanging (see the following section, "Hangings," for an explanation of the difference). Essentially all ligature strangulations are homicides.

If the ligature is soft, such as a towel or bed sheet, it may not leave marks on the neck, though some bruising is not uncommon. A thin ligature, such as an electrical cord, leaves a deep groove or furrow in the tissue of the victim's neck. This furrow's deep impression matches the width of the particular ligature used. Not uncommonly, the ME sees associated bruises and abrasions on the victim's neck. How many of these bruises and abrasions occur and how prominent they are depend on how fiercely and successfully the victim struggles against the attacker. Occasionally, these associated abrasions and bruises reveal the pattern of the ligature used.

Even in severely decomposed corpses, the ligature mark can be preserved. Apparently, the severe compression of the tissues within the furrow closes off the blood vessels underneath. The bacteria that cause a body to decompose tend to migrate through the blood vessels after death. Because the vessels in the furrow have been damaged and bacteria can't pass easily through them, the number of bacteria that reach the area lessens, and thus the putrefaction process within the furrow slows.

The ligature furrow in ligature strangulations tends to be directed horizontally around the neck. Whether the assailant is facing the victim or approaching from behind, the ligature is tightened by pulling laterally on its ends.

At autopsy, the ME examines the victim's hands and nails since hair clutched in the victim's hand and blood and tissue from the assailant beneath the fingernails may be found.

Suicide by ligature strangulation is rare, but it's not unheard of. Because loss of consciousness in ligature strangulations is predominantly due to carotid compression, it can arrive quickly, often in as little as 15 seconds. But, this still gives the victim time to secure the ligature in place by either tying a knot or by wrapping the cord around several times, the overlapping loops securing the ligature in place.

Accidental ligature strangulation is also rare. It typically occurs when a scarf, tie, or other article of clothing becomes entangled in a piece of machinery or a moving vehicle. These accidents often involve ski lifts, elevators, motorcycles, or cars.

Isadora Duncan's famous scarf

Isadora Duncan was famous, an icon in the dance world, and is credited with inventing modern dance. She was also known for the long silk scarves she was fond of wearing. This fashion statement led to her death when, on September 14, 1927, in Nice, France, her scarf became entangled in the wheels of a moving convertible sports car (rumored to be a Bugatti), strangling her.

Hangings

In hangings, asphyxia results from the compression of the airways and the carotid arteries by a noose or other ligature pulled tight by the body's weight. Thus, the victim must be completely or partially suspended. Hangings are almost always suicidal. Most accidental hangings occur in children when they find themselves tangled in a rope or clothing and in a position of complete or partial suspension.

Though hanging compresses the airway and interrupts breathing, the real cause of death in most hangings is compression of the carotid arteries, which blocks blood flow to the brain. Fractures of the *cervical vertebrae* (spinal bones of the neck) happen rarely in hanging deaths, except in judicial hangings, because these fractures require that the body drop a sufficient distance to break them.

In cases of death by hanging, the ME is likely to find the following evidence:

- ✔ **Neck markings:** The neck markings that you see after a hanging depend mainly on the nature of the noose used. Soft nooses, such as sheets, may leave little or no markings. A rope or cord may leave a very deep, distinct furrow in the victim's neck. The longer the body hangs, the deeper the furrow.

- ✔ **Furrow pattern:** In hangings, the furrow has an inverted V pattern. The furrow tends to run diagonally across the neck with its high end at the knot.

- ✔ **Facial changes:** If found several hours after the hanging, the victim's face may be pale, and the tongue may be dark purple and protrude from the mouth. At autopsy, the ME doesn't usually find facial congestion or petechial hemorrhages (see the section "Finding common threads in strangulations," earlier in this chapter, for the details on these reactions) that commonly appear in manual and ligature strangulations.

- ✔ **Lividity:** If lividity appears, it does so in the legs, forearms, and hands. Check out Chapter 11 for more about lividity.

Dying for pleasure: Autoerotic asphyxia

Some people are willing to die for a good time. Autoerotic or sexual asphyxia, in which a person (usually a male) combines strangulation and masturbation, is proof positive.

These misguided adventurers bank on the idea that partial asphyxia somehow accentuates sexual enjoyment. One of the first symptoms of cerebral hypoxia (low oxygen in the brain) is giddiness, and the people who perform this act believe that this sensation accentuates sexual arousal.

Most often, hanging is the method of choice, but nonhanging ligatures and plastic bags also have been used. The victim rigs up a situation where the rope or chosen ligature compresses the neck on demand. This method of masturbation often involves some form of self-rescue device. The victim may be able to move a certain way to relieve pressure or have an instrument with which to cut a ligature or slice open a bag.

Unfortunately, miscalculations can lead to tragedy. Cerebral hypoxia causes poor judgment and coordination, poor assessment of the level of hypoxia, and sudden loss of consciousness. Once unconsciousness occurs, the victim can't save himself.

Officials typically find a male victim, partially suspended by a hanging noose. At times, his hands are bound, which brings up the possibility of a homicide staged to look like an accidental death. But the victim may have used such binding as part of the ritual. An examination of the bindings may reveal whether the victim could have bound himself or not.

✔ **Drugs or alcohol:** The ME should perform a toxicological analysis on all victims of hanging. An assailant may have used drugs or alcohol to subdue the victim in a homicidal hanging, and a suicide victim may have taken alcohol or drugs in order to get the courage to do himself in.

Here, the ME may be able to determine whether the level of drugs and alcohol found in the victim was enough to knock him out or merely enough to impair his judgment. In most cases, making this call isn't easy.

Inhaling Deadly Air: Toxic Gases

Here's a terrifying thought for you: The very air you breathe can kill you. Chances are good that it never will, but if ever you encounter a toxic gas, breathing becomes not a life-giving but a life-taking exercise.

Toxic gases wreak havoc not by keeping oxygen from entering your lungs and bloodstream (as suffocating gases do) but by keeping your blood or body tissues from making use of that oxygen. Carbon monoxide (CO), cyanide, and the combination of hydrogen sulfide, CO, and methane (known as *sewer gas*) are common toxic gases.

That sneaky carbon monoxide

Carbon monoxide is sneaky and deadly. When authorities find a suicide victim in her garage, sitting in a car with the engine running, they can usually chalk up that death to carbon monoxide.

Carbon monoxide is a tasteless, odorless, colorless gas that is completely undetectable by humans. It results from the incomplete combustion of carbon-containing fuels like wood, coal, and gas. Faulty stoves, heaters, and fireplaces can fill the air with CO. Carbon monoxide poisoning kills more people trapped in fires than the fire itself does.

CO is particularly treacherous because it binds to hemoglobin, producing carboxyhemoglobin in your blood. Because carboxyhemoglobin contains no usable oxygen, cells containing this molecule can't supply oxygen to the tissues of the body. Thus, the body's cells become starved for oxygen. Carbon monoxide binds to hemoglobin 300 times more readily than oxygen does and thus takes oxygen's place in the body. Your body can get very high blood levels of CO by breathing air that contains only small amounts of it. For example, breathing air that contains a carbon monoxide level as low as 0.2 percent can lead to blood CO saturations greater than 60 percent after only 30 to 45 minutes.

Most people believe that CO is toxic only in an enclosed area, but that's just not true. People have died while working on their cars in the open air; typically, someone finds the victim lying near the car's exhaust. Similarly, swimmers and water skiers who loiter near the dive platform on the back of an idling powerboat also run the risk of CO poisoning. Carbon monoxide's powerful attraction to hemoglobin explains how people can succumb to CO poisoning in open areas.

The signs and symptoms of CO toxicity correlate with its concentration in the blood:

- The normal level of CO in the blood is 1 to 3 percent, but it can be as high as 7 to 10 percent in smokers.
- At levels of 10 to 20 percent, you experience headaches and a poor ability to concentrate on complex tasks.
- Between 30 and 40 percent, headaches become severe and throbbing, and nausea, vomiting, faintness, and lethargy appear. Pulse and breathing rate increase noticeably.
- Between 40 and 60 percent, the victim becomes confused, disoriented, weak, and displays extremely poor coordination.
- Above 60 percent, coma and death arrive.

In the elderly and those individuals with heart or lung disease, levels as low as 20 percent can be lethal. Victims of car exhaust suicide or those who die from fire in an enclosed room may reach CO levels as high as 90 percent.

Autopsy findings in CO poisoning depend, in part, on carboxyhemoglobin's bright red color. When the ME performs an autopsy on a victim of CO poisoning, the blood and internal organs often appear bright red, and this offers a clue to the possible cause of death.

Individuals who survive CO intoxication can suffer serious health problems. Carbon monoxide mostly damages the brain because it's the organ most sensitive to a lack of oxygen. Symptoms and signs of significant brain insult may begin immediately or be delayed for several days or weeks. The most common after-effects include chronic headaches, memory loss, blindness, confusion, disorientation, poor coordination, and hallucinations. The ME may be asked to evaluate a surviving victim if authorities suspect that the exposure was the result of a criminal act or they want documentation for a civil lawsuit.

Deadly cyanide

I'm sure you've read books and seen movies in which some nasty character uses cyanide to commit murder. In fact, few people use cyanide as a murder device. More people use it for suicide, particularly mass suicides. Individual and group accidental poisoning can occur in industrial settings. Technicians use cyanide salts in metal electroplating, jewelry making, and X-ray recovery industries. The plastic manufacturing industry uses solvents called *nitriles*, which contain cyanide. When burned, these nitriles can release deadly hydrogen cyanide gas.

CASE STUDY

Jim Jones and the People's Temple

Jim Jones was a fundamentalist Christian pastor who established his People's Temple in the 1950s in Indianapolis, Indiana, before relocating to the San Francisco area. Because of his claims that he could cure cancer, heart disease, and other maladies, he drew scrutiny and criticism. When suspicions arose about many of Jones's financial dealings, he moved his followers from the United States to the makeshift town of Jonestown, Guyana.

Rumors of human rights abuses followed him and attracted the attention of some members of the U.S. Congress. In 1978, Congressman Leo Ryan and members of the press visited Jonestown and talked with many of the

People's Temple members, 16 of whom asked to leave with the Congressman and return to the United States. As the departing members and Congressman Ryan awaited a plane at Port Kiatuma Airport, they were ambushed by several of the Temple's security guards. Congressman Ryan and four others were killed, and 11 people were wounded.

Soon after that incident, Jones fed his congregation a fruit drink laced with cyanide and the sedatives Valium and chloral hydrate. More than 900 people died, including more than 250 children. Toxicological testing of the drink and of fluids taken from the deceased proved that cyanide was the culprit.

Hydrogen cyanide gas is the most deadly form of cyanide. Ingesting cyanide salts such as sodium and potassium cyanide produces hydrogen cyanide gas when those powders react with the acids in the stomach. Gas chamber executions use hydrogen cyanide.

Cyanide is a deadly *metabolic poison,* which means that it prevents the body's cells from using oxygen, thus causing the cells to die rapidly. The body acts as if all the oxygen had been suddenly removed. The oxygen is still there, of course, but the cells can't use it. And because the cells no longer extract the needed oxygen from the blood, the blood remains very well oxygenated (rich in *oxyhemoglobin*) and thus bright red.

At autopsy, the ME can see that the blood of the victim is bright red and not the expected dark purple, thus suspecting cyanide or carbon monoxide as the cause of death. Also, any lividity may be pinkish, rather than the usual blue-gray hue, which likewise suggests cyanide or CO poisoning. In addition, the ME may detect the typical bitter almond odor of hydrogen cyanide — that is, if he is capable. Curiously, the ability to detect this odor is genetically determined. Some people can while others can't.

Getting down with sewer gas

Hydrogen sulfide is a byproduct of fermentation and is typically found in sewers and cesspools. Chemists call the combination of hydrogen sulfide, carbon monoxide, and methane *sewer gas.* When you inhale this sewer gas, the hydrogen sulfide takes oxygen's seat on your hemoglobin (much like carbon monoxide does, which I describe in the earlier section "That sneaky carbon monoxide"), and your cells can't get the oxygen they need. Hemoglobin with this gas attached adds a dark purple color to the blood. Sewer gas deaths are almost always accidental and occur when the victim enters an area rich in sewer gas and succumbs to the hydrogen sulfide. At autopsy, the ME finds high levels of sulfide in the victim's blood.

Drowning: Water, Water Everywhere

Drowning is a common fear and a decidedly unpleasant way to go. As you drown, your lungs fill with water, and they lose their ability to transfer oxygen into the bloodstream. While you struggle to breathe, you force water into your sinuses. Coughing triggers an inhalation reflex, which pulls even more water into the lungs. The loss of an air supply combines with the energy you consume in the struggle for survival, and the oxygen level in the blood rapidly falls. You lose consciousness in one to two minutes. The heart stops shortly thereafter.

Finding the manner of death

Drowning is almost always accidental. But MEs often have a difficult time determining the manner of death. Indeed, concluding that the victim actually drowned mostly comes as a diagnosis of exclusion, meaning that the ME starts by determining what *didn't* happen.

The circumstances of the death are often more important than any physical findings. If the ME can't find any evidence of trauma or natural disease to explain the death, and if the victim is found in water, the ME may determine that the death was from drowning. No pathological findings at autopsy can definitely say one way or the other.

Even the finding of *pulmonary edema* (water-filled lungs) doesn't prove drowning because pulmonary edema can occur with deaths from heart attacks and some drug overdoses. If a victim died from a drug overdose and was dumped into water or the person suffered a heart attack and developed *severe secondary pulmonary edema* (water in the lungs arises when a failing heart causes increased pressure in the lung vessels), the autopsy findings may look identical to those of someone who truly drowned. For this reason, the ME should perform a complete toxicological analysis on all suspected drowning victims.

Experts once believed that a classic finding in victims of drowning was a thick, white, or blood-tinged foam in the mouth, throat, and trachea. However, this finding has little evidence to support it, so most modern investigators have dismissed it.

Diving deeper to identify drownings

Drownings are a complicated business for the ME. In fact, the ME may not be able to determine whether the victim was dead or alive when he entered the water. If you place a corpse in water, and it remains submerged for a period of time after death, the lungs passively fill with water, and the ME's examination can't distinguish this postmortem fluid in the lungs from liquid that resulted in death.

As many as 15 percent of drownings can be *dry drownings*. In this situation, the intake of water into the throat causes *laryngeal spasm*. The larynx reacts to the water by *spasming* (constricting or closing). This reaction shuts down the passage of air into the lungs, and the victim asphyxiates. This spasm also prevents water from entering the lungs, so the lungs are dry at autopsy.

But the ME has a few tricks to help him. Finding some or all of the following evidence points the investigation in the direction of drowning:

- **Hemorrhaging:** If a conscious victim enters the water, the struggle to breathe causes a great deal of pressure trauma to the sinuses and the lungs. The ME expects to find *hemorrhaging* (bleeding) into the sinuses and airways, as well as debris from the water, which the victim sucks into the sinuses and lungs while attempting to breathe.

- **Souvenirs from the sea:** Plants or rocks from the bottom of the body of water clutched in the victim's hand may indicate that the victim grabbed them during the struggle to survive. Sort of like grasping for straws.

- **Tiny invaders in the bone marrow:** Though controversial, a search for *diatoms* may indicate whether the victim was alive or not at the time he entered the water. Diatoms are tiny, single-celled organisms that scurry around in salt water and fresh water (diatoms also turn up in many fire investigations — turn to Chapter 8 to find out more). They have silica in their cell walls and are thus very resistant to degradation.

Until cardiac action ceases, any inhaled diatoms pass through the lungs, enter the bloodstream, and are pumped throughout the body. They tend to collect in the bone marrow. Microscopic analysis of the marrow can reveal diatoms, meaning the victim was alive after entering the water, instead of being placed there after death. Because these diatoms are so hardy, this technique is useful for evaluating severely degraded and even skeletal remains, where no lung or sinus tissues are available for examination.

Part IV
Utilizing the Crime Lab

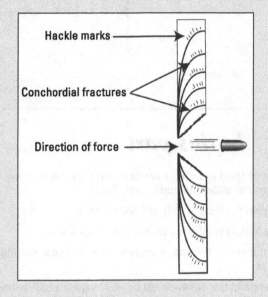

Hackle marks

Conchordial fractures

Direction of force

In this part . . .

- Become familiar with the world of serology, which is the analysis of blood and other bodily fluids.

- Discover the ins and outs of DNA analysis.

- Get a look at what goes on in a toxicology lab.

- Find out more about trace evidence and its use in solving crimes.

- Understand the evidence left behind by guns and firearms.

- Become a skeptic and begin to question the validity of documents.

Chapter 14

Analyzing Blood and Other Bodily Fluids: Serology

In This Chapter

▶ Having a look at what blood is

▶ Discovering forensic uses for blood

▶ Testing for paternity using blood types

▶ Reviewing forensic uses for other bodily fluids

Your identity shows up in more than your driver's license. Blood, sweat, and tears are just a few of the bodily fluids that investigators can use to determine a suspect's or victim's identity through a science called *serology*. These biological fluids are frequently found at the scenes of crimes, particularly violent crimes, and can serve not only to link a suspect to the scene but to identify an individual with a degree of certainty that matches or surpasses fingerprints. This degree of individuality is also useful in cases of questioned paternity and ancestry.

Blood: Life's Most Precious Fluid

Blood is by far the most common bodily fluid left at a crime scene, and it's the most useful, because it opens up many avenues of investigation for the forensics team. Some of these avenues depend upon how blood stains and spatters (see Chapter 6), and others depend upon blood's chemical components and biological behaviors.

Serologists conduct chemical and biological tests on blood samples retrieved from crime scenes with an ultimate goal of determining who the blood came from. That kind of information can tightly link a suspect to the scene or indicate that the suspect was far away when the crime occurred. It can determine whether the blood on a suspect's sock belongs to the victim or whether the blood found beneath the victim's fingernails is that of the suspect or someone else. The coroner uses the science of serology to make these determinations.

Understanding blood

Blood is a complex substance. The liquid portion of whole blood, called *plasma*, contains proteins, enzymes, clotting factors, electrolytes, and various types of cells. Blood cells come in three basic types:

- ✔ **Leucocytes,** or white blood cells (WBCs)
- ✔ **Erythrocytes,** or red blood cells (RBCs)
- ✔ **Platelets,** or tiny cells involved in blood clotting

Whenever whole blood is permitted to clot, and the clotted material is removed, the remaining yellowish liquid is called *serum*. Serum contains most of the proteins and enzymes of plasma, but none of the cells or clotting factors that were consumed during the clotting process.

Blood typing: The ABO system

From a forensic serologist's point of view, the two most important components of blood are the RBCs and the serum. From these, serologists can determine the blood type of any blood samples or bloodstains.

The RBCs contain extremely important molecules called *antigens,* which not only instigate immune reactions within the body but also determine blood type. Antigens are designated as either *A* or *B*. People with Type *A* blood have *A* antigens on their RBCs, and those with Type *B* blood have B antigens. People with Type *AB* have A and B antigens, and RBCs of people with Type *O* blood have neither antigen.

Another antigen in the blood is called the *Rhesus* or *Rh factor,* which sometimes is referred to as the *D* antigen. If your RBCs have these antigens, your blood is deemed *Rh positive,* and if they don't, *Rh negative.* So those with *A*-positive blood possess the *A* antigen and the Rh (D) antigen on their RBCs. People who have *O*-negative blood have neither the *A* or *B*, nor the Rh antigens on their RBCs.

Another important factor to keep in mind is that blood serum contains specialized proteins called *antibodies.* The key point in understanding blood typing is that for every antigen there is a corresponding antibody. An *antibody* is highly specific, meaning that it recognizes and reacts with only its specific antigen. When an antibody meets its corresponding antigen, the two combine to form an *antigen-antibody complex.* This reaction is the basis for the blood-typing procedure.

Serologists test each crime-scene blood sample separately and determine its type. At crime scenes where more than one person sheds blood, such blood-typing helps investigators reconstruct the crime scene. Blood typing was critical to crime-scene reconstruction in the Jeffrey MacDonald case (see Chapter 20).

Identifying a Bloodstain's Source

Forget about identifying the victim or suspect for the moment; identifying a bloodstain is plenty challenging. Depending upon its age and the conditions to which it has been exposed, a bloodstain may look more like a purple paint splotch or a brown grease stain. Even an experienced eye can have a hard time differentiating between blood and, say, dried ketchup.

Whenever the ME and the serologist confront a liquid sample or a stain that might be blood, they work to answer these three questions:

- ✔ Is it blood?
- ✔ Is it human blood?
- ✔ Whose blood is it?

Blood must be found in sufficient amounts and in good-enough condition for it to be useful in testing. Although modern techniques make testing even minute amounts of blood possible, if a sample is severely degraded, it may prove useless. Many chemicals can damage blood to the point that typing and DNA profiling can't be performed. *Putrefaction,* or decay caused by bacterial activity within the cells, is another factor that can degrade a sample beyond repair. Because warmth and moisture promote bacterial growth, putrefaction proceeds much more rapidly under warm and wet conditions.

Most crime-scene samples that reach the serologist are dried and degraded at least to some degree. Dried samples have advantages and disadvantages. Although liquid blood typically offers more useful DNA samples, it's more likely to be degraded or decayed because bacteria that putrefy the blood and tissues thrive in moist environments. Dried samples, on the other hand, lessen bacterial growth and are less likely to degrade.

Answering the first question: Is it blood?

To determine whether a given sample actually is blood (or some other substance), the serologist conducts tests of two basic types: presumptive and confirmatory. *Presumptive tests* typically are cheaper and faster. When they are positive, presumptive tests indicate a likelihood that blood is present but don't establish that as fact. *Confirmatory testing* then is needed to be certain. When presumptive tests are negative, blood is not present, and the more expensive and time-consuming confirmatory tests can be avoided.

Presumptive tests

Presumptive tests for blood fall into two broad categories: those that yield a color reaction and those that cause a fluorescent (glowing) reaction.

Tests that rely on a color change include the following:

- **Kastle-Meyer Color Test:** *Phenolphthalein* is the active compound in the Kastle-Meyer Color Test. When blood, phenolphthalein, and hydrogen peroxide mix, hemoglobin (the oxygen-carrying molecule in red blood cells) causes the peroxide to react with the phenolphthalein, producing a dark pink color.

    The major advantage of the Kastle-Meyer test is that the reaction is quick; the color change appears within a minute or two. The major disadvantage, however, is that certain vegetable products, such as potatoes and horseradish, also can cause the reaction to occur. Of course, potatoes and horseradish are not typically found at scenes where blood has been shed.

- **Tetramethylbenzidine (TMB):** The presumed bloodstain is sampled with a moistened cotton-tipped swab and then applied to a Hemastix strip (a dipstick used to test for the presence of blood) that contains TMB, which undergoes a color-changing chemical reaction in the presence of blood. If the strip immediately turns blue-green, blood may be present.

- **Leucomalachite green (LMG):** Available since the early 1900s, this substance also undergoes a chemical reaction with blood, producing a characteristic green color.

Other tests rely on reactions that cause blood to fluoresce, or glow, under ultraviolet light, revealing blood that can't be seen with the naked eye. Perpetrators often attempt to scrub walls and floors clean, erroneously assuming that if blood can't be seen, it can't be found. Fortunately, that isn't true.

At the crime scene, blood can be revealed by spraying a fluorescent chemical over the area thought to contain blood. The lights are lowered, and an ultraviolet light source is directed over the area, causing the bloodstains to literally glow in the dark. Not only is the likely presence of blood established, but the area of its distribution also is clearly defined. Spurts, spatters, drag marks, and foot- and handprints jump into view.

The following are the most common fluorescent chemicals used:

- **Luminol** is extremely sensitive and can reveal blood that is present in extremely small amounts — even as little as one part per 10 million or less. Luminol also is capable of exposing blood in areas that have been thoroughly cleaned (unless cleansers with chlorine bleach were used), and even on walls that have been painted over. Although it can interfere with some serologic testing procedures, luminol doesn't affect later typing or DNA analysis.

- **Fluorescein** has been around since the early 1900s. Fluorescein doesn't react with household bleach the way luminol does, and that makes fluorescein better suited for exposing bloodstains that have been cleaned up using products that contain bleach. Another advantage of fluorescein is that it's a thicker liquid than luminol, so it tends to drip less, meaning that it sticks better to walls, doors, and other vertical surfaces.

Confirmatory tests

The most commonly used confirmatory tests are the Teichmann and Takayama tests. Both rely on a reaction between a chemical and the hemoglobin molecule found within the RBCs. This reaction results in the formation of crystals, which then are viewed under a microscope. A major advantage of these tests is that they work well with older stains. More recently the Rapid Stain Identification of Human Blood (RSID) test has been employed. This test is more easily and rapidly performed, is more reliable, and can be used with other biological fluids such as saliva and semen.

Knowing when blood's really human

When blood is found at a crime scene, the ME then must determine whether the blood is indeed from a human and not from a dog or cat — or a duck-billed platypus, for that matter. Only after this determination is made can further testing be carried out to discover whose blood it is.

Understanding immunological reactions

Antigen-antibody immunological reactions are part of your body's defense against foreign invaders. The antigen is the foreign invader, and the antibody is the protein that your body constructs to attack the antigen invader. When these two substances react with one another, they *agglutinate,* or clump, producing a large complex that *precipitates* (turns to a solid and falls out of solution [as opposed to being dissolved within the liquid blood]). The precipitate then is gobbled up by the white blood cells of the body and destroyed.

For example, if a bacterium or virus invades your body, your body's immune system recognizes it as foreign and then constructs antibodies against it. In this case, the bacterium plays the role of an antigen, and the antibody attaches to it, forming a large antigen-antibody complex that is easily consumed by the white blood cells. This important reaction to infection helps your body fend off its attackers and return to a healthy state.

Antibodies are very specific. That is, the antibody your body builds to ward off a staphylococcus bacterium recognizes and attaches to only staphylococci and not to streptococci, rhinoviruses, or tuberculosis bacteria. This specificity is at the heart of the tests used for determining the species of blood samples.

Tests used for finding out which species blood came from are antigen-antibody reactions, like the ones used for blood typing (see the earlier section "Blood typing: The ABO system"). The difference, however, is that an *antiserum* (a substance that contains antibodies against a specific antigen) must be created that reacts with antigens specific to humans rather than with the *A* and *B* RBC antigens. That means a specific antibody to a specific human antigen is created so that the resulting reaction, or lack of one, will determine whether the blood is human.

A human antiserum is prepared by injecting human antigen (human blood) into a rabbit or other animal and then allowing enough time for the animal to produce sufficient antibodies against the antigen. The animal's blood, now rich in antihuman antibodies, is removed, and that antiserum is isolated for use in testing blood samples to determine whether they are from humans.

If a solution that contains an antiserum is brought into contact with a blood sample that contains the antigen it was designed to react against, a reaction occurs. This reaction produces an antigen-antibody complex that precipitates or falls out of solution and results in a visible line of precipitation settling out where the two solutions come into contact.

In other words, if an antiserum to human blood comes into contact with a solution that contains human blood, the reaction forms a visible line of precipitant or solid material between the two solutions. If, on the other hand, the blood is not human, no reaction occurs, and no line is created.

The modern crime lab contains antiserums to a variety of common animal bloods. Dog, cat, deer, cow, and sheep antiserums usually are readily available. Using these antiserums, a serologist can determine the species that shed the blood, a factor that can be important evidence in and of itself.

Narrowing the focus: Whose blood is it?

After determining that a blood sample is human, the serologist sets about determining its type. Standard blood typing uses liquid blood, and a positive reaction is indicated by agglutination, or clumping, of the RBCs. Agglutination can occur only if the blood is liquid and if the RBCs are intact.

However, crime-scene blood rarely is liquid; it's more likely to be a stain — that is, clotted and dried — and the RBCs therefore have fragmented. Because the RBCs are not intact, they can't agglutinate, and thus no antigen-antiserum typing reaction can be verified. The serologist cleverly gets around this problem with a technique that draws out the remaining antigens.

Absorption-elution is the process that extracts the antigens in these four steps:

1. **The bloodstained material is treated with blood antiserums.**

   The antibodies in the antiserums combine with the antigens.

2. **The material is washed.**

   This step removes any excess antiserum-containing antibodies.

3. **The sample undergoes elution.**

   Elution is a process that breaks down antigen-antibody bonds by heating them, thus freeing the antigen and the antibodies from one another. The antibodies that were bound to the antigens are washed off.

4. **The eluted antibodies then are tested against known blood antigens, and their reactions are observed.**

   The antigens the antibodies react with reveal which antigens are present in the original unknown sample.

A serologist confronted with a bloodstained shirt determines that the blood is human and goes through the steps in the previous list. If the stain is from someone with Type *A* blood, when the anti-*A* and anti-*B* serums are added in the first step, the blood from the stain reacts only with the anti-*A* antibodies because it has only *A* antigens. After washing (Step 2), only the complex of *A* antigens and the anti-*A* antibodies remains. Elution (Step 3) further separates the antigens and antibodies, thus freeing the anti-*A* antibodies from the stain. Testing the antibodies against blood samples from known blood types then reveals to the serologist a reaction with only Type *A* blood, meaning that the original sample must have been Type *A*.

By simply typing the blood at a crime scene, investigators narrow their suspect list and completely exonerate some suspects by using the population distribution information for the four ABO blood types in Table 14-1.

Table 14-1	Population Distribution of ABO Blood Types
Blood Type	*Population Percentage with Blood Type*
O	43%
A	42%
B	12%
AB	3%

Besides determining the ABO type, serologists are able to further individualize blood samples. RBCs contain more proteins, enzymes, and antigens than those used in the ABO classification system. These include antigens with such catchy names as Duffy, Kell, and Kidd and intracellular enzymes such as adenylate kinase, erythrocyte acid phosphatase, and the very useful *phosphoglucomutase* (PGM).

PGM is an enzyme that appears in many different forms, or *isoenzymes,* and at least ten of them are fairly common. Regardless of ABO type, a particular individual can have any combination of the isoenzymes of PGM. The ME and the serologist use that fact to further narrow the list of suspects for further DNA analyses and confirmation that they were capable of leaving a particular bloodstain.

For example, say that a stain is Type *AB* and has PGM 2. The ME knows the AB blood type is found in only 3 percent (see Table 14-1) of the population, and PGM 2 is found in only 6 percent of people. Because these two factors are inherited independently, the probability of a particular individual being Type *AB*, PGM 2 is only 0.18 percent or less than 2 per 1,000.

If the police find blood at the scene that matches the blood of a suspect who has Type *AB*, PGM 2 blood, the probability that that suspect is not the perpetrator is 2 in 1,000. Although not perfect, those odds still are much better than a coin toss. DNA testing, which I discuss in Chapter 15, then is used to further individualize the sample.

Testing for Paternity

You inherit your blood type from your parents. For that reason, a serologist can assess paternity in many cases. The crime lab is often involved in paternity testing because paternity may be a critical component in determining child support, custody, and visitation. It also may play an important role in crimes and civil proceedings that involve kidnappings, insurance fraud, and inheritance conflicts.

Inheriting your blood type

ABO blood types, or *phenotypes,* come in only four varieties: *A, B, AB,* and *O.* But, for some blood types two *genotypes,* or gene pairings, are possible. A phenotype is what something looks like (in this case the ABO blood type), while the genotype is the underlying genetic pattern. We receive our ABO genes from our parents, one from Dad and one from Mom.

The important thing to know in this system is that *A* and *B* genes are codominant (equally dominant), while the *O* gene is recessive. So someone who receives an *A* gene from one parent and an *O* gene from the other has Type *A* blood, but not Type *O,* because the *A* gene is dominant (see Table 14-2).

Table 14-2	Determining Possible Genotypes from Phenotypes
Phenotype	*Possible Genotypes*
A	AA or AO
B	BB or BO
AB	AB
O	OO

People with Type *O* blood must have an *OO* genotype. They can have neither an *A* nor a *B* gene because having one or the other dominates the *O* gene and produces either Type *A* or Type *B* blood.

A person with Type *A* blood can either receive an *A* gene from each parent and thus have an *AA* genotype or an *A* gene from one parent and an *O* gene from the other for an *AO* genotype. Remember, *A* is dominant, so when it is paired with the recessive *O* gene, the *A* gene determines blood type. People with the *AA* and *AO* genotypes both have Type *A* blood, but genetically speaking, they're different.

Type *A* parents who have *AA* genotypes can provide only *A* genes to their offspring, because all their eggs or sperm have an *A* gene. But Type *A* parents who have *AO* genotypes can provide either an *A* gene or an *O* gene to their offspring, because half their eggs or sperm have an *A* gene, and the other half have an *O* gene. When both parents are Type *A*, several possibilities exist for the genotype their offspring will have. Check out the possibilities in the Punnet Squares in Figure 14-1.

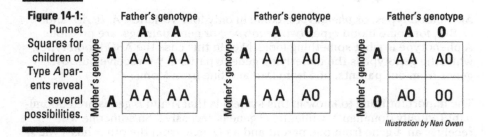

Figure 14-1:
Punnet Squares for children of Type *A* parents reveal several possibilities.

Illustration by Nan Owen

In each of the scenarios presented in Figure 14-1, the child's blood type is Type *A*, except when both parents donate an *O* gene. In the latter case, the child's genotype and blood type (phenotype) respectively are *OO* and Type *O*. These parents can't have any offspring who have Type *B* phenotype or *BB*, *BO*, or *AB* genotypes, because neither parent has a *B* gene to donate.

Determining fatherhood

Blood typing can exclude paternity but cannot absolutely verify it. For example, a man with Type *AB* blood can't father a child with Type *O* blood. So if a child has Type *O* blood, all men with the Type *AB* are ruled out as the child's father. A man with Type *A* (genotypes *AA* or *AO*) blood can be the father, but only if he has an *AO* genotype. Men who have *AA* genotypes also are excluded. Men with the *AO* genotype, however, can't be ruled out at this point.

Another genetic marker, the inherited *human leukocyte antigen* (HLA), is used for paternity testing. If a man and child share the same HLA markers, the probability that the man is the child's father is 90 percent. When testing combines HLA and ABO typing with another genetic marker known as *haptoglobin,* the probability approaches 95 percent.

However, DNA matching (see Chapter 15), which offers 99 percent certainty, when properly administered, is the gold standard for assessing paternity.

Looking at Other Bodily Fluids

Blood isn't the only bodily fluid that can lead crime-scene analysts to a criminal. Semen, saliva, and, in rare cases, vaginal fluid may hold the key to solving a crime. During sexual assaults, semen and saliva commonly are transferred to the victim, the victim's clothing, or nearby surfaces. Saliva can be obtained from food, a cigarette butt, or even from the stamp and envelope of a threatening letter.

The first step in locating these bodily fluids is an examination of the crime scene with either an ultraviolet or laser light source, which causes the fluids to fluoresce, or glow.

These materials must be carefully collected and preserved, because as moist, biological materials, they are susceptible to putrefaction from bacterial growth.

Checking for semen

At the scene of a sexual assault, the search for semen includes the corpse (in cases of murder) or victim, underwear, condoms, bed sheets and mattresses, carpeting, and flooring. A living victim undergoes a *rape exam* by a physician. This exam typically takes place in a hospital emergency room, where standardized *rape kits* are used. Turn to Chapter 12 to find out how investigators handle rape cases.

Tests for semen are either presumptive or confirmatory. Presumptive testing generally is based on the fact that semen contains a very high level of the enzyme acid phosphatase. Confirmatory testing relies on the presence of spermatozoa or prostate-specific antigen (PSA).

Investigators use the following tests to find and analyze semen:

✔ **Presumptive testing:** *Acid phosphatase enzymes* (AP) are a class of proteins that are common in nature and are found in many animals and plants. Semen contains a high level of acid phosphatase, which is produced by the seminal vesicles. This type of AP is called seminal AP or SAP. When SAP is found in a crime-scene fluid sample or stain, it provides presumptive evidence that semen is indeed present. Unfortunately, certain fruit and vegetable juices such as watermelon and cauliflower, some fungi, contraceptive creams, and even vaginal fluid itself can give a false-positive AP test.

Other presumptive tests search for the presence of two other components of semen: *spermine* and *choline.* Each of these tests is positive whenever crystals form after the sample is exposed to certain chemicals.

✔ **Confirmatory testing:** If presumptive testing suggests the presence of semen, one or more of the confirmatory tests are then done. The two most commonly used ones are

- **Microscopic examination:** Because spermatozoa are present only in semen, finding them is absolute proof that semen is present. A sample is placed on a microscope slide and treated with one of several stains. The viewer typically sees a combination of intact and fragmented spermatozoa. Finding a single sperm or sperm head confirms that the sample is semen.

- **Prostate-specific antigen (PSA):** If no spermatozoa are seen, the examiner must resort to testing for *prostate-specific antigen* (PSA or p30), which is highly concentrated in semen. Testing involves an antigen-antibody reaction that is quick and simple. Finding PSA or p30 confirms the presence of semen. Although a vasectomy may markedly reduce or completely eliminate spermatozoa from the semen, it has no effect on the PSA level, because PSA is produced by the prostate gland, which lies downstream from the site of the vasectomy.

Timing intercourse

Finding out when sexual intercourse or rape occurred often is critical in forensics and courtroom proceedings. An accurate determination can implicate or exonerate a suspect.

The duration of sperm motility (movement) in living victims is from four to six hours. In cases of rape-homicide, sperm can remain in the vagina of the victim's body for up to two weeks. The survival of sperm and sperm heads in various body orifices is extremely variable, so no accurate timeline can be established. In general, however, these remnants remain in the vagina for up to six or seven days, the rectum for two to three days, and in the mouth for less than 24 hours. Elevated PSA and SAP levels can be found in the vagina for up to 24 and 72 hours, respectively.

Semen is a fairly resilient substance. Laundering and dry cleaning of stained clothing removes all traces of PSA and SAP, but on rare occasions traces of spermatozoa can be seen through a microscope. If the material is protected from extremes of temperature, harsh chemicals, and other unfavorable environmental conditions, dried semen stains can remain identifiable and usable for DNA analysis for many years. Just ask Bill about Monica's blue dress.

Determining secretor status

Approximately 80 percent to 85 percent of the population are *secretors,* meaning they emit proteins of their ABO blood type in all bodily fluids, including seminal fluid, saliva, and tears. ABO types found in these fluids can be used to eliminate a suspect in a rape, but they cannot accurately identify the individual who secreted them.

Suppose, for example, that a rape victim is a secretor of Type *B,* while the prime suspect is a secretor of Type *A.* Additionally suppose that semen is found in the victim's vaginal swab and, when tested, shows only Type *B* antigens. These *B* antigens can come from the victim, the perpetrator, or both, but they cannot come from the prime suspect, who is a Type *A* secretor and would've left behind Type *A* antigens. The prime suspect, therefore, is exonerated, and police now must search for a suspect who is Type *B,* Type *O,* or a nonsecretor, because the perpetrator either left behind *B* antigens (Type *B*) or no antigens at all (Type *O* or nonsecretor status). In the latter case, the *B* antigens that were found are from the victim.

Thus, matching secretor antigens is similar to blood typing and can eliminate someone but cannot conclusively identify anyone specifically as the assailant, because it's too crude. DNA testing must be employed to make a conclusive match.

Checking for saliva

Saliva is an important bodily fluid to the forensic examiner. It can be recovered from everything from stamps to food and bite marks. More importantly, it can reveal ABO antigens and thus blood types in secretors and sometimes can yield enough DNA for profiling.

Saliva begins the digestive breakdown of carbohydrates into simple sugars as you chew your food. *Amylase* is the enzyme that accomplishes this task. Like AP enzymes, amylase enzymes are found in many animals and plants.

Testing for saliva involves testing for the presence of *alpha*-amylase, the primary amylase found in saliva. No confirmatory tests exist for saliva, only presumptive ones.

Detecting vaginal fluid

Detecting vaginal fluid is difficult, but it may be important in nonejaculatory rapes and penetrations with foreign objects. Swabs can be taken from a suspect's penis or from any suspected foreign object. Testing depends upon the finding of glycogen-containing epithelial cells. *Epithelial cells* line the vagina, and *glycogen* is a starch that is stored within the cells.

Periodic Acid-Schiff (PAS) is a *reagent* (chemical solution) that stains glycogen a bright magenta color. Whenever glycogen-rich epithelial cells are exposed to PAS, their *cytoplasm* (the liquid part of the cell) is stained magenta. In cases of object rape, the suspected object is swabbed, and any material obtained from the swab is spread onto a glass slide and then stained with PAS before being viewed under a microscope. Whenever cells with bright magenta staining show up, the material obtained is likely to be vaginal fluid.

The problem is that not all vaginal epithelial cells contain glycogen. Cells from young girls who have not begun menstruating contain none. Similarly, cells from postmenopausal women rarely contain glycogen. The amount of glycogen found in these cells likewise varies with the stages of a woman's menstrual cycle. As a result, in many cases, the test comes back negative even though vaginal fluids are present.

Chapter 15

Looking Deep Inside: DNA Analysis

In This Chapter

▶ Describing what DNA is and how it works

▶ Understanding the uniqueness of an individual's DNA

▶ Using DNA to identify victims and perpetrators

▶ Looking at paternity and ancestry

The same stuff that makes your eyes green or your hair curly can pinpoint you as the perpetrator of a crime. DNA determines much of who you are (perhaps even whether you're predisposed to commit a crime, according to some), and it's a hot topic in forensic circles. Knowledge of exactly what DNA is and does has been around for a long time, as its chemical makeup and structure have been clearly defined for more than a half century. Its use as a forensic tool is now three decades old.

Opening an Instruction Manual for Your Cells

Your body is made up of approximately 60 trillion cells. Certain cells enable you to see, hear, and feel. Other cells make insulin, sugar, and enzymes to digest your food. Your heart muscle cells pump your blood through your lungs where your red blood cells pick up oxygen and then deliver this precious cargo to all the cells of your body. DNA is the instruction manual that tells each cell what to do.

Understanding the nuts and bolts of DNA

DNA is a complex polymer (any string of linearly joined molecules) arranged in a double helix (like a twisted ladder) and formed into long strands called *chromosomes.* These chromosomes lie within the *nucleus,* or central core, of each cell. Portions of the chromosomes called *genes* are the basic units of heredity. Along the chromosome, each gene has its own specific location, which is called a *locus.* When the chromosomes pair off, so do these *loci* (more than one locus). As a result, your genes pair, too, as you can see in Figure 15-1. Each paired gene is called an allele, and the two together are referred to as an allelic pair.

Figure 15-1:
When chromosomes pair off, so do the loci of the various genes.

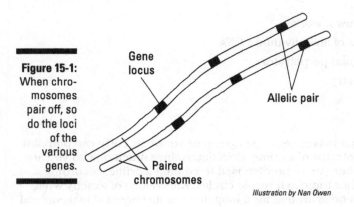

Illustration by Nan Owen

Humans have 46 chromosomes that are arranged into 23 pairs within each cell's nucleus. Surrounding the nucleus is *cytoplasm,* or the fluid portion of the cell, which, along with the nucleus and the rest of the cellular components, is held together by the *cell membrane.* In addition to keeping the cell together, the cell membrane separates each cell from the surrounding environment. In short, each cell basically is a little packet of life.

DNA is a *polymer,* or a molecule of smaller units strung together like a train. The smaller units are *monomers.* Four bases are involved in the production of the DNA polymer: guanine, cytosine, thymine, and adenine. Scientists typically refer to each of these by its first letter: *G, C, T,* and *A.* All life is based on this four-letter alphabet. Millions of bases string together in any given DNA strand, and they can hook up in any conceivable order. The order in which the bases are linked determines the message contained within the DNA. In the same way that the 26 letters of the alphabet can be ordered to form a message, the message that the DNA letters deliver depends upon their order. For example, "abgrtehde" means little, but "aardvark" means a lot. Similarly, a DNA sequence that is C-T-T-G-A-T may mean nothing, while one that's C-G-T-C-T-A may be an instruction to manufacture a portion of a protein that's used in the cell wall of a neuron.

Human DNA is double-stranded, which means that it consists of paired strands of these bases that are wound together into a structure called a *double helix,* a spiral-like structure that looks like a twisted ladder (see Figure 15-2). When these bases pair off to form a double helix, the bases in each strand are a complement of the bases of the other strand. The reason: The rules of *base pairing* dictate that C binds only with G (and vice versa), and A binds only with T (and vice versa).

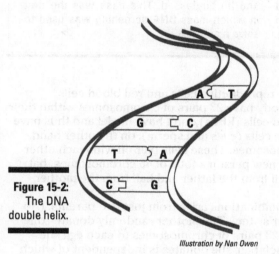

Figure 15-2:
The DNA
double helix.

Illustration by Nan Owen

The base pairing rule that C bonds only with G and A only with T is critical when DNA replicates or reproduces, ensuring that all new DNA strands are exact copies of the originals. The process actually is simple but elegant.

Mine, mine, all mine: Uniqueness and DNA

Each of us has approximately 3 billion base pairs (A-T and G-C pairings within the DNA molecules) in our DNA. That's 6 billion bases in all. Because these bases can be put together in any order, the possible base sequences (series of bases linked in a linear fashion) for any given DNA strand are astronomical. That number, of course, is the basic reason that all humans are different, and it serves as the basis for DNA typing in the forensics lab.

The old blood sample switcheroo

The brutal rape and murder of two teenage girls in the rural English town of Narborough sent a cold panic through that community. When the police investigation hit a stone wall, local officials decided to try the new technique of DNA matching, developed in 1985 by Sir Alec Jeffreys. They believed that the killer lived and worked in the area, so they asked all males in the area to submit a blood sample for testing.

After screening several thousand samples, no match was made. A man came forward, however, telling police that a co-worker, Colin Pitchfork, had persuaded him to give a blood sample in his place. When police obtained a sample from Pitchfork, a match was made, and he confessed. This case was the first in which mass DNA screening was used to solve a crime.

With two notable exceptions — reproductive cells and red blood cells (RBCs) — all the cells in your body have 23 pairs of chromosomes within their respective nuclei. The red blood cells (RBCs) don't have nuclei and thus have no chromosomes. Reproductive cells (eggs and sperm), on the other hand, contain only 23 *unpaired* chromosomes. These cells pair off with each other during fertilization, giving each new person a total of 46 chromosomes that contain genetic information, half from the father and half from the mother.

More than 8 trillion possible combinations arise from just two parents. (No wonder you don't look like your sister.) The mother randomly donates one chromosome from each of her 23 pairs of chromosomes to each egg she produces. Which member of each pair she donates is independent of which member of every other pair she donates.

Of course, the same number of possibilities exists in the father. Because any sperm can combine with any of the mother's eggs, the possibilities become huge.

Fingering Criminals Using DNA Fingerprints

Solving crime means finding out whodunit, so forensic scientists have long searched for ways to absolutely identify individuals from materials left at a crime scene.

The first discovery that provided positive proof was fingerprints, which are absolutely individual. No two people share the same prints, so fingerprinting became and remains an extremely powerful forensic tool. However, fingerprints aren't found at every crime scene. Criminals have learned to wear gloves and to wipe their prints from any objects they touch.

Tracking down every bit of biological debris that gets left behind, however, is impossible for even the best criminals. DNA fingerprinting gives the criminalist an extremely accurate tool for using the tiniest bits of genetic material to identify individuals who were present at a crime scene.

Tracking down and preserving DNA

DNA is found in almost every cell in the human body. Skin, hair follicles, semen, saliva, and blood are common sources of crime-scene DNA. Hair doesn't contain cells, but hair follicles do. Saliva doesn't contain cells, but as it passes through the salivary ducts and washes around the mouth, it picks up cells from the ducts and the mouth. RBCs have no nuclei, so they contain no DNA. The DNA found when blood is tested comes from the white blood cells (WBCs). Using modern techniques, each type of fluid or tissue yields enough usable DNA for testing.

After it's secured from a crime scene, DNA must be handled carefully to keep it from degrading. The best DNA samples are the ones that have been adequately dried and stored in protective containers. When drying isn't feasible, wet samples need to be frozen until they're analyzed.

Imagine trying to read a book in which all the sentences have been reduced to fragments or single words. *War and Peace* might be indistinguishable from *Green Eggs and Ham*. However, if the original books were merely torn into pages, you'd have little trouble distinguishing between the two. Similarly, DNA typing and matching depends upon the preservation of the sequence of the bases that make up the DNA. If the lab has only very short fragments or single bases to work with, much as a book reduced to a pile of single words, it can't effectively type the DNA.

The bigger the DNA sample, the better, and yet usable DNA has been obtained from small and unlikely sources. Even a toothbrush, stamp, or bite wound can yield a usable saliva sample. A single drop of blood or a single hair follicle often is enough. In fact, with the newer techniques available to the DNA analyst, a single cell can supply enough DNA for testing.

In addition, modern technology makes possible the extraction of usable DNA from ancient tissues, even those taken from mummies that are thousands of years old. Scientists have extracted DNA from the bones and teeth of very old skeletal remains and, at times, from severely burned bodies (see the "Who's yer granny and granddaddy? Mitochondria and Y-STR DNA" section later in this chapter).

Looking into the genome

The *genome* is the total DNA within the cell, or the millions of base pairs that make up the long polymers of DNA. Out of that massive number of base pairs, only about 5 percent directly carry out the work of life. These genes are *encoded,* meaning that they direct the *synthesis* (or manufacture) of proteins that the body needs for growth and function. The other 95 percent of the genome is *non-encoded,* which means it doesn't directly code for the production of a protein, but it doesn't simply lie around doing nothing, either. A portion of it regulates how genes function, and much of it is repetitive information whose purpose scientists haven't yet been able to identify. These areas of non-encoded DNA are often called "junk DNA," and it is these segments that are of primary interest to the forensic DNA analyst.

All humans, and indeed all primates, share a large amount of the genome, meaning that much of your DNA is exactly like mine and everyone else's. It's also identical to that of the chimpanzees at your local zoo. Even so, that leaves plenty of unique combinations of DNA to give forensic investigators a keen method of finding out exactly who you are.

In 1984, Alec Jeffreys and his associates at Leicester University discovered that each person's DNA is actually unique. They found that certain areas of the long human DNA molecule exhibit *polymorphism,* a fancy word that means it can take many different forms. These variable areas are unique in everyone, and analyzing these areas allows scientists to make distinctions between one individual and the next. In 1985, shortly after discovering this polymorphism, Jeffreys developed a process for isolating and analyzing these areas of human DNA that he termed *DNA fingerprinting.* The process is also called DNA typing.

Polymorphisms important for forensics can be found in non-encoded, or *junk DNA.* These areas are highly variable in length and base sequence. The variability in length is called *length polymorphism.* It's an important factor in forensic DNA typing because certain base sequences within the non-encoded DNA segments are constantly repeated. As a result, forensic investigators look for two types of sequences:

✔ **Variable Number Tandem Repeats (VNTRs):** The same base sequence repeats throughout a specific locus within the strand. These segments can be hundreds of base pairs long, repeating along the length of the DNA strand a variable number of times. VNTRs are rarely, if ever, used anymore as STRs and SNPs have supplanted their usefulness.

- **Short Tandem Repeats (STRs):** Much shorter than VNTRs — usually three to seven base pairs long — these sections also repeat throughout portions (loci) of the DNA chain. STRs repeat over segments of the DNA strand as long as 400 bases, which means that by using STRs, lab technicians can use even severely degraded samples for testing. Many more STRs are known than VNTRs, which gives forensic scientists many more repeats to analyze.

- **Single Nucleotide Polymorphism (SNPs):** SNPs are the most common DNA variations in humans, and there are literally millions of them scattered along our DNA strands. For example, a known location along the DNA strand might have a cytosine molecule in one person and an adenine or a thymine molecule in another person. A "match" is made if several of these are examined and a suspect's SNPs match those of the crime scene sample. Because SNPs are much smaller than STRs, this technique can be useful in DNA samples too degraded for STR analysis.

The key in DNA typing is that the variability in the pattern of these repeats from person to person is broad, meaning that if technicians can isolate a certain locus of the DNA strand and determine the number of repeats of a given sequence in that area, they can compare it with another DNA strand to find out whether the pattern matches. In addition, research has determined how often a given number of repeats is found at a specific location in the DNA of the general population. Criminalists can use that information to calculate the probability that two DNA samples came from the same person. However, a match from a single locus is not very conclusive. But if several loci match, the probability quickly adds up.

Repeating yourself: How duplication identifies you

In terms of DNA, all of us repeat ourselves, but the specific ways in which we do it make each of us unique. When working to match DNA, investigators look at the repeats on particular loci of DNA. If my DNA were being compared to yours, for example, investigators would look at the same locus on each of our samples. They might find that you received 8 repeats of a particular STR from one parent and 14 repeats from another, and that I received 15 repeats of the same STR from one parent and 23 from another. Your DNA and mine would be very different.

But would your and my DNA be different from everyone else's on Earth? You couldn't tell by looking at only one locus. Other people also may have received 8 and 14 or 15 and 23 repeats for the same locus, but when you look at a dozen loci, the probability that two people received the exact number of repeats from each parent at all 12 loci is only one in several hundred *trillion*.

Looking at another example, if you were to analyze the STRs of a crime-scene sample at five different loci, you might find the following repeats:

Locus 1	12 and 9
Locus 2	6 and 14
Locus 3	23 and 16
Locus 4	5 and 18
Locus 5	8 and 19

Now, say that you already know that each of these STR repeat patterns occurs at these specific loci at respective rates of 1 percent, 3 percent, 8 percent, 1 percent, and 2 percent within the general population. That means 1 in 100 people share the same repeat pattern at Locus 1, 3 in 100 share this same repeat pattern at Locus 2, and so on. Therefore, if a suspect's DNA shows the exact same repeat patterns at all five loci as the crime-scene sample, the probability that the DNA found at the scene came from someone other than the suspect is tiny. In fact, because the inheritance of the STR patterns at each locus is independent of any other locus, the percentages must be multiplied by each other to determine the probability of the DNA coming from someone other than the suspect, which in this case is a whopping 48 out of 10 billion, and that high degree of probability was found using only five loci. Imagine what those odds would be if the suspect's DNA matched the crime-scene sample at 12 or more loci. Book him, Dano.

Understanding the DNA Fingerprinting Process

DNA evidence is incredibly reliable, but it requires some special treatment before it can be coaxed into revealing its secrets. Unlike fingerprint evidence, you can't just "lift" a DNA sample and look at it in the right light to pull answers from it. Getting a DNA sample, and getting that sample into a form that allows investigators to analyze it and compare it with another sample, takes time and a lot of careful work.

The old method of DNA analysis was termed *restriction fragment length polymorphism* (RFLP) and required longer VNTRs. This method has been replaced by STR and SNP analyses in almost every jurisdiction. The reason is simply that RFLP required longer VNTRs (several hundred bases), while STRs are short (4 to 7 bases) and SNPs only a single base, or nucleotide. This means that the DNA to be analyzed can be more degraded and STR and SNP can still be useful as compared to using the old RFLP techniques.

Currently, the standard for DNA testing is STR analysis, coupled with the polymerase chain reaction (PCR). Using PCR, the DNA in even very small samples can be amplified (reproduced) at will. For this reason, the DNA from a single cell can be used to create a virtually unlimited quantity of DNA for testing.

SNP analysis offers an excellent complement to STR analysis, and current research suggests that it might even be able to distinguish identical twins — who by definition have the same DNA — from one another. The reason is that the continuing, lifelong replication of DNA within our cells as they synthesize new cells is subject to copy errors in single nucleotides. So over the years, the DNA of these twins develops variations that can often be exposed with SNP analysis.

This evolution in DNA analysis techniques was underlined by the famous Green River Killer case, as discussed in the sidebar "The Green River Killer."

Looking into the polymerase chain reaction

Criminals rarely are considerate enough to leave behind DNA samples that are large enough to easily analyze in the crime lab. When investigators must make do with only a single hair follicle, or even a single cell, they use the *polymerase chain reaction* (PCR) to turn that tiny bit of DNA into a usable sample.

PCR is a complex series of reactions that basically mirrors what happens in the cells of our body. This process by which DNA replicates (copies) itself is called *amplification*. Each double-stranded DNA molecule is split — separated into its two component strands — and then each half rebuilds its complementary pair. This way, two new identical DNA molecules are produced. Then two become four, and four become eight, and so on.

With PCR, the original small DNA sample quickly grows into a larger, more usable amount. In fact, lab technicians can start with a single copy and before long manufacture millions of exact copies. Replicating DNA enables investigators to test even extremely small samples. In many labs, this process is automated and relatively quick. In fact, with PCR-STR analysis, a profile can be generated in a few hours. There are currently devices that can do this in the field, even before the samples are brought to the lab.

CASE STUDY

The Green River Killer

One of the more notorious serial killers in history was known as the Green River Killer. The moniker came from the perpetrator's habit of dumping his mostly prostitute victims along the Green River near Seattle, Washington. Between 1982 and 1991, nearly 50 murders were attributed to the Green River Killer, and the suspect list was nearly as long.

Police executed a search warrant on April 8, 1987, at the premises of one of the suspects, Gary Ridgway. After obtaining evidence items from his house, police asked him to undergo a polygraph examination, but Ridgway refused. Police then asked for a saliva sample, and Ridgway complied by biting on a piece of surgical gauze. Unfortunately, semen samples taken from many of the victims were too small

for testing, so Ridgway's saliva sample was stored. In the mid-1990s, authorities began using a combination of STR and PCR analysis to identify DNA.

In 2001, the lab tested the sample of Ridgway's saliva, comparing it with semen samples taken from Opal Mills, Marcia Chapman, and Carol Christensen, all of whom were killed in 1982 or 1983. Using the newer PCR-STR techniques, the samples were amplified and compared. Matches were made, and Ridgway was arrested and charged with four of the Green River killings. However, the case took a dramatic and controversial turn on November 5, 2003, when Ridgway pleaded guilty to 48 murders in exchange for a sentence of life without the possibility of parole, thus sparing himself a possible death sentence.

Getting even smaller with SNPs

An even newer technique, *single nucleotide polymorphism* (SNP), uses single nucleotides, meaning that the exact sequence, down to its actual base (nucleotide) sequence, is determined. This means that DNA analysis has evolved from using longer VNTRs to employing shorter STR repeats and now to determining the actual sequence of the bases in the analyzed sample. You can see this makes even more severely degraded samples useful to the DNA analyst.

SNP and similar determinations also make it possible for DNA analysts to distinguish one identical twin from the other. How is this possible? Don't identical twins share the same DNA? Well, almost.

Fraternal twins come from different eggs and different sperm cells. That is, two eggs are fertilized by two different sperm cells at conception. These twins are as different as if born years apart. They are twins simply because they shared the mother's womb prior to birth. Identical twins come from a single fertilized egg. In this case, when the fertilized egg undergoes its first division, the two daughter cells drift apart and then progress to become two distinct individuals. So these twins share the same DNA. Interestingly, even identical twins have different fingerprints, so if these are available, one can be distinguished from the other.

But even without fingerprints, the DNA analyst still has a trick or two to employ. In identical twins, as each of the two identical fertilized eggs produced by the first cellular division continues to multiply and ultimately grow into two different people, the replication of the DNA in each is not perfect. One twin will have a slightly different base sequence than the other. Though with FLRP and STR analysis they may appear identical, and thus indistinguishable by DNA fingerprinting, SNP analysis reveals these minute differences. Perpetrators can no longer blame their crime on their "evil identical twin."

Making the match

Even though the graphs produced by RFLP and STR analysis look very different, they are actually the same. Each visually and numerically presents the DNA analysis in forms that are fairly easy to interpret. Matching the auto-radiographic bands (RFLP) or the peaks (STR) produced from the analysis of a suspect's DNA with that obtained from the crime scene can exonerate or implicate the suspect.

For example, say that a perpetrator shed blood at the scene of a homicide, and the crime lab found and collected it. The perpetrator's blood constitutes an unknown sample because its origin isn't known. When the suspect list includes two people, the lab takes a sample from each of them. The suspects' samples are considered known samples because their origin is known. DNA fingerprinting compares the suspects' DNA with the unknown crime-scene DNA.

In RFLP analysis, bands are created (Figure 15-3), whereas with STR, peaks are generated (Figure 15-4). Even a casual glance distinguishes a match from a non-match.

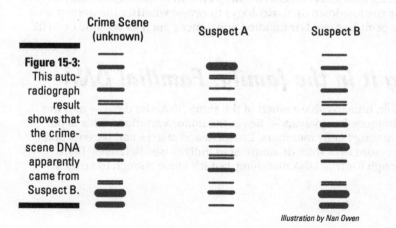

Figure 15-3: This auto-radiograph result shows that the crime-scene DNA apparently came from Suspect B.

Crime Scene (unknown)   Suspect A   Suspect B

Illustration by Nan Owen

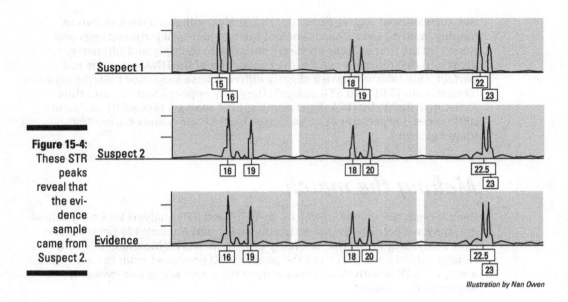

Figure 15-4:
These STR peaks reveal that the evidence sample came from Suspect 2.

Illustration by Nan Owen

Shedding cells: Touch DNA

Did you know that you often leave behind your DNA simply by touching something? Fingerprints left at crime scenes consist of oils, dirt, and grime that has collected on the person's finger pads. The print also contains shed skin cells, and these cells contain DNA. With PCR-STR, even a single cell deposited as part of a fingerprint can lead to a complete DNA profile. So, blood loss by the perpetrator isn't necessary to grab a DNA profile; merely touching something at the crime scene will suffice.

These fingerprint materials can also be subjected to toxicological analysis (see Chapter 16 for the lowdown on toxicology) to reveal whether the person who deposited the print has used or handled substances such as cocaine or GHB.

Keeping it in the family: Familial DNA

As I state earlier, humans share much of the same DNA; the devil — and the crime lab techniques for analysis — lies in the minor variations. This is particularly true among family members. Brothers and sisters and parents and children share more DNA than do nonrelated individuals. Relatives' DNA isn't close enough for true DNA matching, but it's close enough to suggest a connection.

Sometimes the evidence in an investigation strongly points to a particular suspect, but it's not enough to secure an indictment and a successful prosecution. Often DNA from a suspect isn't available, and there isn't enough evidence to obtain a probable cause warrant for investigators to demand a sample. In such situations, investigators may turn to familial DNA by testing the DNA of close family members. If the DNA profile of these individuals is close to the crime-scene sample, this may be enough to get that needed warrant and force the suspect to submit a sample.

Using DNA to Determine Lineage

You have more than your father's ears and your grandmother's hooked nose — you have the DNA that they passed down to you. Because DNA is so individual and because it's passed down from one generation to the next, it's an extremely powerful tool for determining an individual's ancestral background. Whether it's proving or disproving fatherhood or tracking distant ancestors, DNA testing is a reliable tool that provides compelling evidence.

Who's yer daddy? Paternity testing

ABO blood typing can be used to exclude paternity, but it can't absolutely state that a certain man is the father of a certain child (see Chapter 14). DNA testing, on the other hand, can confirm paternity. To determine paternity using DNA, scientists make profiles of the mother's DNA and the child's DNA. These profiles then are compared to the profile of the suspected father. The child's DNA pattern must be a combination of the DNA profiles of the mother and father. The child's DNA profile can't include a band, or peak, that neither parent supplies; however, the child's profile doesn't necessarily have every band that each parent possesses. Remember, each parent only gives half of the offspring's DNA. But, because all of the child's DNA must come from its parents, the child can't have DNA that neither of them has.

Through the union of egg and sperm, each parent donates half of her or his DNA to the new child. Neither, however, donates all of his or her DNA. Chromosomes are arranged in 23 pairs, and each parent donates one chromosome of each pair to the child. Thus, the child is a combination of DNA donated by each parent. Parents may have DNA that the child doesn't have (DNA on the chromosome not donated via the egg or sperm), but the child absolutely can't have DNA that wasn't donated by at least one of the parents. So when the child's DNA is fragmented and separated into bands or peaks, each of the resulting bands or peaks must also be found in the DNA profile of one or the other parent.

CASE STUDY

Paternity and murder

Helen McCourt, a 22-year-old insurance clerk in the small village of Billinge in northwest England, disappeared February 9, 1988. She apparently stopped at the George and Dragon, a local pub owned by Ian Simms, to whom local gossip suggested she had a romantic link. Witnesses reported hearing screams coming from the pub, and when police confronted Simms, he had several scratches on his face.

Police found hair and one of McCourt's earrings in Simms's car. The earring was bloody, and the hair matched that of the missing girl. Within Simms's living quarters, police found bloodstains on the stairway and bedroom floor. Several other items of evidence were found in various parts of the countryside, including

McCourt's bloodstained coat and clothing, which also held hairs from Simms's dog and fibers from his carpet. In addition, the police also found a length of electrical cord that bore strands of McCourt's hair.

The problem facing police was proving that the blood in Simms's apartment was that of the missing girl. Without a body to work with, they turned to the girl's parents. Samples taken from her mother and father were matched with the blood found at the probable crime scene. At trial, Dr. Alec Jeffreys, the father of DNA fingerprinting, testified that the odds against the blood from Simms's apartment being from anyone other than the daughter of the two parents were 14,500 to one. Simms was convicted and received a life sentence.

In paternity testing, if the child possesses a DNA fragment that isn't present in either the mother or the suspected father, then the man is not the child's father. This fragment must have come from someone else (the true father), and paternity for the suspect father is excluded. (See Figure 15-5.)

Figure 15-5: This child has a band that isn't found in the DNA profile of either the mother or the suspect father, who can't be the actual father.

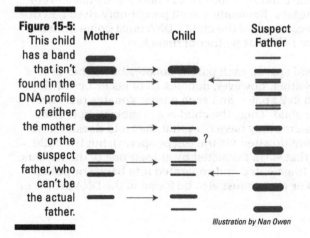

Illustration by Nan Owen

Who's yer granny and granddaddy? Mitochondrial and Y-STR DNA

Mitochondrial DNA adds an extremely useful tool to the forensic toolbox. It helps in identifying perpetrators and human remains and for determining ancestry.

The DNA used in standard DNA testing is nuclear DNA. It can be extracted from any nucleated cell. But cells also contain non-nuclear DNA. This DNA is found within the mitochondria. *Mitochondria* are small organelles that reside within the cytoplasm of the cell and serve as the cell's energy production center. A small amount of DNA is in the mitochondria, but each cell has many mitochondria organelles. Mitochondrial DNA is important for several reasons, including the following:

✔ Passes from generation to generation by the maternal lineage

✔ Mutates rarely

✔ Is found in places where nuclear DNA doesn't exist

✔ Is exceptionally hardy

Your mitochondrial DNA (mtDNA) is inherited unchanged from your mother and only from your mother. She received hers from her mother, and her mother from her mother, and so on.

At fertilization, the mother's egg supplies the cell and half the DNA, but the sperm supplies only half the DNA. The sperm cell breaks down and disappears after passing its genetic material into the nucleus of the egg cell. Thus, all the cell components of the developing *zygote* (fertilized egg) come from the mother, including the mitochondria. As the cell divides and multiplies, these mitochondria are copied and passed on, generation after generation, and that means all the cells of the body contain identical mtDNA.

The rare mtDNA mutation is thought to occur approximately once every 6,500 years. Thus, mtDNA is extremely stable, and that means that your mtDNA is virtually identical to that of your mother, your great-great grandmother, and your maternal ancestors from a thousand years ago. Thus, you can accurately trace your maternal lineage across many generations.

Y-STR DNA is similar to mDNA except that it is located on the male Y chromosome and is passed down along the paternal ancestry line. This means that a male would share his Y-STR DNA with his father, brothers, paternal grandfather, paternal uncles, and paternal nephews if born from a paternal uncle rather than a paternal aunt.

Standing in for the Boston Strangler

The conviction of Albert DeSalvo for a series of rapes and murders attributed to a killer who became known as the Boston Strangler put to rest one of the grizzliest series of crimes in United States history, but there was some question as to whether DeSalvo was the perpetrator of these crimes.

Although he confessed to many of the murders, he frequently got details of some of the crimes wrong, raising suspicion that perhaps he didn't commit all the crimes for which he took credit. Forensic science recently attempted to unravel this mystery.

The Strangler's last victim was Mary Sullivan. In October 2000, 36 years after her death, her body was exhumed from its grave in Hyannis, Massachusetts. Investigators found a semen stain on her body. Tests for the presence of spermatozoa and for prostatic-specific protein p30 were not possible because the sample was

so degraded. However, the material did reveal the presence of mitochondrial DNA (mtDNA).

Investigators obtained blood from DeSalvo's brother Richard. Because brothers have the same mother and thus identical mitochondrial DNA, matching mtDNA from the semen stain with Richard's mtDNA would prove that Albert was indeed the killer. The result? No match. Even though Albert DeSalvo confessed to killing Mary Sullivan, he didn't do it. Or did he?

In 2013, investigators obtained DNA from a bottle discarded by DeSalvo's nephew and subjected it to Y-STR analysis. They got a match. Armed with this evidence, they were able to obtain a warrant, and DeSalvo's body was exhumed. DNA extracted from his bones and teeth matched that of the samples obtained from Sullivan and the crime scene with a probability of 1 in 220 billion. DeSalvo was indeed the killer of Mary Sullivan.

Because mtDNA is hardy, scientists can often extract it from the bones and teeth of very old skeletons and thus use it to identify and determine the ancestry of skeletal remains. Mitochondrial DNA also is found in some tissues where nuclear DNA can't be found. For example, hair predominantly is composed of dead cellular debris. The only living part of hair is the follicle. The cells of the follicles contain nuclear DNA, which can be used for DNA profiling and matching. In other words, hair that's been yanked out or shed with its follicular bulb attached can provide nuclear DNA.

But, what if the hair has been cut, and no bulb is attached? All is not lost.

As hair grows, the cells of the bulb multiply, undergo change, and become incorporated into the growing hair. Part of this transformation is the loss of the nucleus from each cell. Thus, although hair has no nuclear DNA, the dead cellular debris that is incorporated into the hair shaft does contain mtDNA that can be extracted and used for identifying the person who shed the hair.

If a hair is found at a crime scene and it matches the suspect's hair in every physical detail, investigators may reasonably suspect that he shed the hair while at the scene. The problem is that such "proof" is shaky at best. But if the mtDNA from the crime-scene hair matches that of the suspect, the evidence becomes more powerful because the crime-scene hair must have come from the suspect or at least someone who shared the suspect's maternal ancestry.

Indexing DNA: The CODIS system

The FBI's CODIS Unit oversees the Combined DNA Index System (CODIS) and the National DNA Index System (NDIS), which are databases of DNA fingerprints taken from felons and from biological fluids obtained from crime scenes, such as assaults, homicides, and rapes. Forensic scientists hope the database becomes the DNA equivalent of the Automated Fingerprint Identification System (AFIS).

In the same way that a fingerprint can be entered into AFIS and matched against a database of fingerprints from across the country, DNA profiles can be compared through CODIS. Unfortunately, the system isn't yet used in every state and jurisdiction. The FBI is in the process of expanding it into a truly nationwide system.

With CODIS, criminalists are able to compare a crime-scene DNA sample with profiles of known felons and DNA obtained from other crime scenes to establish matches. The DNA in question may match DNA obtained from another crime scene and link the crimes. As a result, evidence from crime scenes can be considered together, which may lead to the identity of a perpetrator. As witnessed by the seemingly constant stream of cold cases solved by DNA matching, CODIS already has enjoyed many successes.

CASE STUDY

Consulting the DNA databank

In March 1989, Debbie Smith was forced from her home and into a nearby wooded area where she was raped. Her attacker warned her that he knew where she lived and that she shouldn't tell anyone or he'd return and kill her. Police tested blood obtained from the prime suspect against seminal DNA obtained from the victim's rape examination but found no match. In 1994, Smith's neighborhood suffered a series of sexual assaults. Another suspect attracted the attention of police, and this time DNA analysis was undertaken. Again, however, they found no match.

Meanwhile, the state of Virginia, where Smith resided, began to develop a databank of DNA profiles taken from convicted felons. As new profiles were obtained, the Virginia Department of Forensic Services periodically tried matching DNA from felon profiles with DNA from unsolved crimes. One of the profiles in the database, identified as belonging to Norman Jimmerman, was matched with the DNA from Smith's attacker. He already was serving time for robbery and abduction. His current sentence is 161 years.

Chapter 16

Testing for Drugs and Poisons: The Toxicology Lab

• •

In This Chapter

▶ Looking into the field of toxicology

▶ Analyzing toxins

▶ Applying test results to forensic problems

▶ Understanding common drugs and poisons

• •

During the millennia since Socrates drank the hemlock that killed him, lethal use of poisons has waned a bit, in part because scientists now know how to trace poisons to those who use them for nefarious purposes. From taking arsenic to overdosing on heroin to drinking too much water (I kid you not), poisoning deaths nowadays are the realm of the toxicologist, who has become a critical component of today's crime labs. Drugs and poisons of all types often are involved in harmful accidents and accidental, suicidal, and homicidal deaths, and they may even be contributory factors in many natural deaths.

Understanding Poisons

Have you ever taken a poison? I bet your answer is, "Of course not!" But you're wrong. You take poisons every day. In fact, you have to take poisons to live. Don't believe me? Try not to drink any water. Try not to breathe.

You see, anything can be a poison. The basic definition of a *poison* is any substance that, when taken in sufficient quantities, causes a harmful or deadly reaction. So a poison basically is a substance that either harms you or kills you. But, the key here is the phrase "sufficient quantities." The degree of toxicity of any substance depends on how much enters your body and over what period of time it does so. For example, you probably already know that arsenic is a poison, but did you know that you probably have arsenic in your body right now? If you're a smoker, you have more than a little bit. Your body also has some mercury and cyanide inside. These substances are in the environment, and you can't avoid them. But they're in such small quantities that they cause no real harm. Take enough of any of them, however, and you're a goner.

I know, I know, you believe the cyanide and arsenic deals, but what's this about water and air?

Both water and oxygen can be toxic. Drinking too much water can kill you. In fact, compulsive water drinking is a psychiatric syndrome often associated with schizophrenia. People with this syndrome drink gallons of water every day. Drinking so much water is called *water intoxication,* and it severely dilutes sodium and potassium in the blood and tissues of the body, damages the kidneys, and ultimately leads to coma and death. Similarly, breathing pure oxygen for too long damages your lungs and leads to death.

The distinction between an intoxicant and a true poison is important. An intoxicant, such as alcohol or carbon monoxide, typically requires that you ingest or inhale a rather large amount to be lethal, while a true poison, such as cyanide, requires only a very small amount.

Even substances that cure can poison. *Digitalis,* for example, is an extremely common cardiac medication derived from the foxglove plant, but it's also a deadly poison. Too much can lead to nausea, vomiting, and death from dangerous changes in the rhythm of the heart. How ironic that it can treat some abnormal heart rhythms but also can cause other, more deadly rhythms. It's all in the dose. The right dose is medication; the wrong dose is poison.

Defining Toxicology

Toxicology is a marriage of chemistry and physiology and deals with drugs, poisons, and other toxic substances, and how these substances alter or harm living organisms, particularly humans. Although toxicology is a relatively new science, the first toxicological test dates back to 1775, when Swedish chemist Karl Wilhelm Scheele discovered a way to prove that arsenic was the culprit in a suspicious death.

Scheele found that chlorinated water converts arsenic to arsenous acid and that adding metallic zinc and heating the acid mixture releases arsine gas. When this gas comes into contact with a cold vessel, arsenic collects on the vessel. In 1821, scientists first used this technique to find arsenic in the stomach and urine of poisoned individuals, and the field of forensic toxicology was born.

Today, the forensic toxicologist's job is to find a toxin and determine its likely effect on the individual who ingested or otherwise came in contact with it. For example, the forensic toxicologist may

 ✔ Assess the state of inebriation of an automobile or industrial accident victim

 ✔ Determine whether someone died from a poison or from natural causes

 ✔ Assess whether drugs played a role in a perpetrator's actions or symptoms

On the other hand, *not* finding a drug may be just as important. Suppose, for example, that the toxicologist finds no drugs in someone who's exhibiting erratic or bizarre behavior. Such a situation may lead to a psychiatric evaluation and ultimately to a diagnosis and appropriate treatment. Similarly, the toxicologist may find that the level of a seizure medication in the blood was too low for the driver of a vehicle involved in an accident, and may conclude that a seizure was the cause of the accident.

Seeking Toxins

Most poisons don't cause visible changes in the body — neither in a living person nor during an autopsy. Some do, but most poisons work their mischief within the cells of the body and leave behind no visible footprints. As a result, the medical examiner (ME) doesn't often see visible evidence of toxins on the corpse or on the microscopic slides of any body tissues obtained as part of the autopsy. Therefore, the ME collects fluids and additional tissues from the body that the toxicologist analyzes for the presence or absence of toxins.

Even when a toxicologist can't find a toxin itself, its breakdown products may be easily identifiable. *Biotransformation* is the conversion or transformation of one chemical into another by the body. This process also is called *metabolism,* and the new products it produces are called *metabolites,* which simply are the results of the body destroying or breaking down chemicals in order to eliminate them. For example, heroin is made from morphine, and when it's injected into the bloodstream, it's immediately converted back into morphine. So looking for heroin is fruitless for the toxicologist, but finding morphine is a good sign that heroin *was* present.

Metallic elements also cause disease and death. Excess iron, mercury, lead, arsenic, antimony, selenium, and many other metals can lead to serious health problems and can even kill you. These metals have caused accidental, suicidal, and homicidal deaths for many years.

Collecting samples

Part of poison's popularity is that it's sneaky. Toxins rarely leave behind visible clues, so finding a toxin, and enough evidence to determine that it was the cause of death, is a tricky business that involves several specialized tests and a variety of bodily tissues and fluids.

The best places to obtain samples for testing are the locations where chemicals enter the body, where chemicals concentrate within the body, and along the routes of elimination. Thus blood, stomach contents, and tissues around injection sites may possess high concentrations of the drug. Analyses of liver, brain, and other tissues can reveal where a drug or its metabolites accumulated. Finally, urine testing can indicate where the drug and its metabolites are concentrated for final elimination. Check out these potential sources of illicit toxins:

✔ **Blood:** Blood by far is the toxicologist's most useful substance. After all, the bloodstream is how toxins, whether injected or absorbed through the stomach or the lungs, are spread through the body. With modern toxicological techniques, you can find essentially any drug and its major metabolites in the blood. Blood examination tells the toxicologist what was going on in the body at the time of death. Concentrations of medicines and drugs within the blood correlate well with levels of intoxication and with levels that are potentially lethal.

✔ **Urine:** Easily sampled with a cup and a trip to the restroom, urine testing is a staple of workplace drug testing. It can also prove useful during an autopsy. Because kidneys are situated along one of the body's major drug and toxin elimination routes, toxicologists can often find such substances in greater concentrations in the urine than in the blood. However, the correlation between urine concentration of a drug and its effects in the body is poor, at best. The urine level can reveal that the drug had been in the blood at some earlier time, but it can't determine whether the drug was exerting any effect on the individual at the time it was collected.

Likewise, toxicologists can't estimate blood concentrations from urine concentrations. The concentration of any drug in the urine depends on how much urine the individual produced. If someone drank a great deal of water, the urine and any chemicals it contains become more diluted than they are for someone who hasn't consumed large quantities of water.

✔ **Stomach contents:** Doctors remove the stomach contents of survivors of drug ingestions by way of a gastric tube, which typically passes through the nose and into the stomach. The contents then are *lavaged,* or washed, from the stomach and tested for the presence of drugs or poisons. During an autopsy, examiners test stomach contents in the same way. Obtaining stomach contents is critical in cases where investigators suspect poison or drug ingestion. However, the concentration of any drugs found in the stomach doesn't correlate with their levels in the blood and thus their effects on the person.

✔ **Liver:** The liver is intimately involved in drug and toxin *metabolism* (destruction). Testing liver tissue and the bile it produces often reveals a drug or its metabolites. Many drugs, particularly opiates, tend to concentrate in the liver and the bile, so investigators can measure them in these tissues, even when blood tests show no traces of them. The liver may reflect levels of a drug during the hours before death, and the bile may indicate what drugs were in the system during the past three to four days.

✔ **Vitreous humor:** *Vitreous humor* is the liquid in the eyeball. It's fairly resistant to *putrefaction* (decay), and in severely decomposed corpses, it may be the only remaining fluid. The vitreous humor is a water-like fluid, which means that water-soluble chemicals dissolve in it. Furthermore, vitreous humor and blood maintain equilibrium, meaning that any water-soluble chemical in the blood also is in the vitreous humor. But substance levels in the vitreous lag behind levels found in the blood by about one to two hours, so testing the vitreous reflects the concentration of the toxin in the blood one to two hours earlier.

✔ **Hair:** Hair absorbs certain heavy-metal toxins (arsenic, lead, and others) and has the unique ability of providing an intoxication timeline for many of these substances. I discuss this fact in greater detail in the "Interpreting the results" section later in the chapter.

✔ **Insects:** Toxicologists can even test insects that feed on corpses for drugs in cases of severely decomposed bodies. Because certain drugs tend to concentrate in the tissues of these bugs, they may supply information about whether a drug was present in the deceased.

Determining the cause and manner of death

The medical examiner ultimately is responsible for determining the cause and manner of death, and toxicological findings can play an important role in making those determinations. Unfortunately, toxicological findings rarely provide a black-and-white, clear-cut answer, because drugs and poisons may be the cause or merely a contributing factor in any cause or manner of death.

Natural

A person may die of natural causes, but drugs may be involved in the mechanism of death. If someone with significant coronary artery disease (CAD), for example, takes an amphetamine or cocaine, that person's heart rate and blood pressure increase, his clogged arteries can't accommodate the demand, and a heart attack can follow. The cause of death would be a heart attack, but the amphetamine or cocaine would be a contributory factor.

When the ME and the toxicologist confront this situation, they must assess the extent of the victim's heart disease, the amount of the drug in the body, and whether a heart attack actually occurred. If the amount of drug is low and the victim had severely diseased coronary arteries, they may conclude that the death was natural and that the drug was only a minor contributing factor. On the other hand, if his CAD was mild but the level of the drug in his body was high, the death likely was accidental, and the drug was the mechanism.

Accidental

Most accidental poisonings occur at home and often involve children. Curious by nature, children eat or drink just about anything — pesticides and paint thinners included. In adults, accidental poisoning most often occurs because a product is mislabeled, usually because someone placed it in a container other than its original one.

Other major causes of accidental death from poisons or drugs are dose miscalculations or dangerous mixtures of drugs. Addicts often miscalculate the amount of heroin or amphetamine they're taking and die from this mistake. In addition, people often have unfounded beliefs, for example: "If one dose of a drug is good, then two must be better." Mixing prescription sedatives and alcohol also is notoriously lethal.

Suicidal

Suicide is the most common manner of death in poisonings. Common agents include, narcotics, sedatives, carbon monoxide, and even prescription drugs. Many suicides involve multiple drugs, and this presents a difficult problem for the toxicologist. Analysis of stomach contents, blood, urine, and tissues taken from internal organs helps determine the levels of each drug and allows the toxicologist to assess how each drug contributed to the victim's demise. If one particularly toxic drug is present in large amounts, it is likely the cause of death; but if multiple drugs are involved, it becomes more difficult to determine that a given combination of drugs was the cause.

Homicidal

Although homicidal poisonings were common from antiquity to the 20th century, they're less common today. Guns now seem to be the preferred method. In the remote past, determining why someone died was difficult, and ascertaining whether a poison was involved was virtually impossible. Modern toxicology, however, has changed all that. Nonetheless, determining that poisoning was the cause of death still is one of the most difficult tasks for the forensic toxicologist and pathologist.

As is true of accidental and suicidal poisonings, homicidal poisonings occur most often at home, meaning that the killer usually knows about the victim's habits and has access to the victim's food, drink, and medications. Knowing who has this type of knowledge can be critical to the ME and police investigators when probing cases of homicidal poisoning.

Examining the Testing Procedures

Literally thousands of drugs and chemicals are harmful, addictive, or lethal — what a headache for the toxicologist! An understanding of the circumstances surrounding a death is of utmost importance for determining how and why it happened. Clues at the scene often point toward a particular drug or poison. For example, finding a young girl on her bed at home with an empty pill bottle at her side would lead to one avenue of testing, and finding a long-term addict in an alley with fresh needle marks would point to another path. The more clues that the circumstances of the death can supply, the narrower the field of possibilities the toxicologist must consider.

When testing for drugs, toxins, or poisons, the toxicologist typically follows a two-tiered approach:

✔ **Presumptive tests** are used for initial screening and typically are easier and cheaper to perform. When negative, they indicate that the drug or toxin in question isn't present, and the toxicologist doesn't need to perform further testing for it. When positive, the results indicate that a particular substance may be present.

In general, these tests are more sensitive but less specific than confirmatory tests. They yield more false-positive results, but are unlikely to give false negatives.

✔ **Confirmatory tests** are used only after presumptive tests find the possible presence of a drug or toxin. They're more expensive and time-consuming, but they establish the identity of the specific drug present.

Presuming the results

Screening, or presumptive testing, comes in many varieties. Common toxicological screening tests include the following:

✔ **Color tests** are chemical tests in which a *reagent* (chemical solution) is added to the substance (usually blood, urine, or tissue) being tested. A color change occurs whenever the suspected chemical is present. The color change results from a chemical reaction between the drug and the reagent, which produces a new compound that imparts a specific color to the mixture. These tests are cheap, easy, and quick, and they determine whether a specific chemical or class of chemicals is present in the material being tested.

✔ **Immunoassays** involve an antigen-antibody reaction. The substance being sought is the antigen, and the testing reagent is the antibody. An antibody reacts only with antigens that it recognizes and ignores all others. In this test, the toxicologist adds an antibody that can specifically identify the suspected substance to the sample. For example, if blood is to be tested for amphetamines, the toxicologist adds an antibody specific to amphetamines to a sample of the blood. A reaction gives him a positive result.

✔ **Thin-layer chromatography (TLC)** is an inexpensive screening test that presumptively identifies hundreds of compounds at once by separating compounds according to how far they move through an absorbent material (usually a silica gel) when combined with a solvent. The compounds are then identified by comparing their respective movements with the movements of known standards. This test uses a color reaction that further identifies the compound. Check out Chapter 19 for more information on this test.

✔ **Gas chromatography (GC)** is a method of separating compounds according to their respective sizes, shapes, and chemical properties. GC can identify the class of an unknown or suspected chemical but can't give its exact makeup. As with TLC, GC is useful as a screening tool, and more importantly, it separates the components of a chemical mixture for later confirmatory testing. Chapter 8 tells you more about gas chromatography.

✔ **Ultraviolet (UV) spectroscopy** takes advantage of the fact that different compounds absorb or reflect light in differing amounts and at varying wavelengths. When exposed to UV light, compounds or classes of compounds absorb UV light more strongly at specific wavelengths and less so at other wavelengths. The magnitude of the light absorption at the wavelength of maximum absorption indicates the concentration of the suspected drug or chemical in the sample.

Working through the possibilities: Drug screening

Every lab has its own protocol for drug screening. What tests are used and the order in which they are performed depend upon what staff and equipment are available, budgetary restrictions, and the biases of the toxicologist in charge. Each has a different way of doing things. That said, most labs have certain standard screens that they employ when first confronted with an unknown sample. These basic screens may include:

✔ **Alcohol screen:** Gas chromatography isolates and identifies the various alcohols and related compounds, such as acetone.

✔ **Acid screen:** Immunoassay of urine samples detects acidic compounds, such as barbiturates and aspirin.

✔ **Alkaline screen:** Gas chromatography screens for substances that dissolve in alkaline solutions. These substances include many tranquilizers, synthetic narcotics, and antidepressants.

✔ **Narcotic screen:** Urine immunoassay reveals opiates, cocaine, and methadone.

✔ **Marijuana and cocaine screen:** Most screens also test for marijuana and cocaine.

Confirming the results

A good confirmatory test is sensitive and specific, recognizes the chemical in question, and can identify it to the exclusion of all others. After a chemical has undergone a screening test and the toxicologist has established a presumptive identity, a confirmatory test can accurately determine the true identity of the unknown substance.

The most important confirmatory test used by the toxicologist is *mass spectrometry* (MS). I discuss this process in detail in Chapter 8. When the toxicologist compares the mass spectrums of unknown and known substances, the identity of the unknown sample comes to light. In the forensic toxicology laboratory, MS usually is employed in combination with gas chromatography. This combination is called *gas chromatography/mass spectrometry* (GC/MS). In GC/MS, GC separates the test sample into components, and MS identifies each of those components.

Infrared spectroscopy also determines the chemical fingerprint of the substance being tested but exposes the substance to infrared light instead of electrons. When exposed to infrared light, each compound transmits, absorbs, and reflects the light in its own unique pattern. These unique patterns determine which compounds are present and thus identify the chemical substance being tested.

Interpreting the results

After testing has revealed the presence and concentration of a chemical substance, the hard part begins. The toxicologist now must assess what the results mean, evaluating each of the drugs present, identifying routes of administration, and determining whether concentrations that are present played a role in the subject's behavior or death. From such determinations, the toxicologist decides whether a drug could have caused the victim to lose control of a car or exhibit violent or aggressive behavior, for example, and whether a drug caused or contributed to the victim's death.

The route of entry of a toxin is extremely important. If a drug was injected into a person who had no means of injecting it or into a site that makes self-administration unlikely, homicide will be a stronger consideration.

In general, the concentration of the drug or poison is greatest at the site where it's administered. For example:

- Ingested toxins show up in the stomach, intestines, or liver.
- Inhaled gases are concentrated in the lungs.

✔ Toxins that are injected intramuscularly linger in the tissues around the injection site. Drugs injected into muscle are slowly picked up by the blood and transported throughout the body.

✔ Drugs that are given intravenously (IV) bypass the stomach and liver, entering the bloodstream directly. Thus, they're quickly distributed throughout the body, and none remain at the IV injection site. The toxicologist may find high concentrations of the drug in the blood and in multiple tissues of the body but little or none in the stomach and liver (as would be seen with ingestion).

Finding a large amount of a toxin in the victim's stomach doesn't necessarily mean that the drug was the cause of death; it may not yet have been absorbed into the blood and distributed to the body. Thus, the level of the drug in the blood is more important than the concentration of the drug in the stomach contents. The toxicologist must see evidence that the drug was absorbed before he can attribute harm or death to the drug.

After determining a blood level of a certain chemical, the toxicologist assigns the level one of these four broad categories:

✔ **Normal:** This level is the one that is expected in the general population under normal circumstances.

✔ **Therapeutic:** This is the level that your doctor wants you to reach when you're taking a prescription medication. It's the blood level of the drug that brings about the most beneficial effect.

✔ **Toxic:** A toxic level is one that may cause harm — nausea, vomiting, or a drastic change in the heart's rhythm, for example — or death.

✔ **Lethal:** This is the level at which the drug in question consistently causes death. In toxicology, the term *LD50* describes the measurement of a chemical's lethal potential. The LD50 of a drug is the blood concentration at which 50 percent of the people taking it die from that intake.

You can see some wiggle room in each of these categories. Everyone reacts to chemicals and toxins differently. Much of this variance relates to age, sex, body size and weight, genetics, and nutritional and health status. A young, robust, and healthy individual usually tolerates more of a given drug than someone who is old, thin, and sickly. Drug addicts commonly ingest or inject doses of cocaine or heroin that would kill the uninitiated in minutes, and alcohol abusers can walk around with blood-alcohol levels that would flatten a nondrinker. Toxicologists must consider these factors when assessing whether a given level of a drug is toxic or lethal and whether it contributed to the subject's behavior or death.

In general, the concentration of a drug or its metabolites in urine doesn't reliably indicate the effects of the drug on the subject. The physiological effects of the drug depend upon its concentrations within the blood and various tissues of the body, including the brain. Many drugs and their metabolites are concentrated in the urine in preparation for elimination from the body, which means the concentration may be falsely high. A time lag exists between when the drug is at maximum concentration in the blood and thus has its maximum effect on the individual, and when it appears in and concentrates in the urine. Simply put, the elimination process takes time, so the urine concentration lags behind the blood concentration.

At times, toxicologists are called upon to determine whether a poisoning is *acute* (quick but intense) or *chronic* (drawn out in small doses). A good example is arsenic poisoning. Arsenic can kill when it's given in a single large dose or when it's given in repeated small doses during the course of weeks or months. In either case, the blood level may be high. But determining whether the poisoning was acute or chronic may be extremely important. The suspect list for an acute poisoning may be long, but the suspect list for a chronic poisoning would include only those who had long-term contact with the victim. A family member, a caretaker, or a family cook would qualify.

Toxicologists use the victim's hair to determine whether a poisoning was acute or chronic. Hair analysis not only reveals exposure to arsenic but also provides a timeline of the exposure. Arsenic, for example, is deposited in the cells of the hair follicles in proportion to the blood level of the arsenic at the time the cell was produced. As hair grows, hair follicle cells undergo changes and are incorporated into the growing hair shaft. In general, hair grows about half an inch in length per month. So the toxicologist can cut the hair into short segments and then measure the arsenic levels of each, thus revealing a timeline of the victim's exposure to arsenic. This evidence can be critical in assessing chronic or episodic poisonings.

Looking at Common Drugs

Every little bit helps when trying to get to the bottom of a possible poisoning, and the ME and the toxicologist use any and all evidence, including the results of toxicological testing, the autopsy examination, and statements from investigating officers and witnesses. To use this information, they must

- ✔ Know the chemical makeup, physiological actions, and byproducts of drugs and potential poisons

- ✔ Understand how drugs are metabolized by the body and the potentially toxic properties of those metabolites

- ✔ Know how these chemicals affect healthy people in addition to people with various illnesses and addictions

- ✔ Recognize the symptoms and signs produced by these chemicals

Although a discussion of every known chemical, drug, and poison wouldn't fit in this book, I provide a peek at many of the poisons, toxins, legal and illegal drugs, and chemicals that the ME and the toxicologist are likely to encounter.

Understanding alcohol

Ethanol, or drinking alcohol, is by far the most commonly abused drug. Its toxic effects are potentially lethal, and the loss of coordination and poor judgment associated with its use can lead to violent and negligent acts. Alcohol is physically addictive, and withdrawal can be an arduous and dangerous process. Without proper medical treatment for alcohol addiction, death rates from withdrawal syndromes such as delirium tremens (DTs) can be 20 percent or more.

Blood-alcohol concentration (BAC) correlates very well with the degree of intoxication. The level is expressed in grams percent, or the number of grams of alcohol in every 100 milliliters of blood. As the BAC level rises, the toxic effects of the alcohol become more pronounced. A level of 0.08 percent is the legal limit for intoxication in most jurisdictions. You may become impaired at a much lower level, but at 0.08 percent, they'll cuff you.

At a level of 0.03 percent, which for most people is the equivalent of consuming a single beer or one highball, you become giddy, but your motor skills show few ill effects. Between 0.03 percent and 0.08 percent, coordination, reaction time, and judgment decline. At a BAC above 0.12 percent, nausea and vomiting can occur, and at 0.25 percent, you're likely to go into a coma. Levels at or above 0.30 percent often lead to deep coma, and above 0.40 percent, death is likely.

A police officer who detains you as a suspect for driving under the influence (DUI) goes through several steps to determine whether you are, indeed, intoxicated. The first is a *field sobriety test,* in which the officer asks you to stand on one foot, stand steady with your eyes closed, repeatedly touch one finger to your nose, or walk a straight line in the heel-to-toe manner. These are done to determine how the alcohol you've consumed is affecting the coordination and balance centers of your brain. Alcohol makes performing each of these tasks clumsy or even impossible. Contrary to what many think, you can't fake a field sobriety test. Physiology conspires against you, and you end up stumbling, wavering, or poking yourself in the eye.

The officer may also ask you to take a breath test (see the sidebar "Exhaling the evidence: Breathalyzer tests"). If so, you're probably cooked. Alcohol passes unchanged through the lungs, going directly from the bloodstream into the air sacs of the lungs and out with each breath, so you can't fake a breath test, either. The alcohol content in your lungs directly correlates with your blood-alcohol level. The higher the level in your blood, the higher the concentration in your exhaled breath. A breath test, therefore, is extremely accurate.

A CLOSER LOOK

Exhaling the evidence: Breathalyzer tests

Indiana State Police Captain R. F. Borkenstein invented the Breathalyzer in 1954. Although it has undergone several alterations through the years, the basic concept remains unchanged. It's a device for capturing and analyzing expired air, and its beauty lies in its simplicity. To use it, just turn a valve to the TAKE position, and the subject blows into a mouthpiece that leads to a collection chamber where the breath is trapped. You then turn the valve to the ANALYZE position, exposing the captured breath to a mixture of water, silver nitrate in sulfuric acid, and potassium dichromate. Any alcohol in the expired air immediately oxidizes into acetic acid, a reaction that destroys the potassium dichromate in proportion to the amount of alcohol — the more alcohol present in the breath, the more potassium dichromate destroyed.

The Breathalyzer also contains a *spectropho-tometer,* a device that measures the absorption of a certain wavelength of light by the remaining potassium dichromate. Thus, as the potassium dichromate is destroyed, its concentration drops, and the amount of light it absorbs decreases. The spectrophotometer measures this change, and the degree of change correlates to the amount of alcohol in the breath. Furthermore, because the amount of alcohol in an expired breath is a direct reflection of the blood-alcohol level, the Breathalyzer gives an accurate, albeit indirect, measure of the level of alcohol in the blood.

If you fail a field sobriety test or a breath test, a blood-alcohol concentration (BAC) test may be performed to determine the exact level, particularly if you've been involved in an accident or caused property damage, bodily harm, or the death of another. Most hospitals and crime labs can accurately and rapidly determine your BACs. The preferred testing method is gas chromatography (see the earlier section "Presuming the results").

In suspected alcohol-caused deaths, the ME measures the alcohol level in cadaver blood to determine whether the intoxication level is high enough to have caused or contributed to the death. However, the blood-alcohol level in some corpses actually *increases* because of the action of bacteria, some of which produce alcohol. To get around this problem, the ME makes a determination of the alcohol level in the vitreous humor of the eye because it reflects a blood-alcohol level with a one- to two-hour lag. So, the vitreous humor can tell the ME what the blood-alcohol level was one to two hours before death.

Embalming a body may make determining the blood-alcohol level at the time of death difficult, if not impossible. During the embalming process, embalming fluid replaces most of the blood, leaving behind little for testing, in most cases. The embalming fluid also contains alcohol, but it's methanol and not ethanol (drinking alcohol). Because the alcohol in the embalming material doesn't enter the vitreous humor after death, the toxicologist can test the vitreous for ethanol. If ethanol turns up in the vitreous humor, it had to have been in the victim's blood before death.

Getting down with depressants

Opiates, barbiturates, alcohol, and other tranquilizers are central nervous system (CNS) depressants that make you sleepy and lethargic and thus are referred to as *downers*.

Opiates

Opiates are chemicals derived from the sap of poppies and are divided into *natural, semisynthetic,* and *synthetic,* depending upon their source and method of manufacture. They are *narcotic sedatives* (sleep producing) and *analgesics* (pain relieving) that produce euphoria, lethargy, and, in larger doses, coma and death from respiratory depression and asphyxia. You can take most either by mouth or injection; all come with great risk of abuse and physical addiction.

Deaths can occur because this class of drugs suppresses the respiratory center of the brain. The victim falls asleep, slips into a deep coma, stops breathing, and dies from asphyxia. This reaction is even more common when an opiate is mixed with alcohol, which is also a brain depressant.

Natural opiates, like morphine and codeine, come directly from the poppy. Heroin actually is diacetylmorphine and is produced by combining morphine with acetic anhydride or acetyl chloride. Heroin is by far the most commonly abused opiate.

In the living, the toxicologist uses the Marquis test to screen samples for the presence of morphine and other opiates. During an autopsy, the ME collects a blood sample for the toxicologist to analyze to determine whether the deceased used heroin.

The toxicologist doesn't test directly for heroin because he wouldn't find any. After heroin is injected, it almost immediately is broken down into monoacetylmorphine and then into morphine, the two chemicals for which the toxicologist tests. If the toxicologist finds monoacetylmorphine and morphine, the victim used heroin. If he finds only morphine, the victim may have used morphine and not heroin (but still may have used heroin). If the victim lived long enough after injecting the heroin for the heroin to be completely converted to morphine, none of the monoacetylmorphine remains, and the toxicologist may not be able to determine which drug was used.

But, the toxicologist can check other sources. Even if all heroin in the blood has been converted into morphine, an examination of the vitreous humor of the eye can reveal monoacetylmorphine, which remains in the vitreous for a much longer period of time and can prove that the deceased did, indeed, use heroin.

Autopsy findings in individuals who die from heroin overdoses are fairly consistent. The ME usually finds evidence of *pulmonary edema,* or water in the lungs; however, that isn't always the case. Curiously, the lungs often show evidence of talc crystals and cotton fibers because those substances are used respectively to cut and filter the heroin. When the drug is intravenously administered, blood carries these crystals and fibers through the heart, and then they filter from the blood and become trapped by the lungs.

Barbiturates

Barbiturates are derived from barbituric acid, and people use them as *hypnotics,* or sleeping pills. Among the five barbiturates commonly used in the past (pentobarbital, amobarbital, secobarbital, butabarbital, and phenobarbital), only phenobarbital remains in wide use today. Phenobarbital is an excellent *anticonvulsive* (seizure-preventing) medication used by many individuals afflicted with epilepsy. The others have been replaced with newer and safer hypnotics. Still, these old drugs are available and frequently abused. Because both barbiturates and alcohol can suppress respiration and even cause a cessation of breathing, their combination is particularly dangerous and may lead to coma and death from asphyxia.

A color test is used to screen for the presence of barbiturates in biological tissues (blood, urine, organs).

Hopping up: Stimulants

The most commonly used *stimulants,* or uppers, are amphetamines and cocaine. They increase alertness, lessen fatigue, and suppress appetite. However, with continued use, they also cause irritability, anxiousness, aggressive behavior, paranoia, fatigue, and depression. These reactions make sense because people who are *hopped up* all the time tend to eat and sleep poorly, overreact to stress, and simply vibrate through life, which is likely to wear anyone out. Furthermore, when it does, physical fatigue and mental exhaustion set in, which may be why one slang name for certain amphetamines is *crank* — they make the user unpleasant and cranky.

Users of stimulants often develop *tachyphylaxis,* which means that the body gets used to them, thus lessening their effects. As a result, people who abuse stimulants must take ever-increasing amounts to get the same kick. One cause of tachyphylaxis is that the body produces more of the enzymes that metabolize these drugs, so they're destroyed and eliminated at faster rates.

Amphetamines, such as crystal methamphetamine, are highly addictive, widely abused, and easily manufactured in garage labs. Because abuse of these compounds is common and widespread, testing for amphetamines is part of virtually every hospital and crime lab toxicology screen.

In the bloodstream, cocaine is converted to methylecgonine and benzoylecgonine. Urine tests target the latter of these two compounds and can find traces for up to three days after the last use. Toxicologists use both immunoassay and the Scott Color Test as screening tests for cocaine.

Taking a trip with hallucinogens

Hallucinogens are trippy. They alter perceptions and mood, lead to delusional thinking, and cause hallucinations. *Delusions* basically are false beliefs that have little or no basis in reality. *Hallucinations* are sensory experiences that aren't real and can affect any or all of the senses; they can be *visual* (sight), *auditory* (sound), *olfactory* (smell), taste, or *tactile* (touch).

The most frequently encountered hallucinogens come either from the plant world (marijuana, peyote, and mushrooms) or the chemistry laboratory (LSD, STP, and PCP).

Smoking Mary Jane

By far the most commonly used (and one of the mildest) hallucinogen is *marijuana.* It goes by many street names including Mary Jane, weed, and pot. It is a cannabinoid, which means it's derived from the *Cannabis sativa* plant. The active ingredient, *tetrahydrocannabinol* (THC), is found in marijuana at a concentration of 2 percent to 6 percent, but higher concentrations are becoming more common. Hashish, the oily extract of the plant, contains approximately 12 percent THC.

The body breaks down THC into a series of compounds, the most important being *9-carboxy-tetrahydrocannabinol* (9-carboxy-THC), which is the major urinary metabolite. Drug testing of the urine looks for this compound, which can be found up to two months after the most recent use. One problem, however, is that even passive exposure can lead to a positive urine test. For example, if you're in the area when someone is smoking marijuana, your urine may reveal low levels of 9-carboxy-THC.

In suspected users, presumptive chemical testing typically involves the Duquenois-Levine test, which shows a purple color change in the presence of cannabinoids. A positive reaction occurs with all cannabinoids and not just THC, so urine testing can't absolutely identify THC. But because most state laws prohibit the possession of any cannabis resins and not just THC, this test typically is all the police need. Other presumptive tests include TLC and GC (see the earlier "Presuming the results" section). The advantage of GC is that it gives an indication of the amount of THC present. Confirmatory testing for THC is done by MS.

Cacti and mushrooms

Peyote is a small Mexican cactus. Its active ingredient is *mescaline,* which is a hallucinogen in the alkaloid family. Many native tribes have used it in their tribal ceremonies for centuries. The surface of the cactus is covered with small round bumps called peyote buttons. These buttons are divided into sections like an orange, and each section contains a cotton-like tuft inside. Either TLC or GC can confirm the presence of alkaloids. Further testing to identify mescaline isn't necessary because possession of the plant material itself is illegal.

Mushrooms present a different problem. The mere possession of marijuana and peyote is illegal, but the possession of mushrooms isn't. And that means the toxicology lab must identify the *psychoactive components* (psilocin and psilocybin) of the mushroom before it can be deemed illegal.

Labs typically use two color-change tests to screen for the presence of psilocin and psilocybin. Van Urk's reagent turns purple, and Fast Blue B turns red in the presence of these chemicals. Often, the toxicologist uses TLC to separate the components, which are then sprayed with Van Urk's solution. Alternatively, the toxicologist views the bands produced by TLC under ultraviolet light, which causes the psilocin and psilocybin bands to glow. Confirmatory tests include GC/MS and infrared spectroscopy. Either test reveals the chemical fingerprints of the compounds and confirms their presence.

Trippy chemicals

A wide variety of chemically-produced hallucinogens are available. The most common ones are *lysergic acid diethylamide* (LSD) and *phencyclidine* (PCP, or angel dust). LSD is potent, and as little as 25 micrograms can produce an acid trip that lasts for 12 hours. Although LSD isn't directly fatal, the hallucinations it produces are typically vivid. Users in many instances have harmed themselves because of these altered perceptions. The primary screening test for LSD is the Van Urk Color Test.

PCP use can lead to aggressive and psychotic behavior. The toxicologist can use either blood or urine for PCP testing. Urine tests may remain positive for a week after the last use.

Dirty deeds: Date rape drugs

You've no doubt heard of the so-called *date-rape drugs* or *rave drugs*. They've been the subject of a considerable number of criminal actions and civil litigations. The conviction of Andrew Luster, the heir-apparent to the Max Factor fortune, was based on his illicit use of *GHB* (gamma-hydroxybutyrate).

The major date-rape drugs are *Rohypnol* (flunitrazepam), *Ecstasy* (3,4-methylenedioxymethamphetamine), GHB, and *ketamine* (ketamine hydrochloride).

These drugs cause sedation, a degree of compliance, poor judgment, and amnesia of events that occur while under their influence. The loss of event memory makes these drugs effective in date-rape situations. A criminal can easily slip a small amount of GHB or Rohypnol into the victim's drink or a bottle of seemingly innocuous water. The victim may then leave with the would-be assailant because the drug impairs judgment and enhances euphoria. Only later does the victim realize that something happened, but memories of events are spotty or even absent altogether.

CASE STUDY

Catching and convicting Andrew Luster

"That's exactly what I like in my room. A passed-out, beautiful girl," Andrew Luster, the great-grandson of makeup legend Max Factor, said into his home video camera right before having sex with his passed-out victim. He apparently had used GHB to sedate the woman. And it wasn't the first time. After an extensive police investigation turned up tapes of several women apparently unconscious and having sex with Luster, he was arrested and charged with multiple counts of illegal drug possession, poisoning, and rape.

Testimony by some of his victims revealed the power of GHB. None of them remembered having sex with Luster, nor were they aware he was videotaping the act. His sensational trial took a bizarre turn when he fled to Mexico. His trial went forward, and he was convicted and sentenced to 124 years in prison. Luster finally was captured by bounty hunter Duane "Dog" Chapman and returned to the United States to serve his sentence.

Recreational use of any of these drugs is a proverbial crapshoot. The quality and purity are variable, even with the pharmaceutically manufactured Rohypnol and ketamine, because they often are *cut* (combined with other materials, such as talc) or mixed with other drugs by the time they reach the street. Thus, users know neither what drugs nor exactly what amounts they're ingesting. And because reactions vary widely from person to person and are unpredictable, you need to make a huge leap of faith to start using these dangerous chemicals — even more frightening when you realize that many people actually use any number of different drugs at the same time. Unfortunately, many young people willingly experiment with them and end up visiting the morgue.

Ecstasy is an amphetamine and appears in most routine drug screens, but the other drugs in this category aren't typically part of such screening. However, they can be easily detected using the combination of gas chromatography and mass spectroscopy (GC/MS — see the earlier section "Confirming the results").

Sniffing and huffing

An odd, but not rare, form of substance abuse is the sniffing of volatile chemicals. This practice also is known as *huffing*. It began with glue and gasoline but has spread to include *napthalene* (moth balls), *toluene* (paint thinners, fingernail polish, and some paints), and *trichloroethylene* (paint thinners and liquid typewriter correction fluid). Other commonly abused gases are gasoline, kerosene, and nitrous oxide (the "laughing gas" used by dentists).

People who inhale the fumes of these volatile chemicals can experience giddiness, euphoria, dizziness, slurred speech, headache, nausea, and vomiting. With continued exposure, loss of consciousness, coma, and death can follow. Permanent damage to the brain, liver, heart, and kidneys also can occur.

Because these gases are volatile, they rapidly break down in the body or are quickly excreted through the lungs. The toxicologist therefore may not be able to find them in the blood or tissues of the user. Often, the toxicologist determines the chronic use of these dangerous chemicals by finding damage to the liver, lungs, and kidneys of the user.

Bulking up

The abuse of anabolic steroids has become epidemic among athletes. These hormones appear naturally in the body in very small amounts, and when taken in large amounts, they cause muscle growth, increased strength, and improved reflexes — exactly what an athlete needs to compete. But steroids are a double-edged sword. They also cause hair loss, impotence, and liver damage (including liver cancer), and can lead to aggressive behavior (called "steroid rage").

Users typically are easy to recognize as they tend to be big, muscular, and athletic. The screening and confirmatory tests mentioned earlier in this chapter detect most synthetic steroid preparations, but unscrupulous chemists constantly create newer and more difficult to detect "designer" steroids. The forensic toxicologist must continually search for new testing techniques to find these banned drugs in athletes.

Checking Out Familiar Poisons

Though poisons aren't used for homicide as often as they once were, the forensic toxicologist is still confronted with cases of accidental, suicidal, and homicidal poisoning.

Here are some of the more common poisons:

- **Cyanide** is one of the most lethal chemicals known. It can enter the body by inhalation, ingestion, or through the skin by direct contact. Cyanide gas, or hydrogen cyanide (HCN), is used for executions.

  Cyanide is a metabolic poison, which means it damages the internal workings of the cells. During autopsy, the ME may suspect cyanide poisoning from the bright, cherry red color of the victim's blood.

- **Strychnine** is a plant-based component of some rat and mole poisons. It possesses an extremely bitter taste, which makes it difficult to disguise in food or beverage. Its well-deserved reputation for causing a lot of pain makes it a rare choice for suicides.

  Strychnine causes powerful convulsive contractions of all the body's muscles. The body adopts a posture known as *opisthotonos,* which means the back is arched, and only the back of the head and the heels of the feet touch the floor. That isn't pretty. Death results from asphyxia because breathing is impossible during such violent muscular contractions. After death, rigor mortis often occurs quickly because the muscles are depleted of adenosine triphosphate (ATP) during their contractions (see Chapter 11).

- **Mushrooms** of the Amanita family are far more deadly than the hallucinogenic variety discussed in the earlier section, "Looking at Common Drugs." Called Death Cap and Death Angel mushrooms, these poisonous mushrooms have been implicated in accidental, suicidal, and homicidal deaths. Just one Death Cap can do you in. During an autopsy, the ME finds severe damage to the liver, and the toxicologist may find a low level of sugar in the blood, in addition to the amantin and phalloidin toxins.

✔ **Ethylene glycol** is the major ingredient in many antifreeze solutions. For some reason, it's a favorite beverage of alcoholics when they can't get ethanol. Unfortunately, it's deadly. All too often, when an ME is presented with the death of a homeless alcoholic, the search for the cause of death includes consideration of antifreeze ingestion. In the body, ethylene glycol breaks down into several compounds, the most important being oxalic acid, which causes oxalate crystals to develop in the brain and kidneys, resulting in irreparable damage and death. During autopsy, the ME finds the crystals in the tubules of the kidney.

✔ **Oxalic acid,** which you can find in raw rhubarb, can lead to accidental poisonings. Ingestion of this plant causes harm in two basic ways. First, it's a powerful irritant to the gastrointestinal tract and causes mouth, throat, and esophageal pain and possibly bleeding. However, its major toxic effects come from the chemical properties of the oxalic acid found in its leaves and stalks. When oxalic acid is absorbed into the bloodstream, it reacts with calcium in the blood, forming calcium oxalate, which can cause cardiac arrest and death. The calcium oxalate produced by this chemical reaction is filtered through the kidneys, where it can clog microscopic tubules and severely damage the kidneys. Survivors often require dialysis or even a kidney transplant.

During an autopsy of someone who dies from this plant, the ME finds a burned and irritated mouth, esophagus, and stomach; low blood-calcium levels; and calcium-oxalate sludge in the kidneys.

✔ **Heavy metals** are not rock bands. They're dangerous metallic elements, and you've heard of most of them. Arsenic, mercury, and lead are the ones that commonly cause illness and death. Others are bismuth, antimony, and thallium. Though each of these metals behaves differently within the human body, they all can cause gastrointestinal injury, which leads to nausea, vomiting, and diarrhea (sometimes bloody diarrhea). Also, each can damage the kidneys, liver, brain, and nerves.

✔ **Insulin** is a lifesaving substance for many diabetics. On occasion, however, diabetics die from accidental overdoses of insulin. It also has been used in suicides and homicides. The injection of a large dose dramatically drops the level of sugar in the blood, and because the brain needs a continuous supply of nutrition, death can occur quickly. Insulin normally is found in all of us, so how, you may ask, could its presence possibly raise suspicion? If the blood sugar level is found to be low and the insulin level high during an autopsy, the ME searches for an insulin-secreting tumor in the pancreas. These tumors are rare and almost never cause a sudden and unexpected death. If no tumor is found, the ME may then suspect that someone administered insulin to the victim.

✔ **Succinyl choline** is an injectable drug that paralyzes all the muscles of the body and prevents all movement, even breathing. Death occurs by asphyxia. Succinyl choline is one of the three drugs used in judicial lethal injection deaths. After injection, it's quickly metabolized by the body and leaves behind little evidence of its presence. Though controversial as to its accuracy, toxicological testing is directed toward finding the drug's metabolites, which can prove that the drug was, at one time, present in the victim.

CASE STUDY

Killing Carmela Coppolino

Carl Coppolino and his wife, Carmela, were physicians who moved from New Jersey to Longboat Key, Florida. On the night of August 28, 1965, Carl called his friend Dr. Juliette Karow and told her he had found his wife dead of an apparent heart attack. Dr. Karow came to the Coppolino home, agreed with Carl's assessment, and ultimately signed Carmela's death certificate, stating that her death was caused by a coronary thrombosis. The Sarasota County medical examiner agreed, so no autopsy was performed. Slightly more than a month later, Carl married wealthy socialite Mary Gibson.

Carl's marriage angered his former New Jersey neighbor Marjorie Farber, who had been having an affair with Carl. After her husband, William, died, Marjorie had followed the Coppolinos to Florida so that she could continue her relationship with Carl. Marjorie visited her friend Dr. Juliette Karow and told her an amazing story: Her husband's death had not been the natural event that everyone thought it was. She said that Carl, who was an anesthesiologist, had given her a filled syringe and instructed her how to inject her husband with it. Her attempt, however, was only partially successful. She panicked and called Carl, who came

over and finished off poor William by strangling him. After Carl returned home, Marjorie called the Coppolinos saying that her husband had died of an apparent heart attack. Carmela went to Marjorie's home, pronounced William Farber dead, and signed his death certificate, stating that the death was caused by coronary thrombosis.

An investigation into both deaths followed, with New York City's then–Chief Medical Examiner Dr. Milton Helpern performing an autopsy on each of the victims. Attorney F. Lee Bailey managed to gain an acquittal for Carl in the death of William Farber, but the more interesting part of the case was that of Carl's wife, Carmela. Helpern was well aware that Carl was an anesthesiologist and had access to many anesthetic drugs, including the muscle paralytic succinyl choline, which essentially was impossible to find in a corpse. Dr. Halpern brought toxicologist Dr. Charles Umberger in on the case. After months of research, Umberger managed to isolate some of the metabolites of succinyl choline, one of which was succinic acid. He then found large quantities of this acid in the brain tissues of Carmela Coppolino, and Carl eventually was convicted of second-degree murder.

Chapter 17

Picking Apart Trace Evidence

• •

In This Chapter

▶ Establishing the value of trace evidence

▶ Checking out some useful microscopic and analytical instruments

▶ Understanding how trace evidence works

• •

C riminals are clever. At least, they think they are. They know to wear
masks and use the dark of night to avoid being identified by any
witnesses. They've seen in movies the importance of wearing gloves or
wiping away fingerprints. They know not to leave behind their own blood
because DNA can hang you. Yet they continue to be tracked down, arrested,
and convicted as the direct result of tiny bits of evidence — evidence perpetrators don't see or realize they're leaving behind or carrying away from the
crime scene on shoes and clothing. As the saying goes, "The devil's in the
details." So is the evidence.

Defining Trace Evidence

From the hair that falls off your head to the carpet fibers that you track in
on the soles of your shoes, *trace evidence* is any very small physical material that can be transferred from person to person or between a person
and a crime scene. Hair, fibers, pieces of glass, chips of paint, and dirt or
plant materials are examples of trace evidence found at crime scenes or
on suspects.

Trace evidence creates links between suspects, places, and objects. In fact,
trace evidence often is the only evidence that connects the suspect to the
crime scene. So investigators must carefully document, photograph (if indicated), collect, and protect this evidence from contamination before it's
presented to the crime lab for detailed analysis.

Trace evidence is predominantly class evidence, rather than individualizing evidence (see Chapter 3): It can exclude a suspect but rarely can it absolutely implicate a suspect. For example, if a blond hair is found at a crime scene and the suspect has black hair, the suspect is exonerated, and police must develop another theory. But, if the suspect's hair matches that found at the crime scene, that person remains a suspect.

An extremely important characteristic of most trace evidence is its transferability. It grabs and clings to clothing, hides in shoe seams, nestles into hair, settles into nooks and crannies, and typically survives for months or years.

In the early 1900s, Edmund Locard of Lyon, France, showed that he could use traces of dust to determine whether a particular individual had been in a certain place. He recognized that everyone constantly picks up and leaves behind tiny pieces of the environment, and that recognition evolved into the Locard Exchange Principle, which is the cornerstone of forensic investigation. Find out more about Locard's principle in Chapter 1.

Locard's principle is the main underlying reason each crime scene is secured and access to it controlled. Everyone who enters the scene takes away and adds trace materials, and this contamination can render any evidence that investigators find useless at trial. Obviously, if the first officers on the scene don't yet know that a crime has occurred, or if they must disarm and apprehend a suspect or assist a victim, some contamination is bound to occur. The same is true for medical and rescue personnel who must help the injured. These situations make the criminalist's job much more difficult.

Understanding Analytical Instruments

The analysis of trace evidence requires a thorough investigation of its physical and chemical properties. Because most trace evidence is very small, investigators can't adequately examine it with the naked eye. Nor can they easily determine its chemical properties. Fortunately, the modern crime lab has a wide array of magnification and analytical systems.

Peering through the microscope

Most types of trace evidence initially are inspected with the naked eye under good lighting. Indirect or angled light brings out details by creating depth and shadows in everything from soil and plants to paint and glass. Ultraviolet and laser lights can expose certain fibers, hair, chemicals, and other substances, but minute details of such evidence must be viewed under magnification.

In addition to the old standard — the compound binocular microscope (the kind you probably used in your high school science classes) — trace evidence examiners use many types of microscopic equipment and techniques to search for and analyze trace evidence:

- **Comparison microscope:** This instrument provides a side-by-side comparison of two pieces of physical evidence. I discuss it in detail in Chapter 7.

- **Microspectrophotometry:** Everyone sees light and color a little differently. One person's red may be another's orange. With microspectrophotometry, the exact color of an object or material and its light transmission, absorption, and reflection characteristics are accurately measured. It works with either standard white light or with infrared (IR) light and is extremely useful for examining paint chips, colored fibers, and dyed or treated hair.

  When comparing two paint chips or fiber strands, an exact color match is an important first step in determining whether they share a common origin. If the colors differ, the two did not come from the same source. Microspectrophotometry allows the examiner to make this determination with extreme accuracy.

- **Polarized light microscope:** Polarized light causes less scatter of the reflected light, making an object appear sharper and its colors clearer. Viewing materials under polarized light can bring out details that you couldn't see under standard light. Examiners use this microscope to examine hair, fibers, and other solid materials.

- **Scanning electron microscope (SEM):** This instrument can attain magnifications up to 100,000 times the original, but rarely do examiners need magnifications above 20,000 to 25,000 times in forensics work. A standard microscope uses light for viewing an object, but an SEM uses an electron beam. This beam sweeps across the object and is viewed through electromagnetic lenses that greatly magnify the image and provide incredible clarity.

  Often, examiners couple an SEM with an *energy dispersive X-ray spectrometer* (EDS), a device that analyzes the light and color characteristics of very small objects. The resulting SEM/EDS is capable of defining structures less than one micron (one millionth of a meter) in size and accurately defining light characteristics of the material.

  This technique is useful in gunshot residue analysis because it can identify the mineral elements, creating a fingerprint of the residue.

- **Stereomicroscope:** *Stereovision* is a result of your eyes being in different spots — you see things from two slightly different angles, and that gives your vision depth. If you look at an object and quickly close and open your eyes, one at a time, you get a good demonstration of this effect. A stereomicroscope works on the same principle. It's a binocular scope (an eyepiece and viewing tube for each eye) in which the point of view of each eyepiece differs by an angle of 10 to 15 degrees, giving a three-dimensional appearance to the object you're examining.

The layers of a paint chip, the texture of a fabric, the surface markings of glass, or the curliness of a hair are best seen in stereovision. For example, the examiner may use a stereomicroscope to analyze the weave, texture, fiber size, and other physical characteristics of two pieces of cloth to determine whether they match.

Testing the chemical makeup of trace materials

When they really need to get down to the nitty-gritty, examiners use more than microscopes. With the following techniques, which are the most common ones, examiners can determine the chemical properties of trace evidence, which helps to determine if the tested samples are identical and thus share a common origin:

- **Infrared spectrophotometry:** This technique involves exposing samples of trace evidence to infrared light. Various substances absorb infrared light at different wavelengths, and these differences distinguish one substance from another.

- **Neutron activation analysis:** This procedure is cumbersome and requires a nuclear reactor. Neutrons fired at the sample collide with its components, causing each component to release radiation at its own unique energy level. Measuring the levels of those radiation emissions reveals the chemical makeup of the sample. This process is useful in the analysis of paint, soil, hair, metals, and many other substances.

   As you can imagine, a nuclear reactor is bulky and expensive. Few labs have them, so this kind of testing usually is conducted by larger regional labs.

- **X-ray diffraction:** In this test, objects or materials are bombarded with an X-ray beam. The way that beam scatters reveals how atoms and molecules in the substance are arranged and thus results in a *chemical fingerprint* of the substance that is useful with materials like paint and soil.

Splitting Hairs: Linking Crime to Coiffure

Investigators frequently find hairs, both human and animal, at crime scenes. The ME must determine whether the hair came from the family dog, the victim, or perhaps the perpetrator.

Although the shaft of the hair alone can't be matched to an individual, it has several properties that make it useful to criminalists. It's small, easily shed, clings to clothing and other materials, and goes unnoticed by perpetrators at crime scenes. Hair is hardy and survives for a long period of time, even years after bodies decompose. Examiners can find many toxins, particularly heavy metals like arsenic, in hair (see Chapter 16). Also, if the follicle is attached to the hair, examiners can often extract DNA and use it to make an exact match (see Chapter 15).

The bulk of hair analysis deals with its structure and chemical characteristics. The value of hair as evidence depends upon how confidently an examiner can match two or more hairs. But hair varies not only from person to person but also from one area of an individual's body to another — the hair on your head is different from the hair on your arms or other parts of your body. Investigators most often examine head or pubic hair as evidence.

Hair analysis is one of the areas of forensic science that has come under fire lately. Lack of standardization of methods and the qualifications of the examiners have led many labs to cease doing these examinations. Yet, if the hair is unique enough and if the examination is properly performed, it can still offer useful evidence. That is, if the judge will allow such testimony to enter the courtroom, and that is becoming increasingly problematic.

Dissecting hair's anatomy

Hair grows out of the skin from a pocket of specialized cells called a *follicle*. The shaft of the hair is made up of three parts (see Figure 17-1), each of which an examiner can use to match hairs. The structure of hair is similar to the yellow pencil you used in school. The lead would be the *medulla,* the wood the *cortex,* and the yellow paint the *cuticle.*

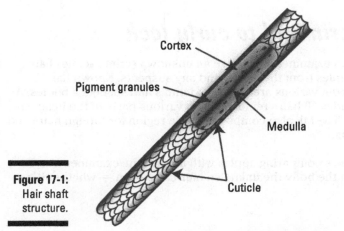

Cortex

Pigment granules

Medulla

Cuticle

Figure 17-1:
Hair shaft
structure.

Illustration by Nan Owen

✔ **Cortex:** In human hair, the *cortex* is the largest portion of the shaft and is the component that contains hair pigment, which gives hair its color. Pigment particles show highly variable colors, shapes, and distribution patterns, all of which help examiners determine race, match known and unknown hair, and identify sources of hair. Under microscopic examination, investigators use the pattern of air pockets and structures within the cortex to seek a match.

✔ **Cuticle:** The *cuticle* is a layer of cells that cover the surface of the shaft and look like scales on a fish or perhaps even roofing tiles. Examiners use scale patterns to determine whether the hair is human or not and to match one hair to another. Scales overlap and always point up the shaft, away from the bulb. These scales are of the following three basic types and vary by species:

- **Coronal** (crownlike) scales give the hair a mosaic surface appearance. Human hair rarely has these scales, but they're common among rodents.

- **Spinous** (petallike) scales tend to be somewhat triangular in shape. These scales aren't found in humans but are typical of cats.

- **Imbricate** (flattened) scales are found in humans and many other animals.

✔ **Medulla:** The central core of the hair, the *medulla* contains a collection of cells but appears as if it's an empty or mud-filled central canal. The width of the medulla relative to the overall width of the hair is called the *medullary index.* In most animals, this index is greater than 0.5, which means that the medulla is more than half the thickness of the hair. In humans, however, the medulla typically is narrow, with an index of approximately 0.3. Whether the material within the medulla appears solid and continuous, interrupted, or fragmented helps criminalists determine the hair's species of origin. Databases of hair types from various animals help them make the match.

Matching criminal to curly lock

To compare hairs, an examiner must have an unknown (crime scene) hair and known hair samples from the victim and any suspects. Known hair samples are taken from various areas of the victim's and suspect's bodies. A typical sample includes 50 hairs removed from various parts of the head and several pubic hairs. The ME also combs the pubic region for foreign hairs and other trace materials.

To make sure that he's comparing apples with apples, the examiner tries to determine where on the body the unknown hair came from — whether it's a head hair, a pubic hair, or a hair from some other location. This determination is essential because the examiner wants to match crime-scene hair with hair taken from the same location on the suspect. In general, hairs taken from different areas of the body have different cross-sectional geometries. Head, eyebrow, and eyelash hairs are more likely to be round, axillary (armpit) hairs are oval, and beard hairs are triangular.

Examiners use a comparison microscope (see Chapter 7) to view known and unknown hairs side by side and work through the following checklist of comparisons:

- ✔ Color and width
- ✔ Distribution pattern of the medulla
- ✔ Color and distribution pattern of pigment in the cortex
- ✔ Cuticle pattern

A study performed by the Royal Canadian Mounted Police shows that if a crime-scene head hair matches a suspect's head hair in all the respects mentioned in the previous list, the probability that the crime-scene hair came from someone other than the suspect is 4,500 to 1. With pubic hairs, the probability falls to about 800 to 1.

Finding further clues

Microscopic examination of the hair may reveal tissue adhering to its root. Because yanking hair from the scalp often rips out follicular tissues, finding tissue suggests that the hair was forcibly removed instead of falling out naturally. A cut edge, of course, indicates that a sharp instrument was employed to cut the hair. In such situations, the examiner can often determine what type of instrument was used.

Dyeing to be matched

If you dye your hair, more than your roots may give you away. With infrared microspectrophotometry, a trace evidence examiner may be able to determine not only whether your hair has been dyed, bleached, or treated but when you last visited the hairdresser — important details for determining your identity. A complete strand of hair reveals the history of your color treatments. Because hair grows approximately half an inch a month, a one-inch segment of undyed or unbleached hair near the root suggests that the last treatment was two months earlier. That pretty much tells you bottle blondes how long it's going to take for those tasteless jokes to stop, doesn't it?

Determining race

Neither age nor sex can be determined by analyzing hair; however, the general nature of the hair (color, thickness, curliness) sometimes separates the source along broad racial lines. Caucasians, for example, tend to have straight or wavy hair with a round or oval cross-sectional shape and a finer and more evenly distributed cortical pigment pattern. People of African ancestry have curly hair that's flat or oval when viewed in cross-section. In addition, the cortical pigment is denser and unevenly distributed. Unfortunately, these characteristics aren't completely reliable, mostly due to racial admixture and individual variations.

Making it individual

You can also find many of the chemicals within your body in your hair. Techniques such as neutron activation analysis (NAA) — see the earlier section "Testing the chemical makeup of trace materials") — can detect more than a dozen different chemicals. Because two people rarely have the exact same chemicals in their hair, comparing the types and amounts of these substances may enable a forensic examiner to determine whether two hairs likely came from the same person.

In certain circumstances, hair can supply DNA, which is highly individualizing. Hair is composed of dead cellular debris that has no nuclei, so you can't find any nuclear DNA within the hair's shaft. The bulb, or so-called root, where hair manufacture and growth take place, is composed of live cells, so examiners can often find DNA there. If hair is pulled from the victim or the assailant, root or follicular tissue, which contains DNA, may be attached. With the newer techniques of PCR amplification and STR analysis (see Chapter 15), a single hair follicle can yield enough DNA for comparison.

This not only works for humans but also for cats, dogs, and other pets and farm animals. Matching DNA from hair obtained from a suspect's clothing to a victim's pet — or vice versa — has proven useful in many cases.

Snowball the Cat: A famous forensic case

In 1994, Shirley Duguay of Prince Edward Island disappeared. A few days later her corpse was discovered in a shallow grave along with a leather jacket, which was soaked with her blood and dotted with white cat hairs. Her estranged husband, Douglas Beamish, owned a white cat named Snowball. DNA in blood taken from Snowball matched that of the cat hairs found at the burial site, proving that those hairs came from Snowball and no other white cat. Beamish was convicted, marking this case the first time that animal DNA was used to gain a conviction.

Matching paint chip to Pontiac in the John Vollman case

Sixteen-year-old Gaetane Bouchard disappeared in 1958. Her body later was found in a nearby gravel pit. She'd been stabbed several times in the chest. Near the pit, police found tire tracks and two chips of green paint that appeared to have been chipped off of a car by flying gravel as the vehicle drove away. Witnesses said that they'd seen Bouchard with a man in a light green car. Friends told police that Bouchard had been seeing a 20-year-old musician from across the border in Madawaska, Maine.

Police visited John Vollman, who owned a light-green 1952 Pontiac. An examination of the car showed that the paint was chipped, and one of

the chips found at the scene appeared to match one of the defects in the car's paint. Microscopic analysis later confirmed the match. During an autopsy, a single hair was found clutched in the victim's hand. That hair and hair from the victim and Vollman were subjected to neutron activation analysis (NAA), a form of nuclear analysis that ultimately showed that Vollman's hair and the hair from the crime scene were similar in chemical content. After prosecutors presented the NAA evidence at Vollman's trial, Vollman suddenly changed his plea from not guilty to guilty of manslaughter. This case was the first in which atomic evidence (as it was called in 1958) led to a conviction.

In the majority of cases, the examiner can extract mitochondrial DNA (mtDNA) from the hair shaft. Because the hair is built from cellular remnants, and because the cell cytoplasm houses mtDNA, you may be able to obtain a usable sample of mtDNA from cut or bulb-less shed hair. Examiners can identify the individual who shed the hair through mtDNA analysis and comparison of its pattern with the pattern of samples from the suspect's siblings or maternal-line relatives (see Chapter 15).

Fiddling with Fibers

Right this minute, countless fibers are on and around you. Some of them originated from your home and some were passed to you when you hugged your friend or bumped into your co-worker on the way to the copy room.

Clothing, carpet, car mats, bedding, towels, and thousands of other things that you use every day are composed of various fabrics. Because they're so common and come in such a wide variety of types, fibers from these fabrics are an important type of trace evidence. Like hair, they're easily shed, transferred, and transported. They stick to skin and clothing and become entangled in hair. Criminalists may collect fibers from the victim's or the suspect's body, hair, clothing, home, or car, or from the crime scene. The crime lab can use these fibers to try to identify the manufacturer or the source of a particular fiber or match one fiber with another.

As with hair analysis, fiber analysis has been under increased scrutiny, again due to lack of standardization of the examination techniques and the examiner's expertise.

Classifying fibers

A *fiber*, basically, is any threadlike element of a material — the threads in your shirt or the tiny pieces twisted together in your carpet. Fibers fall into three basic categories:

- **Natural** fibers come from various animals, plants, and minerals. Examiners can often easily identify and compare these fibers by microscopic inspection alone. Animal hair that is woven into fabric or used to manufacture clothing and other household items is considered natural fiber. Other examples are wool, mohair, cashmere, and silk. Plant fibers include cotton, hemp, flax, and jute.

  By far, the most commonly used natural fiber is cotton. When examined under a microscope, it has an easily recognizable twisted-ribbon pattern. Undyed white cotton is so common that it's of little evidentiary value. Natural fibers derived from minerals include such materials as asbestos.

- **Manufactured,** or regenerated, fibers are fabrics like rayon, acetate, and triacetate. To make them, raw cotton or wood pulp is dissolved, and cellulose is extracted. The cellulose is then regenerated into fibers.

- **Synthetic** fibers come from *polymers,* which are substances made up of a series of *monomers* (single molecules) strung together to make larger molecules that can be thousands of monomers long. Nylon and polyester are synthetic fibers.

Collecting fibers

Time is critical when collecting fiber evidence because studies show that fibers clinging to the clothing of a victim or suspect are lost quickly. After four hours, 80 percent of them may have fallen away, and after 24 hours, 95 percent are likely gone. A search for trace evidence on the clothing of the victim and any suspects therefore needs to take place as soon as possible. Fibers can be lifted from clothing with tape or by vacuuming.

At the crime scene, fibers are most commonly found at the focal point of the crime (the body, a cracked safe, a ransacked desk), particularly if a physical altercation has taken place in that area. Other places that should be thoroughly searched include the points of entry and exit and the routes of approach and escape, if the investigators can identify these points.

Comparing fibers

In the lab, a fiber analyst first examines unknown fibers under a stereomicroscope, assessing their diameters, shapes, colors, shininess, and curls and crimps, and then looking for any attached debris. When matching two fibers, the analyst uses a comparison microscope so that two or more fibers can be compared side by side.

Other tools that help the investigator dig deeper into the fiber's physical and chemical characteristics are

- **Birefringence:** When light passes through some synthetic fibers, it's refracted twice and emerges as two different wavelengths of polarized light, each with its own refractive characteristics. A comparison of the birefringence of two fibers is useful for identification and comparison.

- **Microspectrophotometry:** This process helps the examiner determine a fiber's true color without the problem of observer bias. See the section "Understanding Analytical Instruments" earlier in this chapter for more about microspectrophotometry.

- **Polarized light:** This tool estimates the *reflective index* (the amount and angle of light reflected by an object or substance) of the fiber and helps determine its makeup.

- **Refractive index:** The *refractive index* is measured by directing a narrow light beam at a fiber and calculating the degree to which light is bent as it passes through. This index varies from fiber to fiber.

- **Scanning electron microscope:** Whenever a fiber or piece of fabric is damaged, the fiber analyst can use an SEM to examine fine structural and surface details that can reveal exactly how the damage occurred.

Breaking down the fiber

Two commonly used procedures — the combination of SEM with dispersive X-ray spectrometer (SEM/EDS) and the combination of gas chromatography with mass spectrometry (GS/MS) — can yield the chemical composition of the fiber and of any pigments or treatments that have been added to it during the manufacturing process or as a later alteration. In fact, GC/MS can separate and identify each chemical found in the fiber or in the various applied treatments. For example, the presence of tin and bromide can indicate treatment with a fire retardant. Titanium oxide is found in many delustering products, substances that lessen a fiber's luster or shine.

These chemical determinations can point to the manufacturer of the fiber or serve to more strongly match one fiber with another. After analyzing the physical and chemical properties of known and unknown fibers, the criminalist may be able to say that the two very likely came from the same source. If, on the other hand, the fibers differ in any of their characteristics, the criminalist concludes that they didn't share a common source.

Cracking the Mysteries of Glass

Here's good news for anyone who's tried to sneak in a substitute after breaking Grandma's favorite glass vase: Even a crime lab would have a hard time determining that it wasn't the original. Glass analysis, which is a common undertaking in the crime lab, rarely supplies individualizing evidence, but it can offer class evidence that's helpful to the examiner in determining the probability that two pieces are similar or that they came from a common source. The examiner may confidently say that the original vase and your substitute share the same class characteristics (color, shape, surface characteristics, and optical and chemical properties) and that they may have come from the same source, but he rarely can say that the two absolutely, positively share a source.

Looking into how glass becomes evidence

The glass in your windshield differs from the glass that holds your orange juice. You can easily differentiate between the two by sight, and an examiner who compares the chemical composition of the two also can tell them apart. If either of these kinds of glass breaks, it typically scatters fragments that may attach to weapons, shoes, and clothing, or settle on your skin and in your hair. Perpetrators who shatter a window, break a vase, or drop a glass object risk transferring these fragments to their clothing and thus giving investigators a piece of trace evidence that connects them to the crime.

Glass can trip up criminals in another way: It has a hard, smooth surface that is ideal for retaining fingerprints and shoeprints. For example, an intruder may accidentally touch a piece of glass while crawling through a window or step on a large piece of a broken glass that's fallen to the floor or ground. Either of these situations can yield clear and usable impressions.

In addition, broken glass can injure the perpetrator and result in bleeding. If the point of entry or exit is a broken window or sliding glass door panel, the perpetrator easily can suffer a scrape or cut and yet be completely unaware of the injury, thus leaving behind a DNA sample for the crime lab.

Analyzing and matching glass

Glass is made by heating a mixture of sand (silica or silicon dioxide), limestone (calcium carbonate), and soda (sodium carbonate). During the process, certain other chemicals are added to alter the characteristics of the glass, and various impurities creep into the final product. An investigator can determine the chemical makeup of these additives and impurities, which can be useful in either matching or excluding an unknown sample.

Analyzing the physical, optical, and chemical properties of glass can lead criminalists to its manufacturer. A shard of glass from a car windshield or headlamp may signify the make, model, and even the year of a car used in a crime or involved in a motor-vehicle accident or hit-and-run.

- ✔ **Measuring density:** Comparing the densities of glass samples requires a cylindrical container filled with liquids of different densities. The liquids most often used are bromoform and bromobenzene. They are mixed together, the piece of glass is added, and then one or the other of the liquids is added until the glass is suspended, neither rising nor sinking. At that point, the glass and liquid mixture have the same density. Because the densities of the liquids are known, an investigator can easily calculate the density of the mixture, and thus of the glass. When a known piece of glass is suspended in this manner, and an unknown piece is added, if the latter remains suspended, the densities of the two are identical. If, however, the unknown fragment either sinks or floats, the two pieces of glass don't share the same density and thus aren't from the same source.

- ✔ **Shining light on the subject:** Various glass products transmit, reflect, and refract light in different manners. *Transmitted* light passes through the glass like sunlight through a window. *Reflected* light bounces off the glass, and *refracted* light passes through the glass, but its pathway is bent as the glass slightly changes the direction of the light. Different types of glass differ in one or more of these optical properties. As a result, investigators can show that two pieces of glass are similar, if they share common optical properties.

For example, you can test the refractive index by submerging the piece of glass in a liquid with a refractive index that changes when the temperature of the liquid changes. Silicon oil works. Then, you slowly heat the liquid. The temperature at which the piece of glass seems to disappear reveals when refractive indexes of the glass and the oil are equal. Because the refractive index of a liquid like silicon oil is known at any given temperature, measuring the temperature of the liquid yields the refractive index of the glass.

✔ **Getting chemical:** A forensic chemist can test for additives and impurities in the glass with an eye toward matching the chemical makeup of known and unknown samples. Any differences found enable the chemist to state that the two don't share a common source.

Breaking glass

The way glass cracks often provides clues regarding how it was broken. For example, glass that was broken by a speeding bullet has a different fracture pattern than glass that was broken by a rock crashing through it.

Certain characteristics of a break enable an examiner to determine the direction from which the impact came. Among them are stress-fracture lines that are known as *conchoidal lines,* or lines that radiate from the impact site (see Figure 17-2). Viewed through the thickness of the glass, these lines tend to curve out and away from the point of impact. A closer look reveals smaller lines that radiate in a direction perpendicular to the conchoidal lines. These indications are called *hackle marks.*

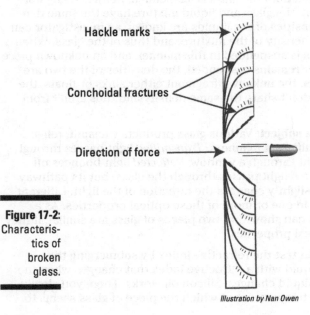

Hackle marks

Conchoidal fractures

Direction of force

Figure 17-2: Characteristics of broken glass.

Illustration by Nan Owen

Cracks in windows and other flat plates of glass tend to be radial and concentric. *Radial cracks* spread outward from the point of impact in a spoke-like configuration. *Concentric cracks* are a series of progressively larger circles around the point of impact. Overall, a cracked window may look like a spider web.

If a projectile, such as a bullet, strikes a window and penetrates it but doesn't completely shatter it, the impact may leave a hole with or without surrounding fracture lines. On the side of the impact, the hole would be rather clean, but on the side opposite the impact, a small cone-shaped plug of glass would have been knocked out. A simple visual inspection of the impact site often reveals the direction of travel of the projectile.

If multiple bullets or other objects break the glass, investigators can often determine the order in which they struck. Radial fractures caused by a second impact typically don't cross fractures from the first impact. In other words, fractures from a second impact end when they encounter glass that's already fractured (see Figure 17-3).

Figure 17-3:
Impact radial fracture lines in glass end abruptly at fracture lines produced by a previous impact. In this case, Fracture B followed Fracture A.

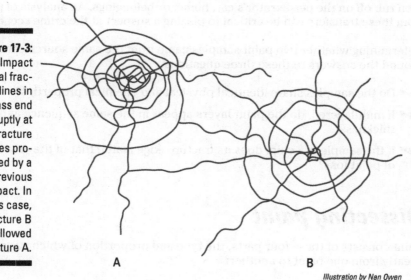

A   B

Illustration by Nan Owen

On other occasions, the lab is asked to determine whether two pieces of glass once were part of the same object. Again, visual and microscopic examinations can be helpful. For example, the fracture line of a piece of glass found at a crime scene can be matched to a similar piece found in the possession of a suspect. Under the microscope, two edges sometimes reveal a perfect fit that indicates the two pieces once were one.

Puttering with Paints

I challenge you to find an environment in which nothing is painted. Unless you live in a cave or a tent on the beach, chances are good that you're surrounded by paint. Your house, your car, and your office have painted surfaces. You come into contact with painted surfaces on a daily basis, and so do criminals. Such paint chips and smears often transfer from one painted surface to another or to a victim or perpetrator during the commission of a crime.

The most common paint samples that are submitted to most crime labs for evaluation come from automobiles. Paint can be transferred from one car to another or from a car to a pedestrian victim. An analysis of the paint's physical and chemical properties often reveals the paint manufacturer and ultimately the make, model, and perhaps even the year of the automobile involved in the accident. This evidence is critical when investigating a hit-and-run accident.

Occasionally, paint or paint chips from a house or other property are submitted. Perpetrators may track through paint on a floor or somehow transfer paint from a freshly painted wall to their clothing or hands. This paint may then rub off on the perpetrator's car, home, or belongings. An analysis of paint from these transfers can be critical to placing a suspect at the crime scene.

Determining whether two paint samples came from the same source centers around the answers to these three questions:

- Do the samples share identical physical and chemical properties?
- If multilayered, do the paint layers appear in the same sequence and thickness?
- If the sample is a chip, does its fracture edge match that of the area of paint loss?

Dissecting paint

Paint consists of these four parts, the type and proportion of which vary greatly from one paint to another:

- **Binders** typically are natural or synthetic resins to which pigments are added.
- **Extenders** add solid bulk, which increases the covering capacity of the paint.
- **Modifiers** change the gloss, flexibility, hardness, and durability of the paint. An example is lead oxide, which toughens paint and makes it resistant to weather.
- **Pigments** add color. They can be organic (most blues and greens) or inorganic (most reds, yellows, and whites) in nature.

Like most trace evidence examinations, paint analysis starts with a simple eyeball test. If samples are of similar color and luster, an examiner checks out the thickness of the layers of paint and the sequence of colors, if several were used.

If the physical qualities match, the examiner then turns to the chemical makeup of the paint or of each layer of paint. This analysis includes any binders, pigments, extenders, and modifiers and is completed using several tools.

Investigators commonly use the combination of GC/MS (see Chapter 8), with a slight twist. Because paint chips are solid, the process that's used is called pyrolysis gas chromatography. *Pyrolysis* is the conversion of a solid into a gas by using high heat. In pyrolysis GC, gas from the pyrolyzed paint chip passes through the GC column and is separated into its various chemical components, which then undergo mass spectrometry. This test reveals a chemical fingerprint of the components of the paint that enables the examiner to make accurate comparisons of submitted paint samples.

Solving the puzzle

By far, the most individualizing evidence in paint analysis is physically matching the edges of a paint chip. If investigators can show that the edges of known and unknown paint chips perfectly fit the way two pieces of a jigsaw puzzle go together, this evidence is fairly conclusive that the two are from the same source. Stereomicroscopic, comparative microscopic, and SEM examinations of the chips can aid in the matching process.

Getting Down and Dirty: Soils and Plants

Remember when your mother scolded you for tracking dirt into the house? You couldn't deny that you did it because the evidence was on your shoes. Criminals face the same situation. Soil from a crime scene, shoes, clothing, car tires, or tools like shovels frequently is submitted to the crime lab for analysis, and the results can substantiate or destroy alibis, refute or support testimony of suspects and witnesses, and place a suspect at or near the scene of the crime — the same way your mother knew it was you.

Identifying soils

Soil is not simply dirt. It's a complex mixture of minerals, plant, and animal matter, and tiny particles of man-made products such as glass, paint, asphalt, concrete, and other materials. The contents of soil vary greatly from one region or locale to another. Soil near the beach in California is much different from the red clay of Alabama, but it also differs greatly from soil found in a downtown Los Angeles park.

Forensic soil analysis begins with visual and microscopic inspections and progresses to determinations of color, consistency, pH (a measure of soil acidity), and mineral content. The examiner also checks out any foreign substances, such as plant material or animal hair. For example, finding patches of beachfront sandy soil on the tires and floor mats of a suspect's car can cast doubt on or even contradict the suspect's claims of never having been near the shore. Likewise, finding horsehair and flecks of horse manure in a soil sample may indicate that the soil came from a horse farm and not from the suspect's backyard.

Chemical analyses can determine whether two samples are chemically similar. X-ray diffraction is useful in examining and comparing minerals that are present in soil samples. GC/MS (see Chapter 8) can identify many constituents of the sample, and investigators find another technique, known as *differential thermal analysis,* useful. The principle behind this form of analysis is that soils absorb and release heat at different rates. In this test, a sample is heated in a specially designed furnace. The point at which the soil breaks down, melts, or boils is determined and then compared with similar thermal properties of other soils to find out whether they match.

Looking at plants and seeds

Plant materials have great forensic significance. They're found in soil samples, on corpses, clothing, flooring, car mats, and tools, and in many other places. As is true of any type of trace evidence, plant materials can link a suspect to a crime or a crime scene. Investigators often look for leaves, stems, pine needles, bark, flower petals, seeds, and pollen because various plants are native to different areas, and materials from them can help determine the origin of a soil sample. For example, if investigators find pine needles on the floor near a homicide victim, but no pine trees grow near the residence, the killer probably brought the needles with him on his clothing or shoes. Determining the particular species of pine tree the needles came from helps narrow the search area.

Pollen, which comes from flowering plants, can be extremely useful to the forensics examiner. Pollen grains are tiny and rarely noticed, yet they're highly distinctive. Pollen may be found on clothing, in the hair of a victim or suspect, and even in envelopes containing threatening letters or ransom notes. Microscopic identification of pollen samples may reveal that the victim or suspect had been in an area where the particular plant was in bloom. Several pollen reference databases provide help with species identification.

Additionally, DNA analysis of pollen and seeds can not only identify the plant species but also can often be linked to a particular tree. Maybe the pine tree growing near the suspect's home.

Chapter 18

Bang! Bang!: Analyzing Firearms Evidence

In This Chapter

▶ Getting to know guns

▶ Analyzing bullets and shell casings

▶ Matching rifling patterns

▶ Handling gunshot residues

*G*uns are a source of pleasure and sport for many people and, when used properly, are safe. But watch a movie, any movie, and odds are that someone, and often several someones, will be shot. Guns have been a movie staple for many years. Old westerns always involved a gunfight or two, and if you view any current TV dramas, you're likely to see that cops, private investigators, criminals, gang members, and just about everyone has a gun. And real life isn't far behind. Watch the news or read a newspaper any day of the week, and you're bound to find that a gun was used in some illegal way.

In fact, guns commonly are used in criminal activities. Besides their obvious capacity for murder and injury, guns are an effective means for gaining control. In armed robberies, abductions, and rapes, having a gun can ensure compliance from the victims. Deaths from gunshots can be accidental, suicidal, or homicidal. In a homicide, evidence from the gun or ammunition often proves to be the perpetrator's undoing.

This area of forensic investigation is often erroneously called *ballistics*. In fact, ballistics is the study of how projectiles — bullets, rockets, mortar shells — travel through space. Gun and bullet examination is actually *firearms examination,* which is performed by specially trained *forensic firearms examiners.* They commonly have to

✔ Analyze bullets and shell casings found at a crime scene to determine what type of weapon fired them

✔ Help with crime-scene reconstruction by estimating the distance between the gun muzzle and the victim or working out the trajectory of the bullets

✔ Match a bullet or shell casing to a particular weapon or to a sample from a different crime scene to link the two

Figuring Out Firearms

Have you ever fired a gun? Most people vividly remember their first time. The sudden explosive discharge is shocking. Even if you expected the recoil, it probably was more of a jolt than you anticipated.

Guns work by instigating an explosion that sends a bullet racing out of the barrel. When you pull the trigger of a gun, its firing pin strikes a cylinder of primer in the shell of the bullet and ignites it, causing gunpowder in the shell to explode. The explosion pushes the bullet through and out of the gun's barrel with tremendous velocity.

Guns typically are classified as handguns, rifles, or shotguns:

✔ **Handguns,** as the name suggests, are held and fired in one hand (as opposed to rifles and shotguns, which you brace against your shoulder to fire) and fall into one of the following three categories:

  • **Revolvers** are the handguns that you see in old westerns. Bullet and shot cartridges (shell casings loaded with a primer, gunpowder, and bullets or shotgun pellets) are placed into a cylinder that revolves with each pull of the trigger, bringing the next cartridge in front of the gun's firing hammer in a sequential manner. After a bullet is fired, its shell casing remains in the cylinder until it's manually removed.

  • **Semiautomatic pistols** (see Figure 18-1) are loaded using a magazine or clip. The clip is basically a spring-loaded device that holds a stack of cartridges that typically slides into the handle of the pistol. This type of weapon, like the revolver, fires once for each pull of the trigger. Some of the explosive energy is used, however, to automatically eject the empty shell casing from the gun, and the spring in the clip seats the next cartridge into the firing chamber.

  • **Machine pistols** are truly automatic weapons. They possess a clip similar to that of a semiautomatic pistol and, when fired, use some of the explosive power from each spent round (cartridge) to expel an empty casing and bring the next cartridge into the firing chamber. The major difference between these pistols and semiautomatics is that machine pistols fire repeatedly as long as the trigger is depressed and ammunition is available in the clip.

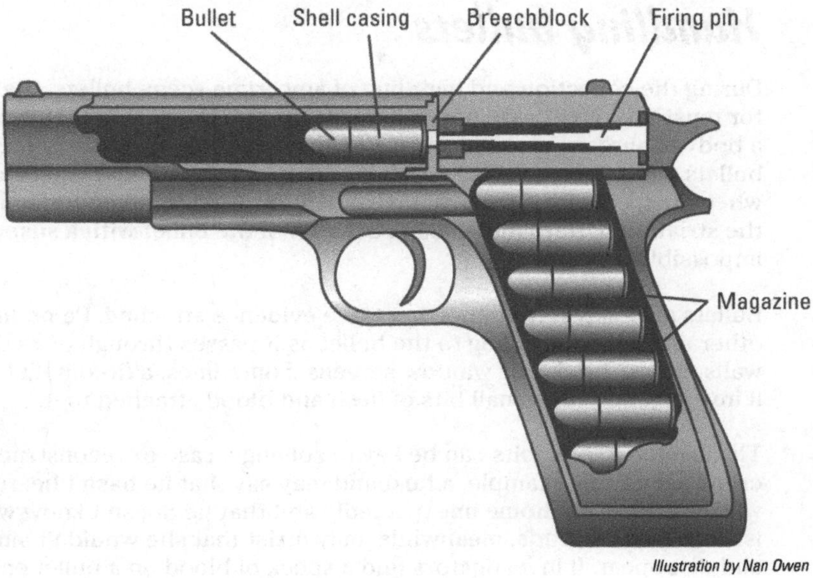

Bullet   Shell casing   Breechblock   Firing pin

Magazine

Figure 18-1:
Anatomy of
a handgun.

✔ **Rifles** often utilize a lever or a sliding bolt to eject a spent cartridge and bring the next one into the firing chamber. Rifles also can be semiautomatic or automatic.

✔ **Shotguns,** in general, don't fire bullets but rather shells filled with groups of pellets *(shot).* As the shot exit the barrel, they spread out in a circular pattern, which means shotguns don't require as much aiming. You just have to point them in the intended direction.

Extracting Info from Ammo

Rarely do investigators find a smoking gun at a crime scene — in large part because most powders used these days are smokeless — but even a metaphorically smoking gun is hard to come by. Bullets, however, are the next best thing and can go a long way toward helping a forensic firearms examiner determine what kind of gun was used, and by whom.

Unfortunately, an examiner often doesn't have an intact bullet for analysis. More often, the examiner gets a severely damaged bullet or a bullet fragment; however, even a bullet or fragment that is not severely deformed or too small to use, still can provide a wealth of information.

Handling bullets

During the collection and handling of any crime-scene bullets, the investigator must take great care not to damage or alter them. Whether removed from a body in surgery or during an autopsy or from a wall at the crime scene, bullets need to be handled carefully. For example, a bullet can be damaged when grasped with a surgical instrument or pried from a doorjamb, altering the striation pattern and making a match of the bullet with a suspect weapon impossible.

Bullets also may have important trace evidence attached. Paint, fibers, and other materials may cling to the bullet as it passes through or ricochets off walls, doors, bricks, or window screens. Sometimes, a fired bullet yields DNA, if investigators find small bits of flesh and blood attached to it.

These microscopic bits can be key to solving a case or reconstructing a crime scene. For example, a husband may say that he hasn't heard from his wife since she left home unexpectedly and that he doesn't know where she is. Family and friends, meanwhile, may insist that she wouldn't simply run off and disappear. If investigators find a speck of blood on a bullet embedded in a basement wall and the blood is matched to DNA obtained from the wife's toothbrush, an indictment may follow, even without a body.

Breaking down bullets

A forensic firearms examiner assesses the chemical and physical composition of a bullet to determine its manufacturer and shorten the list of suspected weapons. You can find most bullet types in weapons of varying calibers and muzzle velocities, but softer bullets are more common in low-velocity weapons, and harder or jacketed bullets usually are used in high-velocity weapons.

Bullets are categorized as follows:

- **Lead bullets** are soft and usually used in low-velocity weapons, like small-caliber handguns and rifles with .22 and .25 calibers. These bullets deform and fragment significantly when they strike a target. Although they penetrate less, the deformation and fragmentation of the bullet can cause severe tissue damage (see Chapter 12).

- **Lead alloy bullets** contain lead and small amounts of one or more other metals that make them harder. Antimony and tin commonly are alloyed with lead to make bullets for high-velocity weapons. Because of their increased hardness, these bullets tend to deform and fragment less and penetrate deeper.

✔ **Semijacketed bullets** have a thin layer of brass coating their sides. The soft lead nose is exposed, enabling the bullet to expand and fragment upon impact. The exposed nose may be slightly hollow, making it a hollow-point bullet, a type that deforms and fragments even more and causes a great deal more tissue damage in the person that it strikes. These bullets are used in low-velocity weapons as well as higher-velocity ones, such as .357 and .44 magnum handguns and high-powered rifles.

✔ **Fully jacketed bullets** are completely covered, even the nose. Brass-covered ones are often called *full metal jackets*. They typically are used in high-velocity guns, such as .44 magnum handguns and high-powered rifles. They have greater penetrating power than other bullets. Besides brass, bullets can be jacketed with Teflon, nylon, and other synthetics. These materials are tough and slippery, serving as lubricants that result in very high muzzle velocities and a high degree of penetrability. Many of these types of bullets can penetrate body armor and thus are known as *cop killers*.

Determining caliber and gauge

The *caliber* of a weapon is a measurement of the internal diameter of its barrel. The caliber of rifles and handguns is measured in inches or millimeters (mm). A .38 caliber handgun has a barrel with an internal diameter of 0.38 inches; a 9 mm has a 9 mm barrel diameter. Shotgun gauges also are measurements of the barrel's diameter; however, they don't reflect a direct measurement. Instead, the gauge of a shotgun is determined by counting the number of lead balls matching the barrel's diameter that it takes to weigh one pound. Twenty lead balls the diameter of a 20-gauge shotgun barrel weigh one pound. One exception is the .410 shotgun, the barrel of which is .410 inches in diameter.

The caliber and type of bullet are important in determining what weapon was used in a crime. If the bullet is intact, or mostly so, the police can determine the caliber by simple measurement. Severely deformed bullets can be weighed, but weighing them doesn't give the exact caliber; it serves only to eliminate some calibers. For example, the weights of .22 caliber and .44 caliber bullets vary considerably. Investigators can often easily determine whether the bullet is jacketed and, if so, with what, thus helping to identify the type of bullet and ultimately the type of weapon.

Shotgun pellets can be extracted from the victim during surgery or an autopsy, and from walls, furniture, and other surfaces. The size of the shot doesn't reveal the gauge of the shotgun but does provide information about the ammunition used. The various sizes of shot are numbered; the lower the number, the larger the pellets within the shotgun shell. For example, Number 8 shot is smaller than Number 4. Pellets vary in size from 0.05 inches for Number 12 shot to 0.33 inches for 00 shot, the largest, which also is called double-O buckshot. An examiner measures the diameter of any recovered shot and estimates what size shot was used.

Shuffling through shell casings

A shell casing is the portion of the cartridge that remains after the powder explodes and the bullet is gone. Shell casings often are the only evidence a firearms examiner has to work with. Fortunately, they retain many marks that are of interest to the examiner, including:

- ✔ **The impression left by the firing pin:** A simple inspection of the base of the casing shows where the firing pin struck, revealing whether the shell had a primer cup *(center-fire)* or had primer around its edge *(rim-fire)*. Knowing where the firing pin struck narrows down the list of possible gun types.

- ✔ **Breechblock patterns:** The *breechblock* is the back wall of the firing chamber (see Figure 18-1). When powder in the casing detonates and pushes the bullet down the barrel, the casing is forced back against the breechblock, leaving an impression on the bottom of the casing.

- ✔ **Headstamps:** Cartridge manufacturers stamp this information into the metal of cartridge casings and shotgun shells when they're made. These impressions sometimes are the manufacturer's initials or logo, the caliber or gauge, or the cartridge type.

- ✔ **Extractor and ejector marks:** Automatic and semiautomatic weapons have mechanisms that pull the next bullet from the clip and seat it in the firing chamber *(extractor)* and that remove the spent shell from the chamber, pushing it from the weapon *(ejector)*. Extractors and ejectors vary among weapons, leaving their own unique scratches and marks on the sides of the shell casings.

Getting Groovy: Comparing Rifling Patterns

Bullets don't pass through gun barrels unscathed but are nicked and scratched along the way. These markings help forensic firearms examiners match bullet to gun type, and maybe even to one particular gun.

Understanding rifling

A spinning bullet is a more accurate bullet, so most guns are *rifled,* meaning spiral grooves are etched or cut into the inside of their barrels to make bullets spin as they're expelled. Cutting the grooves leaves *lands,* or high parts, intact between them. The *grooves* grab the bullet as it travels down the barrel, causing it to spin and thereby greatly increasing its accuracy.

Old smoothbore rifles weren't accurate beyond 100 feet or so, but modern rifled firearms are extremely accurate, some even for thousands of yards.

But the accuracy of spinning bullets isn't what interests forensic firearms examiners. They're more interested in how the lands and grooves of the rifling mark the bullet. As I discuss in the next section, these markings provide class and individual characteristics (see Chapter 3).

When a gun barrel is manufactured, the rifling is cut, stamped, molded, or etched inside of it. The depth of the grooves, the width of the lands, and the direction and degree of the twist vary among different types of weapons and different manufacturers. These characteristics help examiners identify the type of weapon that fired a crime-scene bullet and its manufacturer.

For example, a .32 caliber Smith & Wesson handgun has five lands and grooves with a right (clockwise) twist, and a .32 caliber Colt has six lands and grooves with a left (counterclockwise) twist. Browning weapons also have six grooves, but they twist to the right. Marlin rifles use a technique known as *microgrooving,* which leaves between 8 and 24 narrow grooves inside the barrel. So, if an examiner is given a .32 caliber bullet recovered during an autopsy and he finds grooves consistent with the bullet having traveled down a barrel with five lands and a right twist, the weapon was likely a Smith & Wesson, and investigators can focus on .32 caliber Smith & Wesson handguns and ignore all other types.

The Federal Bureau of Investigation (FBI) maintains a database known as the "General Rifling Characteristics File" to help firearms examiners make these determinations. It lists the land, groove, and twist characteristics of known weapons. Bullet and shell casings likewise can be compared with bullets and casings recovered from other crime scenes that are listed in other databases (see the later section "Searching for answers in databases").

Because smoothbore weapons like shotguns and older firearms aren't rifled, their projectiles don't exhibit any evidence of markings caused by lands, grooves, or twists.

Reading the ridges

When lands and grooves grab and spin a bullet traveling down the barrel of a gun, they also cut into the bullet, leaving behind characteristic markings that are at the heart of firearm comparisons. These markings, called *striations,* are linear and parallel to the long axis of the bullet. They're more prominent on soft lead bullets than they are on metal- or Teflon-jacketed ones. (Check out the earlier section "Breaking down bullets.")

Silencers are devices that muffle the sound of a gun and can range from a towel wrapped around the barrel to a sophisticated sound-absorbing attachment. These attachments may also leave markings on bullets, but these markings are unpredictable. If the silencer does leave behind markings on the bullet but isn't available at the time the crime lab test-fires the gun, these marks can complicate the examiner's attempts to match the bullet to the gun from which it was fired.

As if all these lands, grooves, twists, and striations weren't enough, each rifled barrel has minute characteristics that differentiate it from all others. A rifling tool cuts through each metal gun barrel a little differently; furthermore, cutting or etching equipment becomes worn and damaged with each use. This progressive wear and tear produces rifling patterns that vary from barrel to barrel. In addition, repeated firing wears down and damages the grooves and lands, adding even more individual characteristics to the barrel and thus to any bullet that travels through it.

In short, bullets fired from the same gun share the same striation patterns, but bullets fired from different guns don't. The microscopic striations that the barrel imprints on a bullet often are so distinctive that they indicate that the bullet had to come from a particular gun to the exclusion of all others. Such evidence is individualized.

Comparing individualizing striations is useful in many situations. The first step in making such a comparison is obtaining an intact bullet fired from the suspect weapon. Most firearm labs have a test-firing chamber. An examiner then views the lab-fired bullet next to the crime-scene bullet, using a comparison microscope (see Chapter 7), which places images of the two bullets side by side to facilitate accurate comparisons.

Identifying Dr. Branion's handgun

On December 22, 1967, Dr. John Branion left a hospital in south Chicago, passed by his home, picked up his son from nursery school, and stopped by the house of a friend, before arriving home at about noon. Upon entering his home, he found his wife dead on the floor of a utility room. She had suffered multiple gunshot wounds. Branion called police.

Shell casings were recovered from the scene, and bullets were recovered from the victim during an autopsy. Examining the evidence, firearms expert Burt Nielson determined that the weapon was a .38 caliber. He also noted distinctive ejector markings that indicated the casings could have come only from a Walther PPK. Branion, a gun collector, told detectives that he didn't own a Walther, but a warranted search of Branion's home turned up a Walther PPK brochure, an extra ammunition clip, and a Walther-branded target, all of which bore the serial number 188274. Police also found two boxes of .38 caliber ammunition, one full and the other missing four cartridges. Mrs. Branion had been shot four times.

Police contacted the importers of Walther handguns in New York and found out that a Walther PPK bearing the serial number 188274 had been shipped to Chicago and sold to James Hooks, a friend of Dr. Branion's. Hooks said he'd given the gun to Branion as a gift. Branion was convicted of murder and sentenced to a long prison term.

For example, bullets found at a crime scene can be compared to find out whether they came from only one gun. If not, more than one weapon obviously was used. Likewise, separate bullets, each collected from different crime scenes, can be compared to determine whether the same gun fired them. Such a match strongly connects the two crimes. Most importantly, a bullet removed from a homicide victim can be compared with a bullet that's been test-fired from a suspect weapon. A match means that you have identified the murder weapon, which, in turn, may be the key to identifying the killer.

Two bullets don't have to match in every detail to be considered solid evidence. In fact, they essentially never do. The reason: Each bullet fired from a gun slightly alters the barrel and leaves behind soot and grit. These changes within the barrel and the deposited foreign materials alter the imprinted markings left on the next bullet. In addition, extracting or handling the soft bullet may add or alter some markings. Although two bullets don't need to be identical, you have to find identical patterns on at least three consecutive striations on each bullet for them to be matched with a gun.

Searching for answers in databases

Even with only a single bullet or shell casing and no suspect bullet or weapon to compare them with, the firearms examiner often can determine the type and manufacturer of the weapon that fired the bullet. And thanks to computer technology and firearms databases, it is often possible to compare ballistic markings on the crime-scene bullet with the markings on bullets from weapons used in other crimes. The major database is the Integrated Bullet Identification System (IBIS). Maintained by the Bureau of Alcohol, Tobacco, Firearms, and Explosives' (BATFE) National Integrated Ballistics Information Network (NIBIN), IBIS is by no means complete, but if a bullet or casing from the same weapon is in the system, a match to the crime-scene bullet or casing can connect two or more cases and thus aid in solving them all. This system rapidly compares hundreds of records and indicates any possible matches. An experienced firearms expert then visually conducts the final match.

The Proof's in the Powder: Gunshot Residues

Without a gun, a bullet, or even a shell casing to work with, firearms examiners may be able to draw some conclusions using chemical residues from expended gunpowder. Traces of these residues can linger at the scene and on the victim and shooter. Although it doesn't tell the entire story, finding this kind of chemical evidence on a suspect connects that person to the scene and gives investigators a good reason to dig deeper.

As can be seen with bite marks (Chapter 12) and some types of trace evidence (Chapter 17), the chemical analysis of gunshot residue, as well as the chemical analysis of bullets to help determine manufacturer, has drawn fire — no pun intended. Again, the lack of standardization of testing procedures and examiner training has led the FBI and other labs to reconsider this type of evidence.

Tracing gasses and particles

When a gun is fired, the primer and the powder explode within the cartridge, forcing the bullet down the barrel. Much but not all of the explosive gases and particulate matter produced by the explosion follows the bullet (see Figure 18-2). However, some of these materials escape through openings in the weapon. This factor is particularly true of revolvers, which tend to leak more gases than other types of weapons.

Figure 18-2: Residue from exploding primer and powder when a gun is shot.

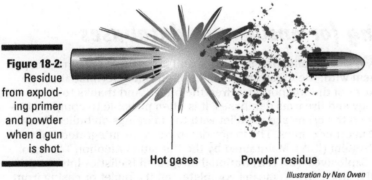

Hot gases   Powder residue

Illustration by Nan Owen

REMEMBER

The chemical and particulate components of these gases, called *gunshot residue* (GSR), cling to the shooter's hand, arm, clothing, face, and hair, They also settle on nearby walls or furniture and on the victim's skin and clothing in close-range gunshots.

Wind and rain can change the pattern of or lessen the spread of the GSR cloud. As a result, an examiner may find GSR in unexpected areas. On light-colored clothing, GSR patterns are readily visible as smudges or smears, but on dark, multicolored, or bloodstained clothing, the patterns can be obscured.

TECHNICAL STUFF

Infrared photography can reveal GSR residues under less-than-ideal circumstances. The *Griess test* may also reveal the pattern. In this test a sheet of photographic paper or a sheet of acetic acid–dampened filter paper is pressed over the area and then immersed in a reagent that reacts with inorganic nitrites in the GSR, revealing the pattern.

Testing for GSR

The goal of GSR analysis is placing a suspect near the gun when it was discharged. Unfortunately, simply being near the gun when it discharges or handling the gun afterward can leave behind GSR on an innocent person. GSR also tends to fade rapidly and usually dissipates after a few hours. It can be wiped or washed away, which is why testing needs to be accomplished as soon as possible after the gun is fired.

Investigators inspect any suspect's hands, face, and clothing and obtain samples. The old paraffin test, where melted paraffin is used to pick up residues from the shooter's hands, rarely is used anymore. Instead, investigators swab the suspect's hands, arms, and clothing with a moist swab or filter paper to obtain samples.

Chemical analysis looks for byproducts of the combustion of the primer and the gunpowder or smokeless powder. These byproducts predominantly are the metals lead, barium, and antimony. The swab or filter paper is treated with *diphenylamine,* a chemical that identifies metals by undergoing a color change. A blue color indicates a positive result. Unfortunately, many other substances, including fertilizer, tobacco, cosmetics, and urine, can yield a false-positive result, and that means the examiner has to confirm the results through more specific testing.

Sometimes GSR is found not on the shooter's hands, but on his clothing or in his hair. A scanning electron microscope (SEM — see Chapter 17) often can locate these tiny GSR particles. Particles that have been exposed to the high temperatures of an explosion are melted and peculiarly deformed, identifying them as products of a weapon's combustion. SEM likewise is often paired with energy dispersive X-ray (EDX), yielding a chemical fingerprint of the substance being tested. Finding lead, barium, and antimony in such small particles while using SEM/EDX highly suggests that the substance is indeed GSR. Unfortunately, it now seems that such testing is less accurate than once thought.

Determining distance

In Chapter 12, I tell you how the distance between the muzzle of the gun and the victim affects the anatomy of entry wounds. When a gun is fired, hot gases and burned and unburned gunpowder particles follow the bullet out of the barrel. The ME usually can estimate the firing distance by the effects of these substances on the wound.

Sometimes, however, the victim is shot through clothing, such as a shirt or jacket, and the tattooing and charring that the gases and unburned powder normally cause on the victim's skin are intercepted by the clothing. The ME therefore is left with few, if any, distance markers on the victim's skin. Enter the firearms examiner.

As is true of gunshot entry wounds on the skin, the residue pattern found on the garment depends upon the firing distance. The farther the distance, the wider the spread of the residue — up to a point. After the firing distance exceeds the distance that the gases and particles can travel, no residue pattern is produced.

The examiner uses the suspect weapon and similar ammunition to perform a series of test firings into similar fabric and accurately estimate the distance. Test firings are made at 6 inches, 1 foot, 18 inches, 2 feet, and 3 feet, and the examiner then compares the residue patterns on the test garments with those found on the victim's clothing to find the closest match.

Restoring serial numbers

Criminals who file off the serial numbers of their guns aren't as clever as they think they are. Investigators have at their disposal several techniques for finding hidden serial numbers. All rely on one simple fact: When metal is pressure stamped, not only is the metal indented with the numbers, but the metal beneath the numbers also is stressed and undergoes structural changes.

Four techniques for finding a missing serial number are

✔ **Magnaflux:** The examiner first magnetizes the gun because ripples in the magnetic forces reveal the disordered metal where the serial numbers were stamped. The examiner then sprays the gun with an oil in which iron-like particles are suspended. The particles tend to collect in areas where the metal's disordered, thus revealing the hidden number. The major advantage of this process is that it's nondestructive and doesn't alter the weapon.

✔ **Chemical and electrochemical etching:** The examiner paints an etching solution over the area in question, and the solution etches the disordered metal faster than surrounding metal, thus bringing the numbers into view. Adding an electric current (electrochemical etching) hastens the process. These processes are destructive, meaning that they change the physical composition of the evidence, and if the examiner uses them to excess or haphazardly, they can destroy the evidence forever.

✔ **Ultrasonic cavitation:** Similar to chemical etching, ultrasonic cavitation also is a destructive process. The examiner places the gun in a special ultrasonic bath and exposes it to very high frequency vibrations, which cause *cavitation,* a process in which tiny bubbles form along the surface of the metal. With continued exposure, cavitation begins eating away at the metal, and does so the fastest in the areas where the metal is in disorder, revealing the serial number.

✔ **Crystal pattern mapping:** This new technique developed by the National Institute of Standards and Technology (NIST) employs scanning electron microscopy (SEM) and reads the pattern of electron backscatter diffraction to reveal obliterated serial numbers.

Chapter 19

Questioning the Validity of Documents

In This Chapter

▶ Understanding handwriting analysis

▶ Identifying forged and altered documents

▶ Analyzing paper and ink

▶ Looking into typewriters and copiers

*I*t has been said that the pen is mightier than the sword, and when it comes to criminal enterprises, this statement often applies. Think about the embezzler who alters a company's books so that he can get away with a large sum of money. Or an altered check, lottery ticket, or will. A critical analysis of any of these documents can be key to solving a crime.

Whenever the source or authenticity of a document is in question, that document is deemed to be a *questioned document*. When investigators are presented with such documents, a *forensic document examiner* enters the picture and may be asked to

✔ Determine whether a document is authentic

✔ Determine whether a document was produced by the person who supposedly produced it

✔ Determine whether a document was produced when it was supposed to have been produced

✔ Assess whether a document has been altered in any way

✔ Compare handwriting, signatures, and typewritten or photo-copied documents

✔ Determine the ages and sources of papers and inks

✔ Expose damaged or obliterated writing

The examiner uses all his skills, his experience, and several microscopic, photographic, and chemical analytic methods to tackle these tasks.

Analyzing Handwriting

No two people write alike. Similarities may exist, but on close inspection, writing varies from person to person in notable ways. An individual's writing style is personal and unique and results from unconscious, automatic actions. You don't think about *how* you write, but only about *what* you're writing.

Likewise, you never write the same way twice. Don't believe me? Sign your name ten times and compare the results. Each signature is a little different, isn't it? Now repeat this experiment while holding the paper up against a wall or while using different types of writing instruments. You find even greater differences between these and the original signatures. Your handwriting and your signatures not only are different each time, but they're also affected by your position and by whether you use a pen, pencil, or crayon. Your handwriting on a tax return doesn't look the same as it does on a bathroom wall, for instance.

This innate variability that everyone has is the bane of document examiners. If they're to compare two samples of handwriting, they must consider this natural variability.

When examining handwriting, the forensic document expert is concerned only with the physical characteristics of the writing and not with determining the writer's personality type. The latter is the job of a *graphologist*, and graphology is not an accepted forensic science.

Developing a personal writing style

Learning to write is a slowly progressive experience. Our lettering goes from big block letters to flowing script only after years of practice. Penmanship doesn't become unique, ingrained, and individual until you reach your late teens. After that, your handwriting style changes little. But it does change, and certain conditions can cause it to change dramatically.

As you age, your style of writing undergoes slow, steady change. The changes are not dramatic, but they're enough to recognize.

Paying attention to these kinds of changes is important when comparing older documents because newer samples of your handwriting may differ from what you wrote 20 years earlier. If you suffer an illness, such as a stroke or Parkinson's disease, these changes may be dramatic. Fatigue, stress, impaired vision, hand or arm injuries, an awkward writing position, and intoxication with drugs or alcohol also can dramatically change your handwriting.

Obtaining standards

A handwriting examiner needs several *standards,* or writing samples, to get a feel for a person's writing style and determine whether that person wrote the questioned document. Complicating matters, standards may have been written with a different instrument and under different circumstances. So comparing a questioned document to a known writing sample on a wall may be impossible.

If no usable *nonrequested standards* (samples that already exist and are known to be authentic) are available, the examiner asks the suspected writer to provide a writing sample, using a similar writing instrument on similar paper, so that the examiner can at least establish a *requested standard.*

Nonrequested writings provide several advantages. The most important is that nonrequested samples reveal the writer's true writing habits and may reveal words and phrases that the writer frequently uses, which can be strong evidence for or against the writer. For example, old letters or notes may contain phrases that are identical to the ones used in a ransom note. The major disadvantage of nonrequested standards or samples is that they also must be authenticated. If they can't be linked directly to the writer, they don't have much value to the examiner.

Handwriting styles aren't static throughout our lives, so examiners try to obtain writing samples from documents written by suspected authors at about the same time as the questioned document. Say that an examiner is asked to determine whether a 20-year-old, handwritten will is authentic and was indeed written by the supposed author. The examiner needs to see other documents written by the supposed author from 20 years ago because those documents reflect his style at or near the time the will was prepared better than documents written just weeks before the examination.

The major advantage of requested writing samples is that no one questions their authenticity. The examiner actually watches the person write. The examiner also can dictate exactly what the individual writes, even a passage taken directly from the questioned document, so that the examiner can compare the samples word for word. If the document contains information that the examiner wants to withhold from the suspect or that is sensitive to an ongoing investigation, the person providing the sample can be asked to write sentences that are quite different but include many words and phrases that were used in the questioned document.

Several disadvantages accompany requested writing samples. Providing a writing sample makes some people nervous or causes them to concentrate too much on the writing process, which can lead to uncharacteristic changes in the way they normally write and sign their names. As a result, minor changes can be introduced that make an accurate comparison much more difficult.

Suspects may also try to disguise their writing style on purpose, not wanting the handwriting sample to match the writing on a forged will, ransom note, or other questioned document. Unfortunately, these attempts to alter writing styles are sometimes successful, making getting a match difficult or impossible.

One way around this problem is to have the suspect write a great deal of material — not just a passage or a page, but several pages. Although altering your style may be fairly easy when writing short passages, the more you write, the more your conscious alterations give way to your natural writing style. Dictating the same material to the writer several times is another trick examiners use to ferret out those who are attempting to disguise their handwriting style. With each attempt, the suspect is likely to use different devices. A good examiner then finds the hidden style elements and the devices that the suspect used to disguise them within the requested writing before making a comparison.

Investigators don't have to worry about a suspect refusing to offer a handwriting sample. Although you may be thinking that providing a handwriting sample violates the suspect's Fifth Amendment right not to incriminate or testify against oneself, the United States Supreme Court decided in *Gilbert v. California* that handwriting is part of identifying physical characteristics that are not protected under the Fifth Amendment. Furthermore, in the case of the *United States v. Mara,* the high court also decided that providing a handwriting sample doesn't violate Fourth Amendment protections against unreasonable search and seizure. So the court can order a suspect to produce handwriting standards even after a refusal.

Comparing handwriting

When beginning the comparisons between two handwritten documents, an examiner looks for points of similarity and points of difference between the known standards and the questioned document. The examiner typically assesses the following features:

- ✔ **Overall form:** The size, shape, slant, proportion, and beginning and ending strokes of the letters are part of the writer's overall form.

- ✔ **Line features:** Writing speed, fluidity, and the amount of pen pressure used provide hints about line features, and so do the spacing between letters and words and how the letters are connected.

- ✔ **Margins and format:** The width of the margins, the consistency of the spacing, and the slant between lines fit into this category, which covers the overall form and layout of the writing.

- ✔ **Content:** Grammar, punctuation, and word choice help point the examiner toward consistent errors, repeated phrases, and other clues that hint at a writer's ethnicity or level of education.

Astute examiners look for all of these features when comparing documents or signatures. No single feature makes an accurate comparison, but a combination of features may enable examiners to determine whether suspect and sample writings came from the same person, which ultimately is a subjective judgment. However, based on the findings, examiners may say that the documents

- ✔ Absolutely match
- ✔ Match with a high probability
- ✔ Probably match
- ✔ Do not match

Not every examination ends in an answer: The examiner may also say that a determination based on the samples is not possible. That outcome isn't too common, though. If the writing in question is *cursive* (with the letters joined) or a signature, a trained examiner usually can usually determine whether a particular individual created it. If, however, the questioned document is printed, this task is much more difficult because many of the distinguishing features of cursive writing aren't present in printed text.

Fortunately for law enforcement officials, most criminals aren't that clever, which is something that often becomes evident in written documents, where misspellings are common. Forensic document examiners use these mistakes to their advantage. When suspected writers of forged documents or ransom notes are asked to produce requested samples for comparison, examiners usually ask them to use the same words that were misspelled in the questionable document. More often than not, if a suspect is the author of a questionable document, any misspellings are also seen in the requested writing.

As is true for fingerprints, firearm rifling patterns, and DNA, several handwriting databases exist. The FBI maintains the "National Fraudulent Check File," the "Bank Robbery Note File," and the "Anonymous Letter File." Examiners can compare some questionable documents with these reference files. High-tech files, like the *Forensic Information System for Handwriting* (FISH), also exist. FISH contains scanned and digitized documents that officials can compare with other similar documents. Forensic document examiners visually check any matches.

Fingering forgers

Forgery typically is defined as writing or altering a document with the intent to defraud. Document examiners may be able to determine whether a document was altered or written by someone other than the stated author, but determining whether the writer's intent was to defraud is left up to a judge or jury.

Even the most careful and gifted forgers leave behind evidence of their efforts. Examiners inspect documents not only with the naked eye but also view them under a microscope, which often reveals telltale signs of forgery.

Two of the more common methods of forgery are freehand simulation and tracing. *Freehand simulation* simply means attempting to copy a signature or handwriting sample, and *tracing* involves placing another document over an original signature and tracing its lines. Each technique leads to various defects in the writing, and an examiner can identify them as the result of forgers writing in a manner that's unnatural. Perfectly matching someone else's writing style is not an easy task.

Common clues that reveal forgery include

- ✔ Evidence of a previous drawing, which can include an underlying tracing of the words or signature

- ✔ Forger's tremors, which are fine yet distinguishable markings that indicate shakiness in the writing and happen when the forger attempts to copy a signature or writing style

- ✔ Uneven writing speed and pen pressure

- ✔ Hesitations

- ✔ Unusual pen lifts, where the forger continually checks his handiwork

- ✔ Patching and retouching, fixing or adding marks

- ✔ Blunt beginnings and endings

Another special form of forgery is *disguised writing,* a deception in which writers attempt to camouflage their own writing. Many ransom notes and threatening letters are written this way in hopes that the author can deny ownership at a later date. Suspects sometimes attempt to disguise their writing when confronted with an incriminating letter they foolishly wrote in their natural handwriting. Check out the earlier section "Obtaining standards" for more information about how criminals try to hide their handwriting.

Exposing Alterations

Forgers often attempt to remove, add, or change portions of written documents for widely varied reasons that range from financial gain to creating an alibi. Alterations can be as simple as changing a date or as complex as attempting to erase and rewrite signatures or portions of documents. These changes are called erasures, obliterations, and alterations.

Wiping away writing

Text that doesn't suit the criminal's needs may simply be erased using a rubber eraser, a knife point or other sharp instrument, sandpaper, or even a fingernail — anything that scrapes or rubs away unwanted marks. You often can easily see erasures with the naked eye, but even when alterations aren't readily apparent, forensic examiners have the following investigative tools at their disposal:

- A simple magnifying glass or a microscope used with *oblique* (angled) lighting uncovers most erasures.

- Ultraviolet or infrared light may expose tiny fragments of eraser and ink nestled into the fibers of the paper whenever someone uses a rubber eraser.

- Lycopodium powder, when dusted over the page, clings to and exposes tiny rubber particles and eraser fragments that invariably remain after erasures.

Exposing erasures is important because, even if the examiner can't see the original words or marks, erasures reveal that someone altered the document, which in and of itself may be proof of a crime and render many legal documents null and void.

Eradicating the original

One way to destroy a document is to obliterate the paper on which it's written. Criminals typically use fire for this purpose. After the paper burns, the writing is lost forever, right? Well, not exactly. If the paper is charred but still intact, reflecting light at various angles off the paper's surface might expose the contrast between the ink and the charred paper background. The page then can be photographed.

Handling charred pages, however, is extremely difficult because they're delicate and easily crumble. Spraying them with a solution of polyvinyl acetate in acetone is one way around this problem. Doing so stiffens the paper and makes handling it much easier. Examiners then float the treated pages on a solution of alcohol, chloral hydrate, and glycerin and photograph them. Alternatively, forensic workers sandwich the pages between two photographic plates and place them in a darkroom for two weeks. They then develop the plates, which may reveal the writing.

Criminals sometimes use chemicals, such as oxidizing or bleaching agents, to remove writing. These chemicals react with ink by producing a colorless compound, and the writing disappears. Well, it *almost* disappears. Using a microscope, an examiner may see remnants of the ink and even a discoloration in the area where the paper was treated.

Using a laser is another modern method of obliterating writing. Although the laser vaporizes the ink, it also burns nearby paper fibers, and the damage shows up under a microscope.

Adding words

Often, a simple obliteration of words or marks doesn't completely serve the forger's needs, so further alteration by replacing obliterated words or numbers with others is required. Common examples are changing the amount of a check or the date on a contract or will. Whenever someone obliterates writing before adding changes, an examiner can see the changes in the underlying paper and analyze the new writing by comparing it with the old for differences in technique. Sometimes, the forgery is so well done that a simple inspection doesn't reveal any changes. Fortunately, the examiner has other tools in his bag of tricks.

Under the microscope, subtle differences between the original and altered portions of the writing may appear. Slight changes in ink color, line thickness, and pen pressure, as well as double lines, often become visible. If the forger used a ballpoint or roller ball pen, distinguishable marks from defects in either type of pen point may show up.

Overwriting is another form of forgery in which the forger doesn't erase anything but rather adds to or overwrites a portion of a document. Maybe a *1* is changed to a *9,* or a *0* is added to a check. If the forger uses the same ink that was used to prepare the original document, these types of changes can be extremely difficult to uncover. But forgers don't often have access to the pen or ink that was used for the original writing, so they make do with a similar pen and ink color. Careful examination of the differing ink might reveal areas that have been altered.

Although two inks may seem identical under normal light, they usually appear much different when exposed to ultraviolet (UV) or infrared light. Each ink reacts differently to UV light; one may fluoresce, and the other may fade from view. Infrared photography, which basically means photographing the page under a blue-green light with infrared-sensitive film, often clearly distinguishes between two kinds of ink. If these lighting techniques don't provide any help, the examiner may have to examine the chemical contents of the inks to show that they are indeed different (see the following section).

Looking for Indentions

You've seen it in movies, and it happens in real life. The criminal scrawls a ransom note, then tears away the note and doesn't give a second thought to the page underneath. Later, police collect the pad of paper and submit it to the document examiner, who exposes the writing, thus proving that that particular pad was the source of the ransom note. The owner of the pad then has a bit of explaining to do.

The movement of a pen over a page indents the second page along the path of the pen, creating *indented writing*. Unlike what you've seen on TV, forensic technicians don't use the old pencil method (rubbing a pencil over the paper to expose the indentions) to uncover indented writing, because the pencil's markings may damage or destroy the evidence.

Sometimes, a simple angled light reveals indented writing. When it does, the technician photographs the page. A more sensitive method is the use of an *electrostatic detection apparatus* (ESDA), which can sometimes uncover indented writing several pages below the original page.

In ESDA, the technician places a Mylar sheet over the page in question to protect it and then places both on a porous metal plate. A vacuum pulls the Mylar tightly against the page. The examiner then passes an electric wand over the sheet and the page, producing static electricity. The charge is greatest in the indentions, so when the technician pours or sprays black toner, similar to that used in copy machines, over the Mylar, that toner attaches to the surface in proportion to the degree of charge and reveals the indented writing.

Examining Papers and Inks

Sometimes, forensic document examiners must determine whether pages have been added to a document or whether the document actually was created at a particular time. In either case, the examiner may resort to analyzing the paper and ink that were used to create the document.

Distinguishing papers

Most paper is made of wood and cotton and often has chemical additives that affect its opacity, color, brightness, strength, and durability:

- ✔ **Coatings** improve the appearance and surface properties of the paper and make the paper better for copiers, printers, or for writing.

- ✔ **Fillers** add color, strength, and surface texture.
- ✔ **Sizings** make the surface less porous to ink, so that writing and printing appear sharp and clear.

The types and amounts of each of these additives vary among manufacturers and paper types, and chemical testing can distinguish one type and manufacturer from another.

Another distinguishing characteristic of paper is its *watermark,* which is a translucent design on the paper that you can see by holding the page up to a light. This design indicates the manufacturer, the date of its production, and often for whom the paper was manufactured. Attempts to forge a watermark usually are easy to spot because true watermarks have fewer fibers than the rest of the page. Forged marks, however, actually are added images and thus have an underlying fiber density equal to the rest of the page.

Identifying inks

Sometimes, the key to determining authenticity of a document lies in the ink that the writer used. Inks that appear the same, physically, may be much different, chemically. This distinction helps the examiner determine whether the same ink was used for each page or word of a document and may even help reveal whether a particular ink existed at the time the document supposedly was prepared.

One nondestructive method of ink comparison is called *microspectrophotometry* (see Chapter 17). This process enables the examiner to accurately determine whether the colors of the two inks match by comparing their light transmission, absorption, and reflection characteristics.

Another method for comparing ink samples is thin-layer chromatography (TLC), which includes following four steps:

1. Very small samples of the inked paper are punched from the written lines using a thin hollow needle.

2. The tiny pieces of paper are placed in a test tube, and a solvent that dissolves the ink is added.

3. A drop of the solvent solution, which now carries the ink, is placed on a paper strip along with drops of several known control inks.

4. The strip is dried and then dipped into another solvent that migrates up the paper strip, dragging the inks along with it.

The distances that all of the inks migrate along the strip are determined by the respective sizes of their molecules. This process separates the inks into bands. Whenever inks from two pages of a questioned document are tested and they yield different bands, the writing on the two pages was done with two distinctly different inks.

An extensive ink reference database is located at the Ink Library, a part of the U.S. Secret Service Forensic Services Division's Questioned Document Branch. In addition, the U.S. Treasury Department maintains an extensive database of the TLC patterns of commercial inks. In a more recent development, many manufacturers began adding fluorescent-dye tags to their products so that they are easier to identify. And because the tags are changed annually, examiners can readily determine the year that the product was manufactured.

The Mormon forgeries

On October 15, 1985, in Salt Lake City, Utah, two pipe bombs exploded. One killed businessman and Mormon bishop Steve Christensen, and the other killed a grandmother, Kathy Sheets. The package that killed Sheets was addressed to her husband, Gary, who also was a bishop in the Mormon Church. The next day, a third bomb exploded in the car of Mark Hofmann.

Hofmann, who survived the blast, told police that he had seen a strange package sitting in his car, and when he reached for it, it exploded. Bomb investigators knew immediately that Hofmann was lying: Evidence indicated that Hofmann had been kneeling in the seat of the car, apparently working with the bomb, when it detonated. Hofmann leaped to the top of the suspect list in the other bombings.

As the investigation progressed, police discovered that Hofmann was somewhat of a whiz at locating ancient documents and had sold many historical documents to the Mormon Church. However, they also uncovered evidence that the documents actually were forgeries, thus raising suspicion that Hofmann planted the bombs in an attempt to cover his forgeries.

The case ended when the police confronted Hofmann with evidence that proved he had forged his discoveries. Document examiners George J. Throckmorton and William Flynn discovered several things amiss when examining a 17th century document Hoffman had uncovered. Letters with tails, or *descenders,* such as *Y* and *J,* seemed to overlap with taller letters, such as *L* and *T,* when the former appeared in lines above the latter. That kind of overlapping wasn't possible with the handset type that was used to make the original documents in the 17th century. The examiners also noted the *alligator effect* — cracking and breaking of the ink from the use of chemical oxidants that were applied to artificially age the appearance of the ink. Natural aging doesn't produce such changes.

Hofmann confessed to the bombings and the forgeries in exchange for a life sentence. He also told investigators how he pulled off the forgeries, which were so realistic that many experts had deemed them authentic.

Dissecting Typewriters and Photocopiers

Not only do pen and paper leave behind clues about the origin of a document but various mechanical devices do also. Typewriters, printers, and copy machines often leave distinguishing marks on the typed or copied page. These marks may reveal that a document has been altered or help investigators find out exactly which machine produced the document in question.

Hunting and pecking for clues

People frequently use typewriters to write threatening letters and ransom and extortion notes. Criminals often are under the mistaken impression that doing so makes the letter untraceable. Not true. When a typewriter is involved, the document examiner tries to

- Determine the make and model of the typewriter
- Match up the note with a suspect typewriter, if one is available

Identifying the make and model means that the examiner must have access to a database of typefaces used in various typewriter models, new and old. Most manufacturers use either pica or elite typefaces, but the size, shape, and style of the letters vary, making identification of the manufacturer and model possible. This greatly narrows the search for the exact machine that produced the document. Unfortunately, typewriters have given way to computers, which connect to printers that may use daisy-wheel, dot-matrix, ink-jet, or laser technologies. These machines vary so little that examiners often can't distinguish one from another.

To determine whether a particular typewriter produced a questioned document, examiners search for individual characteristics that can include misaligned or damaged letters, abnormal spacing before or after certain letters, and variations in the pressure applied to the page by some letters. For example, certain letters can have telltale nicks or spurs that are imprinted on the page, or they can lean to one side or print slightly higher or lower than the others. These defects can be compared to a sample from a suspect typewriter and thus offer powerful individualizing characteristics.

To compare a typed document to a particular machine, the examiner types a comparison document using that machine. When doing so, the examiner uses a ribbon similar in type and condition to the one used to produce the original document. The reason: A worn or lightly inked ribbon reveals minor defects in the typeface, whereas a heavily inked, new ribbon may obscure them.

Typewriters that use ribbons can help the examiner link the typewriter to the document. If the typewriter has a single-pass ribbon and the same ribbon that was used to type the document still is in place, the police can simply read the message from the ribbon itself. Even if the ribbon has been used for several passes, investigators may be able to retrieve portions of the message.

What if the criminal used the original typewriter to add a line or a paragraph to a document? How does an examiner know when that has happened? Because the typeface would be identical, the examiner may not be able to tell whether an alteration occurred. However, when a page is placed into a typewriter a second time, the alignment often is off, and although it may only be slightly askew, the examiner can place a specially made glass plate with an etched grid pattern over the page. This reveals any imperfection in the alignment of the added lines or paragraphs.

Finding distinctive traits in copies

A copy machine duplicates an image from one page onto another through a complex series of events. First, a lens focuses the image of the original page onto a drum that is charged with static electricity and coated with selenium or another light-sensitive substance. The drum retains the image as it's bathed with a toner powder that attaches to the surface of the drum in proportion to the strength of the electrostatic charge. This toner image then is transferred to the blank page, which, in turn, is exposed to a fixing agent.

Investigators can sometimes match a photocopied document to a particular copy machine because the mechanisms within the machine that pull the paper onto and remove it from the copy surface can leave marks on the page. Likewise, the cover glass, camera lens, or drum may have scratches or defects that mark every page that it produces. Occasionally, these marks appear on a photocopied page, and investigators can identify and match this marked page to the machine that produced it.

Part V
The Part of Tens

If you're finding the field of forensics to be pretty interesting, check out a list of ten additional resources for further study at www.dummies.com/extras/forensics.

In this part . . .

- ✔ Discover ten famous forensic cases.
- ✔ Get the lowdown on ten ways Hollywood gets it wrong.
- ✔ Check out ten great forensic careers.

Chapter 20

Ten Famous Forensic Cases

- -

In This Chapter

▶ Linking tool marks, bite marks, and firearms to criminals and crimes

▶ Identifying and tracing sources of poisons

▶ Identifying criminals and remains with fingerprints, blood, and DNA

▶ Solving cases by digitally aging old photographs

▶ Analyzing papers and inks

- -

Some crimes seem to capture the public's interest. You need look no further than a certain double homicide case against an internationally famous football player and a bloody glove to know what I'm talking about. The Lindbergh kidnapping was the crime of the century long before O.J. Simpson was born. The Sacco and Vanzetti case seemed as if it never would end, and the same can be said of the murderous rampage of Ted Bundy, one of America's most famous serial killers. This chapter gives you a glimpse at a few of the cases that made headlines and forensic history.

Using a Homemade Ladder: The Lindbergh Kidnapping

Colonel Charles A. Lindbergh was an American hero. On May 20, 1927, the Lone Eagle, as he was known, became the first person to fly solo across the Atlantic in his single-engine airplane, the *Spirit of St. Louis*. Less than five years later, on the night of March 1, 1932, his son, Charles, Jr., was abducted from the second-floor nursery of his Hopewell, New Jersey, home.

Clues were meager. A ransom note was left on the nursery windowsill, and a ladder lay on the ground beneath the window. Dusting the ransom note envelope revealed no latent fingerprints, but analysis of the writing led investigators to believe that the writer was poorly educated and likely of German descent. The ladder was homemade, suggesting that the kidnapper had tools and was skilled in carpentry.

As the case progressed, communications began between the kidnapper and John F. Condon, a public school principal who had publicly offered a reward for the return of the child. Condon turned over a $50,000 ransom in exchange for a note stating that the child could be found near Martha's Vineyard Island onboard a boat named *Nelly*. Unfortunately, no such boat existed, and on May 12, 1932, the decomposing body of the child turned up in a wooded area near Lindbergh's home. The cause of death was either asphyxiation or blunt-force head trauma.

Police had recorded all the serial numbers of the bills used for ransom, and during the next 2 1/2 years, the money occasionally surfaced between New York and Chicago, with a higher concentration of it turning up in the Bronx.

As the investigators' attention turned to the ladder, Arthur Koehler, an expert in wood and wood products, was brought in on the case. During his examination of the ladder, he found that four different types of wood were used in its construction: ponderosa pine, North Carolina pine, birch, and fir. The fir appeared to be a section of flooring that had been used to finish the left upper part of one of the ladder's rails and indicated the builder of the ladder had run out of wood and used a piece of flooring to complete the construction.

Koehler microscopically examined portions of the ladder and discovered marks that suggested that a planing machine had been used to smooth the side rails. He discovered several distinctive marks on the wood that had been made by the machine. Koehler asked for planed wood samples from more than 1,500 mills across the country and discovered the same marks on wood milled by Dorn Lumber in McCormick, South Carolina. From there, he traced the wood used in the ladder to National Lumber and Mill Work Company in the Bronx, where much of the ransom money had turned up.

Meanwhile, a service-station operator wrote down the license plate number from the vehicle of a suspicious-looking man from whom he had taken a ten-dollar bill and called the police. The bill, it turns out, was part of the ransom money, and Bruno Richard Hauptmann, a carpenter of German descent, was arrested.

In the attic of Hauptmann's home, investigators discovered a floorboard missing from a joist that had four nail holes that exactly matched holes found in the piece of fir used to finish the ladder. Koehler also found a handheld wood plane in Hauptmann's home that sported defects that matched distinctive marks left on certain areas of the ladder during the smoothing process. Koehler then applied a well-known trick of the forensics trade. He wrapped a piece of paper around the wood from the ladder and rubbed a pencil back and forth until a black-and-white replica of the pattern left by the wood plane appeared. He later applied the same technique to another piece of wood that he'd smoothed with the same plane. They matched.

Based on the evidence provided by Koehler and the fact that some of the ransom money turned up in Hauptmann's garage, Hauptmann was convicted of the kidnapping and murder of Charles Lindbergh, Jr., on February 13, 1935. He was executed April 3 of the same year.

Sacco and Vanzetti and Sacco's Gun

During the afternoon of April 15, 1920, security guards Alessandro Berardelli and Frederick Parmenter were transferring payroll funds for a shoe factory in South Braintree, Massachusetts. Two men opened fire on the guards, killing them both and fleeing with more than $15,000, a tidy sum in those days. Witnesses told police the two gunmen were "Italian looking" and that one of them sported a dark handlebar mustache. The only bits of evidence found at the scene were several shell casings that were manufactured by three different firms: Remington, Winchester, and Peters.

Two days later, the getaway car was found and traced to an earlier robbery that police believed had been arranged by Mike Boda, a local criminal. When police went looking for Boda at his hideout, they found not him but two men, Nicola Sacco and Bartolomeo Vanzetti. Vanzetti had a dark handlebar mustache, and Sacco possessed a .32 caliber handgun, the same caliber as the murder weapon. Sacco also had 29 bullets for the gun, all manufactured by Remington, Winchester, or Peters. The two men were arrested and charged with the double murder.

Police also discovered that Sacco and Vanzetti belonged to an anarchist movement that advocated violent political change. By the time the trial opened on May 31, 1921, before Judge Webster Thayer in Dedham, Massachusetts, the case had become America's first Red Scare. The defense team put together an alliance of anarchist, communist, and union leaders called the Sacco-Vanzetti Defense Committee, which labeled the trial a witch-hunt.

The case hinged on proving that the bullets that struck down the two guards came from Sacco's gun, but those bullets were so outdated that forensic examiners were unable to locate any unspent ammunition to test-fire for making a comparison. Ultimately, they resorted to using the ones they'd found on Sacco at the time of his arrest. A match was made, and Sacco and Vanzetti were convicted and sentenced to death. But the story didn't end there.

Albert Hamilton, an expert of questionable honesty, came forward saying that he had no doubt the bullets used to kill the two guards *did not* come from Sacco's gun. The defense petitioned for a retrial and, during the hearings, Hamilton showed his true colors. In an odd performance, he brought two new .32 caliber Colt handguns to court and disassembled them, along with Sacco's gun. He then attempted to secretly exchange one of the new gun barrels for the one on Sacco's gun. Judge Thayer caught him, ordered that

Sacco's gun be reassembled, and denied the petition for a new trial. Still, the story didn't end.

Because of continued protests by anarchists, in June 1927, a committee was formed to look into the case. America's leading firearms expert, Dr. Calvin Goddard of the Bureau of Forensic Ballistics in New York, entered the fray. At his disposal were two new forensic tools: the comparison microscope and the helixometer. The former enabled scientists to microscopically inspect and compare two different bullets, and the latter was a probe fitted with a light and magnifying glass that enabled them to examine details of the inside of a gun barrel. Again, the match was conclusive.

On August 23, 1927, the two killers died in the electric chair. Yet the controversy persisted. In 1961, and again in 1983, the case was reexamined, and on each occasion, Goddard's findings were confirmed.

Ted Bundy's Bite Marks

Between 1969 and 1975, a series of brutal sexual homicides swept through the Pacific Northwest, Utah, and Colorado. The victims were strikingly similar in that each had dark hair that was parted down the middle. The suspected killer, a male, often wore a fake cast and feigned an injury, thus seeking his victims' help with some task. After the unsuspecting women stepped into his tiny Volkswagen bug, the killer overpowered them and took them to a remote area where he tortured, raped, and murdered them.

As police in various jurisdictions worked their respective cases, one name kept appearing: Theodore Bundy. On November 8, 1974, Carol DeRonch, an 18-year-old woman, found herself inside Bundy's VW. When he attempted to handcuff and bludgeon her, she fought him off and escaped. Nearly a year later, on August 16, 1975, police stopped the driver of a VW for suspicious behavior. They found handcuffs and a crowbar in the car and identified the driver as Ted Bundy. Carol DeRonch fingered him, and he was convicted of kidnapping and sentenced to 1 to 15 years in prison.

Bundy then was extradited to Colorado to face a murder charge. In June 1977, he escaped but was apprehended only eight days later. He again escaped on December 30, 1977, but this time, he headed to Florida.

In the dead of night on January 15, 1978, Bundy entered the Chi Omega sorority house on the campus of Florida State University in Tallahassee. He assaulted and raped four coeds, killing Lisa Levy and Margaret Bowman. Less than two hours later another student was attacked. She survived.

A month later, police arrested Chris Hagen for driving a stolen vehicle. They soon found out that the person they thought was Hagen actually was Ted Bundy, who was wanted for murder in several states.

Unfortunately for prosecutors, Bundy left little evidence at the sorority house. They found no fingerprints, and none of the surviving victims could identify their assailant. When the police dusted Bundy's apartment for prints, they found none.

The only piece of evidence that police had to work with was a bite mark on the buttocks of Lisa Levy. Bundy at first refused to give an impression of his teeth, but a court order soon forced him to comply. Bundy's teeth were misaligned and chipped, and they matched the bite-mark bruises found on Lisa Levy perfectly. On July 23, 1978, Bundy was convicted of murder, a crime for which he was put to death January 24, 1989, in Florida's electric chair.

Stella Nickell's Trail of Fingerprints

Sue Snow suddenly collapsed on June 11, 1986, in the bathroom of her home in the Seattle, Washington, suburb of Auburn. Paramedics found her unconscious and gasping for breath. They transported her to the hospital, where she soon died. One possible explanation for the young woman's death was a drug overdose, but she was not a known user and had taken only a couple of Extra-Strength Excedrin, a safe medication.

During her autopsy, examiners noticed a faint odor of almonds emanating from the corpse. A toxicology exam revealed the presence of cyanide. An examination of the Excedrin capsules followed, and they too tested positive for cyanide. The Food and Drug Administration (FDA) and the manufacturer, Bristol-Meyers, moved quickly to remove all Extra-Strength Excedrin bottles from shelves across the country. Seattle police found two other contaminated bottles, one in Auburn and the other in nearby Kent.

In a separate turn of events, Stella Nickell told police on June 17 that her husband had died suddenly just a few days earlier and that he too had taken Excedrin. Already buried, Bruce Nickell's death certificate stated that he'd died of emphysema. However, because he was a registered organ donor, a sample of his blood had been retained, making an exhumation unnecessary. Tests done on his blood sample showed that he too died from ingesting cyanide.

While police searched for a connection between Sue Snow and Bruce Nickell, the FDA examined more than 740,000 Excedrin capsules from the Pacific Northwest and Alaska. They found cyanide in only five bottles, two of which were in the possession of Stella Nickell. Asked whether she bought the bottles at the same time and from the same store, she said no, she had purchased them on different days at different stores. The odds against such bad luck are astronomical.

In addition to cyanide, FDA examiners detected another odd chemical in the contaminated capsules: traces of an algaecide known as Algae Destroyer, which is used in fish tanks. Stella Nickell had a fish tank and immediately became the focus of the investigation. An in-depth look into her background revealed that she had a history of forgery, fraud, and child abuse. In addition, she had purchased extra insurance on Bruce that would pay her $176,000 in the event of an accidental death.

Stella Nickell denied any involvement in the product tampering but failed a polygraph examination. Then her own daughter came forward, telling police that her mother had often mentioned killing Bruce, even going so far as indicating that she'd researched the use of cyanide. This information led police to the local Auburn library, where they discovered that a book Stella had checked out was overdue. The title? *Human Poisoning.* They also found that she had twice checked out *Deadly Harvest,* a book on toxic plants. At the FBI crime lab, 84 of Stella's fingerprints were found on the book's pages. Most of them were found in the section dealing with cyanide. On May 9, 1988, Stella was sentenced to a 99-year prison term.

Finding Fibers on Jeffrey MacDonald

At 3:40 a.m. on February 17, 1970, U.S. Army Captain Dr. Jeffrey MacDonald summoned military police (MPs) to his home at Fort Bragg, North Carolina. When the MPs arrived, they found Dr. MacDonald lying on his bedroom floor next to his wife, Colette. He wore only blue pajama bottoms. A matching pajama top lay across the chest of his wife, who had been brutally and repeatedly stabbed to death. Above them on the bed's headboard was the single word "Pig" written in blood. Down the hall, the bodies of the MacDonalds' two children, 5-year-old Kimberly and 2-year-old Kristen, lay in pools of blood. Only Jeffrey MacDonald was alive, having suffered just a single knife wound to his chest.

MacDonald said he'd fallen asleep on the living room sofa only to be awakened by screams from Colette. He was immediately attacked by three men and a woman, whom he described as hippies chanting, "Acid is groovy" and "Kill the pigs" as they slashed him with a knife. They tore his pajama top, which he then wrapped around his hands, using it to parry the thrusts from the knives. He was ultimately knocked unconscious, later awakening to find his family slaughtered. He attempted mouth-to-mouth resuscitation on each of his daughters before finding Colette with a knife protruding from her chest. He removed the knife, covered her with his pajama top, and phoned the MPs.

The MPs immediately were suspicious, questioning why MacDonald's injuries were minimal when his family had been severely brutalized; why the living room, where MacDonald alleged he'd been attacked by four people, was so neat; and how MacDonald, who needed glasses to correct his poor vision, could provide such detailed descriptions of four assailants he'd seen only in the dark. They also wondered why the torn fingertip of a latex surgical glove was found in the MacDonalds' bloodstained bed.

Interestingly, the MPs found a copy of *Esquire* magazine with an article on the recent Manson family murders in the living room. In those murders, the murderers wrote messages, including the word "pig," in blood at the crime scenes.

Unfortunately, the investigation was less than perfect, evidence was lost, and charges against MacDonald were dropped. The story might have ended there, except that MacDonald went on a television talk show, berating the military and accusing the MPs of gross incompetence. The television appearance led to a renewed interest in Captain MacDonald.

The FBI entered the investigation and turned up a wealth of new information. First of all, in a coincidence that defies odds, each family member had a different blood type. This factor enabled investigators to track the movements of each person and particularly those of Jeffrey MacDonald. His blood was found in small quantities in only three places: on his glasses in the living room, on a cabinet where a box of surgical gloves was stored, and on the bathroom sink, where investigators believe he inflicted his own minor wound. Neither blood nor fingerprints were found on the two phones MacDonald used to call for help, and no prints were found on the knife MacDonald said he removed from his wife's chest. Furthermore, no prints were found on the knife and ice pick that were discovered outside near the back door. Had they been wiped clean?

Blue fibers from MacDonald's pajamas were found everywhere. *Almost* everywhere, that is. They were in the two girls' rooms and all over, around, and even beneath Colette's body. Yet, none were found in the living room where MacDonald said he was attacked and his pajama shirt was ripped.

The most damning evidence, however, came from the FBI crime lab. Analysts showed that 48 holes in the blue pajama top exactly matched 21 wounds to Colette when the garment was folded over her chest. More importantly, each puncture was round and smooth, an indication that the garment was stationary when the blows were struck. Had the pajama top been in motion, the way it would have been with MacDonald using it for defense, the punctures would have been ragged with irregular holes.

To top matters off, Collette's blood stained both pieces of the torn pajama top. When the two pieces were placed side by side, the stain patterns matched, suggesting that the staining occurred before the top was torn; moreover, it directly contradicted Capt. MacDonald's statement that he'd placed the top over his wife's body *after* it was torn.

In July 1979, nearly a decade after the murders, Jeffrey MacDonald went to trial for the triple murder. His conviction resulted in a sentence of three consecutive life terms.

Georgi Markov and the Lethal Umbrella

In 1971, Georgi Markov defected from Communist Bulgaria to London. An outspoken critic of the regime in his homeland, he continued his assaults in antigovernment broadcasts on the BBC. The Bulgarian government was less than pleased with his diatribes.

While walking on the Waterloo Bridge on September 7, 1979, Markov felt a sharp pain in his right thigh. He turned to see a stranger with a furled umbrella. The man apologized in a thick accent and hurried to a cab. Inspecting his leg, Markov discovered a red puncture mark on his thigh.

That night Markov fell ill, and by the next morning, had a high fever, rapid pulse, and low blood pressure. His wound was severely inflamed, and his white blood cell count soared. X-rays of his leg revealed nothing, and despite large doses of antibiotics, his condition worsened during the next two days, and he died. During an autopsy, a section of the skin around Markov's wound was removed and sent to Dr. David Gall, an expert in poisons at the top-secret government Chemical Defense Establishment at Porton Down.

Within the submitted tissues, Gall found a metal pellet the size of a pinhead with two tiny holes drilled into it. He assumed that the pellet, containing a lethal substance, had been injected into Markov by a gas gun hidden within the assailant's umbrella. The nature of Markov's demise made bacterial and viral entities unlikely culprits and favored a chemical toxin.

Only *ricin*, a substance derived from castor beans, seemed to fit the scenario, but the police had no reliable test for ricin. The body's natural enzyme systems quickly break down ricin, leaving no trace of it. In an ingenious experiment, investigators injected an amount of ricin equal to what the pellet could hold into a live pig. The animal quickly became ill and died in less than 24 hours. An autopsy of the pig showed organ damage identical to that in Markov's organs, suggesting that ricin was indeed the agent injected into him.

The Hendricks Family's Last Meal

David Hendricks was a successful Bloomington, Illinois, businessman who traveled frequently to meet with customers. One such trip was planned for Friday, November 4, 1983. Hendricks planned to leave late November 4 and drive all night to be ready for meetings the next day in Wisconsin. According to Hendricks, while his wife attended a baby shower, he and their three children arrived at a local pizza parlor at 6:30 p.m. for dinner, which they finished by 7:30. The children went to bed around 9:30, his wife returned at 10:30, and Hendricks departed on his trip at approximately 11:30 p.m.

During the weekend, Hendricks called home several times, but received no response. He called friends and relatives to find out whether they'd seen his wife or children. He finally called the police, expressing concern that maybe his family had been in an accident. Police informed him that no one by the name of Hendricks had been involved in any accidents.

Hendricks returned home on the evening of Tuesday, November 8, to find the police and several neighbors at his home. His family had been brutally murdered with a knife and an axe, both of which had been found neatly cleaned and lying at the foot of his bed. Hendricks was too shaken to enter the house, and police, sensing his shock, spared him the grisly details.

Had Hendricks kept his mouth closed, the story might have ended there, but the next day, he told reporters that burglars had broken in. He even listed items that had been taken. Police wondered how he knew what had been taken when he hadn't entered the house and they hadn't told him of their findings.

Autopsies of the children proved Hendricks was lying. The stomach contents of the three children revealed undigested pizza, which means they died within two hours of eating because that's approximately how much time it takes for the stomach to empty. Digestion ceases at death and essentially freezes stomach contents in the state they were in at the time of death. Because the children finished their meals at 7:30 p.m., this finding indicated that Hendricks probably killed his children around 9:30 p.m., about an hour before his wife returned home. He then killed her and left on his trip, thinking he had the perfect alibi. Forensic evidence proved to be his undoing, and he was convicted of murder and sentenced to four life terms.

Picturing John List

In 1971, John List lived in a large home in Westfield, New Jersey, with his wife, three teenage children, and his mother. Neighbors noticed that they hadn't seen the List family for some time and that the home seemed deserted, except for the fact that lights throughout the house blazed brightly every night. On December 7, police dropped by to investigate and found four bodies neatly placed on sleeping bags on the floor of a room near the back of the house. The bodies were John List's wife, Helen, and their three children. In an upstairs bedroom, they found the body of John's mother, Alma. Each had been shot. John List, however, was nowhere to be found, and even more disturbing were five addressed envelopes that police found taped to a filing cabinet.

John List, an influential member of the local Lutheran church, explained his rationale for committing the multiple murders in letters found in the envelopes. He said he was not good with money, his mismanagement had driven the family to the brink of bankruptcy, and he didn't want his family subjected to a life on welfare, so he spared them this humiliation by killing them.

Two days later, List's car turned up in long-term parking at New York's John F. Kennedy International Airport (JFK). Wanted posters were spread immediately from coast to coast, and because of John List's fluency in German, throughout West Germany and German-speaking areas of South Africa. The result: no leads and no John List.

Two years later, Bernard Tracey joined the Westfield Police Department and quickly became interested in the case. Thirteen years later, he was no closer to finding the fugitive. In an attempt to rekindle interest in the case, Tracey approached *Weekly World News,* and the supermarket tabloid ran a story on the John List case on February 17, 1986. Again, no new information came forth.

In the meantime, however, Wanda Flanery of Aurora, Colorado, thought the photograph that accompanied the tabloid story closely resembled her neighbor, Bob Clark. She mentioned her suspicion to his wife, Delores, who scoffed at the idea that her church-going husband could be a murderer. Shortly thereafter, the Clarks ran into financial difficulties caused by Bob's poor handling of their money, and they relocated to Richmond, Virginia.

Still frustrated by his inability to crack the case, Tracey approached the television show *America's Most Wanted,* which initially showed little interest in the case. However, when Tracey contacted them once again a year later, the show's producers decided to look into the situation, which proved to be the major turning point in the case. They hired forensic sculptor Frank A. Bender to fashion a bust of what John List might look like some 18 years after his last known photograph. Dr. Richard Walter of the Michigan Department of Corrections was brought in to offer a profile of John List as an aid to reconstructing his likely current image. Walter thought that List's religious background made it unlikely that he'd ever undergo any plastic surgery and that his lifestyle wouldn't be one of diet and exercise — valuable information considering that either factor could alter List's pattern of aging.

FBI specialist Gene O'Donnell then entered the picture. Using the latest computer technology and the old photograph of John List, he digitally aged the likeness in the photo by adding gray and receding hair and fleshy jowls. He also included thick-rimmed glasses similar to the ones List wore in the photo. When *America's Most Wanted* aired the John List case along with the aged photo May 21, 1989, more than 250 calls came in. One from an anonymous caller in Colorado said that John List was living in Richmond, Virginia, under the name of Bob Clark. The caller, it turns out, was a relative of Wanda Flanery. Fingerprints proved that Bob Clark and John List were the same person, and on April 20, 1990, nearly two decades after murdering his family, John List received a life sentence.

Being Anastasia Romanov

The Russian Revolution of 1917 was a bloody affair that included the execution of the royal family. On July 17, 1918, by order of the Bolshevik leader Vladimir Lenin, Czar Nicholas II, his wife Alexandra, their five children, and four others were executed in the basement of a house in Yekaterinburg, Siberia. This act ended three centuries of Romanov rule. During the ensuing years, the house became a *de facto,* or unauthorized, shrine, and pilgrimages to see the Czar's final resting place became commonplace. In 1977, however, the Soviet government put an end to the practice by bulldozing the structure.

For Gely Ryaboy, locating the Czar's burial site became an obsession. Being a filmmaker with the Interior Ministry, he had access to many secret archives, which he searched for evidence of where the czar and his family might be buried. Through this research, he located the children of Yakov Yurovsky, a guard who had witnessed the executions. Yurovsky's son gave Ryaboy a note from Yakov, describing the disposal of the bodies in a swamp near the bulldozed house in Yekaterinburg. Working under cover of darkness, Ryaboy finally amassed a collection of bones and clothing fragments that he thought might represent the executed royal family. However, instead of the expected 11 skeletons, only 9 were found.

In 1991, as the Soviet Union disintegrated, the task of identifying the remains was undertaken more openly. Superimposition of photos of Nicholas and Alexandra over two of the skulls suggested that, indeed, they were remains of the czar and czarina. DNA testing showed that five of the nine skeletons were from one family; however, it didn't conclude whether skeletal remains of the man, woman, and three children were, in fact, the Romanovs. So the investigation turned to mitochondrial DNA (see Chapter 15) for the answer. Because mitochondrial DNA is passed down unchanged from generation to generation through the maternal line, a maternal relative was needed. As it turns out, Prince Philip, the husband of England's Queen Elizabeth, is a direct descendant of Czarina Alexandra's sister. The prince offered a blood sample, and the match was made, proving that the remains were indeed those of Nicholas, Alexandra, and three of their children.

But what of the two other children? The bones of Crown Prince Alexei and his sister, Anastasia, were not among the remains. Their skeletons were missing from the swamp. Rumors suggested that Anastasia and Alexei survived the execution and escaped, but no one knew where the two ended up.

In 1920, a Berlin woman named Anna Anderson claimed to be the missing Anastasia. Many people believed her, but others considered her a fraud. Although Anderson died in 1964 in Charlottesville, Virginia, the truth didn't come to light until 1994. Anderson had undergone a surgical procedure before her death, and the hospital kept a sample of her tissue. DNA testing of the sample revealed that she wasn't Anastasia but rather a Polish peasant named Franzisca Schanzkowska. Finally, in 2007, the remains of two children were found in a shallow grave not far from where the remains of the Romanov family had been discovered, and mtDNA, STR, and Y-STR analysis suggested that the remains were those of Anastasia and Alexei.

Faking Hitler's Diaries

On February 18, 1981, staff journalist Gerd Heidemann presented his boss, Manfred Fischer, director of the German publishing giant Gruner and Jahr, with the literary find of the century — Adolph Hitler's diaries. The documents were handwritten in almost illegible German script. Heidemann said he had received them from a wealthy collector whose brother was an East German general. Without consulting any historians or document experts, Fischer agreed to purchase the 27-volume diary along with a previously unknown third volume of *Mein Kampf* for 200,000 marks.

After receiving the works, Fischer set about authenticating them. He gave portions of the documents and samples of Hitler's handwriting to Dr. Max Frei-Sulzer of the forensic department of the Zurich police and to Ordway Hilton, a world-renowned document examiner in Landrum, South Carolina. Unbeknownst to Dr. Frei-Sulzer and Hilton, the handwriting samples came from the same source as the diaries. Both men determined that the writings were from the same hand and that the documents, therefore, were authentic.

Bantam Books, *Newsweek,* and Publisher Rupert Murdoch entered into a bidding war for worldwide publication rights. Murdoch flew in Hugh Trevor-Roper, a renowned British historian, who, while working under the same deception as Frei-Sulzer and Hilton, reached a similar conclusion. *Newsweek* won the bidding, however, agreeing to pay $3.75 million.

Fortunately, at the request of Gruner and Jahr, the forensic department of the West German police conducted its own evaluation, and what it uncovered shocked the publishing world. The paper on which the diaries were written contained *blankophor,* a whitener that didn't exist until 1954. The bindings contained threads of viscose and polyester, neither of which existed in the 1940s. Furthermore, none of the four types of ink that were used were widely available during World War II, and a measurement of chlorine evaporation from the ink revealed that the documents were less than a year old. The manuscripts, it turns out, were fake.

Chapter 21

Ten Ways Hollywood Gets It Wrong

T hese days, much of what people know about history, geography, and world cultures comes from what they see on TV and in movies. Because forensics is such a hot topic these days, millions of viewers also are becoming armchair experts on that subject. But is Hollywood reliable? Sometimes yes, sometimes no. In this chapter, I cover some of the common forensic mistakes that Hollywood puts on the screen.

The Quick Death

A gun is shot or a knife is thrown and down goes one of the bad guys, perhaps clutching his chest or taking one last dramatic breath, but either way, he's instantly a goner.

The problem: No one dies instantly in those circumstances. Well, *almost* no one. Instant death can occur from heart attacks, strokes, extremely abnormal heart rhythms, and with cyanide and other *metabolic poisons* (toxins that perform their mischief inside the cells of the body). Trauma from gunshot wounds (GSWs) and knife wounds, however, rarely causes instant death. Yet, how often has a single shot felled a villain? Bang, and he drops dead. For something like that to occur, the bullet would have to severely damage the brain, the heart, or the *cervical* (neck) portion of the spinal cord. A shot to the chest or abdomen normally leads to a bunch of screaming and moaning, but death comes from bleeding, and that takes a while. Check out Chapter 12 to see how trauma really affects victims.

The Pretty Death

I call this example the *Hollywood Death*. The actor looks calm and peaceful, and not a single hair is out of place. And what about blood? Not a drop. Well, unless it's a Freddie or Jason slasher movie, where blood is almost another character unto itself. The deceased is often nicely dressed, lying in bed, with perfect makeup and a slight flutter of the eyelids when you look closely. This description is particularly true when the deceased happens to be one of the good guys.

Face it: Real dead people are ugly. It doesn't matter what they looked like during life. In death, they're pale, waxy, and gray. They have dead-looking eyes, dark-blue lividity (see Chapter 11), and pale faces. Their eyelids don't flutter, and they don't look at all relaxed and peaceful. They look dead.

And fairly quickly they smell bad. When a movie detective ventures into the Louisiana swamp and finds the girl who's been missing for four days, she might be damp and dirty, but she's still beautiful. How else can the audience sympathize with her demise? The fact that she's been lying in a wet, 90-plus-degree environment for four days seems to make little difference in her appearance. The facts: They'd smell her before they saw her, and she'd appear something less than pleasant.

The Bleeding Corpse

A detective arrives at a murder scene a half hour after the deed and sees blood oozing from beneath a door. When the detective pushes the door open, a corpse lying on the floor oozes blood from the mouth and from the gaping GSW in the chest.

TILT! Blood clots within minutes of leaving the body and, surprise, dead folks don't bleed. When you die, your heart stops, and your blood no longer circulates. When blood stops moving, it clots, and, you guessed it, clotted blood doesn't move. It doesn't gush, ooze, gurgle, flow, or trickle from the body, and it neither oozes beneath a door nor flows from a wound.

A clever example of how to do it right can be found in the movie *Blood Simple,* the first commercial movie from the Coen Brothers of *Fargo* fame. In one scene, a man enters his lover's husband's office at night and finds the husband slumped in a chair behind his desk. Blood and a bullet wound to his chest tell the story. The man believes his lover has shot her husband and decides to cover for her by disposing of the body. But, as the camera angles in on the deceased man's dangling hand, you see a trickle of blood slide down one finger. He's not dead! The man places what he thinks is the husband's corpse into the back seat of his car and drives far from civilization to bury it. It's the dead of night, and as an astute viewer, you're on the edge of your seat, waiting to find out just when the husband will wake up and surprise the unwitting man. Rent it.

The Exact Time of Death

How many times have you seen the detective or the ME confidently announce that the victim "died at 10:30 last night?" I always wonder exactly how the ME made that determination. Was it rigor mortis, body temperature, or lividity? Was it the presence or absence of certain bugs? Of course, the problem is that none of these forms of evidence reveal an exact time of death. Each of them may provide an estimate of the time of death, but not even a combination of these factors enables the ME to exactly pinpoint the time of death.

In real life, the ME says that the death "*likely* occurred between 8 p.m. and midnight." But that obviously makes the ME appear wishy-washy, and Hollywood likes its heroes to be smart — sometimes even smarter than they can possibly be.

The One-Punch Knockout

The hero socks the bad guy's henchman in the jaw. The henchman goes down and apparently is written out of the script because you never hear from him again. It's always the henchmen because antagonists, like most real people, require a few solid blows to go down.

For a little perspective, think about a boxing match. Boxers are guys who are trained to inflict damage, and even they have trouble knocking each other out. And when they do, the one on his back is up in a couple of minutes, claiming the punch was a lucky one. James Bond may be able to knock someone out with a single blow, but real people (with the possible exception of Mike Tyson) can't, and neither can a car salesman turned amateur-sleuth or a recovering-alcoholic, cigarette-smoking private eye. He may knock down the bad guy, perhaps stun him, and maybe even render him unconscious, but the bad guy will awaken quickly, shake off the cobwebs, and come after the hero, even angrier and more hostile than before.

The Disappearing Black Eye

The beautiful, made-for-TV movie actress is subjected to a pop in the face from the bad guy. In the next scene, she hides her obvious black eye behind a pair of sunglasses, but in the following scene, there she is again, back to her porcelain-complexioned self.

The reality is that a character who gets a black eye in Act 1 has it for two weeks, which likely takes you a long way past the end of the movie. That character can't look normal later that day in Act 2.

A black eye is a *contusion* (bruise) caused by blood leaking from tiny blood vessels that are injured by the blow. Your body takes about two weeks to clear all that out of the tissues. After you're hit, the resulting bruise darkens for about two days, fades during the next four or five days, and turns greenish, brownish, and a sickly yellow before disappearing. Yet, you've seen the hero get a black eye that looks significantly better by the next morning and is gone by the next day. I guess actors don't like to be seen with black eyes.

I call this superhuman bruise reduction a part of "The Quick Healing." A character with a back injury from a fall down a flight of stairs can't run from or chase the bad guy or make love to a new lover the next day. In the real world, you need a few days to heal, and you limp around and complain in the interim. When you break an arm, you need four weeks minimum to heal, but because a movie is only two hours long, characters must heal almost instantly.

The Fast-Acting Poison

Within seconds of drinking arsenic-laced tea, a concerned, then frightened look comes across the victim's face, she clutches at her throat, and falls dead. Very dramatic. Also, very unlikely, but that hasn't stopped it from being a Hollywood staple for decades.

Acute arsenic poisoning doesn't kill that quickly. In fact, it may take several days. The victim develops sudden abdominal pain, nausea, vomiting, and possibly bloody diarrhea. Not a pleasant visual, so it's better to simply portray victims grabbing their throats and then collapsing.

Cyanide and other metabolic poisons block the ability of the body's cells to use oxygen or other needed chemicals. This process can cause severe shortness of breath and a constriction of the chest or throat. And because it works rapidly, the victim may indeed grab his throat and collapse. In the age of terrorism, you've probably become familiar with several other fast-acting toxins: sarin and VX gas, for example. However, these substances are hard to come by, and most readily available poisons work much more slowly and don't cause a sudden collapse and death. But you can't beat a sudden death for high cinematic drama, so the movie industry has adopted this sequence of events for essentially all poisons. Check out Chapter 16 for more information about poisons.

The Untraceable Poison

The clever big-screen evildoer gets away with murder by using a poison that doesn't leave a trace of evidence. No such thing. In Chapter 16, you find out that a diligent search by the forensic toxicologist can reveal traces of virtually any chemical or its metabolites. With fancy equipment like gas chromatography/mass spectroscopy (GS/MS), forensic scientists can determine the fingerprint of virtually any chemical. Because the Hollywood poison is untraceable, there's no need for an expensive and time-consuming full toxicological examination.

Another common scenario is for the ME to find a strange and unusual poison in about 20 minutes. Sorry, folks, it just doesn't work that way. First, the ME must use screening tests to determine whether a poison is present, and if so, what type of poison it is. The ME then uses more definitive testing, such as GC/MS, to identify exactly which poison is present. These processes take time.

The Instant Athlete

The hero chases the bad guy down streets, over bridges, through tunnels, up stairs and ladders, and over fences and rooftops, barely breaking a sweat or breathing hard, and certainly without a hair out of place. More often than not, the hero is a cop or a private investigator who drinks too much, smokes too much, rarely sleeps, and eats donuts on a regular basis. You see the hero in disheveled clothing, not gym attire. You see the hero sitting in a bar, not pumping iron or running on a treadmill. When you're out of shape, adrenaline takes you only so far — a block, maybe two on a good day. The same goes for the bad guys.

An example of how a situation like this was handled correctly is found in the movie *Marathon Man.* Remember Babe Levy (played by Dustin Hoffman)? He ran and ran for his life as Dr. Christian Szell (portrayed by Sir Laurence Olivier) and his Nazi bad guys chased him endlessly. Early in the film, you discover that Babe was a distance runner who ran around the reservoir in Central Park every day. So you know that he actually *can* run for his life.

The High-Tech Lab

Beautiful people stroll through one high-tech, sleek-looking lab after another, solving crimes (involving more beautiful people) with the newest and best equipment and at lightning-fast speed. That's how it works on TV, but the real world is not like *CSI*. Visit your local crime lab, and you don't see plasma-screen TVs, top-of-the-line computers, or beautiful people. The personnel in most crime labs are beautiful for the incredible and often thankless work they do, not necessarily because they have pretty faces.

Real labs are likely to be in windowless basements of police departments, where the norm is institutional green walls and secondhand, patchwork equipment held together with spit and chewing gum. Such are the budgets of most labs.

Unlike the guys and dolls on *CSI,* who get their results in a New York minute, technicians working in crime labs need real time to get real results. The same test that takes place almost instantaneously on the big screen actually takes days or even weeks in the real lab. Although you can do a preliminary or presumptive test quickly, most confirmatory testing takes time. Rarely does a lab get key results within only minutes, thus enabling the hero to use those results to nab an evil master criminal just before he boards a plane to Colombia.

Chapter 22

Ten Great Forensic Careers

*I*f you like science and law enforcement, you can probably find a career niche in the field of forensics. One caveat: By definition, forensics deals with law enforcement, meaning that if you have a criminal record, you may as well look for another line of work.

In this chapter, I offer information about how you can get your foot in the door and a few of the more interesting areas of forensics. Many of the careers I mention are illustrated throughout this book, and Chapter 2 gives detailed descriptions of the most common jobs.

By no means is this list complete, and the information I give you is general in nature. Every jurisdiction has its own way of doing things, including official job descriptions and educational requirements for the various jobs that are available. Likewise, all forensics offices and labs have different levels of sophistication supported by budgets of varying sizes. Smaller departments can't afford to offer some services, and larger regional offices and labs may employ personnel in almost every forensic area.

Some forensics jobs require an extensive education, but others require only a strong interest. Some require certification by a board, and others have no certification requirements whatsoever. Some require considerable experience, but others are considered entry-level positions.

In any event, before you embark on any of these paths, I suggest that you research your field of interest and check out the jurisdiction where you think you want to work. Doing so can tell you what is required and may even provide you with suggestions for which local schools and training programs you need to attend. Another way that you can approach a career in forensics is to check with local colleges to find out what forensics classes they offer. They may be able to tell what jobs are most needed in the area that you want to pursue. Better yet, do both.

Criminalist

Criminalist is a modern term that encompasses workers in many fields of forensic science, but it most often refers to crime scene and crime lab workers. If you like law enforcement and laboratory work, this field is ideal for you. Your duties depend on your education, experience, and interests. As a criminalist, you can specialize in fingerprinting, firearms, tool marks, questioned documents, trace evidence, or crime-scene analysis. Many criminalists have experience in or come directly from law enforcement, a background that obviously is useful in any of these areas.

The only real requirement for becoming a basic criminalist is a bachelor's degree in forensic science, biology, or one of the laboratory sciences, such as chemistry. Many colleges and universities offer a full forensic-science curriculum. Expect to face courses in chemistry, biology, microbiology, math, physics, pharmacology, and other scientific areas. After you have your degree, you can seek employment with a forensics lab. You don't need an advanced degree to get the position of basic criminalist, and you get most of your knowledge and skills while on the job.

If, however, you want to specialize in a specific area, you need to pursue a postgraduate education or work as an apprentice in your particular area of interest. For example, if you want to become a firearms expert, obtaining a postgraduate education in the field and then entering the workforce is best. Otherwise, you need to work in the firearms department of a crime lab for a minimum of one to two years. After that, you can seek employment as a firearms examiner. Be warned, however, that someone with the extra education and on-the-job experience is a more attractive job candidate than someone with only a bachelor's degree and the same on-the-job experience.

Crime Scene Investigator

A *crime scene investigator* or *crime scene technician* (also called a criminalist in some jurisdictions) goes to the crime scene and collects the evidence. Entering this field, you can expect to work at odd hours because criminals don't typically work on a 9-to-5 schedule. You also help police secure the scene and protect, preserve, and collect the evidence. You must know how to work a crime scene, recognize, collect, and transport evidence, and maintain the chain of custody of the evidence. More specifically, you need to know how to expose, photograph, and collect latent fingerprints, using specialized light and chemical techniques. In short, crime-scene technicians deal with all types of evidence at the scene.

You can typically come by this job by obtaining a degree in forensic science or becoming a police officer. Some jurisdictions hire only police officers as crime-scene specialists. You can enhance your employability in this area by joining the police force *and* obtaining a forensic-science degree. Being proficient in crime-scene photography also helps. Remember, most jurisdictions can't afford to hire someone for every job, so the more skills you have, the better.

Forensic Investigator

In the same way that you can view a crime-scene investigator as the on-scene extension of the crime lab, you can view the forensic investigator, or coroner's investigator, as an extension of the coroner or medical examiner (ME). By choosing this field, you can expect to work at all hours, too.

As a *forensic investigator,* you visit scenes where deaths occur, and you're responsible for handling the body; the crime scene belongs to the police, but the body falls under the jurisdiction of the coroner. You identify the deceased whenever possible by collecting personal belongings and interviewing family members, friends, and witnesses. You examine and perhaps collect evidence from the body and prepare it for transport. You may also have to prepare reports about your activities and discoveries and testify in court regarding your findings and observations.

You need at least a high school diploma or equivalent, two or three years' experience in law enforcement or investigative work, and a basic understanding of medical terminology and crime-scene investigation protocols, including the basics of evidence collection and preservation, chain of custody, and applicable laws. Becoming a police officer and obtaining a degree either in forensic science or one of the physical sciences is the best way to prepare for this job.

Forensic Pathologist

The *forensic pathologist* is at the apex of the forensic system of investigation — the top dog, so to speak. But the work of the forensic pathologist isn't for the faint of heart. Just because you like *Quincy, M.E.* reruns doesn't mean that you're cut out for this profession because, frankly, it's dirty, smelly, and grotesque. But it's also fascinating and rewarding.

As a forensic pathologist, you're eligible to serve as ME or coroner or to work in the ME's or coroner's office, examine human bodies to assess the cause and manner of death, perform autopsies, supervise the pathology lab, perhaps supervise an entire crime lab, examine crime scenes, assist law enforcement officials with body search-and-recovery procedures, provide expert testimony in court, and represent the coroner's office in various public and legal arenas. To perform these duties, you must possess a medical license and knowledge of anatomy, pathology, anthropology, dentistry, microscopy, X-ray and laboratory testing, evidence rules and court procedures, crime-scene evaluation, and federal, state, and local laws.

The educational track for this job is long and grueling. You have to go through (at minimum) college, followed by four years of medical school, a one-year medical internship, and a four-year pathology residency. Afterward, a one- or two-year forensic pathology fellowship can help you, although some locations accept one or two years of work experience in a forensic pathology lab. However, most leadership positions require board certification in anatomic pathology and forensic pathology. This certification requires an examination by the American Board of Pathology.

Forensic Pathology Technician

If being a forensic pathologist interests you, but medical school and years of specialty training don't, you may want to consider being a *forensic pathology technician*. In that capacity, you work side by side with the forensic pathologist and assist with all of that person's duties. You help with and actually perform portions of the autopsy. You also may take X-rays and obtain samples from the body for *toxicology* (drugs and poisons), *histology* (tissue microscopic examination), *serology* (blood), *microbiology* (infectious materials), fingerprinting, and trace evidence analyses. You recover bullets and other foreign objects from the corpse, photograph the body, remove specimens, and help maintain the chain of evidence. You may even be asked to discuss autopsy procedures and results with the victim's family members, law enforcement officers, and mortuary personnel.

For this job, experience counts more than education. Most labs require only a high school diploma or equivalent, but having college-level experience in any of the laboratory sciences also helps. Moreover, one or two years of experience in a medical laboratory and, even better, a forensic pathology lab, give you a real leg up. The key is obtaining a working knowledge of general and medical laboratory procedures, medical tools and equipment, and an understanding of lab-safety and infection-control procedures.

Forensic Anthropologist

If you like the biological sciences, history, anthropology, and archeology, *forensic anthropology* may be right for you. The major duties of this position are helping the ME or coroner with the recovery and identification of human remains. This work includes estimating biological profiles (age, sex, height, race, and so on) of skeletal remains and assessing the causes of skeletal trauma. You may have to visit an internment site, help excavate it, and examine tissue or skeletal remains for the purpose of identifying the deceased person and helping to determine the probable time and cause of death.

Being a forensic anthropologist requires a great deal of educational preparation. You need a bachelor's degree in a subject such as chemistry, biology, anatomy, physiology, or anthropology, and a graduate degree, preferably a doctorate in anthropology or human biology. You need a PhD and at least three years of experience in forensic anthropology when seeking board certification in the field.

Although you may be able to work in the field with fewer credentials, having the postgraduate education makes you a more attractive candidate. Most forensic anthropologists work at universities and serve as consultants to MEs and the courts.

Forensic Toxicologist

Toxicology combines chemistry, pharmacology, physiology, and biology. If you have an aptitude for science and an interest in chemistry, forensic toxicology may be of interest to you.

As a *toxicologist,* you deal with postmortem toxicological evaluations as they relate to causes of death and drug testing in criminal and workplace situations. You may examine seized materials (marijuana, cocaine, heroin, and other illicit drugs) to determine their chemical nature. To do this examination, you need to be familiar with sample collection and laboratory equipment and procedures used for analytical drug testing. Your actual duties may be those of either an assistant or supervisor, depending on your education and experience. Most forensic toxicologists work in crime, government, or private laboratories.

You need a bachelor's degree in one of the laboratory sciences, such as chemistry, toxicology, or pharmacology, as a minimum, but the lab may prefer master's and PhD degrees. You may enter the field with a lesser level of education, but you can enhance your chances for advancement with a postgraduate education in the field. For example, in many areas, forensic toxicologists are classified in three different levels. Level I, the entry level, requires only a bachelor's degree and little, if any, experience. Advancment to Level II may follow after you complete two or more years of experience in the lab. Level III requires four years of experience or two years of postgraduate study in toxicology. You probably need a master's degree or PhD and four years of experience to serve as a supervising or head forensic toxicologist.

Fingerprint Examiner

Fingerprint examiners are a critical component of most crime labs. If you enter this field, you compare fingerprint evidence obtained from crime scenes with similar evidence obtained from suspects and from large databases. You also visit crime scenes and help with exposing, photographing, and lifting prints, which means you must be familiar with all the light and chemical methods for exposing latent prints and all the procedures for protecting and collecting them.

In the section "Criminalist" earlier in this chapter, I say that a criminalist can pursue extra education or experience in fingerprint analysis and become a fingerprint examiner. Although that's true, doing so isn't the only way to reach that goal. Some jurisdictions hire you if you have a high school diploma or equivalent and you've taken a few college courses in chemistry, biology, or mathematics. Check with your potential employer to be sure. When following this route, you can expect to work for several years before achieving any advancement.

Forensic Document Examiner

If you love books and letters, the highly specialized work of a forensic document examiner may be for you. As a *forensic document examiner,* your primary duties are examining documents and other written and printed materials with an eye toward determining their authenticity, age, and authorship. You must have good eyesight, extreme patience, a dedication to detail, and the ability to pass many hours working alone. You also need some skills with language, photography, and laboratory testing procedures.

You don't need to fulfill any specific educational requirements to enter this field, but if you expect to be certified by the American Board of Forensic Document Examiners (ABFDE), you must meet certain criteria, which include earning a college degree and amassing work experience in the field. As is true of other forensic areas, earning your degree in forensic science or one of the laboratory sciences, particularly chemistry, can really help you. Chemical testing is an integral part of the job of the document examiner.

Your work experience needs to be in a questioned-documents lab, where you can learn the trade as an apprentice. Several federal agencies maintain such labs, including the Bureau of Alcohol, Tobacco, Firearms, and Explosives (BATFE), the FBI, the CIA, the IRS, the U.S. Postal Service, the U.S. Secret Service, and any of the branches of the armed forces. Many state and local crime labs also have questioned-documents sections.

Forensic DNA Analyst

If science is your interest, you might be drawn to the relatively new and exciting field of DNA analysis. DNA analysts work with biological materials obtained from suspects, victims, and crime scenes with an eye toward creating a DNA profile and matching it to other DNA evidence. This work requires patience, a meticulous attention to detail, and adherence to strict protocols if usable evidence is to be forthcoming.

To enter this field you will need at least a bachelor's degree in biology, chemistry, genetics, forensic science, molecular biology, or biochemistry. Many employers require an advanced degree (masters or PhD) in one of these disciplines as well as at least two years of experience in full-time case work.

Index

• H •

hackle marks, 288
hair
  analysis of, 279
  anatomy of, 279–280
  cortex of, 280
  cuticle of, 280
  DNA, 282
  dyed, 281
  John Vollman case, 283
  matching criminal to, 280–283
  medulla of, 280
  mitochondrial DNA in, 250–251, 283
  source of, 278–281
  toxins in, 257, 263
hallucinations, 268, 269
hallucinogens, 268–270
hand guard, 186
handedness, 158
handguns. *See also* firearms evidence; guns
    and gunshot wounds
  class and individual characteristics, 37–38
  definition of, 294
handprints, 76
hands, rape exam, 200
handwriting analysis, 306–309
handwriting examiner, 307
handwriting style, 306–308
hangings, 211–212
haptoglobin, 231
Hare, William, 206
Hauptmann, Bruno Richard, 322–323
head, blunt-force trauma to, 193–196
headspace vapor extraction, 124
headstamps, 298
heavy metals, poisoning, 273
height, estimating, 158
Helmer, Richard, 166
Helpern, Milton, 274
hematoma, 188, 189
Hendricks, David, 328–329
Henry, Sir Edward, 76, 81
Henry System, 81
heroin, testing for, 266–267
Herschel, Sir William, 76
hesitation wounds, 143
high-risk victims, 70
high-velocity spatters, 97

hip replacement surgery, 153
Hitler's diaries, 332
HLA (human leukocyte antigen), 231
Hofmann, Mark, 315
Hollywood films, forensic mistakes in
  the bleeding corpse, 334–335
  the disappearing black eye, 336
  the exact time of death, 335
  the fast-acting poison, 336–337
  the high-tech lab, 338
  the instant athlete, 337
  the one-punch knockout, 335
  the pretty death, 334
  the quick death, 333
  the untraceable poison, 337
Holmes, Reginald, 152
homicidal choking, 205
homicidal fires, 126–129
homicidal incised wounds, 185
homicidal poisonings, 258
homicidal smothering, 205
homicides
  definition of, 136
  ligature strangulation, 210
  rape-homicides, 201
huffing, 271
human leukocyte antigen (HLA), 231
humerus, 158
hydrogen sulfide, 215
hyoid bone, 209
hypnosis, 54, 57
hypocalcination, 193

• I •

icons used in this book, 2–3
identification of evidence, 39
identifying unknown victims
  artifacts, 151
  bones and skeletons, 155–160
  cause and manner of death, 163–164
  DNA analysis, 155
  fingerprints, 153–154
  individual characteristics, 160–161
  mass graves, 165
  overview, 150–151
  reconstructing faces, 164–165
  scars, birthmarks, and tattoos, 151–152
  teeth, 154

About the Author

D. P. Lyle, MD, winner of the Macavity and Benjamin Franklin Silver awards and a nominee for Edgar, Agatha, Anthony, Scribe, Silver Falchion, and USA Best Book awards, is the author of many nonfiction books *(Murder & Mayhem, Forensics For Dummies, Forensics & Fiction, More Forensics & Fiction, Howdunnit: Forensics,* and *ABA Fundamentals: Understanding Forensic Science)* as well as numerous works of fiction, including the Samantha Cody thriller series *(Devil's Playground, Double Blind,* and *Original Sin);* the Dub Walker thriller series *(Stress Fracture; Hot Lights, Cold Steel;* and *Run to Ground);* the Royal Pains media tie-in novels *(Royal Pains: First, Do No Harm* and *Royal Pains: Sick Rich);* and the upcoming Jake Longly thriller *(Deep Six).* His essay on Jules Verne's *The Mysterious Island* appears in *Thrillers: 100 Must Reads;* and his short story "Even Steven" appears in International Thriller Writers's anthology *Thriller 3: Love Is Murder.*

He has served as guest of honor at Killer Nashville, SleuthFest, and other writers' conferences. He teaches extensively; is International Thriller Writers's (ITW's) vice president for education; and runs CraftFest, Master CraftFest, and ITW's online Thriller School.

Along with Jan Burke, he is the co-host of *Crime and Science Radio.* He has worked with many novelists and with the writers of popular television shows such as *Law & Order, CSI: Miami, Diagnosis Murder, Monk, Judging Amy, Peacemakers, Cold Case, House, Medium, Women's Murder Club, 1-800-Missing, The Glades,* and *Pretty Little Liars.*

He was born and raised in Huntsville, Alabama, where his childhood interests revolved around football, baseball, and building rockets in his backyard. The latter pursuit was common in Huntsville during the 1950s and '60s due to the nearby NASA/Marshall Space Flight Center.

After leaving Huntsville, he attended college and medical school, and served an internship at the University of Alabama; followed by a residency in Internal Medicine at the University of Texas at Houston; and then a fellowship in cardiology at The Texas Heart Institute, also in Houston. For the past 40 years, he has practiced cardiology in Orange County, California.

Website: www.dplylemd.com

Blog: writersforensicsblog.wordpress.com

Crime and Science Radio: http://www.dplylemd.com/crime--science-radio.html

Dedication

This book is dedicated to all the wonderful and hardworking people in the world of forensic science and law enforcement. Your work often goes unrecognized and unrewarded, yet it is essential in the delivery of justice for all. Thank you one and all.

Author's Acknowledgments

I must thank my wonderful agent Kimberley Cameron of Kimberley Cameron and Associates for many years of hard work and dedication to my writing career and for her always helpful advice — and friendship. Thanks, KC, you're the best.

To my editors Christina Guthrie and Tracy Boggier and all the professionals at Wiley. You made this update painless.

To my friend, fellow author, and *Crime and Science Radio* co-host Jan Burke for her help with this book. Her research materials and advice were indispensable in the preparation of this work.

To Nan Owen, my better half, for supplying the artwork for this book.

Publisher's Acknowledgments

Executive Editor: Lindsay Lefevere

Senior Acquisitions Editor: Tracy Boggier

Editorial Project Manager: Christina Guthrie

Development Editor: Christina Guthrie

Copy Editor: Christine Pingleton

Technical Editor: Susan Walsh, PhD

Art Coordinator: Alicia B. South

Production Editor: Antony Sami

Illustrator: Nan Owen

Cover Image: Andrey Kuzmin/Shutterstock